CULTURAL CONTEXTS AND LITERARY IDIOMS
IN
CONTEMPORARY IRISH LITERATURE

THE IRISH LITERARY STUDIES SERIES
ISSN 0140-895X

CULTURAL CONTEXTS AND LITERARY IDIOMS

IN
CONTEMPORARY IRISH LITERATURE

edited by
Michael Kenneally

Studies in Contemporary Irish Literature 1
Irish Literary Studies 31

BARNES & NOBLE BOOKS
Totowa, New Jersey

First published in the United States of America in 1988
by Barnes & Noble Books, 81 Adams Drive, Totowa, N.J. 07512

Library of Congress Cataloging in Publication Data

Cultural contexts and literary idioms/edited by
Michael Kenneally.
     p. cm. — (Irish literary studies; 31-)
Bibliography: v. 1, p.
Includes index.
Contents: v. 1. Studies in contemporary Irish literature.
ISBN 0-389-20792-6 (v. 1)
1. English literature—Irish authors—History and criticism.
2. English literature—20th century—History and criticism.
3. Ireland—Intellectual life—20th century. 4. Ireland in
literature. I. Kenneally, Michael. II. Series: Irish literary
studies: 31, etc.
PR8754.S78   1988
820'.9'89162—dc19

Originated and published in Great Britain
by Colin Smythe Limited, Gerrards Cross, Buckinghamshire

Produced in Great Britain
Set by Crypticks, Leeds,
and printed and bound by Billing & Sons Ltd. Worcester

CONTENTS

STUDIES IN CONTEMPORARY IRISH LITERATURE

General Editor
Michael Kenneally

INTRODUCTION

This collection is the first in a four-volume series devoted solely to critical analysis of Irish writing since the 1950s. *Studies in Contemporary Irish Literature* will present essays which, taken together, should provide a solid foundation for scholars and students interested in the extraordinary literary achievement of Irish writers during the past three decades. Essays in volume one have been commissioned to map out aspects of the cultural, social and political context of contemporary literature and to set forth some of the defining characteristics and predominant concerns within a given genre. The three subsequent collections in the series will focus, respectively, on poetry, drama and fiction.

As several essays of this first volume make clear, the contemporary Irish writer confronts a reality defined by a complex array of issues, some of which are the universal questions posed for all artists as they attempt to find an individually appropriate and coherent means by which the self can find expression, while others are uniquely bound up with the nature of Irish life and the Irish literary tradition. The changes wrought in Irish society since the early sixties have been fundamental in nature and far-reaching in implication. In broadest terms, they can be described as a shift from a primarily tradition-bound and inward-looking society to a more open and flexible nation. The exigencies exerting pressure on Irish life have their roots in such diverse causes as rapid economic growth and technological development, the emergence of a substantial middle-class energetically committed to consumer values, inexorable rural to urban migration, an awakening feminist consciousness, the fading of national ideals, the decline in traditional moral imperatives, and the demographic crisis of an expanding population and declining job opportunities.

Social historians and cultural commentators can readily identify those public events which might be perceived as symbolically signalling the shifts in the collective Irish psyche over the last quarter of a century: the profound reverberations initiated by Vatican II; the establishment of a national television network in

1961; the renewal of sectarian violence in the North in 1969; and the economic prosperity stemming from 1973 membership in the European Economic Community. These factors were compounded by such universal phenomena as the revolution in international communication and travel, along with the widespread influence of popular American culture. When continually refracted and, in the process, reinforced by the pervasive mirror of the media, such changes put enormous strain on the social fabric of the nation and constituted a sustained challenge to the reality which obtained since the inception of the state. The ideology which had prevailed since 1922 was based, to a large degree, on a romanticisation of the rural, a glorification of native Irish traditions, and an idealisation of history, particularly those moments that could be viewed as significant steps in the long struggle leading to Easter 1916. Frequently marshalled to define and control postcolonial reality, this ideology — reinforced by the inherently conservative values of small-town shopkeepers and farmers, and the disproportionate influence of Jansenist Catholicism — lead to political isolation, economic stagnation, and a social atrophy compounded by successive waves of emigration.

As Fintan O'Toole's essay makes obvious, the economic prosperity of the sixties and seventies produced an inevitable clash between former values and those of an increasingly prosperous and liberal-minded middle class society. Disregarding, if not rejecting, certain cherished national ideals, Irish society readily embraced the social and moral attitudes that had found international favour — a less rigid interpretation of religious dogma, a more open attitude to sex and an unabashed commitment to consumerism. This rupture with previous perceptions of nationality placed serious pressures on the Irish psyche which, in the literature of the period, manifested themselves in diverse images of dislocation, estrangement and discontinuity.

The past two decades in Northern Ireland have also, as we know, seen serious challenges mounted against established social and political structures. In the pre-1969 North, the values of the Protestant majority predominated, shaping a society firmly grounded in evangelical fundamentalism, industrialisation, a vigorous defence of the status quo and an exaltation of those Ulster figures — from the Boys of Derry to Carson and beyond — who had defended union with Britain. This ideology had been used since the establishment of the Northern political entity in an attempt to cement over obvious differences in the community and to promote a single vision of Northern life. But the civil rights movement of the late 1960s — initially a protest against the use of housing, jobs and the franchise as instruments of hegemony by the Protestant majority — soon yielded to older, more divisive questions of one's relationship to place, history, community and language.

It is one of the ironies of recent Irish history that at the moment in the sixties when society in the Republic began to evince the first shifts away from the values derived from a nationalist ideology to a more pragmatic, ahistorical, even secular perspective, the renewal of the Northern conflict served as a powerful reminder that, in fundamental ways, the decades since 1922 constituted, for both the North and South, a social and political hiatus, a period when essential questions of national identity and affiliation had been postponed, not solved. Over the last two decades, then, both societies have been stalled at critical junctures; neither is able to subscribe wholeheartedly to former ideologies nor to commit itself to a vision based on common values and assumptions. In the North, this impasse is all too obvious in a society where, for many individuals, questions of identity and allegiance are frequently reduced to principles based on repudiation and exclusion. In the South, the conflicting loyalties fostered by the economic rejuvenation and social changes of the sixties and seventies have necessarily precluded an unencumbered response to the present or a clear articulation of the nation's future. The sharp decline of the Republic's economy in recent years, with its attendant social and political implications, along with the stalemate in the North, are symptomatic of the unresolved issues bedevilling both societies. The fact that any significant break in the Northern deadlock must originate in London, and that the fortunes of the Southern economy are largely dependent on policies made in Brussels, New York or Tokyo highlight the extent of national disability.

For a variety of complex social and historical reasons, Irish literature has traditionally displayed an inordinate concern with questions of cultural identity and nationalistic ideals. In more recent years, the urge to define oneself in relation to nation, community, history and language has been complicated by the impact of shifting social, economic and political realities. The pressure on the artist to respond imaginatively to such phenomena has been all the more intense, given the unrelenting attention of the media on public affairs, and, in particular, its ability to create the illusion that gradual and subtle shifts in national consciousness are already established phenomena and therefore require response. The methods by which contemporary writers deal with questions of cultural identity are influenced, in no small measure, by the changed role of the artist in Irish society. In contrast to its predecessors, the current generation of Irish writers is engaged with its reality in a way that was impossible and, perhaps, would have been inconceivable for Joyce, O'Connor, O'Faolain, Flann O'Brien or Kavanagh. Unlike those estranged and often beleaguered figures, whose vision was blatantly at odds with the existing ethos and whose literary voice was sometimes distorted by the critical stance forced upon them, contemporary writers suffer no such social isolation. With the virtual elimination of censorship, the introduction of beneficial tax laws and the exposure to constant — too much, perhaps — media attention, the literary artist has become an entirely acceptable figure in contemporary Irish life. In fact, self-imposed exile and the banning of one's works have been replaced as the hallmarks of Irish literary accomplishment and artistic integrity by star billing at public events and appointment to Aos Dana, an exclusive group of government-selected artists, membership in which guarantees a certain public stature as well as a modest State income.

In his essay on literature and culture in the North, Anthony Bradley begins from the recognition that writing in modern Ireland has been preoccupied with the intersection of literature with Irish history, society and politics. He examines the manner in which recent Ulster writers embody, reject or refract the conflicting cultures in the North, the extent to which literature is rooted in an affiliation with a cultural tradition defined by religion, history, politics, and by attitudes to place, class and language. Several essays in this collection have identified, as perhaps the single most recurring impulse in current Irish writing, an obsession with the past, be it personal biography, national history or literary tradition, which in the process of imaginative exploration frequently takes on mythic and archetypal dimensions. As Edna Longley's essay establishes so forcefully, Irish writers are frequently engaged in obsessive encounters with a past which must be rejected, transformed or accommodated. For many, the legacy of genealogy and nuance of personal history constitute the primary obstacles restricting release of the self into the open spaces of possibility and fulfilment. The psychic landscape where this struggle finds its most frequent and fertile expression is the tangled emotional relationship between father and child, a paradigm readily apparent in the work of, among others, John

McGahern, Brian Moore, Bernard MacLaverty, Maurice Leitch, Brian Friel, Thomas Murphy, Hugh Leonard, Seamus Heaney, Michael Longley and Paul Muldoon.

While the exploration of patrimony has traditionally been associated with the desire to establish one's posture toward ancestry, to discover the foundations on which legitimate self-knowledge might grow, it also has other implications. An examination of the plethora of fathers — actual, religious and symbolic — and the emphasis on father/child relationships in contemporary Irish writing, reveals that they tend to be identified with the values of community and economics, with social acceptability, religious conformity and material well-being. As such, they are often depicted as the immediate barriers to the individual's progression, whether it be from a rural to an urban, working-class to a middle-class, or an Irish to a foreign world. More tellingly, especially when viewed in the context of diminished maternal images, the preponderance of fathers suggests a lessening of interest in traditional ideals of nation and perspectives on history. In the past, as we know, the personification of the country as Cathleen Ni Houlihan, the Sean Bhean Bhocht or some such female embodiment of Ireland's tragic past was employed to consolidate a specific vision of the nation's future. As Christopher Murray makes clear in his discussion of the Irish history play, however, such mythic perceptions of country and history now appear to offer little imaginative nourishment to writers burdened under the weight of a chronically fragmented present and uncertain future. Indeed, the past as an historical continuum determining the present is frequently depicted as the most debilitating influence limiting individual freedom and controlling personal options. The sectarian conflict in the North has been used, by Bernard MacLaverty, Graham Reid, John Montague and others to underline the deterministic nature of life in that province, how its citizens are at birth already victims of genealogy and environment, and must contend with the impingement of public events on private lives, of historical forces on individual predilections.

Closely allied to the need to situate oneself in relation to the past is the Irish writer's concern with place, with awareness of geographical as well as historical relationships. The *dinnsheanchas* tradition of Gaelic poetry, which emphasises the poet's knowledge and celebration of the historical and community associations with physical environment, is still a vital characteristic of Irish writing. Much of Seamus Heaney's poetry, for example, is a meditation on the significance of locality, particularly those places judged to be emotionally and intellectually connected with stages of consciousness and personal evolution, and even perceived as themselves generating awareness because they are a common symbolic means of expression. Similarly, the poetry of John Montague restlessly examines the palimpsestic features of the Irish landscape, attempting to define the nature of his relationship to, and kinship with, successive Irish cultures. Yet, while the concern with locality may shift from the lexicography of personal history to the cultural strata of nation, community and tribe, it derives its essential energy from the desire for self-knowledge and self-definition. The poetry of place is frequently motivated by the urge for metaphysical placement.

This obsessive concern with locality ultimately becomes, in the view of Pat Sheeran and Nina Witoszek, a reflection of a desire for the transcendent, with its attendant neglect or suppression of the claims of objective reality. Fuelled by a *contemptus mundi*, on the one hand, and a yearning for unity and harmony on the other, it is a striving for the ideal and the absolute which stand outside of time and are in such appealing contrast to the fragmented and chaotic. This yearning finds expression in much contemporary Irish literature (the poetry of Heaney, Montague and Kinsella; plays such as Friel's *Faith Healer*, Kilroy's *Talbot's Box*, and Murphy's *The Sanctuary Lamp* and *The Gigli Concert*; and, with some qualifications, certain novels of Francis Stuart, John McGahern, John Banville, Aidan Higgins and Brian Moore) in the recurring image of the individual rejecting the demands of social, economic and political reality, and seeking manifestation and integration of the self in the symbolical and metaphysical. Sheeran and Witoszek believe that the repression of this desire for an imaginative 'fifth province', a realm beyond the temporal and physical, finds release in the two characteristic Irish tendencies towards verbophilia and mythomania. It produces a literature marked by an extraordinary emphasis on language and a transformation of subject matter into myth.

Gerald Dawe finds the Irish poet's inordinate interest in language, place and cultural affiliation as problematic. He sees this predisposition as a potentially debilitating pressure, a thematic bias and cultural conditioning which can restrict and undermine the poet's ability to maintain artistic integrity. The very colloquialism of poetic idioms and images, rooted as it is in a perception of language as a static, even sacred object, is in danger of becoming merely a rhetorical end, a convention which can inhibit full imaginative freedom. Dawe finds the tendency to thematic predictability in, for example, Tom Paulin's concern with the poet's role in public debate, Montague's delineation of nostalgic landscapes of home, and Heaney's poetic exploration of the very practice of being a poet. Over and against these, Dawe proffers the poetry of Derek Mahon, Thomas Kinsella and Padraic Fiacc. For example, he praises Mahon for his exploration of a poetic voice in language stripped of sentimentality and devoid of any appeal to rhetoric; in Dawe's view, it is 'a poetry of manner highly-tense, yet balanced, and formally set within the conditions of definite times and places', but yet imaginatively confronting those universal conditions of estrangement and discontinuity which are the inheritance of the writer in the modern world.

However, while some writers may attempt to find imaginative liberation through a direct, untrammelled response to individual situation and consciousness, the complex relationship between language and identity remains of vital importance to others. It is, therefore, central to critical discourse on contemporary Irish culture and literature. Michael Toolan's essay looks at present-day Irish writing in the context of the critical theories of Derrida, Barthes and Said, particularly the claim that language, because of its inherent inadequacies and inherited associations, is collective, and consequently is an inescapable imposition beyond the individual's power to shape and imprint. The essay offers a defence and celebration of Irish English as a rich, authentic and desirable resource, powerfully 're-made' by Joyce, Friel, Heaney, Montague and others. From a somewhat more specific perspective, Colbert Kearney focuses on those writers who wrote in both the Irish and English languages, and struggled between the pull of two linguistic traditions, one ancient the other modern, one national the other international. For those possessing no direct knowledge of Irish, the language could, through its influence on Hiberno English, prove to be a valuable resource, enabling a transformation and revitalisation of English. But for writers like Flann O'Brien, Brendan Behan and Eoghan O'Tuarisc problems of ambiguity and alienation surfaced, highlighting the cultural schizophrenia and complex issues of affiliation and voice which haunt the modern Irish author, writing in the shadow of a domineering culture, first English, then American. To examine one aspect of this predicament, John Wilson Foster attempts to unravel some of the tangled relations between Irish and English writers, particularly the unique status of Ulster poets over the last several decades, situated as they are in a province geographically Irish but constitutionally British. He sees Ulster poetry since the war as 'a case-study in the history of Anglo-Irish literary relations, with their mutual incursions, and their two-way traffic in poetic reputation and critical reception.'

Terence Brown focuses on the current critical debate on the ongoing relationship to Irish life of the literature of the Anglo-Irish Ascendancy as represented primarily by Yeats, Lady Gregory and Synge. While this issue has been part of the Irish critical tradition since the literary revival, it has been intensified in recent years in publications such as *The Crane Bag* and the Field Day pamphlets. The dichotomy has been reduced to a polarity between Yeats and Joyce, between what is perceived, on the one hand, as a literature of subjective, idealistic and romantic tendencies, heightened by Yeats's interest in an effete Celticism and the otherworldliness of the occult, and, on the other, a literature concerned with the objective reality of modern Irish society, unadorned, and carrying no prescribed vision of national identity, no sense of seeking continuity with the past as a means of substantiating either cultural or literary strategies. In the revisionism of recent years, Yeats has been seen as a magnificent anachronism who attempted to establish a cultural and literary tradition which would provide a legitimising context for his own writing. Central to this critical discussion has been Thomas Kinsella's 1966 essay, 'The Irish Writer', a seminal work whose influence is manifest in several of the essays in this collection, and which articulates the Irish writer's sense of being cut off from his literary inheritance, of confronting a tradition that is gapped, discontinuous and terrifyingly disabling, particularly so because of the loss of the Irish language. While acknowledging Yeats's ability to create his own tradition in isolation, 'a coherent entity, at a graceful elegiac height above the filthy modern tide', Kinsella saw Joyce as the writer who represents a continuity or healing of the Irish tradition because he deals directly with Irish reality, with the 'lumpen proletariat, the eloquent and conniving and mean-spirited tribe of Dan'. Consequently, he argued that Joyce is the first Irish writer to speak for Irish life since the death of the Irish language. Terence Brown's position is not merely that such dialectical manoeuvring distorts to make its point but that the time has come to admit a less reductive estimate of Yeats, while also acknowledging that Joyce's creative consciousness and literary strategies also lack full enabling significance. Such a procedure would clear the way for new readings of both writers, and in the process allow contemporary writers to move beyond a dialectical tension which has been inhibitive and prolonged.

Those essays in the collection dealing with specific literary topics initiate the process of charting the predominant forms, idioms and thematic issues which define much of contemporary Irish writing. In poetry, for example, Dillon Johnston sees the pluralism and multiplicity of voices associated with Joyce's writing, the desire to escape from the myths and attitudes fostered by the literary revival, being manifested in present-day Irish poetry. Kinsella, Muldoon, and to a lesser degree, Heaney, Montague and Mahon, all have begun this process of deconstruction and revisionism. The predominant features of this poetry are a markedly distinct and dramatic form, a changing and usually unidentified persona, a neutral and amoral tone, a stark message, and a suppression of lyricism or any tendency to music or rhetoric. In fiction, Andrew Parkin sees the enduring tradition of the Big House novel not as an anachronistic literary form artificially resuscitated from an Ascendancy culture now dead, but as a literary phenomenon that can be explained as imaginatively rooted in nostalgia, or in the desire for revenge on an exploitative class, or, most importantly perhaps, as the testament of the tenacious hold of a form of rural culture over the modern, urban imagination, an Irish version of pastoral.

In contrast to the persistent appeal of the Big House world is the decline in imaginative attractiveness for dramatists of historical, particularly political, figures. Christopher Murray traces the abandonment of the once-popular history play to the decline in appeal of patriotic values and nationalist sentiments, to the profound shifts which have occurred in the psyche of the nation. Yet, as Claudia Harris's essay shows, Irish playwrights do have a continuing fascination for the theme of sacrifice and martyrdom, of expiation and atonement, though the point of view of the dramatist can range from sympathy to irony, and the tone can vary from tragedy to comedy. The inability to deal with contemporary issues by way of an exhortatory treatment of Irish historical events and public figures has been partially compensated, it would seem, by re-workings of Sophocles' *Antigone* which, in recent years, has been adapted for the Irish context by three playwrights and a film director. As Anthony Roche's essay makes clear, the Antigone myth, with its exploration of the rival claims of the status quo and the urge to revolution, justice and the law, tribal loyalties and allegiance to the body politic, respect for the dead and the needs of the living, the dreams of youth and the realism of maturity, and the sexual dialectic of male and female, provides a convenient imaginative vehicle for dealing with many of the conflicting loyalties at the heart of contemporary Irish life.

The thematic concentration on issues related to individual consciousness, on the emotional and psychological dimensions of subjective reality, is a particular characteristic of Irish women writers, who must wrestle with questions of identity and self-understanding in an environment that does not readily accommodate a satisfactory vision of life. Contemporary Irish women recognise that the old mores prevent unfettered self-manifestation but that new, potentially liberating options are still resisted by powerful social, religious and political institutions. Tamsin Hargreaves in her essay on women novelists and Art McGuinness in his discussion of three women poets examine some of the procedures by which the female self seeks expression and fulfilment, devises strategies of survival and fortification, and attempts to ascribe meaning to disparate experiences, a struggle which is all the greater because it must be conducted in the context of the wider tensions of Irish life. Indeed, the attempt to negotiate a viable path through a social, cultural and political landscape that is cracked and fissured under the powerful strain of opposing forces is paradigmatic of the divisions in society at large. Because contemporary Irish writing probes a wide range of issues related to individual consciousness and national identity, insistently examines the individual's reponse to metaphysical uncertainty and cultural estrangement, and does so with vigour and in a variety of literary idioms and forms, it commands our attention and scrutiny. The four volumes of *Studies in Contemporary Irish Literature* will provide a forum in which this critical discussion can take place.

ISLAND OF SAINTS AND SILICON: LITERATURE AND SOCIAL CHANGE IN CONTEMPORARY IRELAND

FINTAN O'TOOLE

In *Cathleen Ni Houlihan*, a play which contributed a great deal to the romantic ideology of the emergent Ireland, W. B. Yeats has Mother Ireland transformed from an old woman to a young girl 'with the walk of a queen'. By 1966, fifty years after the 1916 Rising, Mother Ireland, after the bitter experience of the years of Independence, is an old woman again. The stage directions for Brian Friel's play of that year, *The Loves of Cass Maguire* describe the old woman who is sitting on the stage: 'Were she able to walk around, she would have the authority and self-possession of a queen, but because she is invalided, she just looks monumental.' The walk of the queen has petrified into immobility. She is crippled, deaf and rambling, as striking but as useless as a monument. She is deaf to her grandson, seventy years her junior, who tosses her the occasional grudging insult as he reads aloud, not from *The Love Songs of Connacht*, but from *True Detective* magazine: 'O'Shea flung his men around the building and dashed inside. The startled Samoan girls in varying forms of undress ran screaming into Madame Lulana's.'[1] Between the Ireland of Yeats's dreams and the Ireland of stupefied awakenings, there is an unfathomable gulf. In Friel's vignette, staged as the Irish state was wallowing in sentimental celebration of its own romantic origins, the old Ireland is unable to listen to anything but its own ramblings, the new one unable to talk in anything but a borrowed voice. *The Loves of Cass Maguire* had its premiere, not in Ireland, but, appropriately, in America.

The distance of sixty four years between *Cathleen Ni Houlihan* and *The Loves of Cass Maguire*, however, is not the significant one. The transition was much more truncated. Take this vision of Dalkey, a village to the south of Dublin which has now become one of its suburbs, written in the nineteen fifties:

Dalkey is a little town, maybe twelve miles south of Dublin, on the shore.
It is an unlikely town, huddled, quiet, pretending to be asleep. Its streets
are narrow, not quite self-evident as streets, and with meetings which
seem accidental. Small shops look closed but are open . . . The road itself
curves gently upward and over a low wall to the left by the footpath
enchantment is spread — rocky grassland falling fast away to reach a toy-
like railway far below, with beyond it the immeasurable immanent sea,
quietly moving slowly in the immense expanse of Killiney Bay.[2]

Then take this description of the same place:

Today the only green spaces are pocket-handkerchief gardens and a
sloping football pitch fronted by a sports stadium. Not long ago I was
asked to open a fashion show in the stadium. There was an audience of
six hundred and among them I recognised faces I had not seen in a third
of a century. Then they had belonged to urchins like myself; now they
were light years away from the dinginess and the scrimping: they drove
fast cars, played bridge and had been to Spain in August. From the relative
luxury of their present world, they could afford to look back with an
affectionate longing for the one from which they had escaped.[3]

The first of these passages is from Flann O'Brien's novel *The
Dalkey Archive*; the second from playwright Hugh Leonard's
autobiography *Home Before Night*. The distance between them,
between the depopulated village and the crowded station,
between O'Brien's view of the immanence, immensity and
majesty of nature dwarfing the insignificance and impermanence
of the urban settlement and making even the railway 'toy-like'
and Leonard's vision of nature parcelled, coralled, neutered by
people who have clawed their way to material success at the
expense of an ambivalent relationship with their own past, is the
distance that modern Irish literature has had to travel. It has had
very little time in which to make the journey.

To talk of the collapse of old ways of making literature under
the strain of radically altered social and political circumstances is
not to talk of the corruption of something pure, noble and innocent
by the vulgar, tainted and ravenous forces of an alien culture. The
social and political forces which shaped the mainstream of the
Irish Literary Movement were not sprung spontaneously from
the native soil like the shamrock. They were themselves shaped
by an intersection with foreign political cultures, particularly the
British and American. Irish political nationalism, the cement of
the Irish Literary Movement, had a major element of American

influence, even in the way it understood its own most sacred concept, republicanism. Crucially, Irish nationalism adopted the vague and flexible American usage of the term rather than the radical and secular republicanism of France.

Britain was the enemy, America our ally: the cultural bulwarks of Anglophobia constructed by the Gaelic revival constituted a Maginot Line against attack from one direction only. The notion of a pure, simple peasantry which fed both the literary and political movements needed to be protected by the new Irish state from foreign influences, but in doing so the very basis of cultural independence was denied. The ironies abound. The possibility of a native literature with a mass readership was cut off by censorship — the shelves emptied of banned Irish books were filled largely with American cowboy novels and their healthy, rural, asexual cameraderie. The basis of native music, the informal dances at crossroads or in houses, was destroyed by de Valera's Public Dance Halls Act of 1935 which ensured that dances had to be held in licensed halls, where they could be supervised, particularly by the clergy, and where Irish music was for the most part replaced by American style dance bands. Slug and Shorty, the Dublin cowboys punching cattle along the ringsend trail in Flann O'Brien's *At-Swim-Two-Birds* are legitimate inhabitants of the Irish cultural world in the years after Independence.

The momentous social changes which have taken place in Ireland since 1959, then, were drastic but not sudden. They made clear and official a process which was already at work, and this is why they were accepted and contained by Irish society. If modern industrial society had not really come to Ireland before the sixties, Ireland had been going to modern industrial societies for the previous century. At the time when de Valera was pouring forth his famous 1943 St Patrick's Day vision of cosy homesteads and comely maidens in a bucolic paradise, 25,000 of his fellow countrymen were leaving the country every year for the cities of America and Britain. Mass emigration had been the central economic fact of life for a century before that. But this was the unofficial Ireland, not the material of the Literary Movement. When Lady Gregory wrote a play called *Fifty*, the title referring to the number of pounds with which the hero returns home after two years in America, the Abbey company objected that this might make America sound too attractive. She changed the title to *Twenty Five*.

The most important author of the contemporary Irish canon is T. K. Whitaker, secretary of the Department of Finance at the end of the fifties, and its seminal work is his *First Programme of Economic*

Expansion, published in 1958 and going into effect the following year. The thrust of Whitaker's plan was to recognise that Independent Ireland was a failed economic entity, to dismantle the tariff barriers which were supposed to nurture native and self-reliant industry and to do everything possible through tax advantages and grants to attract foreign investment. It was a plan for industrialisation, and inevitably for urbanisation, and as a shot in the arm it had a heady effect. American multinationals began to arrive: Hallmark Cards in 1958, Burlington Textiles in 1960, General Electric in 1962, until, by 1983, foreign firms had invested nearly six billion pounds in the Republic, four and a half billion pounds of which came from America. Ireland stopped thinking of itself as an island of saints and scholars and started to try on the image of what the Industrial Development Authority's advertisements would call the Most Profitable Industrial Location in Europe.

The author of that industrial policy, T. K. Whitaker, also held strongly anti-protectionist cultural views which underpinned his willingness to see the state opened out to foreign influences. His own cultural ideology, based on a long view of Irish history, stressed Ireland's ability to assimilate and make her own the cultures of invading peoples. His combination of reverence for Ireland's Catholic cultural past and confidence in its ability to absorb foreign influences was a useful ideological frame of mind for a man who was about to open the floodgates. When Whitaker made a pilgrimage to the shrines of the Irish saints and scholars who had evangelised the Germanic tribes in the seventh and eighth centuries, he found that their statues shared altars in St Gallen or Salzburg with native German saints. He was able, however, to console himself with the thought that 'Irish initiative and devotion needed eventually to be underpinned by German organization and method!'[4]

Imagine a poet in Whitaker's Department of Finance, watching and taking part in this revolution. Imagine him deeply concerned, as any poet might be, with ideas of tradition and continuity. Imagine him watching and writing, as Thomas Kinsella, Department of Finance civil servant, does in the title poems of his 1968 collection *Nightwalker and Other Poems*:

> Robed in spattered iron
> At the harbour mouth she stands, Productive Investment,
> And beckons the nations through our gold half-door:
> Lend me your wealth, your cunning and your drive,
> Your arrogant refuse;

Let my people serve them
Bottled fury in our new hotels,
While native businessmen and managers
Drift with them, chatting, over to the window
To show them our growing city, give them a feeling
Of what is possible; our labour pool,
The tax concessions to foreign capital,
How to get a nice estate though German,
Even collect some of our better young artists.[5]

How would such a poet differ from his predecessors? For one thing his concern for continuity, the concern which caused Yeats and his colleagues to establish the myth that their movement was a revival rather than a synthetic creation, would be twisted into a painful awareness of discontinuity. Kinsella becomes absorbed with what, in his 1971 Thomas Davis Lecture he calls 'The Divided Mind':

I recognise that I stand on one side of a great rift, and can feel the discontinuity in myself. It is a matter of people and places as well as writing — of coming from a broken and uprooted family, of being drawn to those who share my origins and finding that we cannot share our lives.[6]

The source of that sense of discontinuity, in its public manifestation, is made clear in *Nightwalker*: it is economic change. Kinsella's failure, however, is that he came to locate that rift in the linguistic divide between the old Gaelic poets and the later Irish poets writing in English instead of in the immediate political social changes which he had himself recorded. His project became merely linguistic and he tried to pursue a lost sense of cultural continuity by translating the Gaelic poems in *The Tain* and *An Duanaire*. (The latter is dedicated to T. K. Whitaker 'who gave the idea'). His own poems suffer the discontinuity, fragmentation and indeed confusion of the new Ireland without coming to terms with them. He obscures the meaning of the sense of breakdown which he reflects. His failure is all the more pointed because it was Kinsella himself who, in 1966, identified the task of the contemporary Irish writer — to follow 'Joyce's act of continuity: he simultaneously revives the Irish tradition and admits the modern world' by directly confronting in his writing 'what he sees shaping the new Ireland'.[7]

Kinsella's dislocation of the sources of continuity from the immediate and political to the historical and literary is not a unique response in contemporary Irish writing. A similar response to discontinuity is evident in the plays of Brian Friel,

where a sense of loss and rupture is located first in the immediate
social and political circumstances of the early sixties, is then
evaded, and finally is located in a historical and linguistic context
which allows it to be dealt with at a distance, keeping the writer's
hands free from the vulgar grime of contemporary Irish reality.
Friel's sense of the divided mind is dramatised in a clear social
context in the 1964 play, *Philadelphia, Here I Come!* where it is the
tension of the real and contemporary Irish dilemma — emigration
— which makes it appropriate to split the main character Gar
O'Donnell into two parts, Gar Public and Gar Private, played by
two different actors, and to take soundings in the spiritual
schizophrenia engendered by the pull between home and the
small town on the one hand and dreams of success in the big city
on the other, exactly mirroring the beginnings of urbanisation
and industrialisation in the early sixties.

In the play which follows *Philadelphia, The Loves of Cass Maguire*,
the elements of the social contradictions in Ireland in 1966 are
clearly present. There is the opening of the play described above,
with its tension between a rambling Mother Ireland and a young
man of the new generation; there is the appearance of W. B. Yeats
only as a figment in a mad woman's fantasy; there is Cass talking
in an entirely American idiom, a kind of patter that was beginning
to be heard in Ireland and that would become the new *lingua
franca* in the years to come; there is the fact that 'Colonel Johnson's
place',[8] the local Big House, is said to have been bought by the
people who own the dancehall, signalling the rise of the new
Irish middle class on the high tide of foreign investment; and
there is Tessa, the girl who works in the nursing home, whose
fiancé is going to build her a bungalow 'with bay windows and
venetian blinds, and a big garage and red-tiled roof',[9] the first
reflection in contemporary literature of the rash of brash new
bungalows which began to replace the quaint but mean thatched
cottages as money was injected into the countryside. These
incidentals set out the lie of the land in an Ireland which is changing economically and socially. Above all, there is the central concern
of the play with a past which has now become problematic. Cass
tries to insist that 'yesterday's dead and gone and forgotten', but
is immediately warned by her son that 'You may think you can
seal off your mind like this, but you can't. The past will keep
coming back to you'.[10] The past becomes problematic only when
it is being broken with, and in the Ireland of 1966 there was an
unprecedented break with the past in progress.

The Loves of Cass Maguire, however, is a slight play which goes little beyond a statement of its dilemma, and in the end tidies its heroine away in her past rather than trying to have her confront her future. Cass is left rambling in an old folk's home and the sharpness of Friel's vision is blunted by sentimentality. And having identified the social rupture caused by economic change in Ireland in the sixties, Friel effectively left it there. As the sixties wore on, the explosion of civil conflict in Northern Ireland became a more pressing context for his work and he eventually abandoned the Southern Question of economic and social change for the Northern Question of identity and a different sense of dislocation. By a different route, he arrived at the same dislocation of discontinuity as Kinsella had done. Like Kinsella, he came to abstract the sense of discontinuity from the real and immediate economic change and locate it in language, most explicitly in his companion pieces of the early eighties, *Translations* and *The Communication Cord*. *Translations* deals ostensibly with the same situation as one of Friel's very first works, a radio play called *To This Hard House*. Both plays concern a small rural school threatened by change. But the shift of concern within the same basic story, apart altogether from the maturation of Friel's skills in the interim, is significant. *To This Hard House* was written in 1958, the first year of the new economic policy, and its concerns are with social change. It is set in its own time and the threat to the school is explicitly from 'population trends, new industries etc.' *Translations*, twelve years later, and after the explosion of the Northern conflict, is set in a small rural hedge-school, but now the story is located in the distant past, in 1833, and the pivotal point of rupture and discontinuity is also put back 125 years. Crucially, the nature of the rupture is changed from a primarily economic one to a primarily linguistic one. Friel chooses 1833 because it is the year in which the English language invades the bucolic life of Ballybeg. The 'divided mind', as in Kinsella, is no longer the schizophrenia caused by rapid economic and social change in the late fifties and early sixties of this century, but a hiatus between mind and tongue caused by the switch between one vernacular and another in the last century. An economic and cultural problem becomes merely a cultural one.

The evasive action taken by Kinsella and Friel in relation to the economic and cultural schizophrenia of the Republic of Ireland after Whitaker is not, however, a matter of mere wilfulness. Their reaction in the face of Ireland's belated industrial revolution is not untypical of the way writers in more developed countries reacted to their own, earlier, industrial revolutions. They decided, literally, to mind their own business, to retreat into their own domain of culture, language and history. This retreat is motivated by a crisis in the relationship between the writer and the audience which is itself a part of the greater cultural problem which followed on the modernisation of the Irish economy.

The great force which united culture and politics, literature and economics, writers with their audience, was Irish nationalism. The strength of the nationalist movement was its inclusiveness, the way in which it managed to find a place within its political goals for everything from economic demands to religious right-eousness, from the words the Irish were to speak to the games they were to play, taking literature effortlessly into its broad sweep. The advantage, albeit a highly problematic one, from the point of view of the literary movement was that writers could see themselves and their concerns as allied to those of the public, external world. The writers embraced, and were embraced by, a single broad movement which, by and large, also included their audience. Even for those writers like O'Casey or Frank O'Connor, who chose to dissent from the glorification of the national struggle, there was a language of discourse in which the audience could share.

The same forces, however, which led to the abandonment of economic nationalism, made for an increasing scepticism among the cherished political ideals of nation. Ireland, the Ireland whose future under independence was meant to be noble, had become a huckster economy, its ruling class not noble Gael but jumped-up jobbers. The contrast between aspiration and actuality had become so bitterly ironic that, by the early sixties, Thomas Kinsella was able to parody Yeats's 'Easter 1916' thus:

> Around the corner, in an open square,
> I came upon the sombre monuments
> That bear their names: McDonagh & McBride,
> Merchants; Connolly's Commercial Arms . . .[11]

We had, said Kinsella in the same poem, 'Downstream', 'exchanged/ a trenchcoat playground for a gombeen jungle'.

The nationalist experiment had been deeply undermined by emigration, and Paul Durcan's poem 'The Girl With The Keys To Pearse's Cottage' again makes ironic play of the failed aspirations of the 1916 leaders:

> She was America-bound, at summer's end.
> She had no choice but to leave her home —

The girl with the keys to Pearse's Cottage.[12]

By the early sixties, it was impossible for Irish writers to talk of 1916 and its leaders in tones other than ironic ones. A combination of the vainglorious fiftieth anniversary celebrations of 1966 with the newly endorsed scepticism of the Whitaker/Lemass era made possible the exuberant impudence of Tom MacIntyre's story 'An Aspect of the Rising', a calculated act of blasphemy against the man who was still President of the Republic, Eamon de Valera. At the end of the story, a Dublin whore, about to entertain a client on a spot in Phoenix Park overlooking the president's residence, works herself up into a sexual frenzy through a stream of invective against the Chief himself:

You crawthumpin' get of a Spaniard that never was seen . . . with your long features and your long memory and your two and twenty strings to your bow, what crooked eggs without yolks are you hatching between rosaries tonight? . . . Diagrams — more of them you're amusing yourself with maybe, proving that A is B and B is C and a Republic is Jazus knows what until Euclid himself'd be cracked in Dundrum trying to make y'out. . . . it was damn all diagrams or anything else we got from you above in Boland's Mills when Simon Donnelly had to take over the command, you sitting there with your heart in your gob and your arse in a sling . . .[13]

As the sixties gave way to the seventies, indeed, de Valera would be symbolically replaced as an icon in Irish literature. For Thomas McCarthy, writing about de Valera on the occasion of his funeral, his 'austere grandeur' is mixed with the memory of a 'decade of darkness/A mind-stifling boredom'. For Neil Jordan in *The Past*, de Valera is the rigid embodiment of 'the doctrines of eight centuries' a figure already, in his lifetime, frozen in the vaults of history:

The windows in Dev's car are tight though as he is forced gently against the door and then forced away again with the car's movement. His face is abstract and expressionless, though somewhat kindly, eternally fixed in that gaze with which it met photographers, as if now anticipating a photograph. It never changes.[14]

More typically, for Paul Durcan, de Valera's austerity, the quality on which the heart of a generation of Irish people were fed, is merely absurd:

But even had our names been Diarmaid and Grainne
We doubted De Valera's approval

> For a poet's son and a judge's daughter
> Making love outside Aras an Uachtarain.
>
> I see him now in the heat-haze of the day
> Blindly stalking us down;
> And, levelling his ancient rifle, he says 'Stop
> Making love outside Aras an Uachtarain.'[15]

As a public hero, de Valera is replaced by Durcan with another President of the Republic, and an infinitely more cosmopolitan figure, Cearbhall Ó Dálaigh:

> A Gaelic Chinaman whose birthplace
> At 85 Main Street, Bray,
> Is today a Chinese restaurant.[16]

de Valera's imaginative dethronement as the presiding deity of public life is much more than an expression of political preferences. It is the rejection of independent Ireland before Whitaker and, as such, a direct reflection of the impact of the new Ireland on the literature of the sixties and seventies. It is also a mark of the degeneration of nationalism as a binding force behind the literature.

If Irish nationalism and its demigods became a soft target for writers after the *First Programme of Economic Expansion*, the element of that nationalist ideology which most influenced modern Irish literature, the notion of the countryside and its attendant peasant as the essential Ireland, though it did not by any means cease to be prevalent, did at least attract an increasing scepticism. As late as 1954 it had been possible for an Irish writer like Paul Vincent Carroll, regarded as a realist, to extol the myth of the impoverished but wise Irish peasantry, unselfconsciously creating an image of Ireland as a place which existed primarily for foreigners:

She [Ireland] may well be destined to be the saviour in a world jungle of rank material weeds, and perhaps distracted foreigners, driven to despair by the ever-multiplying complexities of a machine- and gadget-ridden age, will visit her to try to relearn, from that tattered woman trudging her way to the slum hospital to have her baby, or from that peasant lost in wonder at the yellowing barley, the unutterable simplicities of living ... If *that*, instead of prosperity, population and efficiency, is the destiny of Ireland, then surely she is the divine instrument of a pitying God, and I, as one Irishman, will be well content.[17]

After Whitaker, however, Anthony Cronin in his poetry articulated the resentment of writers whose milieu was essentially urban at the glorification of rural literature which had been a major part of Irish ideology since the Literary Revival. His tart scepticism about the literary myths is to the fore in 'The Man Who Went Absent from the Native Literature':

> He did not think that the cabin where the rain came in under the
>   door was free from sordidity;
> And thought that in any case the sordid we had always with us.
> But that when it came to the sordid
> Metropolitan sordidity was richer and more fecund.[18]

And again in 'Homage to the Rural Writers, Past and Present, At Home and Abroad':

> The endurance of the rural breed
> Seems, like the rugged landscape, stoical.
> Rural grasping, rural greed,
> Are somehow, unlike ours, heroical.[19]

While Cronin attacked the literary icon of the peasant, however, it was left to writers with their origins in Ulster, the centre of urbanised, industrialised culture in Ireland, to attack the thing itself, to try to show the cruelty and ignorance of the previously idealised peasantry. Patrick Kavanagh in *The Great Hunger* and Flann O'Brien in *An Béal Bocht* had already effectively attacked the notion of a pure and happy peasantry, but there was nothing in the literature with the same deep aversion to the peasantry *per se* as is found in, say, James Simmons' 'Peasant Quality' or in Michael Longley's 'Mayo Monologues'. Simmons watches drunken, Gaelic-speaking countrymen disporting themselves in 'this hideous Bloody Foreland pub':

> Their fields are full of stones
> when they want bread and a job and so much more
> than tvs and cinemas and telephones . . .
> Possessed by three unities they will never escape —
> ignorance, poverty and hate — they definitely are
> stylish, passionate and in great shape.[20]

Longley, in his three monologues, moves from a residual memory of the archetypal peasant to a vision of a dark, vicious and disturbed sexuality which seems to go with the land to an ultimate image of the degradation of the pure peasant living in harmony with nature: a poem about a bestialist.[21]

What the economic revolution of the early sixties meant to Irish literature was therefore a removal of the cultural reference points which had shaped its earlier period. With neither nationalism nor its concomitant ideology of rural life to act as a binding force, it became impossible to think of an Irish literary movement. Movements need common reference points, and in the Ireland of the sixties and after, it was precisely the fixed cultural notions which were being called into question. New class forces, new divisions of urban and rural, new consumer choices were making themselves felt in Ireland, so that 'Ireland' itself, as a fixed and coherent notion, ceased to exist, either in social life or in literature. What we are dealing with in contemporary Irish literature is a series of variations on Ireland, a series of individual responses to discontinuity, disruption and disunity. In 1959, Year One of Whitaker's revolution, John B. Keane included a prophecy at the end of his play *Sive*, spoken by Pats Bocock who acts throughout the play as a Chorus:

'There is,' he says, 'money making everywhere. The face of the country is changing. The small man with the one cow and the pig and the bit of bog is coming into his own. He is pulling himself up out of the mud and the dirt of the years. He is coming away from the dunghill and the smokey corner. The shopkeeper is losing his stiffness. 'Tis only what I see on my travels. The farmer will be the new lord of the land. What way will he rule? What way will he hould up under the new money? There will be great changes everywhere. The servant boy is wearing the collar and tie. The servant girl is painting and powdering and putting silkified stockings on her feet and wearing frilly small clothes under her dress. 'Tis only what I see on my travels. The servant will kick off the traces and take to the highroad. Money will be in aplenty. *(He points to Sean Dota, the villain of the play)* The likes of him will be the new lords of the land. God help the land!' [22]

Keane may not have been entirely accurate in identifying the farmer as the new lord of the land, but the questions he posed about the way the challenges of new money would be faced were the pertinent ones of his time. In three major areas there would be agonising changes whose effect on Irish society and its values was unpredictable. The opening up of the country to outside influence on a wider scale than heretofore in the context of rapid social change created new attitudes to emigration and urbanisation; new attitudes to sexuality; and the rise of a new class, the *arriviste* urban middle-class. For those writers who chose to reflect these developments, they created fertile tensions which were played out most directly in the theatre, but also in the poetry and fiction of the sixties, seventies and eighties.

Urbanisation was problematic from the start for an Irish literary movement which had at its heart the vision of a peasantry, materially poor but culturally rich. With the exception of Joyce, Irish urban life was either ignored or assimilated to rural forms and ideals. The city, most clearly in the novels of Liam O'Flaherty but just as significantly in the work of a whole range of Irish writers, became the focus of corruption and impurity, set against the innocence and simplicity of the peasant. Emigration, which involved not just an exodus from Ireland, but an abandonment of the countryside for the city, was bemoaned precisely because it led to contact with the dangers of urban life, seen as sordid, unhealthy and unnatural. In the years after the Second World War, when the unwanted young of rural Ireland were getting the necessities of life denied to them at home in the English cities of London, Birmingham and Coventry even an intelligent novelist like Bryan McMahon could be heard to wail 'The pattern of Irish life in the shoddy towns of industrial England has yet to reveal itself; it seems rather a pity that the rural Irish did not emigrate to rural England'.[23] The automatic characterisation of city life as shoddy, the staggering ability to miss the point that the emigrants actually wanted jobs in the city and the accompanying belief that it was not so much emigration but emigration to cities that was the problem, all say much for the enduring power of the rural myth. It was hardly accidental, therefore, that within five years of the Programme of Economic Expansion being put into effect and the drift towards urbanisation on the part of the Irish population being made explicit, a number of plays on the subject of emigration had been written by a new generation of Irish playwrights. Neither can it be said to be accidental that only one of these plays — John Murphy's *The Country Boy* — was produced in 1959 at the Abbey. The attempt of Brian Friel in *Philadelphia, Here I Come!*, of Tom Murphy in his trilogy *On the Outside, A Whistle in the Dark*, and *A Crucial Week in the Life of a Grocer's Assistant* or of John B. Keane in *Many Young Men of Twenty* and *Hut 42* to dramatise the tensions of emigration was not in keeping with the official world view of the Irish literary establishment.

Murphy's *A Whistle in the Dark* was produced first at the Theatre Royal, Stratford East in 1961, having been forcefully rejected by the Abbey's manager, Ernest Blythe. His short play *On the Outside*, set outside a dancehall on a quiet country road in 1958, had ended with the words of an embittered young man, excluded from the smug society of small-town Ireland: 'Come on out of here to hell.' *A Whistle in the Dark* takes us to that hell, the hell of the Carney family's violent existence in Coventry. The pattern seems to fit into the established significance of country and city in Irish literature: the city which the characters are forced to take refuge in is a hell, the locus of an inbred corruption. But Murphy establishes the pattern only to turn it on its head. For it is not Coventry or England which causes the Carneys to destroy each other in their fierce need to assert themselves as proud men. The move from Mayo to Coventry has meant for the Carneys only an intensification of the tribal family ties and of the struggle for survival in a brutish world which they knew at home. The immediate fountainhead of their aggression is Dada, their father, who comes from home to visit them at the start of the play. The source of their tragedy is not, as it would have been if this were a Liam O'Flaherty novel for instance, their displacement to the city, but something in themselves and in the world at home which has formed them.

A Whistle in the Dark shows the flight of emigration to be impossible, the hostility of the world in Murphy's vision having very little to do with place. It destroys once and for all the myth that Irish anguish sprang from the tainting of rural simplicities with urban complications. The play in one sense matched the national mood which was against emigration and in favour of making Ireland a fit place for its people to live in, but in another sense it went strongly against the central illusion of the new era, the belief that material progress was possible in a vacuum, that happiness could be founded on a pursuit of consumer goods without a fundamental self-appraisal and a realistic self-consciousness to go with it. The dream of material progress is precisely what motivates Michael, the eldest of the Carney brothers who tries to make a new life for himself on the basis of respectability and hard work. The dream is shown to be illusory because it is someone else's dream, a fantasy which depends on ignoring, not on coming to terms with, the past. At a time when Ireland was beginning to dream someone else's dream, which would itself prove illusory within two decades, Murphy's Michael could not but be a deeply disturbing figure for an Irish audience. Nearly a quarter of a century later, the Irishman in another Murphy play, *The Gigli Concert*, a figure who is very much like one of the Carney brothers twenty years on, finds that having made a fortune as a corrupt builder, his yearnings remain unsatisfied.

In the play which followed *A Whistle in the Dark*, *A Crucial Week in the Life of a Grocer's Assistant*, (written in 1962 though not staged until 1969) Murphy enacted precisely the process of a young man coming to terms with the reality of his own life and place and refusing the flight of emigration. John Joe dreams of America at night:

Yes, I got here, I got here! See that box over there? Treasure, gold. Big box — the big box — bigger box — the biggest one! To be sent home to Mammy, 'cause now I'm of use.[24]

But in the course of the play he awakens and begins to see what is around him, the sordid, in-turned claustrophobia of the small town:

Wives and husbands up and down the roads, pots calling kettles black; the poor eating the poor. Anybody's business but our own. Not content with the hardships of today, the poor mouth whining about yesterday as well. Begrudging, backbiting, hypocrisy: smothering and slobbering in some cunning nineteenth century way.[25]

Out of this grim realisation of reality, however, comes not the strengthening of his fantasies of emigration but the freedom to choose to stay and build a life for himself. In *A Crucial Week*, the possibility of a decent life at home is founded on a realistic vision of what home is, not on borrowed dreams.

Murphy did not, however, leave the schizophrenia of the migrant there. As the sixties progressed and the rate of economic growth accelerated, large numbers of Irish emigrants began to return home from the cities of England, lured by the promise of stable employment and the residual lustre of the country they had grown up in. Murphy's work of the seventies and eighties is full of homecomings, in *The Blue Macushla, Conversations on a Homecoming* and *Bailegangaire*,[26] and less literally in the search for a neutral ground, a space somewhere between home and abroad where the yearnings of his characters can be unfolded. Murphy's metaphysical concerns — the search for wholeness and transcendence — arise directly from the social and economic changes taking place in the country, the sense of dislocation and division which rapid industrial development produced. What has made Murphy extraordinary is his consistent refusal to seek the wholeness nostalgically, as something which existed in the past and can be regained. In fact, in his plays, it is only by the ruthless and relentless jettisoning of such illusions that a leap towards transcendence becomes possible. Despair, not nostalgia, is the route to wholeness. In a country feeding itself on the American dream,

Murphy's apocalyptic advocacy of despair has been a consistent counter-current. More than any other Irish writer he has dealt directly with the contemporary reality of the country without being imprisoned by it.

Hugh Leonard, on the other hand, has arguably become a prisoner of the reality he has tried to reflect. Leonard has been the most direct product of the social changes of the sixties, writing out of the experience of the new urban middle-class which arose from the increased affluence of the country. His work has embodied a different kind of schizophrenia from that engendered by emigration, the schizophrenia of a middle-class which is close enough to its own less affluent past to be terrified of it, insecure enough to be in danger of returning to it. The obsession with the past which haunts Leonard's characters is social and economic, rather than metaphysical in origin.

One of the immediate effects of the economic revolution of the sixties was that it made farce, for the first time, an available form for the Irish dramatist. Eugene Labiche invented farce for the *parvenu* culture of the second Empire, finding in it a way of poking fun at the bourgeois while endorsing the bourgeoisie. Leonard performed the same function for the Irish theatre, at once, in a play like *The Patrick Pearse Motel* exposing the insecurity and vulgarity of the Dublin *nouveaux riches*, and at the same time providing a cushion of laughter and resignation on which to ease their sufferings. The central characters of Leonard's plays are at the terminus of their desires. They are successful products of the economic revolution, the ones whose boats have been lifted by the consumer tide. Their primary problem is that of achievement in a society which is still half-formed. Only a generation away from poverty, their riches too newly acquired to have accumulated the sanction of time and tradition, they are gripped with fear of being sucked back into what they came from. They have no aspirations anymore, just neuroses. Caught in the truncated transition from the old Ireland to the new, they are so deeply ambivalent about their own past that they can hardly sustain a single identity and, like Friel's Gar O'Donnell, they begin to dissolve and divide before our eyes, becoming two people on the stage.

The splitting of character into two roles is Leonard's characteristic stage device. In his most successful play, *Da*, the division between the past and the present is made explicit by having the character of Charlie (who to a large extent represents the author) played by two different actors: one for his present self and another for his younger incarnation. Returning home for the funeral of his adoptive father, Charlie is haunted by his childhood and the figure of Da. He has tried but failed to lay the ghost of his origins by using money as an exorcising power:

Since I was born, 'Here's sixpence for the chairoplanes, a shilling for the pictures, a new suit for the job. Here's a life.' When did I ever get a chance to pay it back, to get out from under you, to be quit of you? . . . The only currency you'd take you knew I wouldn't pay.[27]

Charlie, split, haunted by his own past, drawn to what he came from but terrified of its ignorance and poverty, is a new kind of man in Irish literature. It is fitting that he should be an orphan, making his personal past an image of the fractured continuity of his society.

In most of Leonard's plays since his return to Ireland from working in England, in 1970, the past is vividly present on stage, defying his characters' efforts to shake it off. *Time Was* (1976), set in a new affluent housing estate in south Dublin, presents a living room which 'reflects the delight of PJ and Ellie on discovering, five years ago, that they could afford this kind of house: it has been furnished with one eye on comfort, the other on visitors'. The dreams and fantasies of childhood years, embodied now in Hollywood idols, not in Celtic mythology, slip into the present to assault two comfortable, respectable couples. The past here is positively dangerous: the couples end up literally under siege from the fantasy figures of their earlier years. In *A Life* (1979), the main characters are again split in two, with different actors playing their past and present selves. In *The Patrick Pearse Motel*, Irish history plays a farcical role, the collective past flitting about the characters as they seek moments of sexual pleasure outside of the ravages of time. The motel in question, where a sexual encounter is to take place, has rooms named after the great Irish patriots and a restaurant called the Famine Room. The joke emphasises the fact that Leonard's *nouveaux riches* have no sense of history, as rapid social mobility displaces them in relation to the past. The same ironic point is re-inforced by giving the characters names from the fenian sagas: Dermod, Grainne, Usheen, Fintan. Tradition becomes a bitter joke as the discontinuity of rapid social change shatters the connections which normally act as anchors to the world.

Strongly related to this is the way in which Leonard's plays reflect on the new sexual mores of the middle-class, another product of the economic and consumer revolution. In plays like

Summer (1974) and *The Patrick Pearse Motel*, Leonard's characters try
to substitute individual moments of excitement for coherent ties
with reality. If history is problematic, sex offers, however fleet-
ingly, a way of standing outside of time. Speaking of her husband,
Grainne in *The Patrick Pearse Motel* says

'he is so bloody dull and this house is dull, and I would love to have a
man just once, just once before my throat gets wrinkles and people look
at my brooch first and then my ring, and then me, and I swear, I swear I
will never ask for another thing as long as I live — just one short fleeting
night of harmless innocent adultery'.[28]

Grainne, awakening from the consumer dream that engulfed
Ireland in the sixties is afraid that she will become identified
merely with the material tokens of her wealth, her brooch and her
ring, and seeks a moment outside of time and contingency which
would make sense of her dislocation.

   In *Summer* we see three married couples, first in 1968, then in
1974, Richard and Jan having passed the intervening years in an
adulterous affair with each other. Between the two acts of the play
they have aged physically, as time wreaks its destruction on their
flesh. Sex is a means of suspending time and finding some kind
of union with the world, a substitute for ties of class, nationality,
religion or history. The *nouveaux riches*, having attained what they
set out to attain — money — want time to stop so that no change
can rob them of that attainment. But sex is not efficacious in
stopping the clock, and the torment goes on. Richard in *Summer*
comes to understand this:

'It takes so many years and you do so much harm before you own up to
it that in your whole life there is you and there are strangers and there is
no one else. There's a clock in a room, and you invite people in for drinks,
and hope the chat and the laughing will drown out the noise of it. Well,
it doesn't and after a while you realise that they're listening to it too. You
wish they'd go home.'[29]

   Leonard has diagnosed the same discontinuity as Friel, Murphy
and Kinsella did, the same psychological result of social change.
But where Friel dealt with that by positing a sense of wholeness
located in the past, and Murphy by placing that wholeness in the
future, Leonard has failed to find any such place where the
divided mind might be healed. Having plumbed the neurosis of
his own audience, the Dublin middle-class, he has remained
locked in to that neurosis, offering only resignation and comfort
in laughter, a sense that since nothing else is possible, things

might as well be as they are.

If the irruption of new sexual mores had its problems in middle-class Dublin, the sexual revolution in the countryside was infinitely more problematic and it was again in the theatre that the problems were played out. John Montague in his 1963 poem, 'The Siege of Mullingar', parodied Yeats and put forward an ironic view of the sexual liberation of the young:

> In the early morning the lovers
> Lay on both sides of the canal
> Listening on Sony transistors
> To the agony of Pope John
> . . .
> *Puritan Ireland's dead and gone,*
> *A myth of O'Connor and O'Faolain.*[30]

But the change in sexual attitudes was not so easily assimilated as the poem suggests. John B. Keane, above all, sought both to reflect and contain the contradictions of the countryside's sexual life in a series of plays dealing with sex, property and the family.

The ideology of Independent Ireland, enshrined in the 1937 Constitution, placed enormous emphasis on the importance of the family, but this emphasis could co-exist with the Church's Jansenistic disgust at manifest sexuality, because the basis of the family was seen as being economic rather than sexual. In the early peasant plays of the Abbey Theatre, marriage is a major theme, but it is seen as being inseparably bound up with the transfer of land. Romantic love is a luxury of the landless. One important aspect of the general economic crisis of the fifties, however, was that the transfer of land through the 'made' marriage (where sex played no part in the match) had been overwhelmed as a social force by emigration. When the young preferred emigration to a life of holding on to the land at the cost of a late marriage, the question of finding some other incentive to marriage — sex — became a crucial one to the very survival of the state. One of the central results of the modernisation of Irish society in Whitaker's Programme was the accommodation of economics to sexuality in the countryside. The rural economic order needed sex, but not too much of it.

One of the great ironies with regard to marriage and sexuality was that the church had done much to create a crisis which threatened its own future in Ireland. In its attempts to keep sex out of the reckoning, the church had focussed on the dangers inherent in social and cultural activities. Its position on the matter was summed up with admirable clarity in the New Catechism: 'What are the chief dangers to chastity? The chief dangers to chastity are: improper dances, immodest dress, company keeping, and indecent conversation, books, plays and pictures.' The problem for the church was that it was all too successful in this attempt to ensure that social intercourse did not become sexual. Where marriage was meant to be economically motivated, and economic motivations had been defeated by emigration, marriage itself simply went out of fashion. By the time that John B. Keane started to write plays, 64% of the Irish population was single; 6% widowed and only 30%, representing the lowest marriage rate in the world, was joined in holy wedlock, producing tomorrow's souls for heaven. The position in the mid-fifties was so bad that the Catholic magazine *Ave Maria* proposed

that all the culpable Irish bachelors in country districts be taken into custody and held in prison until such time as they made a promise to find a mate within six months. This may seem drastic, but Ireland's falling population, due to infrequent marriages, calls for definite action to diminish widespread bachelorhood.

Just at the point where Ireland was about to surrender its protectionist economic chastity to the advances of foreign multinationals, John B. Keane declared the need, in a play premiered in 1959, for Irish marriage to accommodate the new romantic sexuality or else face its own destruction. In *Sive* he attacked the system which saw money and property as the primary force of marriage and held up romantic love in its stead. Crucially, however, Keane was not an advocate of sexual revolution, only of an accommodation of the new forces to the old forms, of sexuality to marriage. His concern is as much that the new forces of sexual liberation should be channelled into wholesome healthy social purposes in the institution of marriage as that the old matchmaking system should be attacked. For instance, he summed up his second play, *Sharon's Grave*, written in 1960, as 'a conflict between a physically abnormal sex-crazed delinquent and a young upright lad whose heart is pure . . . an extension of the everlasting clash between the diabolical and the angelical'. The frame of mind which associates physical deformity and delinqency with 'sex-crazed' is one informed by the categories of the Redemptorist preachers against the evils of sex. Dinzee Conlee, the sex-crazed delinquent himself, is a grotesque embodiment of the forces of sexuality, rampant and waiting to be unleashed on the unsuspecting Irish countryside at the beginning of the sixties.

Keane is not sure what to do with him and has him go off and fall down a hole, though as the decade went on he would learn to domesticate the demons of Irish sexuality.

Sive had an extraordinary impact in Ireland, finding a vast popular audience around the country through the amateur drama movement, after the Abbey had rejected it. It is easy to see now that its appeal came from its dissection of the Irish family as an institution under stress. The play deals with the family in an almost schematic way. There are three different models on the family and sexuality at work: the extended peasant family based on land and kinship which is present in Mena's obligations to house her husband's mother Nanna and her illegitimate niece Sive; the nuclear family of Mena and Mike; and the illegitimate family of Sive and her dead parents. The drama of the play derives from Mena's attempt to move from one model of the family to the other, from the extended family to the nuclear family, just as was happening in the society as a whole. She tries to do this by getting rid of both Sive and Nanna and getting the money to set herself and Mike up as a normal, nuclear family, prosperous enough to take advantage of the coming good times. Her tragedy is that she is a woman crushed in the wheels of social change.

As the pace of that social change gave an increasing urgency to the need to put a durable shape on sexuality within the family, Keane probed deeper into the rural family in crisis. If *Sive* was an attack on the tribal family in the name of the domesticated sexuality of the nuclear family, the plays of the sixties, most notably *The Year of the Hiker* and *Big Maggie*, are attacks on the old matriarchy in the name of the ideal unit of man, woman and children in which sexuality is tamed and rooted. In *The Year of the Hiker* the sickness in the family is laid at the door of a frustrated and man-hating woman. In *Big Maggie*, Maggie is an image of Ireland itself, and her failure to keep her family together forms a parable of the need for sexuality and marriage to adapt to the changing times. Like Ireland after Independence from England, Maggie is given her freedom with the death of her husband. But like the Irish state before the sixties she uses that freedom to keep her children under rigid control, denying and thwarting their sexuality, largely for economic reasons. She is bent on getting her two daughters married respectably and on preventing her two sons from marrying at all until they have worked long enough for her. This attempt at control creates a boilerhouse atmosphere where sexual tensions build up to an explosive level. One of the daughters is caught sleeping with a married man, the other is

susceptible to the blandishments of a ravenously sexual commercial traveller who himself has a reputation with women. One of the
sons storms off into exile; the other wants to marry a local girl but
has not enough money to allow him to do so. In this imagined
family, Keane dramatises the entire rural society in its sexual
dilemmas. Maggie fails to hold the Niagara of sexual tension in
check, and the family falls apart, giving a grim warning of what
will happen if a way to accommodating sexuality to social stability
is not found.

The comparison of Keane's treatment of sexuality with Leonard's
is instructive. For one thing it marks the extent to which the rural
continued to dominate over the urban in the literature of the sixties
and seventies, even though in this period urban living became
the typical Irish experience. For Keane is able to use sexuality to
dramatise an entire society, while Leonard is still keenly aware of
the particularity of his characters' situation. Keane is able to
make Big Maggie a Mother Ireland figure because all of the literary
conventions allow for the dilemmas which she faces — family,
property, sexual tension — to be seen as essential experiences of
an essentially rural nation. Leonard's characters never take on
these symbolic resonances. Their sexual quest is a search for
momentary personal salvation, not, as in Keane, a crucial question
of the survival of the nation. In Leonard sex is an escape from
time, in Keane it is an historical phenomenon, a question which
arises at a very specific time in the development of a society. In
Leonard sex is a release from containment; in Keane it is that
which must be contained.

In line with literature everywhere else, Irish literature began to
treat of sexuality in an increasingly matter of fact way. A case in
point is the treatment of homosexuality. In spite of having written
an explicitly and movingly homosexual story, 'After the Wake',
published in Paris in 1950, Brendan Behan still felt compelled to
sanitise homosexuals through outrageous stereotyping in *The
Hostage*, premiered six years later. By 1969, however, there could be
a decent and sympathetic portrayal of a homosexual on the Dublin
stage in Thomas Kilroy's *The Death and Resurrection of Mr Roche*. By
1976 and *Night in Tunisia*, Neil Jordan's first book of stories, there
is, in the story 'Seduction', a completely deadpan treatment of
youthful homosexual impulses. In the eighties, the condition of
homosexuality itself, as opposed to the situation of individual
homosexuals, could be used by Frank McGuinness as a physical
metaphor for states of national consciousness — division, intro-
version — in plays like *Innocence* and *Observe the Sons of Ulster*

Marching Towards the Somme.

But the change in the treatment of sexuality brought about by
the general social changes is more than a matter of frequency or
frankness. The nature of sexuality itself as envisaged in Irish literature has changed. In the essentially romantic configuration of
Irish literature since the revival, sexuality is frequently identified
with the forces of nature. Before the sixties, in a climate of sexual
repression, sexuality is idealised, turned into a heroic, pantheistic
metaphor. Liam O'Flaherty, Austin Clarke, James Stephens and
Sean O'Casey turn sex into a God or Goddess roaming the countryside — Pan, Angus, Queen Gormlai, Eros. Stephens in *The Crock
of Gold*, Clarke in many of his poems, and O'Flaherty in *The
Ecstasy of Angus* and elsewhere, specifically identify their deity of
sexuality with the countryside and with Ireland itself. Cathleen
Ni Houlihan, the Ireland of the aisling visions is eroticised by
Clarke in his 'Aisling':

> . . . I thought her clothes
> Were flame and shadow while she slowly walked,
> Or that each breast was proud because it rode
> The cold air as the wave stayed by the stream.[31]

When we get direct sexuality in Clarke, it is most often filtered
through the cleansing strain of translation from the Gaelic poets
of the eighteenth century. As with Stephens and O'Flaherty, sex,
being absent in reality, is mythologised and assimilated to the
dominant myths of the countryside, nature and Ireland.

This, too, became impossible with the belated industrial revolution. Sex ceases to be an animistic life-force and becomes
socialised, mediated by the details of a consumer society. An
important landmark in this change is Patrick Kavanagh's long
poem *The Great Hunger* in which the conjunction of sexuality and
natural world, instead of being a benevolent form of pantheism,
becomes a nightmarish and surreal miscegenation. In *The Great
Hunger*, the sexualisation of nature is intimately linked with the
reality of sexual frustration. Here 'The twisting sod rolls over on
her back/The virgin screams before the irresistible sock' or 'They
put down/the seeds blindly with sensuous groping fingers' or
'He saw his cattle and stroked their flank in lieu of wife to handle'.
Kavanagh's recognition of the blunt facts of Irish sexual life
before the sixties makes mythology impossible. After the sixties,
when the sexual dam has burst, the treatment of sex in literature
is governed by the disillusioning realisation that it is, as Tom
Murphy's J. P. W. King says in *The Gigli Concert* 'a disappointing

answer to the riddle of life'. No one has reflected this more
directly than John McGahern in *The Pornographer*.

The problem in *The Pornographer* is no longer that sex is not
available, but that it is to no avail. The narrator sleeps with two
women shortly after he has met them. There is nothing, in the
book, special or extraordinary about this. Times, in the novel,
have changed. The woman he meets in the dance hall looks down
on the dancers and recalls

'My uncle taught chemistry. He was the Professor, a light in Maria Duce
[a right-wing Catholic organisation]. He certainly wouldn't approve of
this place' . . . Some of the couples were so wrapped round one another
on the floor that except for the drapery of clothes they might be dancing
in coitus.[32]

But the change has not brought wholeness. Far from being an
untrammelled life force, sex is itself conditioned by consumerism.
The narrator's sexual experiences are packaged as pornography
and sold, and they are utterly tainted by this fact. Whereas in the
mythologised sexuality of O'Flaherty or Clarke, sex is aligned
with nature, in *The Pornographer* the couple make love on a tourist
boat on the Shannon river — nature is, like the sex of the narrator's books, distanced, formalised and packaged for consump-
tion. In McGahern, as in Murphy, the sixties liberation is a false
one.

With that disillusion, the force which might have taken the
place of the old certainties as a unifying factor in the culture of the
nation — consumerism, the American dream — has been effectively written off by Irish literature. Aside from its inherent falsity
and hollowness, it has now, as the stream of emigration becomes
a flood again and the receding tide leaves more and more boats
beached on the desolate economic shore, become obviously ineffectual. Since the old definition of Irishness (Corkery's three
marks of distinctiveness in *Synge and Anglo-Irish Literature* are
Catholicism, Nationalism and Land) proved no more viable, the
current generation of Irish writers is one for whom Irishness
is a fractured, disunited state. In expressing this, at least, the
open influence of American and British popular culture has
provided a useful resource. From McGahern's use of pornography
in *The Pornographer* to Tom Murphy's use of the movie gangster
genre in *The Blue Macushla* and from Paul Durcan and James
Simmons' use of American musical rhythms to the European
influence on young writers like Dermot Bolger, Michael
O'Loughlin or Niall Quinn, the common cultural currency of

Anglo-America, of which Ireland is now a part, has proved a useful literary resource.

The colloquial note, far removed from any attempt at a neatly shaped, formalised artistic creation, has served Paul Durcan well in writing about a reality which is itself unshaped and chaotic:

> We live in a Georgian, Tudor, Classical Greek,
> Moorish, Spanish Hacienda, Regency Period,
> Ranch-House, Three-Storey Bungalow
> On the edge of town:
> 'Poor Joe's Row' —
> The Townspeople call it —
> But our real address is 'Ronald Reagan Hill'.[33]

Writers such as Bolger, O'Loughlin or Quinn, are creating a literature out of the new realities, confirming that the Irish young are part of the subculture of Europe, drifting in and out of the shifting army of industrial gastarbeiters in Germany or Amsterdam. Sex, drugs and rock and roll are more important in their work than religion, nationalism and land. In the plays of Paul Mercier, writing out of the north side of Dublin and its sprawling working-class housing estates, the young still have dreams, but they are the same dreams as are dreamt by the young in any city of the industrial world: soccer stardom, rock stardom, being someone, getting noticed. And Mercier, too, to reflect this world, has adapted the fast, brash style of cinema and pop videos. What is important is that these influences from international consumer culture are used, refashioned and shaped in such a way that they can contribute to a critique of the received values.

What remains of distinctiveness is the quest. Ireland, after the failure of the Whitaker era, is more unformed than ever. Whereas in post-imperial Britain there is a sense that history has ended, a sense strongly reflected in the literature, in Ireland now there is a sense that history is still only beginning. The very lack of a formed modern culture is itself a strength, a demand that things be seen anew. The evidence suggests that the new literature of urban Ireland will be less carefully honed than what had gone before, but that it will draw on new realities. Its journey will be without maps.

LITERATURE AND CULTURE IN THE NORTH OF IRELAND

ANTHONY BRADLEY

Literature in modern Ireland has traditionally been preoccupied with the question of cultural identity and has borne much of the burden of social and political expression. Of course, neither the literature of the Irish Renaissance nor of what has been described as the Ulster Renaissance is completely defined by its Irishness, but both bodies of literature exist in a particularly intimate relation to Irish history, society and politics. It is the connection between Ulster writing and the divergent cultures of Ulster that I am concerned with in this essay.

Literature is a manifestation of culture, to be sure, but precisely because it is art, literature contains and distances itself from culture. So we are able to experience its cultures through the poems, plays and novels that come out of Ulster, but cannot simply equate the literature with the particular cultural situation in which it originates.[1] My aim is, then, to see how some of the better-known Ulster writers, writing mainly in the last 25 years, embody or reject or refract the conflicting cultures of the North; to determine the extent to which the work of those writers is rooted in an affiliation with a cultural tradition defined by a particular religion, history and politics, attitude to place, class, and language. Each one of these topics could be, perhaps should be, the subject of a separate, exhaustive essay or book chapter, so my treatment is, given the limitations of space, highly selective.[2]

To use the terms 'Catholic' and 'Protestant' to describe writers from the North of Ireland may seem to contaminate literary criticism with the sectarian crudity that bedevils social and political life in that part of the world. A general reluctance to see literature in its social and historical contexts becomes particularly pronounced in the case of the North, presumably because the nature of the conflict there seems archaic and tribal. So I use 'Catholic' and 'Protestant' reluctantly but advisedly, as the least unsatisfactory shorthand to indicate the two separate cultural

36

traditions out of which Ulster's writers come. I should add the qualifications that, in every case where I use 'Catholic' or 'Protestant' to describe a writer, I really mean 'from a Catholic [or Protestant] *background*', and I do not impute religious belief (or disbelief, either). My point is that if none of the writers I discuss stands in a simple relation to the world-view implied by the terms 'Catholic' and 'Protestant' in the Ulster context, their sensibility and consciousness can nonetheless scarcely fail to have been shaped by their social and political experience in Ulster, granted that the differences between the two cultural traditions have been recognised as extending, historically, into virtually every aspect of life — not only one's religion, education, place of habitation, politics, interpretation of Irish history, but also which foot one uses to lever a spade, and in the popular mind, at least, one's pronunciation of the letter 'h'.[3]

What Ulster writers from the two cultural traditions have most in common is that they are both at odds with the dominant culture in the North — that Calvinistic blend of religion and politics that not only characterises the more extreme manifestations of public life in Ulster, but also affects the whole quality of life, personal as well as public; what John Montague describes in *The Rough Field* as 'a culture where constraint is all'. It is not only the bitterness and violence of that ideology, the particular nightmare of history created by this mentality that the Ulster writer finds himself confronting, but also the other more subtle manifestations of the same outlook that result in the crippling of creative possibilities for the human spirit, and the complication it introduces into almost every aspect of personal life and human relations.

Writers from a Protestant background usually engage in a more intimate and confrontational encounter with this dominant culture of the North; by and large, Catholic writers view this culture as alien from the outset, and if they tend to resist the claims of Irish Catholicism and nationalist ideology, there is a greater degree of acceptance by Catholic writers of their cultural and religious background than by Protestant writers of theirs. Perhaps the sense of belonging to a larger Irish culture has always been the Ulster Catholic's way of compensating for an inimical political and social system. Writers from a Protestant background, on the other hand, are faced with the fact that their culture, historically defined by the emphasis on Calvinism, has been invoked as the rationale for Protestant economic and political supremacy, and has a history of indifference or antagonism to art:

This simple culture was, for most of its adherents, a non-literary one which did not encourage either the reading or the writing of imaginative literature . . . Social and cultural values were increasingly determined [with the advent of the Industrial Revolution] by a Presbyterian middle class with one eye firmly fixed on God and the other as firmly fixed on Mammon, and imbued with the determination to live honest, sober lives from which anything resembling art for art's sake would be rigorously excluded.   (Lyons, pp. 129-30)

II

Not men and women in an Irish street
But Catholics and Protestants you meet
                William Allingham (*Blackberries*, 1884)

Since I use the terms Catholic and Protestant as meaningful if unsatisfactory labels for Ulster writers, I had better begin by asking to what extent their writing can be perceived to be shaped by the dogma and ritual of their religious affiliation. While Ulster writing is not subordinate to religious belief (although it was so among the early Protestant colonists, just as it was in Puritan New England), both bodies of literature are arguably identifiable as Catholic or Protestant much more so than other strains in modern literature. Contemporary Ulster writing consistently draws on religion for subject matter, theme, metaphor, style, language, titles, allusions and analogies. While this use of religion as a literary source is natural in a society which stresses so emphatically religious belief and practice, (as Michael Longley points out, 'Ireland must be one of the very few remaining areas in the English speaking world which are still likely to produce poets who write out of a response to religion'), it should be apparent that in Ulster writing today orthodox belief is resisted, transformed and subordinated to the purposes of art rather than the other way around.[4]

An essay on Gerard Manley Hopkins by Seamus Heaney demonstrates a keen and clearsighted awareness not only of Hopkins' aesthetic limitations, but also of a body of poetry limited precisely because it is 'in the service of an idea'.[5] All the Ulster Catholic writers would seem to follow Joyce's lead in transforming their religion into art, in becoming priests of the imagination. At the same time, however, their minds (like Joyce's) are imprinted with the liturgy and teaching of Catholicism, and Catholicism provides both subject-matter and metaphors for their writing.

Brian Moore is the most obvious apostle of Joyce in his rejection of the repressiveness of Catholicism, in seeing Catholicism as a force that limits and constrains the growth of the free individual. Moore is the only writer from an Ulster Catholic background to dramatise the crisis of belief, a theme that is of enduring interest for Irish audience in particular, it would seem, though probably it is also a compelling subject for many lapsed Catholics in North America. Moore's treatment of this crisis, as it is suffered by Judith Hearne, by the abbot in *Catholics* (a novella revived in dramatic form at the Lyric Theatre in Belfast in the spring season of 1985), by the protagonist of *Cold Heaven* who is reluctant witness to a latter-day miracle in California, and by the Jesuit protagonist of his recent novel *Black Robe* (1985) suggests that ultimately Moore is less interested in the question of belief *per se* than in Catholicism as an anachronistic yet enduring faith that compels respect because it resists, even if unsuccessfully, the secularism and moral vacuity of the modern world (the savagery of the new world, in the case of *Black Robe*). That opposition is especially clear in *Catholics*, which is set in a future when the rock-like dogma of the Church is being eroded from within by a secular humanism originating in the edicts of the Second Vatican Council.

Moore may very well be perennially interested in Catholicism, but in his treatment of it, he reminds one of Graham Greene: in *Cold Heaven* especially, he seems to want to have his cake and eat it too — to see to what extent even a faith one disbelieves in might be stretched to account for the emptiness of a world without God. Moore is an existentialist for whom Catholicism has never had much validity in terms of its teachings, but it has always fascinated him as a belief-system, as an ideology according to whose dictates other people live their lives and resist the emptiness of the modern world. But Moore is impatient with Ulster Catholicism, a system of belief which he sees as irredeemably repressive. In a comic exorcism of Ulster Catholicism in *Fergus*, Moore's protagonist attributes to his brother-in-law the type of Puritanism associated with Cotton Mather that is more usually attributed to Ulster Protestantism. And even given that *Fergus* is comic in spirit, there is little sympathy or understanding of the impulse that drives the protagonist's sister and her husband to pilgrimages at Lough Derg, merely mockery.

A pilgrimage to Lough Derg is, of course, the occasion of Seamus Heaney's recent book, *Station Island* (1984). In an earlier quasi-pilgrimage to monastic sites on the islands of Lough Erne, which is bisected by the political boundary between Northern

Ireland and the Republic of Ireland and therefore often under army and police surveillance, Heaney's response seems to be shaped not only by the spirit of Catholicism embedded in the monastic remains (and by a more primitive religion that preceded Christianity), but also by the 'thick rotations' of the military helicopter overhead:

> Everything in me
> Wanted to bow down, to offer up,
> To go barefoot, foetal and penitential,
>
> And pray at the water's edge.
>   (*Field Work*, 1979, 'Triptych III: At the Water's Edge')

The passage encompasses, first of all, the learned response of Catholicism, inspired by the site, to humble oneself, to sublimate personal unhappiness and suffering in the aim of a higher good; to abase oneself, to punish oneself in a tradition of strict asceticism. But the passage also includes a response to the armed force represented by the helicopter, the emblem of another imperial power that requires a similar response — to 'creep' rather than 'walk' in the language of the poem, where 'walk' refers to a prohibited civil rights march in the aftermath of Bloody Sunday. What the poet faces in the Church and in the civil and military power of Britain are the twin masters faced by Stephen Dedalus in *Ulysses*: 'The imperial British state . . . and the holy Roman catholic and apostolic church.'

As with Joyce, so with Heaney, art takes the place of a faith that seems to require only self-abasement. In contrast to the anointing with ashes on Ash Wednesday, another oppressive reminder by Catholicism of our mortality, 'poetry wiped my brow and sped me'. In 'Field Work IV', when the poet presses a leaf of flowering currant on the back of a woman's hand, and rubs it with brown earth, it leaves a pattern of the leaf's veins. The poem suggests, allegorically, that art is a making palpable of the design inherent in nature. And in this version of the ceremony of Ash Wednesday, the poet, in bringing out the leaf's design on the woman's hand, celebrates her fruitfulness as part of the wider pattern of nature's fecundity; if he must acknowledge that the mark of the earth, like that of the ashes, is a stain that reminds us of our mortality, it is a mortality whose chief ingredient is not simply degeneration and decay, but a 'perfection' attributable to the stain of art and nature:

> I lick my thumb
> And dip it in mould
> I anoint the anointed
> leaf-shape. Mould
> blooms and pigments
> the back of your hand
> like a birthmark —
> my umber one,
> you are stained, stained
> to perfection.

The 'machinery' of *Station Island* is thoroughly Catholic; but the Dantean framework for this 'peasant pilgrimage' (as the ghost of Joyce, who appears in the poem, sneeringly calls it) is a literary mechanism that enables the poet to deal with various claims on his allegiance in a more dramatic form than he has employed to date. Heaney first employed the Irish Catholic ritual of stations as a metaphoric structure for a series of prose-poems in a pamphlet called 'Stations' in 1975. He conceived of these prose-poems, he tells us in the preface, 'as points on a psychic *turas* [Irish for 'journey'], stations that I have often made unthinkingly in my head'. The stations have now been incorporated, in *Station Island*, into the larger, accommodating structure of an actual Irish place reputed to be Saint Patrick's Purgatory, and into the literary structure modelled on Dante's *Purgatory*. For literary precedents nearer home, there are Patrick Kavanagh and William Carleton, both of whom wrote pieces on Lough Derg, and whose ghosts both appear in Heaney's poem.

Heaney's attitude to what he sees on Lough Derg is guarded, as though the atmosphere were both comforting and oppressive:

> I was back among bead clicks and the murmurs
> from inside confessionals, side altars
> where candles died insinuating slight
>
> intimate smells of wax at body heat.   ('Station Island', III')

Like Dante's purgatory, Heaney's is a framework or setting that contains his society's bitterness and hatred. In the Station Island sequence of poems at the centre of this volume, Heaney confronts or is confronted by the ghosts of friends murdered in Ulster's sectarian strife, by his own vague guilty sense of 'broken covenants' (personal? political? religious?), by literary ancestors who cajole, blame and offer advice. There is little reverence displayed for conventional pieties, though: indeed, the ghost of a missionary priest is surprised to see the poet and speculates that his presence in this place may be a farewell to Catholicism — perhaps he is here 'taking the last look'.

John Montague, too, frequently makes religious ceremonies the occasions for his poems, especially in *The Rough Field* (1972); the metaphor he uses for his art in the following quotation, however, characteristically plays on the social organisation (rather than the belief system) of his religion:

> I break again into the lean parish of my art
> Where huddled candles flare before a shrine
> And men with caps in hand kneel stiffly down
> To see the many-fanged monstrance shine   ('The Bread God')

There are, in this volume, poems with such descriptive titles as 'The Crowds for Communion' and 'After Mass' juxtaposed with quotations from Protestant sectarian literature. Montague's feeling in these poems is one of sympathetic identification with the people involved in the ritual, with their collective historical experience of oppression and a sharp awareness of their minority status, rather than with belief *per se*. That he recognises his own aristocratic name as a form of the despised 'Tague', the disparaging identification of anyone in the North who is Catholic, suggests how deeply felt is Montague's identification with his co-religionists in Ulster:

> Tague
> my own name
> hatred's synonym   ('A New Siege')

But Montague portrays Catholicism not only in its socio-political aspect, but also as a faith that sustains rather than oppresses the lives of his people. Montague has no inclination to condescend to or be ironic about the rituals and icons of a provincial Catholicism. Yet he sees that religious belief as valuable because it is embedded in the everyday lives of these people, and not because it is some transcendent, other-worldly system. Characteristically, religious imagery in Montague's poems is assimilated into everyday life. In the lovely 'Silver Flask' (in *The Dead Kingdom*, 1984), Montague's family, reunited after long years, experiences a feeling of communion that *includes* the ceremony at midnight mass, blending images of the eucharist melting on the tongue and wet snowflakes melting in the headlights of the car returning home. In the lives of these Ulster Catholics who inhabit Montague's poems, we encounter the unconscious embodiment of human dignity amid the harshness of their everyday lives, a virtue their church has neglected in its other-worldly icons of piety. In a moving tribute to an aunt who reared him, Montague makes us feel that her devotion to St. Theresa, the Little Flower, is not only a thoroughly typical aspect of a provincial variety of Catholicism, but more importantly, that the aunt's selfless embrace of her difficult life makes her more genuinely saint-like than the image of St. Theresa, garlanded with flowers, which is the object of her veneration:

> The thongless man's boots
> the shapeless bag apron:
> would your favourite saint
> accept the harness of humiliation
>
> you bore constantly.   ('The Leaping Fire')

In another vein, Montague will use the form of a Catholic litany of the Virgin, enlarging its function to invoke earthly and human nature in a pagan celebration of fertility ('For the Hillmother'). But what Montague does most memorably (in this context of his Catholicism), one might argue, is to people a landscape: to give us, with some of the richness and fullness of fiction, the cultural landscape of provincial Catholicism in the North.

Both Montague and Heaney also people their landscapes with their Protestant neighbours, and one can find in the poems of both writers the community of rural Ulster, its neigbourliness and its non-sectarian sense of solidarity with people of the same class who can even, inoffensively, joke about their religious differences; but one finds too, that sense of unease and suspicion, of sad distrust that so frequently infects such relationships. In Montague's 'The Errigal Road', he co-celebrates the mythology of a Tyrone landscape with an 'old Protestant neighbour' in a walk through their 'shared landscape', and laments the violence afflicting the countryside. As the two part, Montague to return to what is now his home in the Republic, his fellow Ulsterman urges him to tell the people there that Catholics and Protestants in the North share a way of life, and enjoy mutual respect despite the Troubles:

> 'Tell them down South that old neighbours
> can still speak to each other around here'
>
> & gives me his hand, but does not ask me in.

That last, disappointed phrase registers the subtle unease exacerbated by the violence even among 'old neighbours'.

In Heaney's 'The Other Side' (the obliqueness of the phrase as a way of referring to those who are not one's co-religionists is pure Ulster), there is a comparable conversation with an old Protestant neighbour. Here, however, the neighbour unwittingly embodies a separate tradition: he is, in fact — in his language, in the difference between his farm and the poet's, in his religious beliefs — the living embodiment of the Planter tradition. He dismisses the Catholic neighbour's 'scraggy acres':

> 'It's as poor as Lazarus, that ground,'
> and brushed away
> among the shaken leafage:
>
> I lay where his lea sloped
> to meet our fallow,
> nested on moss and rushes,
>
> my ear swallowing
> his fabulous, biblical dismissal,
> that tongue of chosen people.

The whole ethos that this man's historical identity has created is something formidable, prophetic, and judgmental in his observation that Catholics are not guided by the Bible:

> 'Your side of the house, I believe,
> hardly rule by the Book at all'.

If the historical irony with which the poem resonates (the mythology of colonialism that the natives neglected their land, that they elected poverty and ignorance of the word of God) is lost on Heaney's Protestant neighbour, the poem nonetheless celebrates the attempt at community, empathises with the neighbour's feelings of strangeness as he stands in the yard of his Catholic neighbour's farmhouse, embarrassedly waiting for the rosary to end before paying his social call. The poem is, indeed, paradigmatic of other encounters between Catholic and Protestant in Ulster writing, where the difference between the two mentalities is understood to be the sour residue of a colonial situation infinitely more than it is a matter of disputed religious doctrines.

Brian Moore's description of the city centre of Belfast (in chapter six of his first novel, *The Lonely Passion of Judith Hearne*, 1955) is filled with anger and impatience, but there is in the passage an awareness of the historical process of colonialism which has left this legacy of antagonism in Ulster down to the present day; this psychic landscape captures the Catholic's resentment of the religio-political world-view of the Ulster Protestant establishment — the garrison mentality, the complacent alliance of trade and religion, the urge to dominate (presented here in a sexual image):

There, under the great dome of the building, ringed around by forgotten memorials, bordered by the garrison neatness of a Garden of Remembrance, everything that was Belfast came into focus. The newsvendors calling out the great events of the world in flat, uninterested Ulster voices; the drab facades of the buildings grouped around the Square, proclaiming the virtues of trade, hard dealing and Presbyterian righteousness. The order, the neatness, the floodlit cenotaph, a white respectable phallus planted in sinking Irish bog. The Protestant dearth of gaiety, the Protestant surfeit of order, the dour Ulster burghers walking proudly among these monuments to their mediocrity.

Heaney's Protestant neighbour in 'The Other Side' is a more subtle and complex embodiment of the Protestant ethos in Ulster, an ethos which is, in the main, rejected by the writers who emerge from the Protestant tradition. In its style and attitude, the work of writers who come out of the Ulster Protestant tradition reflects and largely rejects that tradition's mentality, especially its interpretation of the Bible as justification for its world view, its particularist interpretation of God's word as a guarantee to the Ulster Protestant that he is one of the chosen people, that his tribe is elect, that only his austere and uncompromising view of the world is correct, that man is innately depraved, and finally that God is on his side politically and militarily, that He will help vanquish his ungodly enemies.[6]

There was a great deal in the poetry of Louis MacNeice (1907-63), probably the most important figure in the Ulster literary pantheon for poets born into the Protestant tradition, and in the work of his contemporary W. R. Rodgers (1909-69), that struggled with the dark imperatives of Ulster Protestantism and its puritanical emphasis on sin and guilt. Not only were their formative years spent in Ulster, but both had an intimate connection with religion in that MacNeice's father was a clergyman and Rodgers himself was, for more than a decade, a Presbyterian minister. Michael Longley succinctly describes MacNeice's poetic career: 'MacNeice's poetry began and continued as a reaction against darkness and a search for light' ('The Neolithic Night', p. 103). If this darkness was not wholly attributable to Ulster Protestantism, it certainly was closely associated with that variety of religion.

For Rodgers, the Calvinism of his upbringing was something he came to subvert joyfully in his love poetry and other poems on biblical themes. Nonetheless, he remained haunted by the nightmare of a Calvinist God:

> God broke into my house last night
> With his flying squad, narks, batmen, bully-boys,
> Proctors, bailiffs, aiders and abettors —
> Call them what you will — hard-mouthed, bowler-hatted.
>
> ('Scapegoat')

Here the echoes of metaphysical poetry recede before a social and psychological reality in which God is imaged in a peculiarly Ulster configuration of 'Special Branch [police], local party hack and Orange Lodge'.[7]

Contemporary Ulster poets continue to wrestle with the life-denying aspects of Calvinistic Protestantism. Derek Mahon's ironic expounding of scriptural texts in 'Ecclesiastes' and 'Matthew V. 29-30' is exemplary. 'Ecclesiastes' recognises and excoriates the appeal of the fanatical denial of life, the insistence that all is vanity, in the bleak landscape of a Sunday in Belfast; the 'dank churches, the empty streets,/the shipyard silence, the tied-up swings'. (The battle over observance of the Lord's Day still occasionally flares up in Ulster, though it has shifted from playgrounds to such issues as the Sunday opening of leisure-centres; a few years ago the city council of Lisburn, a small town on the outskirts of Belfast, successfully prevented a circus from profaning the Sabbath by putting on a Sunday performance. Catholics have long been considered inveterate breakers of the Sabbath for their attendance at sporting events and dances on a Sunday — in Heaney's 'Stations' a prose-poem called 'The Sabbath-breakers' describes a Gaelic-football match sabotaged by Puritan neighbours: 'the goalposts had been filled by what roundhead elders, what maypole hackers, what choristers of law and liberty.')

Mahon's 'Matthew V. 29-30' is a witty *reductio ad absurdum* of Christ's injunction to deny the self. 'Lord, mine eye offended/So I plucked it out' is only the beginning of a blackly comic annihilation of the self and others that follows from a strict interpretation of Christ's words. It is this sort of text that makes possible the implacable convictions of religious fanaticism, Mahon seems to be saying. If Catholic writers tend to react most obviously to the oppressiveness of their church as a social institution, writers from an Irish Protestant background like Mahon or Beckett are able, more radically, to see the blight to the spirit or the absurdity involved in the precepts of religion.

Mahon's evocative urban pastoral, 'Courtyards in Delft' (in *The Hunt by Night*, 1982), is the verbal embodiment of one of those cityscapes which are so characteristic of Dutch genre painting of the seventeenth century, a genre that celebrates a distinctly Protestant middle-class culture, taking as its subject the common-place and familiar life of the material world, essentially celebrating the release in art from a Catholic iconography of madonnas and angels, and from political domination by Catholic Spain. Mahon's poem may be read as an analogue for the ethos of the Protestant spirit as it manifests itself in Ulster.

The poem replicates and savours, though through a filter of astringent irony, the virtues of the mentality depicted in the portrait: the cleanliness that competes with Godliness, the tidy-mindedness, the pride in one's house, the complacent sense of order and tranquility. And it ultimately rejects that mentality because it is seen as inimical to the life of the individual and especially the life of the artist. If Mahon's urban imagination lingers not on bogland, but on

> the coal
> Glittering in its shed, late-afternoon
> Lambency informing the deal table,
> The ceiling cradled in a radiant spoon

his mind also registers the antagonism to the spirit associated with that culture, sees it, once again, as justifying its virtues in violence:

> I must be lying low in a room there,
> A strange child with a taste for verse,
> While my hard-nosed companions dream of war
> On parched veldt and fields of rain-swept gorse.

Mahon's language as well as his themes reflects his cultural inheritance. Terence Brown penetratingly remarks on Mahon's use of the word 'foreknowledge' in 'Gipsies Revisited': 'theologically Calvinist in its provenance, [it] suggests a puritan's exactitude of definition and solemnity of judgement.'[8]

Tom Paulin's poems register more harshly than Mahon's what he perceives as the 'manichean geography' of Ulster. His poems project the impoverishment of spirit he sees in Ulster Protestantism onto the Ulster landscape:

> Here, the word has withered to a few
> Parched certainties, and the charred stubble
> Tightens like a black belt, a crop of bibles.   ('Desertmartin',
> *Liberty Tree*)

Paulin also sees the characteristic mixture of theology and politics that distinguishes Ulster Protestantism as deluded. The revolutionary politics and religious tolerance of Ulster Protestant radicals in the eighteenth century, the United Irishmen, celebrated in Paulin's *Liberty Tree* (1983), stand in stark contrast to the 'theology of rifle butts' which has dominated Ulster Protestantism before and since.

The controlling ideas of much of the prose fiction by writers from a Protestant background also involves, like poetry, a rejection of an oppressive Calvinism that threatens the passional fulfilment of the self and the free spirit, as in that classic of Ulster fiction, Sam Hanna Bell's *December Bride* first published in 1951, but reprinted in 1974, and given renewed attention in the light of the contemporary vitality of Ulster writing. However, it's not only that such fiction rejects Calvinism in its more extreme forms as blight to the spirit — the imagination and art of the authors are also shaped in a positive way by the spirit of Calvinism. What I am trying to describe here has affinities with the New England Calvinism that colours the imagination and style of Nathaniel Hawthorne and Emily Dickinson, both of whom nonetheless resisted the Puritan God created by their community.

Perhaps it is this sort of quality that John Cronin had in mind when he aptly described *December Bride* as 'like some sombre woodcut come wonderfully to life'.[9] The novel is a brooding pastoral tale set on the shores of Strangford Lough. It evokes a whole way of life, that of the Ulster Protestant small farmer whose first allegiance, as Mr. Isaac Sorleyson, the local Presbyterian minister, experiences to his chagrin, is not always to the letter of holy law, but rather to the exigencies of farming. In the midst of this community live, isolated but without much active intolerance from the community, the quasi-incestuous *ménage à trois* of Sarah Gomartin and the two Echlin brothers. Mr. Sorleyson's strictures are vitiated by what emerges as not always successfully repressed sexual interest in Sarah — he has little such interest in his wife. Sarah's mother represents the austere and homely high-mindedness that evades Sorleyson, though her simple adherence to the standards of conduct set by the Protestant martyrs is portrayed with gentle irony.

December Bride has been compared to Hardy's fiction, presumably because of the pastoral element, the sense in which the lives of these characters are subordinated to their way of life, are part of the background of the changing seasons and the agricultural calendar. But *December Bride* is reminiscent, too, of Hawthorne's *The Scarlet Letter*, both in its content and style. There are surely affinities in the general situation of both novels, in which a strong-minded and passionate woman is involved with two men, is virtually isolated in a Puritan community, and is a sexual magnet for the community's religious leader at the same time as he must condemn her sin. The style of both novels, moreover, seem to have absorbed some of the more attractive qualities that suffuse the way of life of their characters — a sober and chastened use of language whether in narration or dialogue.

But of course *The Scarlet Letter* is more emphatically allegorical and symbolic in its structure, and the character of Hester Prynne, though Sarah Gomartin shares some of her characteristics, is more intellectual and noble than the heroine of *December Bride*. Bell's characterisation of Sarah and her world verges at times on the naturalistic: while he is sympathetic to her courage, passion and integrity, he also registers the extent to which she is capable of being selfish, calculating and prejudiced.

*   *   *   *   *

One might see in the sobriety of John Hewitt's poetry also a characteristic that could be described as Protestant, even though Hewitt is a resolutely secular man of the left. The tone of his poetry is suggestive of the testimony of the individual conscience, aware that it is, in the Ulster context, a voice in the wilderness. The resolutely unadorned language of his verse eschews whatever might be considered showy in favour of the plain, even the austere, emulating perhaps the Ulster rhyming weavers of the nineteenth century whose work he has written about.[10]

Hewitt aims to incorporate the native Irish tradition of Ulster into what he describes as his own Planter tradition. He uses the monastic round tower and an Ulster Protestant church tower (in the style known as Planter's Gothic) as symbols of the two religious and artistic traditions, and seeks to blend them in his own work: 'I may appear Planter's Gothic, but there is a round tower somewhere inside, and needled through every sentence I utter.'[11] Whether Hewitt achieves this synthesis or not is a matter for debate, but the idea of Gothic is interesting and relevant as an expression of the Ulster Protestant identity. F. S. L. Lyons sees Planter's Gothic, the 'fortress-like' architectural style of seventeenth-century Protestant churches built in Ulster during the Plantation as 'the visible expression of that seige mentality which is never far from Ulster Protestantism' even today (*Culture and Anarchy*, p. 120).

The Gothicism that originates in the English eighteenth-century novel is a more literary and intellectual defence than Ulster's garrisons against the intrigue and superstition of Catholicism, but its source also is in Protestant belief, as Leslie Fiedler has pointed out.[12] Gothic fiction assumed a life of its own, of course, and the horror, sexuality and violence became self-perpetuating conventions, relished merely for their own sake or employed for more complex literary purposes than the refutation of Papist superstition. The Gothic has always been an important element in American literature from its beginnings down to the present day, from Charles Brockden Brown's *Wieland* (1796) to the fiction of the mid-twentieth century that has been characterised as Southern Gothic. The earlier phase of American Gothicism, which would include the fiction of Hawthorne, Poe, and elements in the fiction of Henry James and the poetry of Emily Dickinson, is distinguished by its pronounced tendency towards symbol and allegory; in these works, as in *Paradise Lost*, evil is possessed of a certain seductive grandeur. In the later phase, the fiction of William Faulkner, Flannery O'Connor, Carson McCullers, Erskine Caldwell and others, there are aspects of both realism and melodrama; evil manifests itself in and through a sordid and corrupt society, which is spiritually deformed and grotesque. At the same time, this second phase of American Gothic shares the metaphysical absolutism of the first in that it sees human experience essentially as a struggle between good and evil. And also like the earlier body of literature, Southern Gothic to some extent internalises Calvinism in its implicit acceptance of man's sinfulness and depravity, of the predominance of evil and the difficulty of redemption; its realism, moreover, is most frequently subordinate to the modes of symbolism and allegory.

Fiction by Ulster writers from a Protestant background might thus be seen as constituting a sort of Northern Gothic, occupying an imaginative territory somewhere between Puritan New England and the Calvinist South. As in its American counterpart, the setting for Ulster Gothic is a brooding, rural landscape that emanates decay and corruption. The 'good country people' who inhabit this landscape are collectively involved in incestuous relationships, homosexuality, obsessive and compulsive behaviour, violence, rape, various forms of sadism and masochism. Published mainly in the 1950s and 1960s, Ulster Gothic runs the gamut from melodramatic fiction that may involve a relatively unsophisticated use of these motifs through a sophisticated and artfully controlled disposition of them — from Jack Wilson's *The Tomorrow Country* and *Dark Eden* to the novels of Maurice Leitch, the fiction of Anthony C. West, and Bell's *December Bride*.

The title of a novel by Leitch is couched in that biblical idiom ('it's as poor as Lazarus') that Heaney wondered at in his poem 'The Other Side', an idiom which provides inspiration for a good deal of writing by Ulster Protestant writers, and which is such an important source for the Gothic imagination.[13] The title of Leitch's *Poor Lazarus* (1969) may have been mediated, its epigraph suggests, by Chekhov's *Ivanov*, but there isn't much that is recognisable as Chekhovian in Yarr, Leitch's protagonist (except perhaps the neurasthenia he shares with Ivanov). Yarr is the only Protestant shopkeeper in a Catholic village in the border area of Armagh: he is sexually impotent, unhappily married, shows paranoid and schizoid traits, suffers a breakdown and presumably commits suicide at the end of the novel. The only meaningful relationship in the novel is the latently homosexual one between Protestant Yarr and Catholic Quigley (a Canadian filmmaker), a relationship that ends disastrously, with Yarr justifiably feeling exploited and betrayed. The area might well be the rural Mississippi of American fiction rather than rural Ulster: it is a landscape of sleazy bars and dancehalls, failing stores, grotesque characters and incidents, a panoply of moral aimlessness, of meanness, stupidity and cruelty. There is no redemption for the human spirit in the world of this novel; rather there is only a despairing sense of the corruption that contaminates both the individual and the society as a whole, and a prescient intuition of that society's disintegration. It is hard to avoid the conclusion that *Poor Lazarus* is an admonitory parable or allegory that is of intimate relevance to the Ulster situation.

There is a more recent and hopeful instance of this genre in a very fine television drama by Leitch, *The Gates of Gold* (1983), which is reminiscent of Flannery O'Connor's fiction. The plot involves a mute, retarded girl living on a farm in County Antrim with rather joyless, older foster parents. She is enabled to speak by an ageing, alcoholic evangelist who seems to be having a homosexual liaison with a younger evangelist. Their tent crusade smacks of charlatanism, but is actually the agency for a very human grace and redemption.

III

> The present state of Ireland bears so strongly
> on the past, that in delineating the one we
> seem to portray the character of both.
>
>> Charles Teeling, Introduction, *History of the*
>> *Irish Rebellion of 1798: A Personal Narrative*
>> (c. 1828).

For Ulster Catholic writers especially there is, in George Steiner's phrase, 'a past tense to the grammar of being'; there is a focus within their work on the Irish past, and of course their interpretations of the past have a more or less direct bearing on the present.[14] History in Ulster *is* politics. But although Ulster Catholic writers ultimately see the present predicament as the outcome or repetition of a process that has gone on for centuries, they are sharply aware, unlike the writers of the Irish Literary Revival, that our interpretation of history, as Steiner and others have reminded us, depends less on literal facts than on 'images of the past'. Indeed, the hedge-schoolmaster Hugh in Brian Friel's play *Translations* actually *says* this (and there are other instances of quotation and paraphrase from Steiner in the dialogue which buttresses another central theme of the play, the extent to which any act of communication is, even when the would-be communicators share the same language and culture, an interpretation between privacies). And Ulster Catholic writers are also as self-conscious as Thomas Kinsella about the difficulty of recovering their cultural inheritance from the Gaelic world because that tradition is available to them only as something that is discontinuous and fragmented.[15] (One also senses in Ulster writers some of Joyce's reluctance to trust the native tradition.)

One image of the past shared by Heaney, Friel and Montague is the peasant institution of the hedge-school. Heaney uses it as a metaphor for a certain way of life that is encountered in modern Irish poetry for the first time in Patrick Kavanagh: 'Kavanagh's grip on our imaginations stems from our having attended the intimate hedge-school that he attended' ('The Sense of Place', *Preoccupations*, p. 137).

That metaphor of the 'hedge-school' for a way of life experienced by so many of the Irish people is suggestive of a shared legacy of experience in rural Ireland's small farms, its social organisation, its pastimes, its work, education, religion, its emphasis on what Kavanagh would have called the 'parochial' in an approving way. So that what begins to get into print with Kavanagh and continues in contemporary Ulster writers from a rural background is a social and historical realism that gives expression to a way of life that had not really been expressed before. It is a literature written by a recently emerged class in Irish society, a democratising version of pastoral that eschews the heroic mythology of the Revival and is a much more accurate and intimate representation of the social structure of modern rural Ireland than anything written by Yeats or the Revival writers.

The image of the hedge-school in Heaney's poems (he gave the title *Hedge-School* to the Glanmore sonnets of *Field Work* when the sequence was published separately) is emblematic of the way of life of the people, a way of life with its own pieties and art and institutions, a Hardyesque native and peasant tradition of which Heaney feels a pàrt, a tradition which is not part of the high literary culture of the middle classes:

> Then I landed in the hedge-school of Glanmore
> And from the backs of ditches hoped to raise
> A voice caught back off slug-horn and slow chanter
> That might continue, hold, dispel, appease
>
> (Glanmore Sonnets, II)

Yet this quotation is taken from a sonnet, a form whose genealogy is decidedly literary and non-Irish. Of course, Heaney marries both traditions, the native one with that other to which he also belongs, which includes books, universities, cities and the European and American literary traditions in its broader view of the world.

In *Translations*, Friel seems painfully aware that what was left of the native Irish culture by the 1830s was an anachronistic peasant culture, symbolised by the hedge-school, to which English Victorian colonialism, via the national school and the ordnance survey, put a swift rather than lingering end. Indeed *Translations*, like Friel's other political plays, seeks to alter the nationalist context in which 'the Irish problem' is to be understood. In *Translations*, Friel sees Irish history in the wider context of the history of colonialism, just as in *The Freedom of the City* (1973) he portrayed the involvement of poor Catholics in the civil rights phase of the present Troubles as part of the context of third-world struggles.

Heaney has mythologised the historico-political plight of Ulster Catholics in another image of the past that bears obliquely on Ulster's present. Those astonishing archaeological finds in Danish peat bogs, the miraculously preserved bodies of men and

women from the early Iron Age who were ritually murdered as
sacrifices to the Earth Mother, offered Heaney (in the volume
North especially) a powerful if ambivalent mythology to which, in
some measure, contemporary history in the North of Ireland
might be assimilated. Heaney seems to have been obsessed in
his series of bog poems with the need to find metaphors which
would register the pathological aspect of the minority's identity
in the North, an aspect which is partly elective, deriving from the
potent nationalist mythology of sacrifice to a female principle
called Ireland, but which is also (more often, perhaps) unsought,
a matter of victimisation.

Yet while the Danish bog people are reckoned to have been
sacrificed for the common good, there is, by and large, little sense
of renewal in Heaney's poems even when it is clear that he is
focussing on the preserved bodies of Iron Age victims as distinct
from the corpses of Ulster's political violence. Rather, both sets of
victims are regarded with a kind of fascination and awe, with an
equivocal mixture of horror and reverence. One might see the
'repose' (a word that recurs in these poems) of these bodies
preserved by the chemistry of the bogs as a way of immobilising
complex loyalties in the Ulster situation by seeing that violence as
in some way natural and recurrent. The overwhelming emotional
effect of the bog poems, however, is the sense that contemporary
Ulster, like Iron Age Denmark, is an atavistic, tribal society in
which violence, hatred and barbarous murder are deeply en-
grained in the whole way of life.[16]

If the analogies of the bog poems are, however powerful in
their emotional effect, somewhat generalised in their connections
with political murder in Ulster, there is something profoundly
and directly affecting about Heaney's elegies for the individual
victims. In these poems (in *Field Work*) there is a vivid realisation
of the individual human being, of the particular shape and meaning of his life, and of the horror of his murder; most of all, there
is the calm confidence of the poem that the spirit of the dead
person lives on. Yet part of Heaney must feel that even those
elegies need to be demythologised, to be challenged because the
comfort they offer is an evasion of human and political realities.
So in *Station Island*, Heaney confronts himself with the accusation,
uttered by the subject of one such elegy in *Field Work*, that he has
used art as an evasion of reality:

> 'The Protestant who shot me through the head
> I accuse directly, but indirectly, you

who now atone perhaps upon this bed
for the way you whitewashed ugliness and drew
the lovely blinds of the *Purgatorio*
and saccharined my death with morning dew.'

('Station Island', VIII)

Both this ghost and that of another, 'the perfect, clean, unthinkable victim', reject the mystique of victim and Heaney's guilt at his own 'timid circumspect involvement'.

John Montague's account in *The Rough Field* of Ulster history is the most explicit and some would say the most tendentious in its nationalism of the attitudes toward the past found in Ulster writers. In Montague's sequences in *The Rough Field*, he assumes the responsibility of speaking for his people in an almost tribal sense — his is the voice of the minority in the North at a critical moment in their history. He thinks of himself as the first poet from his background for two hundred years: 'I would appear to have been the first poet to have come from the Hidden Ulster, so to speak, from the anonymity of the Ulster Catholic population.' [17]

Montague's history is a traditionally nationalist one that sees the origins of Ulster's present difficulties in the seventeenth century, in the dispossession of land in the Plantation, the persecution of religion, the loss of a native culture; the eighteenth century offers the brief and defeated unity of Presbyterian and Catholic in the United Irishmen, the nineteenth a sectarian bigotry expressed in the Orange Order and Protestant religious leaders that has continued into the present. In *The Rough Field*, the present Troubles, as well as the poet's own family history, are deliberately set into the larger context of Ulster history. The sequences of poems that make up *The Rough Field* are ornamented with marginalia — historical accounts, letters, wood-cuts, quotations from Spenser and Davies (those Elizabethan humanists whose affiliation with colonialism helps to remind Irish writers that they cannot belong unambiguously to an English literary tradition), as well as from Engels and Che Guevara. All this insists on the fact that the present is given meaning by the past, that the mentality of the present inhabitants of Ulster has been shaped by its past.

The Rough Field resists the temptation to short-circuit history by merely tracing the source of the present Troubles to the seventeenth century, but instead traces the dissension from the seventeenth through the intervening centuries to the present.

And if Montague's history is clearly a nationalist one, it is the intimacy of the connection between, on the one hand, personal and family history, and on the other hand, the history of Ulster, that validates the sequence imaginatively. The personal feeling that animates 'A Grafted Tongue' makes it *not* a poetic commentary on an historical tradition the condition of which is felt to be mutilated, but rather a poem that expresses an intense, personal realisation of that historical experience. The difficulty of articulation which that poem embodies is a subject shared by other Ulster Catholic writers: by Heaney, who sees the hanged body of Henry Joy McCracken (in 'Linen Town') as 'a swinging tongue', and connects reticence and silence with the political and cultural identity of the Ulster Catholic, and by Friel in *Translations*, in the mute character of Sarah.[18] The context for Sarah's muteness is, as in Montague's poem, the switch from hedge-school to national school; the fact that her muteness is a given at the beginning of the play does not change the basic connection in Ulster Catholic writers between a repressive political and cultural situation and the failure of articulation. Finally, the tendentiousness of *The Rough Field* as history (and here it fills the vacuum in recent scholarly historiography of Ulster which is copious and diverse in tendency, but contains no traditionally nationalist account of Ulster history) is offset by other themes: by the prevailing note of dismay at the decay of the rural community, both Catholic and Protestant, and by the note of exile that separates the poet from the world of his childhood and youth.

Despite recent revisionist histories of Ireland, the society of United Irishmen, founded in Belfast in 1791, persists as the only hopeful image from Ulster's past of the transcendence of sectarianism in common revolutionary purpose. The insignia of the United Irishmen (a harp encircled by the motto 'It is new strung and shall be heard') adorns the cover of Montague's *The Rough Field*; Heaney's 'Linen Town' reflects the 'tang of possibility' that characterised this period of the North's history. Tom Paulin's poems in *Liberty Tree* (1983) and Stewart Parker's play *Northern Star* (1984) are also focussed on this unique moment in Ulster's past. Paulin looks back to Ulster's eighteenth century Protestant radicals for an answer to the question that monotonously dominates the present in Ireland. 'And Where Do You Stand on the National Question?' may put that question in a mockingly naive way, but the answer is serious and genuine:

I want a form that's classic and secular
the risen République
a new song for a new constitution

John Hewitt is Montague's Protestant counterpart in the explicitness of his concern with Ulster's history from the vantage point of an inheritor of the Planter tradition. He is also keenly aware of the colonial history of Ulster, of the origins of Ulster's Protestant population in the Planters of the seventeenth century, of their dispossession of the native Irish, and of the persistence into the present of states of mind that have their origins, at least, in the determining historical situation of the Plantation. Hewitt's long poem 'The Colony' (1950), though it is ostensibly concerned with a Roman colony in some outpost of empire, is a fairly circumstantial account of the process of colonisation in Ulster, and a clearsighted yet sympathetic rendering of the colonial predicament of Protestants who were, in the words of another poem's title, 'once alien here', but now feel as native as anyone else.

Other Ulster writers, both Catholic and Protestant, are impatient with what seem to them an archaic history and definition of the modern self. The nationalist tradition holds no attraction, for example, for Brian Moore. The characters in *The Emperor of Ice Cream* (1965) who are associated with that tradition are seen as self-deluding, sanctimonious relics of a creed that is faded if not outworn, led into foolish sympathies with Germany during the Second World War because of their anti-English sentiment. That is, if they belong to the middle class. If they are proletarian types with the self-destructive courage of their foolish conventions, like Gallagher in the same novel, who tries to signal to assist German planes in the blitzkreig of Belfast, they are moronic. For Moore, Irish history is clearly irrelevant to the longed-for disaster of the Second World War which 'confers meaning' on the dull town of Belfast by making it part of world history, and affording his autobiographical persona the opportunity to show all who contested his passage to adulthood how wrong they were. It is possible to see Moore's tendency in this novel, like that of the poets frequently cited in it, as symptomatic of what George Steiner describes as 'the phenomenology of *ennui* and of longing for violent dissolution' (*Bluebeard's Castle*, p. 23).

If there is in Moore a rejection of the images of the past that compose Irish history, there is also an acceptance of a greater nightmare, as though *that* would strip away all false consciousness, destroy bourgeois pretence and enable one to live authentically.

Derek Mahon would seem to share Moore's impatience with
Irish history, especially in its more contemporary manifestations:
thus he rejects the demands of his 'fire-loving/People . . . that I
inhabit,/Like them, a world of/Sirens, bin-lids/And bricked-up
windows' ('The Last of the Fire Kings'). There is an emphatic
yearning in Mahon to be 'through with history' (the phrase
occurs in both 'Rathlin Island' and 'The Last of the Fire Kings'),
to be safe from 'the historical nightmare' ('The Apotheosis of
Tins'), and many of Mahon's poems take place in some post-
apocalyptic setting. Indeed, to be through with history, not just
Irish history, almost demands the apocalypse. What is it in Western
culture that he and Moore should so cry out against it, should
anticipate, almost vengefully, its destruction? It is not so much
disgust with the barbarities and stupidities of Irish or European
history as anger and impatience with bourgeois society's stagnation and infuriating complacency. It is as though the elimination
of bourgeois beliefs and values requires wholesale destruction.
The implicit argument would seem to be that only if the middle
class and its fetishistic concerns with 'fitted carpets, central
heating/And automatic gear-change' ('Poem Beginning with a
Line by Cavafy') is destroyed, '. . . may [we] give our attention at
last/to things of the spirit' ('The Apotheosis of Tins'). The bombing
of Belfast in Moore's *Emperor*, 'the twilight of cities,/the flowers of
fire' ('The Golden Bough') in Mahon are the wish-fulfilment (in
Moore's case gratified by history) that derive from alienation,
ennui, loathing and nausea provoked by bourgeois society.

The Second World War in which, of course, Eire (what is now
known as the Republic of Ireland) was neutral, and Ulster engaged
because of its constitutional link with Britain, was a catalyst
that tested not only the divided loyalties of Anglo-Irish writers
like Elizabeth Bowen (who sent secret reports from Eire to the
British government on the attitude of the Irish people to the war),
but also the loyalties of writers from an Ulster Protestant background, like Louis MacNeice.[19] Their plight is essentially the
same: as Heaney points out, it is the problem of belonging to two
nations.[20]

MacNeice's love-hate for Ireland was uncomprehending of
Irish neutrality and dismissive of the new state's assertion of
independence. For him, 'the kiss of the past is narcotic' ('Western
Landscape'); history is not the inward-looking Ireland and its
Gaelic past, but the present exigencies of Europe and Hitler; Irish
neutrality is a treacherous betrayal of the lives of Ulstermen and
British soldiers and sailors:

The neutral island facing the Atlantic,
The neutral island in the heart of man,
Are bitterly soft reminders of the beginnings
That ended before the end began.

Look into your heart, you will find a County Sligo,
A Knocknarea with for navel a cairn of stones,
You will find the shadow and sheen of a moleskin mountain
And a litter of chronicles and bones.

Look into your heart, you will find fermenting rivers,
Intricacies of gloom and glint,
You will find such ducats of dream and great doubloons of ceremony
As nobody today would mint.

But then look eastward from your heart, there bulks
A continent, close, dark, as archetypal sin,
While to the west off your own shores the mackerel
Are fat — on the flesh of your kin.

Ulster Catholics were suspected, as were their co-religionists in neutral Eire, of advancing the cause of a united Ireland at the traditional time of England's difficulty; in fact, the English government in 1940 offered the unification of Ireland to de Valera if Eire would come in on the side of the Allies — de Valera refused (Fisk, pp. 159-88). Seamus Heaney's prose-poem 'England's Difficulty' recalls a very early memory of being taken outdoors to ness, a great distance away, the conflagration of Belfast in the aftermath of the German bombing. The piece reflects the awareness of the Ulster Catholic, sharpened during the Second World War, and, no doubt even more so during the present Troubles, that his position in the Ulster state is potentially treacherous, that he is one of 'the scullions outside the walls'. The psychological consequences are the mixture of reticence and evasiveness, even in peacetime, that some see as typical of the Ulster Catholic character: 'An adept at banter, I crossed the lines with carefully enunciated passwords, manned every speech with checkpoints and reported back to nobody' ('England's Difficulty').

IV

. . . there is almost an inverse proportion, in the twentieth century, between the relative importance of the working rural economy and the cultural importance of rural ideas.

Raymond Williams, *The Country and the City*

If the sense of place in writing by Protestant novelists and poets tends to register a bleakness of spirit, and perhaps is the correlative for a culture with which they feel out of sympathy, in Catholic writers place is conceived of in a more positive, more physical and primitive sense. If the Protestant imagination reflects an alienated sense of its native place and inclines toward the gothic mode (at least, in fiction), the Catholic imagination celebrates the atavistic power of place and tends toward the pastoral mode in poetry and fiction.

The negative connotations of the term 'pastoral', unfortunately, have been uppermost for a long time now. One thinks first of a false naiveté, of tame and artificial literary conventions. But there are versions of pastoral which inform modern literature (the fiction of Lawrence and Hardy, for example, or the poems of Robert Frost), in which certain kinds of feelings are connected with the rural world, feelings which have been formed under the pressure of individual and collective experiences before they have been shaped by literary conventions. The representation of the rural world and its values in these writers (involving a certain relation to the natural world, and a particular experience of community and work that Raymond Williams describes as 'rural ideas') has an intrinsic importance for our time, when we are increasingly separated from those feelings.[21] But the rural world also functions in these writers, just as importantly, not only as subject but also as setting for complex ideas which are not intrinsically rural. The pastoral mode in Ulster writing is also pastoral in both senses: it connects us with a way of life that is rapidly disappearing from our increasingly urban and industrialised culture, and it also employs that rural way of life as a framework for other sorts of ideas — is pastoral, in short, according to Empson's definition of pastoral in *Some Versions of Pastoral* as a structure that contains the complex within the simple.

Seamus Heaney's international popularity surely derives in part from his 'rural ideas', from the rich sense his poetry gives the reader of the energy and vitality of the natural world and a whole way of life associated with its cultivation. But even the early poems with such titles as 'Digging', 'The Forge', 'The Thatcher', and so on, not only put us in touch with the beauty and fear of the natural world, and with a traditional way of life that is vanishing from our western culture, but also involved analogies between that world and the world of ideas.

There are various strands to this version of pastoral in Heaney. There is something of the same 'surge toward praise' in his own nature poetry that he detects in early Irish poetry. And there's a whole series of poems in *Wintering Out* that have affinities with the Irish genre called *dinnsheanshas*: 'poems and tales which relate the original meaning of place names and constitute a form of mythological etymology' ('The Sense of Place', *Preoccupations*, p. 131). Heaney's celebration of the identity of places as embodied in the musical and linguistic phenomena of their names (in 'Anahorish', 'Toome', 'Broagh', 'Gifts of Rain', and 'A New Song') uncovers the Irishness of the Ulster landscape, or reveals the intersection of the North's conflicting cultures as it is reflected in these names.

A similar attention to place-names is a major focus of Brian Friel's play *Translations*, which focuses on Ulster in the 1830s, just at that critical point when Irish Catholics are disconnected from the Irish language and the native culture by the introduction of the National schools ('sham' national, as Engels described them), and by the enterprise of the ordnance survey which altered or Anglicised so many of the island's place-names.[22] These names, as John Montague is also keenly aware, can net a world of associations; this is as true of Montague's Garvaghey as it is of Heaney's Mossbawn.

Montague's poems also take us into a rural world, the melancholy landscape of his native country Tyrone:

> the rushy meadows
> small hills & hidden villages —
> Beragh, Carrickmore,
>
> Pomeroy, Fintona —
> placenames that sigh
> like a pressed melodeon
> across this forgotten
> Northern landscape.   ('Last Journey')

The elegaic tone in Montague, his sense of melancholy at the decay of a community, is frequently associated with pastoral, and especially with Goldsmith's work (the subject of an unpublished study by Montague). But if the tone of such poems as 'The Mummer Speaks', 'A Lost Tradition', 'Hill Field', 'The Road's End', 'The Errigal Road' and other poems is distinctly elegiac, Montague's technique and his sense of the immanent value of ordinary people's lives is more reminiscent of William Carlos Williams than Goldsmith. In Montague, moreover, this elegiac quality assumes a political edge as the poet registers what both Heaney and Montague, paraphrasing Corkery, have described as the 'hidden Ulster', the Gaelic identity of Ulster which preceded the Plantation and survives only in remnants in the present. Montague surveys the townland of Garvaghey in Tyrone and sees glimpses of a civilisation that was dislodged in the seventeenth century, but that survives in the political and cultural affiliation Ulster Catholics have made with it, and the note of elegy is mixed with bitterness and anger as he contemplates the enduring process of colonial history in Ulster.

There is another aspect to this version of pastoral by Ulster Catholic writers which Heaney, Montague and others share, a version that was anticipated by Kavanagh. Yeats's version of pastoral was conventional and anti-historical: the social and economic structure of Irish life was utterly different than the quasi-feudal Ireland he imagined in so many poems, which are pastoral in their marriage of the peasantry and the aristocracy, and blind to the revolutionary social changes which made Ireland a country, essentially, of small farmers who owned their land, were increasingly middle class, and had little to do with the Anglo-Irish Ascendancy, which by Yeats's day had lost its economic and political power. (Despite this movement in Irish history and society, the 'big house' persists as a powerful residual theme in modern Irish literature.)

But Kavanagh was the first Irish poet from this representative background of rural Ireland, and his significance for subsequent Irish poets, as well as for the Irish people, was immense, as Seamus Heaney points out:

Kavanagh's fidelity to the unpromising, unspectacular countryside of Monaghan and his rendering of the authentic speech of those parts gave the majority of the Irish people, for whom the experience of life on the land was perhaps the most formative, an image of themselves that nourished their sense of themselves in that serious way Synge talked about in his preface.   ('The Sense of Place', *Preoccupations*, p. 137)

The mode of pastoral in Ulster writing is not limited to poetry. In the fiction of Michael MacLaverty we have what looks like a simple strain of pastoral, expressing a nostalgia for the countryside from the prison of Belfast's narrow streets. But MacLaverty's short stories and novels reflect the historical predicament of Ulster Catholics who settled hopefully on the fringes of Belfast as it grew into an industrial centre but who always felt alienated by a city that seemed inimical to them. As MacLaverty's characters raise their eyes from the slum streets to the hills surrounding the city, there is the feeling that they have lost something precious in the transition from country to city, whenever it occurred; at the centre of this feeling is the incongruous historical awareness urban working class Catholics frequently carry with them down to the present day, of the dispossession of the land of Ulster, their land, by the Plantation of the seventeenth century.

MacLaverty documents the social experience of Catholics living in Belfast's slums, particularly in the 1920s and 1930s, lovingly representing the whole subculture of their poverty and the way they act, think, feel and speak. There is in his novels and stories a powerful but not a grim sense of the narrow lot of these people, because they accept 'the central place of suffering and sacrifice in the life of the spirit'.[23] Poverty and sectarianism are consequently endured, usually without question. To take arms against this state of affairs by joining the IRA ends in disaster in the short story 'Pigeons' and the novel *Call My Brother Back* (1939). It is not surprising that MacLaverty's stories and novels have enjoyed a renewed readership in Ulster today (many of them had been out of print for twenty years), for so much of what he describes in the works I have mentioned is familiar to people living in Belfast's Catholic housing-estates, who are conditioned by deprivation, a sacrificial ideal of nation, and the oppressive apparatus of the Ulster state. The confrontation in 'Pigeons' has taken place so many times in the present Troubles that one might conclude not much has changed in fifty or sixty years:

Three men along with my Daddy carried the yellow coffin down the stairs. There was a green, white and gold flag over it. But a thin policeman, with a black walking stick and black leggings, pulled the flag off the coffin when it went into the street. Then a girl snatched the flag out of the peeler's hand and he turned all pale. At the end of the street there were more peelers and every one wore a harp with a crown on his cap.

(*Collected Short Stories*, p. 24)

The naïve point of view and style puts the quarrel very succinctly. The tricolour of the Irish Republic asserts the irredentist claim that Ulster is Irish and the armed struggle of the IRA morally legitimate, whereas the emblem on the policemen's caps asserts that Ulster is British.

Ulster's most famous novelist, Brian Moore, is unique among Catholic writers in that he was born into an urban, professional middle class family. So his experience and imagination have not been nourished by the countryside or by writers who belong to the rural tradition — Joyce clearly is Moore's master. And yet in Moore's novella *Catholics* what we have is essentially another

version of the pastoral. The piece is set on an island off the coast
of Kerry, and is reminiscent in its celebration of Catholic monas-
ticism to poems by Montague or Heaney. In *Catholics*, past and
present are played off against each other, as are the rural world
and the urban, the community and rootlessness, religious ritual
and political engagement, and by implication, a desexualised
world and a more complicated 'real' world.

With the notable exception of Moore, Ulster Catholic writers,
unlike their Protestant counterparts, tend to be from the rural
parts of Ulster: they are the children of small farmers, shopkeepers,
schoolteachers, working people in rural occupations, who move
through the university, usually the first of their family to do so,
and then migrate to Belfast/Dublin, or more exotic and foreign
places. Montague and Heaney are the pioneers here, Muldoon and
Ormsby representative of a more recent generation. In the preface
to his excellent anthology *Poets from the North of Ireland*, Frank
Ormsby cites himself and Muldoon as examples of 'educated
Northern Irish Catholics growing away from their background
but finding their poetry permeated by its attitudes, traditions,
and minority status'.[24] One should remember, however, that it is
quite possible, if not entirely common, for a member of the
younger generation of poets in Ulster to grow up in Belfast, as
Ciaran Carson did, speaking Irish as his first language and
deeply immersed in Irish traditional arts. The extraordinary
thing is that this cultural sense of one's Irishness should be
sustained, with this kind of purity, in a large industrial city, that
a certain consciousness be available within the general character
of modern, urban social experience which runs counter to it. So
Carson's poems reflect both a Gaelic tradition (in his poems on St.
Ciaran), as well as the city life of Belfast. The situation of Ulster
poets, then, like that of Irish poets generally, only more so, is
fecund in the imaginative territory it occupies between country
and city, past and present, Irishness and non-Irishness, rural
community and isolated individual, dumb natural world and
articulate world of education, rural middle class and urban
professional class, and between religious faith and faith in art.

V

'And it can happen — to use an image you'll understand — it can happen
that a civilisation can be imprisoned in a linguistic contour which no
longer matches the landscape of . . . fact.'   Brian Friel, *Translations*

Most Ulster Catholics, like the vast majority of the citizens of the Republic, do not grow up speaking Irish as their first language. But many of them learn it in Catholic secondary schools, a process which is complemented by stays in the Gaeltacht area of Donegal. Both Heaney and Montague record the strangeness of their first encounters with their mother tongue. But if most Catholic writers have to learn Irish, it is clearly something that is of great importance for their work. Even if they write in English, and are nurtured by the English literary tradition as well as the American, they are also haunted by the language, poetry, mythology and world-view of that other tradition. One might point to the affinities with Gaelic of Michael MacLaverty's prose style as an example. John Cronin eloquently describes how the style of MacLaverty's prose 'seems in some way to have captured the muted, undemonstrative, pastel serenity of the native language as it is used in these books (*Twenty Years a-Growing* and *The Islandman*) to tell of the daily lives of fishermen and small farmers in lonely places' (Cronin, p. 76). Whether in Heaney's *Sweeney Astray* or his etymological place-poems, or Montague's translations, or their common concern with the language of landscape, shared by Friel in *Translations*, the massive structural irony of which is that the staple of its dialogue is imagined to be in Irish — all these writers thus feel obliged in various ways to come to terms with the Irish language. In some measure, at least, they graft the native Irish tradition onto the modern Anglo-American one.

There are, moreover, some few Ulster Catholics even in Belfast for whom Irish is their first language. And while there have always been Irish language schools in Belfast, and individual families whose strong sense of cultural identity led them to speak Irish at home, this commitment has spread because of the political trouble in the North. The learning of Irish in evening classes, the existence of several streets in West Belfast whose inhabitants speak Irish as their first language, the success of a new Irish school in the same area, and of course the learning of Irish in jail by political prisoners — all this suggests how significant and vital Irish is as an emblem of cultural and/or political identity in the North of Ireland.

The Irish language, then, is connected in Ulster with a sense of the past and of place that insists Ulster is Irish. Donegal, one of the counties of the historical province of Ulster excluded from the modern political unit now known as Ulster, has a particular significance for Irish nationalists in modern Ulster (as did the West of Ireland in general for Irish nationalists around the turn of the century). Donegal has this significance for Ulster Catholics precisely because it exists in such close proximity to them and is so clearly Irish in certain ways: it was part of the old province, is now part of the Republic, has pockets of Gaelic speakers, is overwhelmingly rural, possesses a wilder and more romantic landscape, and, until recently anyway, had a more depressed economy than most of the six counties. Many Ulster Catholics who were born in Belfast and have actually spent most of their lives in that large industrialised city are still able to feel that Donegal is their spiritual home even if they only visit it for an occasional holiday. The same situation is more understandable in the case of Derry, Ulster's second city, because it is only separated from Donegal, which is its natural hinterland, by the political boundary. Although Brian Friel spent many years in Derry, it was Donegal that took hold of his imagination: almost all of his plays, including *Translations*, are set in Ballybeg (Irish for 'small town') in County Donegal.

Writers from a Protestant background (MacNeice, Mahon, Longley, for example) are also attracted to the West of Ireland, though usually they see the West as a place beyond time and history. There are, however, sensitive reactions to the Irishness of the cultural landscape of the West, as in the dedicatory poem of Michael Longley's *Selected Poems* ('For Ciaran Carson: On Hearing Irish Spoken') or his 'Letter to Derek Mahon' recalling a journey to Inisheer, a poem which recalls Synge's awareness of being an outsider in the West (even though he knew Irish):

> We were tongue-tied
> Companions of the island's dead
> In the graveyard among the dunes,
> Eavesdroppers on conversations
> With a Jesus who spoke Irish —

In 'Once Alien Here', John Hewitt expressed the linguistic plight of the Ulster poet who feels at home in neither the English nor the native Irish tradition — 'lacking skill in either scale of song,/the graver English, lyric Irish tongue'. More recently, Tom Paulin has redefined the language question to point up the literary and political significance of English as it is spoken in Ireland and especially in Ulster.[25] Protestant writers, however, are more apt to reflect the language and mythology of classical Greece and Rome, and/or an acquaintance with modern European languages and philosophy. Louis MacNeice was a university teacher of classics before he went into broadcasting: it's not surprising that the titles and allusions of many poems reveal a sensibility at home in classical Greece and Rome as well as the modern world. Some of the outward manifestations of that sensibility are indicated also in his translations of the Agamemnon, of classical and medieval Latin lyrics, of French and German verse, and a notable translation of *Faust*. In Michael Longley's work we find an imitation of Tibullus and a poem entitled 'An Image from Propertius'. And if in Mahon we find a diverting updating of the Irish 'I am Raftery', we are much more likely to discover references to Ovid and translations or versions from Horace, Villon, Rimbaud, Corbière, Pasternak, and Cavafy.

Paul Muldoon is arguably the first poet from a Catholic background in Ulster to use the same psychic raw material as Heaney and Montague in a consciously modern idiom that is suggestive of Borges rather than any Irish mentor. Muldoon's Irishness is demonstrably there in his subject matter (bomb-scares in Belfast, assassinations, Irish history, religion, even the series of poems on his father) and to a much lesser extent in his technique (involving the use of *aisling*, translation from the Irish, meditations on place-names). But the Irish subject matter co-exists with the history of the American Indians, the landscapes of North American cities, voyages up the Amazon, wrestling on TV; and the traditional Irish form is wickedly subverted — 'Aisling' concerns an encounter with a goddess who seems to be infected with venereal disease and a consequent visit to a hospital where a hunger-striker who has ended his fast is on a kidney-support machine. What comes first in Muldoon is the cool, witty, surreal art of the individual poem, and its implied acceptance of the crazed nature of the Irish situation as no different than the modern world's craziness elsewhere. In Muldoon are joined the Irish rural tradition and a dandified literary cosmopolitanism: 'I flitted between a hole in the hedge/And a room in the Latin Quarter' ('The Mixed Marriage').

VI

Ireland still remains the *sacra insula*, whose aspirations must on no account be mixed up with the profane class struggles of the rest of the sinful world.   Engels to Marx, December 9, 1869

In Irish society, allegiances to nation and church have historically taken precedence over class relationships. It is clear that the root cause of this state of affairs is colonialism, and that from one perspective, this situation may be seen as a kind of arrested development whereby Ireland's growth was thwarted not only economically but ideologically as well. One consequence for Irish literature is that it tends to be preoccupied by those issues which dominate Irish society as a consequence of colonialism:

The indigenous conflict between classes, which has been such fruitful material for the English novelist, was, in Ireland, retarded and subverted by, on the one hand, the presence of colonialism, which had transformed the Anglo-Irish and the Protestant middle class into a 'garrison' class, for ever sniffing the smoke of the Boyne, and, on the other, by the way the Catholic middle class had taken over the national ideal and incorporated other groups and classes within it.[26]

Ulster society and most literature that is produced by that society continues to emphasise national and religious affiliation at the expense of class identity. When a writer (or a social scientist, for that matter) focusses on class, it tends to be a matter, inevitably, of specifying that class as Catholic or Protestant, nationalist or unionist. The same thing is true of class antagonisms, which are insulated within one or the other ideological camp.[27] So in fiction by Ulster writers, we find a revealing portrait of the Catholic middle class in the work of Brian Moore; for a portrait of the Protestant middle class, we must turn to Janet McNeill.

Brian Moore provides us with a masterful exposition of the mentality of the Catholic middle class in his novels — the doctors, lawyers, schoolteachers and priests who espouse a genteel, politically important form of Irish nationalism almost as a concomitant to their Catholicism, but whose first allegiance is to the middle class idols of respectability and worldly success. Since Moore has little or no sympathy with the working classes, Catholic or Protestant (both are viewed with distaste), his protagonists are alienated not only from Protestant Ulster in this largely segregated society, but from the larger part of the Catholic population by reason of class difference, from their class counterparts in the rest of Ireland by a political boundary, as well as from their own suffocating middle class existence. The consequence is, inevitably, that they reach a level of alienation which is unbearable.

Janet McNeill might be seen as a counterpart to Moore in her preoccupation with middle class alienation, but again the class issue is complicated by religion. John Cronin rightly praises her 'ironically sympathetic depiction of middle-class Protestant Belfast . . . More powerfully than any other writer I know, [she] conveys the very feel of middle-class, Protestant Belfast and mercilessly explores both its complacency and its unease' (Cronin, pp. 79-80). If MacNeill's novels are a great deal more muted than Moore's, and if she lacks his dramatic ability in creating character, she does convey in *The Maiden Dinosaur* the ennui of a class that has insulated itself from anything but its own immediate familial and personal problems, and a strong sense of futility about personal relationships (that is, in *As Strangers Here*, at odds with an improbable, highly-coloured action that seeks to involve the city's setting and Ulster's recurrent political violence). The protagonist of the latter novel, Rev. Ballateer, shares with Moore's protagonists a distaste for and incomprehension of the working classes.

For the depiction of class as the most significant element in Ulster society, and for a more sympathetic portrayal of the working class, one must turn to a strain of Ulster drama by writers mainly but not exclusively from a Belfast working class Protestant background that sees unionism and nationalism as equally irrelevant to the plight of the people, as manufacturing the sectarianism, indeed, that separates natural allies. Here again, though, the focus tends to be on the *Protestant* working class or the *Catholic* working class. At present, Graham Reid's plays, widely disseminated on television or enjoying long runs and attracting new audiences for the theatre, reject the supremacist ethos of Ulster unionism, the hold of paramilitary groups on Protestant working class community that no longer forms an aristocracy of labour, and an outmoded and class-ridden educational system. Reid's plays possess a particular value as a vivid and authentic rendering of contemporary working-class life in Protestant Belfast, registering anger, bitterness and despair at the entrapment it constitutes. Ironically the only course of action open to Reid's characters, it seems, is emigration, the traditional resort of Catholics driven to flee the oppressive political and economic straits of life in Ulster.

The critique of Ulster life from a leftist perspective, the sense that the conflicting ideologies of unionism and nationalism mask the real issues that should unite the working class communities of both sides, has been a hallmark of the Ulster theatre since the days of Sam Thompson, at least. The direct treatment of sectarianism in *Over the Bridge* (1960) was profoundly threatening to the Ulster establishment, political and artistic. John Boyd is, as it were, the middle term between Thompson and a younger generation of playwrights like Reid and Martin Lynch (from a working class Catholic background): the work of these playwrights is more or less naturalistic in method, and its O'Casey-ish structure of feeling attempts to subvert what it sees as the false consciousness of unionism and nationalism, which precludes any real true community for the Irish working classes. Stewart Parker's sympathies are leftist also, but Parker's technique is clearly more sophisticated and more interesting than the naturalism of his contemporaries, more reminiscent of Brecht than O'Casey.

It is worth remarking, as some evidence for the 'unpartitioned intellect' (and imagination) of Irish life, that a number of these Northern playwrights found an audience and a theatre in Dublin before they could in Belfast: Stewart Parker and Graham Reid both enjoyed their initial successes at the Dublin Theatre Festival.[28] Given a tradition of indifference or even hostility to the arts in Ulster, and given the political tensions which have never been far from the surface of life there, it must have seemed incongruous to local playwrights that the Lyric, Ulster's finest theatre was (at least formally) dedicated to the poetic drama of W. B. Yeats, a drama which, generally speaking, repudiates the social and political world in favour of 'the depths of the mind'. Under the pressure of events in the North, however, and especially with its new management, the Lyric Theatre has shown itself more appreciative of local talent (Martin Lynch was a recipient of its fellowship award). Other institutions traditionally associated with high culture have also recently supported local writers — Graham Reid was recently writer-in-residence at Queen's University. One might argue that at least these Ulster dramatists and their audiences, see through the prevailing ideologies of unionism and nationalism.

On the other hand, a poet from a working class Protestant background, Johnston Kirkpatrick, will acknowledge in his aptly titled 'Another Country' that the question of which country one owes allegiance to is one that continues to dominate working class consciousness, and minimises any potential solidarity between Catholic and Protestant; even when they live side by side in the same working class neighbourhood, the sharp religious and cultural differences of the present can be seen still to be shaped by a colonialism dependent on the garrison mentality, on the idea of belonging to a mother country, of being at home in another culture than that of the country you inhabit. Even the children's transforming the actual antagonism of the situation into a game of cowboys and indians indicates only another story of settlers and dispossessed natives:

Didn't we know them on sight?
Devious eyes close set
for blowing out candles
Wasn't theirs another country?
'No queen here' defiant gables
claimed in paint at the foot
of our street. 'Indian
territory' we named the place,
risked our covered wagons
home from the matinee
through their foreign canyons
by the poisoned river, clotted
smelly with domestic waste,
the air bitter with smoke.

Their totems, a thorned scalp,
sacred hearts crimson
in the gloom of sitting rooms,
anorexic images,
their poetry alien
to our protestantism
washed and aired on the pulpit
that chinstrapped the spirit
on locusts and wild honey;
loyal to a mother country
whose cavalier faces hung
in halls beside the coats;
and on the roofs of both our houses
the short swords of close combat.[29]

VII

The cultural differences reflected by Ulster writers are indisputably real. Whether from a Protestant or a Catholic background, the Ulster writer displays an historical consciousness of his situation, and a clearsighted awareness of the ideologies by which his fellow-citizens live and die in their native place. Yet both sets of writers are united in opposition to the dominant religio-political culture which has shaped life in Ulster for centuries, both are affiliated in various personal and literary relationships, and their work might be considered to represent an honest if highly civilised political discourse by virtue of which 'the Irish psyche is being redefined'.[30]

Literature by Ulster Catholic writers offers to readers who come out of the Protestant tradition a way of experiencing a culture which is, given the nature of Ulster society, familiar yet alien; the reverse process is, of course, equally true. So the reading in Ulster schools (with one notable exception, still segregated on the basis of religion) of poems, plays and fiction by Northern writers, combined with the study of Irish history, may yet lead to a greater understanding of 'the other side' than has existed to date. Perhaps, one day, the bitterness and hatred of Ulster's present divisions will, in Derek Mahon's words, 'amaze the literate children/In their non-sectarian schools' ('Afterlives'). Yet the literature that has been produced in Ulster in the last generation or so is of compelling interest to a larger audience than Ulster or even Ireland can offer. This is a matter of individual talent to be sure, but also of the rootedness of Ulster writing in a social and historical world which is felt to be typical and microcosmic of the modern world rather than aberrant. Like all Irish writers only more so, writers from the North are in what John Montague describes as 'a richly ambiguous position, with the pressure of an incompletely discovered past behind . . . and the whole modern world around'.[31]

IRISH CULTURE:
THE DESIRE FOR TRANSCENDENCE

WALENTINA WITOSZEK AND PATRICK F. SHEERAN

E. F. Schumacher (*Small is Beautiful*) in his posthumous *A Guide For the Perplexed* recounts an experience of being lost while sightseeing in Leningrad. His street-map failed to show the presence of several enormous churches which were visible from where he stood. An interpreter came to help him. 'We don't show churches on our maps', explained the guide. Schumacher contradicted him by pointing to one that was very clearly marked. 'This is a museum', responded the guide 'not what we call a "living church". It is only the "living churches" we don't show.'[1]

Similarly with cultural and literary maps. The obvious is frequently either simply ignored or veiled in some way. A case in point is the absence of any serious discussion of the transcendent as it influences Irish culture. The most valuable generalisations we have had — *The Irish Comic Tradition*, 'The Literary Myths of the Revival: A Case for their Abandonment', *The Profane Book of Irish Comedy, Culture and Anarchy in Ireland 1890-1935* stress the anarchic, profane, irreverent, 'bottomifying', ironic elements of our tradition — its 'barbarous sympathies'.[2] *Per contra* we wish to point to the presence of the opposite and complementary pole, the desire for transcendence rather than the appetites of gravity.

Newton, we recall, studied the fall of the apple and drew some large conclusions. Goethe, by contrast, wanted to know how the apple got up there in the first place. The draw of levity as opposed to the pull of gravity remains unstudied, not least in the Irish cultural context.

II

An example will best reveal both the direction of our Goethian quest and place the discussion in the appropriate context.

The Crane Bag — the most influential as it is the most comprehensive of intellectual journals recently published in Ireland —

set itself the task of cultivating 'the fifth province'. Modern Ireland is composed of four provinces yet the Irish word for province is *coicead* meaning a fifth. This ancient fifth province, about the actual location of which there is some uncertainty, stands for the middle or centre. If Tara was the political centre of Ireland, the middle or fifth province — sometimes described as a secret well known only to the druids — acted as a second centre. The first editorial of *The Crane Bag* explains:

It seems clear to us that in the present unhappy state of our country, this second centre of gravity must be restored in some way. The obvious impotence of the various political attempts to unite the four geographical provinces would seem to indicate another kind of solution, another kind of unity, one which would incorporate the 'fifth' province. This province, this place, this centre, is not a political or geographical position; it is more like a disposition. What kind of place could this be?[3]

'What kind of place could this be?' A brief review of the sources of *The Crane Bag* image of the fifth province will reveal its true dimensions.

The image derives, most immediately, from a scholarly work which, unfortunately, has had little impact on Celtic Studies but has provided imaginative sustenance and excitement for many — Alwy and Brinley Rees' *Celtic Heritage* (London: Thames and Hudson, 1961). The Rees brothers reinterpreted Celtic tradition in the light of comparative studies in religion and mythology, notably Hindu mythology. Their chapters 'A Hierarchy of Provinces' and 'The Centre' set out the evidence for a 'fifth province' not only in early Celtic Ireland but in Wales and Britain and beyond that to vedic India. They demonstrate the existence of 'a conceptual framework which was by no means confined to the Celts and which could be impressed anew upon whatever territory was considered a unit'.[4] A footnote refers to 'the first writer to draw attention to the cosmological significance of the provinces of Ireland' — René Guénon in *Le Roi du Monde* (Paris: Gallimard, 1927). Guénon was, first and last, a metaphysician working within the tradition of the *Sophia Perennis*. He sought out the timeless metaphysical truth underlying the diverse religions which he studied: Hindu, Moslem, Christian, Amerindian. His many monographs explore, in particular, the metaphysical principles embodied in traditional symbolism. In the Primordial Tradition, the fifth province is the 'spiritual Pole', 'the heart of the world', 'The Holy Land', 'The Land of the Living', 'The Terrestrial Paradise' or its symbolic equivalents. The Fifth Province stands to the four provinces as the Absolute to the relative, the Transcendent to the empirical, the Spiritual to the temporal.[5] This is the fullest amplification of its meaning.

Like the Holy of Holies, it is veiled in *The Crane Bag* discourse. Seamus Heaney, writing the prefatory note to a collection of the first ten volumes, states: 'In formulating the idea of a fifth province of the imagination, a second centre for the country independent of the centre of power, *The Crane Bag*, then, does not seek to evade the contingent realities.'[6] But there is, as we suggest elsewhere, a characteristic avoidance of the noncontingent reality of the *sacrum*.[7] Only if 'imagination' is granted its full Coleridgean force 'as a repetition in the finite mind of the eternal act of creation in the infinite I AM' will the term have the amplitude implicit in invoking the traditional symbolism.

'The work of constituting the fifth province' remains an esotericism, not least within the pages of *The Crane Bag* itself. Perhaps, given the dominant positivism of our times, a certain obfuscation is necessary. And doubtless the symbol has received valid, if partial, exoteric (political, social, cultural) interpretations. Witness Tom Paulin's recent self-dedication to the ideal in his *Ireland and the English Crisis* where he claims that 'this other, invisible province offers a platonic challenge to the nationalistic image of the four green fields'.[8] If the Marxists can dismiss — and they do — this image/concept because it lacks the necessary substratum 'in reality',[9] those who approach it from the standpoint of traditional metaphysics can both enlarge and sharpen its referent. In consonance with our theme, our approach will be to deal with the phenomena under scrutiny, not in terms of reductionism, but by the method of *amplificatio*. Our purpose is to put religion back on the Irish map, to unveil the mystery.

III

Transcendence is best defined in the words of one whose consciousness has been encompassed by it. The testimony of authority is unavoidable in this context. There are passages in Yeats and A.E. which offer such a definition but we turn for preference to the work of one who subjected his experience to the rigours of Kantian analysis: Franklin Merrell-Wolff's *The Philosophy of Consciousness Without an Object* and *Pathways Through to Space*. The glossary to the latter 'experiential journal' defines the Transcendent as follows:

In the broadest sense, the Transcendent stands in radical contrast to the empirical. It is that which lies beyond experience. Hence Transcendent Consciousness is non-experiential consciousness; and, since experience may be regarded as consciousness in the stream of becoming or under time, the form is of necessity a timeless Consciousness.[10]

It is, then, timelessness as opposed to time, the limitless to the bound, unity to multiplicity, knowledge through identity as opposed to subject-object knowledge, the absolute to the relative.

The essence of modernity, its characteristic note, is a loss of faith in transcendence, in an encompassing and surpassing reality. The traditional definition of man which accommodates the transcendental dimension is that he is three-fold: body, soul and spirit (corpus, anima, spiritus). And the world by reciprocal relation is likewise three-fold: terrestrial, intermediary and celestial. Our naturalistic metaphysics have left us with but one level of being and, by consequence, a pervasive nihilism. Viktor Frankl has suggested, with a great deal of clinical evidence to support the contention, that 'repression of the Transcendent' lies at the root of modern pathology.[11] Both the desire and its repression, especially strong in Ireland, accounts, we believe, for much that is powerful and aberrant in Irish life and letters.

We will endeavour to document this assertion and — given the limitations of space — do so with lamentable brevity. What are the manifestations of this desire and its repression on the political, existential, psychological, architectural and literary planes?

IV

Margaret Thatcher, in angry dismissal of Irish calls for national unity, commented recently that the 'Irish thing was all metaphysics' anyway and hence incapable of resolution. She may have been more accurate than her critics allow, though in a sense she hardly intended. (Longman's Dictionary of Contemporary English would support her usage: 'Metaphysics — of ideas or thought, at a high level and difficult to understand'). The Irish 'nostalgia for unity' (Edna Longley) is, at bottom, a nostalgia for Unity, for illo tempore before the fall into multiplicity and division, a sort of misplaced neo-Platonism. Thus the 'preferred option' of the New Ireland Forum is for unity rather than a federal/confederal state or joint authority (there were, in all, 317 different submissions). The mythic archetype which lies aback of much discussion on these matters in Ireland — including the Forum's — is precisely the neo-Platonic fall from original unity. Thatcher's sense that the desire cannot be assuaged by any empirical arrangement is perceptive as far as it goes. Perhaps she had been reading (it is the wildest speculation) Oliver Mac Donagh on the Irish consciousness of time? In *States of Mind* Mac Donagh appropriates Ranke's phrase, 'Every generation is equidistant from eternity' to typify the Christian sense of history as opposed to the Whig interpretation in terms of progress.[12] In Ireland the passage of time, we suggest, goes back to *illo tempore* itself.

On the existential level, the Irish are credited with a perfect mania for freedom. But freedom is something that, in Ireland, is almost always thought of as coming from outside. It is hardly ever an inner condition exfoliating outwards. The geometry of the Irish mind is Projective rather than Euclidian.[13] The long history of colonial oppression can go someway to account for the peculiarities of the Irish sense of freedom. In those countries which were for centuries prisons or mad-houses the sources of freedom lie not so much in man as in the outside, supernatural factor: God, Fate, History, Providence. Freedom is associated, therefore, with salvation or redemption. 'Róisín Dubh' (Little Black Rose), one of Ireland's most popular political songs, captures this sense exactly:

> A Róisín ná bíodh brón ort tár éirigh duit —
> tá na bráithre ag dul ar sáile is iad ag triall ar muir,
> tiocfaidh do phardún ón bPápa is on Róimh anoir
> is ní spáraílfear fíon Spáinneach ar mo Róisín Dubh.
>
> (Róisín have no sorrow for all that has happened you:
> the Friars are out on the brine, they are travelling the sea,
> Your pardon from the Pope will come, from Rome in the East
> and we won't spare the Spanish wine for my Róisín Dubh).[14]

Freedom here has religious connotations, its sources are transcendent rather than immanent, it derives from faith rather than human rights. As such it stands in contrast to the American ideal as it is enshrined in, let us say, the work of the New England Transcendentalists and their descendents, where freedom is a subjective condition and the Self is immanent and supreme above all contingent circumstances. (The immanence of the American Deity, too, contrasts sharply with the transcendence of the Irish Catholic God). Its modern day versions, shorn of metaphysical roots, are to be found in Abraham Maslow's 'self-actualizing person' and, more flamboyantly, in Wayne Dwyer's no-limits person who has rid himself of his erroneous zones and wins one hundred per cent of the time. Yeats in 'A Prayer for my Daughter' asks that Anne Yeats be endowed with the American virtues:

> Considering that, all hatred driven hence,
> The soul recovers radical innocence
> And learns at last that it is self-delighting,
> Self-appeasing, self-affrighting,
> And that its own sweet will is Heaven's will;
> She can, though every face should scowl
> And every windy quarter howl
> Or every bellows burst, be happy still.[15]

It is a poem/prayer against the Irish perception of the human condition (it contains, incidentally, a number of echoes of Emerson's famous essay 'Self Reliance' with its motto '*Ne te quaesiveris extra*'). So too the lonely impulse of delight which animates the Irish Airman aligns him less with Sidney than with Emerson and the perfect man. 'Every true man is a cause, a country, and an age.'[16]

One philosophical implication of the Irish desire for the transcendent is *Contemptus mundi*. Deirdre and Naoise playing chess in the face of imminent disaster is an archetype of the Irish situation. Instead of building a fortress against their enemy, trying to organise help or, simply, making love, they play at chess. Transcendence is inscribed in the very image of an action which is no action, which enables the actors to refuse to take reality for arbiter. 'A King and Queen at chess' are impervious to calamity, indeed they enter into a complicity with death. Much of contemporary Ireland is contained in this image — a neglected countryside, a derelict economy, a refusal to exercise taste or discernment where material objects are concerned, an abandonment of re-construction. What are the people doing all this time? They are still playing chess (readers will substitute their own version of the ludic metaphor) while waiting for death. Pragmatic action to save themselves loses any compelling force in this perspective. Not for nothing has John Jordan remarked on 'that streak in the Irish character which seeks by temporary denial of life to hold death at bay: what we might call, irreverently, *contemptus mundi* on the instalment plan'.[17] He cites as 'purer forms' of that contempt Yeats's 'Cast a Cold Eye . . .', Pearse's 'Naked I Saw You' and Austin Clarke's 'Tenebrae'.

Two forms of escape, on the psychological level, are permissible in Ireland from quotidian reality: madness and religion. It is customary since Leszek Kolakowski's famous essay 'The Priest and the Jester' — an essay that has exerted a profound, if subterranean influence on Irish writers — to oppose the two allegiances as Kolakowski does:

The antagonism between a philosophy consolidating the absolute and a philosophy questioning the accepted absolutes, appears to be incurable, as incurable as the existence of conservatism and radicalism in all areas of human life. It is the antagonism of a priest and a jester; and in almost every historical epoch, the philosophy of the priest and the philosophy of the jester have been the two most general forms of intellectual culture. The priest is the guardian of the absolute who upholds the cult of the final and the obvious contained in the tradition. The jester is he who, although an habitué of good society, does not belong to it and makes it the object of his inquisitive impertinence; he who questions what appears to be self-evident.[18]

Thus Mad Sweeney harries the Saint; Ossian abuses St. Patrick; Christy Mahon defies the repressed people of darkest Mayo and so on. What's more to our purpose, however, is to note that Mad Sweeney and St. Ronan aspire to the same condition but employ different rhetorics. Both create for themselves a secondary reality which surpasses the limits of the empirically given. Priest and Jester are both outsiders; one escapes into madness, the other into religion — and the common factor is the desire for transcendence. It is the only thing they have in common, but it is an important thing.

The Jester, in his latest incarnation in Ireland — Heaney's 'Sweeney Redivivus' allows that 'The Cleric' and himself have been engaged on a not dissimilar project:

> History that planted its standards
> on his gables and spires
> ousted me to the marches
>
> of skulking and whingeing.
> Or did I desert?
> Give him his due, in the end
> he opened my path to a kingdom
> of such scope and neuter allegiance
> my emptiness reigns at its whim.   ('The Cleric')[19]

In many cases it is enough to study material signs — the gables and spires of the country's architecture — to discern the specific orientation of a society. For many peoples architecture is the supreme expression of their spiritual life — recall the aspiration of the Gothic Cathedral, the alignment with sacred mountains of the Hopi pueblo, the delicacy and strength of Japanese domestic buildings. In Ireland, what does that jumble of Spanish style villas, mock Tudor residences, 'Georgian' estates, avant-garde Churches, squat bungalows on a quarter acre of ground and psuedo-vernacular thatched cottages signify? The fundamental implication is that external surfaces are of no importance, that the luxury of aesthetic form is almost unknown. Scattered over the Irish countryside there is a great clutter of different idioms, styles, and architectural languages without any effort to harmonise them. If surfaces are unimportant, what of interiors? What goes on behind the ugly facades? Transcendental Meditation? Our writers have suggested imbecility and paralysis.

The landscape too drives to transcendental longings. Despite the padding of the Tourist Board, it is a minimal landscape. It impels the imagination to do something with it, to go beyond the given. The penitential hills of the Burren, the open bone-stone graveyard of Connemara cry out for imaginative completion. By contrast, the landscape of California or Norway overwhelms the imagination, renders it passive in the face of majesty. So too with the ruins which are everywhere in Ireland. Before a Chartres or Ely Cathedral the eye is drawn to explore a plenitude of forms. Before a broken chancel arch or solitary bee-hive cell the mind is drawn to *create*, not *discover*. The landscape has the quality which Mark Patrick Hederman has described in the word *uaigneas*, an Irish word 'that sounds like the sharp slanting cry of a curlew over a bog'.[20] He finds the quintessence of this quality in the peculiar lighting of the country. 'The lighting somehow withers and shrivels the root. That to me is *uaigneas*. It influences us towards a religious or metaphysical dimension. It makes the ground of our beseeching too narrow to be taken seriously. It places us upon the last ditch'.[21]

Two images drawn from this secretive countryside, the well and the bog, have provided Irish poets with dominant images. The well image (Richard Murphy's 'Brian Boru's Well', John Montague's 'The Well Dream', Seamus Heaney's 'Personal Helicon', Máirtín Ó Direáin's 'Na Tuarais') expresses both a sacral view of nature — it is always a Blessed Well — and the transcendent, hidden source of poetic inspiration, the manifest emanating from the unmanifest. The bog image has been put to a number of secular uses; by turns it can suggest the layered strata of different cultures in Ireland or the search for the final bottommost 'authentic' foundation to which all else must yield precedence. But it is also our closest equivalent to the desert, the vacancy where transcendence becomes possible. Bog and Well coalesce in Heaney's 'Bogland':

> Our pioneers keep striking
> Inwards and downwards,
>
> Every layer they strip
> Seems camped on before.
> The bogholes might be Atlantic seepage.
> The wet centre is bottomless.[22]

Inward and downward to a bottomless centre — to the fifth province.

Finally, it is literature which, in a multiplicity of ways, reconstructs the model of the world prevalent in a given society. A *prima facie* case that the recurring image of a man striving for transcendence is central to the best contemporary drama in Ireland can be established by pointing to Brian Friel's psychodrama *Faith Healer*, Tom Kilroy's *Talbot Box* and Tom Murphy's *The Sanctuary Lamp* and *The Gigli Concert*. The aberrant forms in which this striving occurs — the magic of the faith healer, the masochism of Talbot, the blasphemy directed at the sanctuary lamp, the desire to sing like Beniamino Gigli — lie precisely in the fact that the rhetoric and imagery of traditional, institutional religion is no longer found adequate to accommodate the religious impulse. The Church and its representatives are flayed and mocked but the repressed desire for transcendence emerges for all that. Murphy is the most bitter in his denunciation of Irish Jansenism ('Holy medals and genitalia in mortal combat with each other') and the God of *The Sanctuary Lamp* is a 'metaphysical monster'. Yet Harry, who admits to keeping madness as a standby in case all else fails, has his own intimations of transcendence. It is couched in a purely private language:

'The soul — y'know? — like a silhouette. And when you die it moves out into . . . slow-moving mists of space and time. Awake in oblivion actually. And it moves out from the world to take its place in the silent outer wall of eternity.'[23]

The 'return of the repressed' as we know from other contexts, takes monstrous, aberrant forms.

Talbot in Kilroy's *Talbot Box* speaks of his quest in a way that has a greater traditional sanction. ''Tis because I wanta meet the darkness as meself' he tells the uncomprehending Priest Figure when he goes to take the pledge. And to the Woman in her role as Everywoman the lineage of the 'misfortunate little man' who bound his body with chains and ropes is clear. She dwells on the matter with a Synge-like gusto and relish:

Woman (*High*) He is in the company of St. Anthony who wrestled for twenty years in the desert with a nightmare circus of demons, St. Catherine of Sienna whose self-flagellations astounded Satan. From the deserts south of Alexandria to the upper reaches of Cappadocia, across the Spanish plateau and out to the Western rim of our own Irish islands, stylites, anchorites in incredible exercises of penance, chains, poles, hairshirts, beds of nettles, motionless for hours with arms out-stretched in the shape of the Cross![24]

The deserts *south* of Alexandria to the *upper reaches* of Cappadocia — the precision and the wildness go marvellously together. And as the Author's note to the play implies it is the 'essentially irreducible division' between the claims of society and the demands of vision which is central to the play. No synergic relation between individual and community is possible in the 'primitive, enclosed space, part prison, part sanctuary, part acting space' (Ireland in short) of *Talbot's Box*.[25]

Poetry, perhaps more than any other literary form, can give immediate expression to transcendent longings. It certainly provides us with the most quotable evidence.

At the pivotal point of our most politically involved long poem — John Montague's *The Rough Field* — a super-sensory experience (only Mr Montague's humility forbids us to call it a mystical experience) is described. This moment, when 'the bird of total meaning/Stirs upon its hidden branch', occurs when the poet has been to visit a Well (what else?) reputedly inhabited by a monster trout:

> Was that
> The ancient trout of wisdom
> I meant to catch?

Returning home, he describes his 'fierce elation':

> My seven league boots devour
> Time and space as I crash
> Through the last pools of
> Darkness.[26]

It is a remarkable moment in a poem that otherwise maintains a minute and painful fidelity to empirical time and space.

Seamus Heaney's recent *Station Island*, 'a sequence of dream encounters with familiar ghosts', like Montague's poem is faithful to place and circumstance yet it too deepens to a well — the 'living fountain' of St. John of the Cross's *'Cantar del alma que se huelga de conoscer a Dios por fe'*. The studied formality of Heaney's translation amid the freer verses which surround it alerts the reader to the change of significance. (The passage from René Guénon quoted in note 5 provides and excellent gloss on the text.)

> That eternal fountain, hidden away,
> I know its haven and its secrecy
>   although it is the night.
>
> But not its source because it does not have one,
> which is all sources' source and origin
>   although it is the night.
>
> I am repining for this living fountain.
> Within this bread of life I see it plain
>   although it is the night.[27]

Nowhere in Irish letters is that repining more anguished than in the work of Thomas Kinsella, the darkest as he is the most determinedly modernist of Irish poets. Yet even he penetrates through desolate surfaces to the Jungian archetypes. The Voyager of 'Downstream' (Shelley's *Alastor* is relevant) is swept 'into a pit of night'.

>   Now, deeper in,
> Something shifted in sleep, a quiet hiss
> As we slipped by. Adrift . . . . A milk-white breast . . .
> A shuffle of wings betrayed with a feathery kiss
>
> A soul of white with darkness for a nest.
> The creature bore the night so tranquilly
> I lifted up my eyes. There without rest
> The phantoms of the overhanging sky
> Occupied their stations and descended;
> Another moment, to the starlit eye,

> The slow, downstreaming dead, it seemed, were blended
> One with those silvery hordes, and briefly shared
> Their order, glittering.[28]

That 'soul of white with darkness for a nest' recurs in the most
desolate of Kinsella's long sequences — *Notes from the Land of the
Dead*. It too secretes a well from which flow the four rivers of the
Terrestrial Paradise out to 'th'encircling sea, that bitter river' of
mundane reality:

> . . . down among the roots like a half-
> buried vase brimming
> over with pure water,
> a film of clear brilliancy
> spilling down its sides
> rippling with reflections
> of the four corners of the garden.[29]

Clearly there is an homology between the image of the 'fifth
province' as presented by *The Crane Bag* intellectuals, Guénon's
formless centre and the wells, fountains and springs of the poets.
All relate to the Transcendent/empirical opposition formulated
earlier.

Prose fiction is more refractory. The work of our leading
novelist, Francis Stuart (*Redemption*, *The Pillar of Fire*) deserves
special notice in this context. But the case can be made on wider,
more comprehensive grounds. The absence from our literature of
anything approaching the Catholic Novelists in France or the
Polish Christian Writers is hardly a stumbling block. It is form
rather than content which is of prime significance here.

The Irish novelistic tradition, as has been argued elsewhere, is
more properly described as a romance tradition.[30] The romance
form as opposed to that of the bourgeois realistic novel is less
engaged with the social, more concerned with symbolic and
metaphysical representations of experience, '. . . less interested in
redemption than in the melodrama of the eternal struggle of good
and evil, less interested in incarnation and reconciliation than in
alienation and disorder'.[31] The central, essential relationship is
not that of man to society or to his fellow man, as it is in the novel,
but rather the individual's relationship to a demanding absolute.

The thin, realistic surface of Irish fiction is everywhere
punctured and corrugated by the subterranean forces of religion,
superstition, metaphysics and madness. Henry James's strictures
on the lack of variety and complexity in American life as an

explanation for the dominance of romance forms in the American tradition are sometimes invoked to account for the Irish situation. We would suggest that it is rather the effort to accommodate the 'vertical' aspirations for transcendence within a 'horizontal' form resistant to such obsessive desires that accounts for the pervasiveness of grotesque and romance elements in our tradition.

It is increasingly difficult, once again, to separate an Irish tradition in fiction from that of others. John Banville, Aidan Higgins, John McGahern, Francis Stuart and Brian Moore have a cosmopolitan reach to their work which is resistant to a purely native reading. Moore's *Cold Heaven* is a case in point. It stands at the confluence of American and Irish romance and is the richer for both. The epigraph from Yeats ('Suddenly I saw the cold and rook-delighting heaven/That seemed as though ice burned and was but the more ice') captures the irruption of visionary experience into the life of a modern post-Christian American. Marie, who dislikes priests and denies being a Catholic, who 'hated school and the Mass and prayers and all of it' has a vision of the Virgin Immaculate near the Point Lobos Motor Inn. But she has her own life to lead and holds out against 'ineluctable forces, inexplicable odds' in the name of her 'known and imperfect existence'. She chooses to refuse the transcendental experience. But that does not mean that it is elided. Apart from her resolve to remember it in silence for the rest of her life the vision is renewed for Sister Anna, a nun from the nearby convent of the Sisters of Mary Immaculate. What for Marie was a source of nightmare and paranoia is for Sister Anna an occasion of 'indescribable adoration'. 'It's Sister Anna's vision now' Marie tells the Monsignor. 'Don't you see what's happened? I refused it, and now it has gone on to Sister Anna. She's a nun, she's the right person. I'm the wrong person. There was some mistake.'[32] Point Lobos joins the Irish visionary archipelago from south of Alexandria to our own Irish islands.

V

Two characteristic Irish impulses — verbophilia and mythomania — express the condition we have attempted to describe. The extraordinary emphasis on the Word, most notable in the Irish dramatic tradition but finding its supreme exemplar in Joyce, can be traced back to idealist premises. The line of distinction was firmly drawn by Leon Trotsky in a different context when he

opposed the Formalist writers (Viktor Shlovsky, Boris Eichen-
baum) in Russia in the name of Marxism:

Just as Kantian idealism represents historically a translation of Christianity into the language of rationalistic philosophy, so all the varieties of
idealistic formalization either openly or secretly, lead to a God, as the
Cause of all causes . . . The Formalist school represents an abortive
idealism applied to the question of Art. The Formalists show a fast
ripening religiousness. They are followers of St. John and they believe
that 'In the beginning was the Word'. But we believe that in the beginning
was the deed. The word followed, as its phonetic shadow.[33]

Those 'idealistic formalizations' were openly avowed by an earlier
generation of Irish writers — Yeats, A.E. and, despite the overt
denials of Joyce, they are implicit in his own explorations of the
Word. Today they are more covert.

Mythology in the Irish context hardly needs any substantiation.
It is not only our literature but our politics and geography which
have expanded or contracted to meet mythological demands.
From another perspective it operates as a *mytho-therapy* — what
cannot be resolved in fact can find its resolution in myth. A
number of our intellectuals — Deane, Kiberd, Kearney — have
urged the necessity for a balancing and correcting *logotherapy*. The
dominant motive is to de-mythologise and to call for recourse to
the pragmatic rather than the transcendent (vide, *The Field Day*
pamphlets). It is they (O'Brien, Deane, Kiberd, Kearney — they
would hardly want to appear in the same sentence together) who
now arouse the ire once reserved for playwrights and novelists.
Fiction and myth have been largely domesticated. It is logic
which hurts now.

The key word from Tone to Joyce to Deane to describe the Irish
condition is 'paralysis'. Paralysis is the wrong word: it is rather a
suspended energy. In Norway there is a meteorological condition
known as the *Dis*, a chronic mist which never contracts into rain
or dissolves into sunlight. It is energy in the state of passivity
refusing a phase transition into something else. At the core of the
Irish *Dis*, we would argue, is the desire and the repression of
transcendence. The benign consequence of this is an exquisite
verbal art. The malign is that the whole of reality is reduced to the
verbal sphere, to words, words, words. There is, in Ireland, a lack
of action. Most Irish 'deeds' are failures — and they evoke a myth
or story to render the failure magically effective. (Again Norway
provides an illustration this time by way of contrast. Norwegian
culture is the opposite extreme — it is a culture of the deed, of

action despite the meteorological *Dis*). In Ireland the word is more real, more efficacious than the deed (Irish politicians have been draining the Shannon for upwards of fifty years). The word, finally, is the *Dis* — a suspended action, an imperfect act of transcendence. And this imperfect act does not lead to religion but rather to a religious fixation, for religion can do without words. Ireland is the country in which the desire for the transcendent leads to a lack of religion.

'WHEN DID YOU LAST SEE YOUR FATHER?': PERCEPTIONS OF THE PAST IN NORTHERN IRISH WRITING 1965-1985

EDNA LONGLEY

I

In Irish literature the past as history, as a continuum, looms larger than the past as mortality. Edward Thomas said that Villon 'inaugurated modern literature with the cry — *Mais où sont les neiges d'antan?*'.[1] That cry pervades Hardy's poetry, for instance, which Seamus Heaney partly misreads in this Irish-angled comment on 'The Garden Seat':

The poem is about the ghost-life that hovers over the furniture of our lives, about the way objects can become temples of the spirit. To an imaginative person, an inherited possession like a garden seat is not just an *objet,* an antique . . . rather it becomes a point of entry into a common emotional ground of memory and belonging. It can transmit the climate of a lost world and keep alive in us a domestic intimacy with realities that might otherwise have vanished.[2]

But the point about all Hardy's ghosts, unlike Heaney's, is that they are dead:

> Here was the former door
> Where the dead feet walked in.   ('The Self-Unseeing')

Whereas Hardy is obsessed, to use Samuel Hynes's phrase, with 'the irreversible pastness of the past',[3] Irish writers are more likely to be obsessed with its irreversible presentness. David Martin punctuates his novel *The Ceremony of Innocence* (1977) with symbolic appearances by Shellshock Sam, still fighting the battle of the Somme in his head:

> Lieutenant Sam Ogilby, of the 36th (Ulster)
> Division, made up primarily of the Ulster
> Volunteer Force.

> Has he found his ghosts?
> His ghosts are real.[4]

Notoriously, the two communities in Northern Ireland cannot arrive at an agreed version of the past, let alone the present or future. (Prehistoric Navan Fort has been proposed as the mystic point where parallel lines might meet.) The increasingly subtle findings of historians have inspired no revisionist orange banners of West Belfast murals. A soldier in Frank McGuinness's play *Observe the Sons of Ulster Marching Towards the Somme* (1985) — once again a gathering of ghosts in a character's head — speaks for many. As his comrades in the trenches pass the time by re-enacting the battle of the Boyne (a play-battle within a play-battle) he calls anxiously 'Don't change the result'. This scene registers both historical cause and effect, and the sacrosanct tribal tableau which has contributed to it. The Somme itself, of course, figures on Orange banners; while the play, as a less immobilised account of history, indicates yet again how 1969 re-activated the past in the imagination of writers. The artistic consequences need not only be painful or on the grand scale. An unprecedented flood of personal and local reminiscence[5] signals some effort at more total communal recall: to set down or set straight small bits of the record. A recent addition to this literature is *The Last Romantic Out of Belfast* (1984), a first novel by Sam Keery (b. 1930), who evokes his Second-World-War childhood. When the hero Joe McCabe finally emigrates, he compared Belfast viewed from a distance with Carlyle's history of *The French Revolution*, and contrasts both with the intimate close-ups in his own memory and by implication in the novel: 'The thought occurred to him that history, like mountains, can be seen whole only from afar.'[6]

But if memoirs in the form of fiction, poetry and drama, as well as 'straight' autobiography are complicating the map of the past, for most Ulster people the changed present has rendered the past more unchanging, confirmed the stories the tribes have always told themselves. Graham Reid's play *Remembrance* (1984) centres on the intensified habit of mutually exclusive commemoration. A stylised cemetery dominates the stage, and the mother of a dead IRA man and the father of a dead RUC man tend hostile graves. Paul Muldoon's poem 'Come into my Parlour' also uses a cemetery to represent history as not only fixed, but fixed in advance. The poem hits at 'the vanity of ruling beyond the grave' by making the graveyard rule, and pre-empt the individual's life history. Coulter the gravedigger, predeterminantly named after his spade,

itself an Ulster cultural determinant, 'knows' where everyone
belongs:

> What Coulter took as his text
> Was this bumpy half-acre of common.
> Few graves were named or numbered
> For most were family plots.
> He knew exactly which was which
> And what was what . . .

'This bumpy half-acre of common' symbolises Ulster, Ulster
history, and history in Ulster: the past as the future. Muldoon
obviously supplies a 'text' and a reading (or moral) which diverge
from those of Coulter. This essay will conclude with a discussion
of Muldoon's poetry as historical and literary-historical revisionism. For instance, 'Come into my Parlour' might be read as an
inversion of Seamus Heaney's 'Digging'. More generally, it
suspects all invitations issued by ancestral voices.

II

   'Come into my Parlour' exemplifies a tension between creative
dynamic and historical stasis which contributes to the strengths
of Northern Irish poetry in particular, and which has various
issues in the work of Brian Friel, John Montague, Seamus Heaney,
Michael Longley, Derek Mahon, Tom Paulin, Brian Moore, Maurice
Leitch, David Martin and Bernard MacLaverty. My quotation,
'When did you last see your father?', suggests a means of getting
at the various configurations the past assumes in their imaginations. It implies, first, the amazing popularity of this motif;
secondly, that father-figures may bear a changing relation to
actuality even in Ulster. It's through parents that the individual
locates himself in history, and Irish history remains in many
respects a family affair. (The different Unionist parties sometimes
call themselves 'the Unionist family', presumably à la Mafia.)
Ulster society too is intensely familial. In 'Come into my Parlour'
the speaker sees history's web as 'family plots' — punning on
graves, conspiracies, and tales of the predictable: 'the grave of my
mother,/My father's grave, and his father's . . .'
   Introducing his anthology *Irish Poets 1924-1974* David Marcus
notes 'the profusion of poems about the poets' fathers or mothers
or other near-relations', and surmises 'that such ancestral homage

could be a substitute for the fervorous patriotic themes beloved of earlier poets and denied by the changed times to their successors'.[7] It could indeed or, since times change so slowly in the North, might mark a staging-post. Of course the relationship between father and son (as increasingly between mother and daughter) has often focused new definitions of social and imaginative identity — for example, in British literature of the 1950s. However, Ulster 'conservatism complicates filial rebellion, whether in fact or fiction. In Dan Magee's play *Horseman, Pass By* (1984) a father and son violently quarrel about the latter's involvement with the IRA.[8] In Bernard MacLaverty's story 'Father and Son'[9] silent parallel monologues voice the same issue. Both works end in violence without essentially resolving the question of how the generations divide up reaction and revolution between them. Twenty years ago Brian Moore's novel *The Emperor of Ice-Cream*, set during the Second World War, affirmed the values of freedom from the sectarian past. Gavin Burke's authorially endorsed rebellion reaches fruition amidst an apocalyptically bombed Belfast. His father, given to 'pious prate about Catholicism' and pro-Hitler 'fascist leanings in politics'[10] finally admits error, while Gavin thinks: 'His father was the child now; his father's world was dead.'[11] Maurice Leitch's *The Liberty Lad* published in the same year (1965), and also a *Bildungsroman*, follows Frank Glass's growing distance, as an upwardly mobile schoolteacher (courtesy of the 11-plus), from a Protestant working class background. The novel ends with his mill-worker father's funeral, and these sentences:

He thought that I was at last weeping for the loss of my father, but I wasn't. I was crying for the loss of someone else, me, as I had been once, three, four years . . . a year ago.[12]

The Liberty Lad features a Unionist MP, yet hardly touches on political matters. The MP resembles power-figures in British fifties and sixties fiction (such as *Room at the Top*) to whose class-patterns, and pattern-breaking, the novel adheres.

The social findings of *The Liberty Lad* are not necessarily contradicted by Leitch's later novel *Stamping Ground* (1975); but progress, mobility and growing pains are replaced by heavily emphasised circularity, the 'smug circling continuum' deplored by local historian Barbour Brown.[13] The novel's setting steps back in time to 1950, and in place from the small-town Ulster of *The Liberty Lad* (between country and city) to a Protestant rural heartland. And instead of Frank Glass's exploited father, sick and working in a dying trade, we meet a clutch of powerful and unpleasant patriarchs: notably, Henry Gault whose

> existence was as undeviating as a furrow he would set himself to plough
> ... He moved through each day along a similarly straight course from
> dawn to an early bed-time and he judged everything and everyone he
> came in contact with — wife, son, servant, beast, implement — by the
> same standards he set himself.[14]

All the patriarchs in the novel blight the social, personal and sexual development of their offspring. Any prospect of 'liberty' is minimal.

Outside my period, Sam Hanna Bell in *December Bride* (1951) created a more likeable Presbyterian farmer-patriarch; as does Seamus Heaney in 'The Other Side', which relishes 'each patriarchal dictum'. However, Presbyterianism and Protestantism have no monopoly of patriarchy, although Heaney elsewhere revives the allegory of Ireland as female and England as conquering male:

> To some extent the enmity can be viewed as a struggle between the cults
> and devotees of a god and goddess. There is an indigenous territorial
> numen, a tutelar of the whole island, call her Mother Ireland, Kathleen ni
> Houlihan, the poor old woman, the Shan Van Vocht, whatever; and her
> sovereignty has been temporarily usurped or infringed by a new male
> cult whose founding fathers were Cromwell, William of Orange and
> Edward Carson.[15]

This is of course a mythic, religious version of history (to be discussed later). But if the female metaphor fits Catholic vulnerability in the North, it sometimes masks the masculine and authoritarian character of Catholic as well as Protestant Irish culture.[16] de Valera as 'the chief', national founding-father and custodian of the past, managed to fuse the auras of father as paterfamilias and father as priest. Muldoon's poem 'Cuba' makes this link, together with an Irish-American political connection. A father telling off his daughter for 'Running out to dances in next to nothing' goes on:

> Those Yankees were touch and go as it was —
> If you'd heard Patton in Armagh —
> But this Kennedy's nearly an Irishman
> So he's not much better than ourselves.
> And him with only to say the word.

> If you've got anything on your mind
> Maybe you should make your peace with God.[17]

In the last stanza the girl confesses 'Bless me, Father, for I have sinned'. But the poem in fact exposes the sins of fathers, men laying down the law. Another poem 'Anseo' makes a similar point through the irradicable effect of an authoritarian schoolteacher — 'the Master' — on a boy he has mentally and physically persecuted. 'Joe Ward' is now 'fighting for Ireland', and

> His volunteers would call back *Anseo*
> And raise their hands
> As their names occurred.[18]

In any case fathers in Northern Irish literature calibrate tradition and transition, small shifts in the land of 'Not an Inch'. Muldoon calls it 'writing about what is immediately in front of me, or immediately over my shoulder'.[19] If I now concentrate chiefly upon poetic fathers, it is because poetry more radically transmutes the autobiographical into the symbolic, sees further round the corner of the *status quo*. The actual fathers of poets include the following mixed bag: a Belfast shipyard worker, a South Derry cattle-dealer and small farmer, a Brooklyn exile, a market-gardener in Armagh orchard-country, and an English furniture salesman who fought in both world wars. The generation gaps span movements from country to city, from country to country, and in all cases to a university education never achieved by the father.

Brian Friel's drama has close associations with poetry, and the fathers in his plays since 1969 represent one extreme of perception. In *Aristocrats* and *Translations* they personify the inadequacy of what the past has transmitted. The 'aristocratic' O'Donnells of Ballybeg Hall are described, with Friel's evident sanction, as:

Four generations of a great Irish Catholic legal dynasty . . . a family without passion, without loyalty, without commitments; administering the law for anyone who happened to be in power; above all wars and famines and civil strife and political upheaval: ignored by its Protestant counterparts, isolated from the mere Irish . . .[20]

Symbolically maimed by a stroke, the current head of the house focuses the play's attack on collaborationist, Redmondite traditions in Irish politics. Hugh, the hedge-schoolmaster father in *Translations*, is much more positively conceived. Far from the O'Donnells' amoral deracination, he hands on authentic qualities and traditions of 'the mere Irish'. Nevertheless the play criticises his pandering to colonialist expectations about the drunken, verbalising Irishman, who speaks a 'language . . . full of the mythologies of fantasy and hope and self-deception'.[21] Hugh's son Owen, once a literal and metaphorical 'collaborator' in the Anglicising Ordnance Survey, finally rejects his own compromises and his father's 'confusion',[22] when the British soldiers threaten the community. In both these plays the sense of fathers having let down their children makes a political comment on the history of Northern Catholics since 1921.

The work of three poets from Protestant backgrounds expresses a range of filial feeling: rejection, reinvention, acceptance. Derek Mahon's poetry takes as its premise, even its *sine qua non*, alienation from familial and tribal origins. In 'Ecclesiastes', which satirises the Protestant religious and political will to domination, the reader resists blood-calls to 'nourish a fierce zeal' and

> love the January rains when they
> darken the dark doors and sink hard
> into the Antrim hills, the bog meadows, the heaped
> graves of your fathers.[23]

'Fathers', with its biblical ring, is a common Protestant word for ancestry and history. John Hewitt's best-known poem begins 'Once alien here my fathers built their house',[24] and Mahon's 'Canadian Pacific' evokes Ulster-Scots and Scots nonconformist emigrants to the new world as 'Those gaunt forefathers'. Mahon has written no poem based on his actual father; but his first collection *Night-Crossing* (1968) includes celebrations of a 'Grandfather' and 'Wicked Uncle'. Tribal renegades, childishly anarchic, they imply a son's revolt by subverting 'adult' bourgeois Protestant respectability; the former 'discreetly up to no good', the latter indiscreetly.

Tom Paulin's *Liberty Tree* (1983) attacks Protestant culture in more narrowly political terms: Protestantism as Unionism. In 'Father of History' he seems to invent an ideal alternative to his own headmaster father. This schoolmaster builds

> Lisburn like a warm
> plainspoken sermon on the rights of man.
> A sunned Antrim face, he maybe prays
> to the New Light in a relished dialect . . .

Certainly a sunnier Antrim than Mahon's. This prelapsarian vision of the Protestant United Irishmen who *should* have begotten history, names the specific Republican fathers of its attitudes: 'Munro, Hope, Porter, and McCracken.'

In Michael Longley's poetry the father focuses questions of belonging rather than longing: an Englishman who fought twice for his country. The poem 'Second Sight'[25] imagines a disorienting visit to London during which the speaker asks: 'Where is my father's house, where my father?', what of an English dimension in Ireland, an Irish dimension in England? There is a contrast between two poems about the father's war-service written before and after 1969. The earlier, 'In Memoriam',[26] sets out to 'read' the father's personal 'history' as a means of comprehending the 'death and nightmare' of the Great War. The later poem, 'Wounds',[27] uses the father's witness of the war — 'the Ulster Division at the Somme / Going over the top with "Fuck the Pope"./ "No surrender" ' — as a perspective on civil war in Ulster, on the still more quintessential futility of deaths such as a bus-conductor

> shot through the head
> By a shivering boy who wandered in
> Before they could turn the television down
> Or tidy away the supper dishes.
> To the children, to a bewildered wife,
> I think 'Sorry Missus' was what he said.

Paul Fussell comments: 'the irony always associated with the Somme attack remains to shade that conclusion. But at least the Somme attack had some swank and style: one could almost admire, if afterward one had to deplore.'[28]

To digress briefly from fathers: the Somme appeals to the imaginations of Longley, Martin, Leitch (Barbour Brown reflects: 'So many of his friends' names in the Deaths column of *The Ballymena Observer*'),[29] McGuinness. The latter, who comes from Donegal, is unique in approaching the theme from a background supposedly alien. More commonly, the world wars divide imaginations, if more subtly than the way Remembrance Day every November divides Dublin. Denial of any Catholic Irish participation in the wars resembles the cultural suppression that obliges Paulin's Protestant United Irishman to 'endure posterity without a monument'. By a nice paradox, Stewart Parker's play about McCracken, *Northern Star* (1984), attracted Belfast audiences as much as *Observe the Sons of Ulster* drew Dublin. This may help to change something, if not any results. However, Seamus Heaney's poem 'In Memoriam Francis Ledwidge'[30] finds this Irish Catholic's involvement in the war imaginatively unresolvable, although the theme clearly compels him. Whereas for Longley the English 'soldier-poets' such as Isaac Rosenberg and Edward Thomas are literary-historical touchstones, Heaney's 'In Memoriam' regrets: 'In you, our dead enigma, all the strains / Criss-cross in useless equilibrium' ('strains' puns on another genetic definition of history). Nevertheless the poem's own bloodline includes one trope of First World War poetry, the haunting rural flashback, in the beautiful image: 'ghosting the trenches with a bloom of hawthorn'.

Another line, 'You were not keyed or pitched like these true blue ones', which may impute undue patriotism to the British dead ('True Blue', incidentally, figures on Orange banners), manifests a deep Northern assumption about tribal inheritance. John Montague's *The Rough Field* is grounded on such assumptions. 'The Cage'[31] introduces the poet's father as 'My father, the least happy man I have known' and also refers to 'the lost years in Brooklyn'. 'Molly Bawn', in *The Dead Kingdom* (1984) still more explicitly places the father in the context of 'the embittered diaspora of / dispossessed Northern Republicans'. The next poem, 'A Muddy Cup', explores the poet's separation as a child, not only from his father, but from his mother who gave him to be fostered. This family 'diaspora', echoing in the repeated adjective 'lost', both underlies and underlines the historical losses mourned by *The Rough Field:* 'shards of a lost tradition'; a dead Gaelic civilisation; the vanished, vanquished O'Neills; the Flight of the Earls; the 'Loss' column of the New Omagh Road balance sheet; 'Our finally lost dream of man at home / in a rural setting.'

Montague's distinctively Tyrone terrain shows how local as well as family history influences the shape of the past in a poet's imagination. Local historical societies are much thicker on the ground in the North than in the South, perhaps for obvious territorial reasons: every Northerner is an amateur local historian. Barbour Brown's obsessive researches into his 'valley' parallel Leitch's own curiosity. Brown progresses from church records to 'lists of rocks and plants and buildings' to a voyeuristic interest in 'the forked animal again', thus becoming 'this spy creeping about the hedgerows'.[32] Paul Muldoon's parodic parish the Moy at once ironises and exploits the literary aspect of local-historical allegiance. For instance, his sonnet-sequence 'Armageddon, Armageddon'[33] (pun) ponders the inflation of a country into a war-zone, or war-poetry zone:

Why not brave the planetarium?

Seamus Heaney's poetry presents South Derry as a lusher field than Montague's Tyrone, and as the product of more complex geographical and historical co-ordinates. 'Terminus', from the pamphlet *Hailstones* (1984), ends on a vista of less than total loss:

> Baronies, parishes met where I was born.
> When I stood on the central stepping stone
> I was the last earl on horseback in midstream
> Still parleying, in earshot of his kernes.

Heaney's midpoint 'parleying' gives rise to more than one version of the past in his poetry, even different fathers. At the outset (mid-sixties) the figure based on his actual father sums up a positive inheritance of skills and values which the poet transmutes within his own medium. Several poems emphasise the responsibility of 'following', and being followed by, earlier generations. In 'Follower' qualities of the father define qualities of the poetry: technical 'expertise', weight: 'His shoulders globed like a full sail.' The sense of ancestral solidity, rich rural continuity, in *Death of a Naturalist* (1966) is disturbed by those literal 'skeletons' from the past who appear in two Famine poems. Later, *Wintering Out* (1972) leads Heaney 'into [the] trail' of more insubstantial forebears than his farming fathers. Flitting wraiths symbolise discontinuities rather than continuity: the deprivations and repressions both of Irish history in the long term, and Ulster history in the short term. Heaney's gloss on 'The Tollund Man' initiates him into this tragic family: '[he] seemed to me like an ancestor almost, one of my old uncles, one of those moustached archaic faces you used to meet all over the Irish countryside.'[34] ('Moustached archaic faces' is, curiously, a quotation from Philip Larkin's poem 'MCMXIV'.) In contrast with the Tollund Man's condition, the early poem 'Ancestral Photograph' begins: 'Jaws puff round and solid as a turnip.' Heaney's most celebrated poem about his father, 'The Harvest Bow' in *Field Work* (1979), might be read as a tentative reconciliation of his two family histories. A renewed vision of poetry as calling on the father's 'gift' and 'mellowed silence', poetry as peace-maker despite the changed 'spirit' of the times, attaches to

> a drawn snare
> Slipped lately by the spirit of the corn
> Yet burnished by its passage, and still warm.

III

Northern Irish poetry contains 'perceptions of the past' and philosophies of history, also articulated by historians and politicians, yet modified within the larger whole of poetry. What might be termed 'the aspirational approach' tends to receive least modification. Exemplified by Paulin's *Liberty Tree* this approach derives from the corporate Field Day cultural attitude, including more complex manifestations in Friel's drama. Seamus Deane's introduction to Friel's *Selected Plays* stresses how sundered Donegal haunts his imagination as 'a powerful image of possibility'.[35] This image crystallises Friel's protest against what Deane calls 'the sense of a whole history of failure concentrated into a crisis over a doomed community or group'.[36] Pointing to the sources of Friel's themes in a community robbed by history, robbed of history, Deane repeats such words and phrases as 'depressed and depressing atmosphere', 'apathy', 'desolation', 'failure', 'crisis', 'socially depressed and politically dislocated'. This language partly derives from psychology: the terminology for depressive psychosis. Friel in *Translations* applies a kind of therapy to this psychosis by offering Northern Catholics an alternative history, cultural self-respect, however 'doomed' that Gaelic culture itself may be. *Translations* can be read as less a historical play about Ireland and England, than an 'image of possibility' to redeem the more recent past in the North: an aisling. It fits Oliver MacDonagh's phrase for the goal of Gaelic revivalists in the twenties: a 'land . . . repeopled, in imagination, by a precolonial society, free of the stains and shames of anglicisation'.[37]

Liberty Tree, too, sets out to 'father history', to sire the future on 'images of the past'. Paulin's 'image of possibility' for Ireland, for the Protestant people of the North, is a date — 1798. Another date, 1912, represents the contrasting nadir, and completes his vision of Ulster history as decline and fall from an ideal. 'Desertmartin' '[sees] a plain / Presbyterian grace sour, then harden, / As a free strenuous spirit changes / To a servile defiance'. Decline and fall, like failure and possibility, rules out merely developmental and evolutionary understandings of history. Even Paulin's 'critical position . . . is founded on an idea of identity which has as yet no formal or institutional existence. It assumes the existence of a non-sectarian, republican state which comprises the whole island of Ireland.'[38] The aisling as literary criticism? Similarly, Paulin's Field Day pamphlet, *A New Look at the Language Question*, proposes a more 'institutional existence' for the English language in Ireland, a dictionary to codify what he regards as linguistic and literary 'anarchy'.[39] This aspiration towards an ideal language often distracts the actual language of Paulin's poetry. Words, on the whole, take an evolutionary view of themselves, 'Worn new' in Edward Thomas's paradox. Paulin's impatience to establish a new vocabulary, partly based on 'a relished [Ulster] dialect', gives words like the following no time to settle: 'glooby', 'scuffy', 'claggy', 'choggy'. As well as adjectives which aspire to exist, Paulin also repeats adjectives of aspiration 'green', 'sweet', 'equal'. And his poetry's general dependence on adjectives seems to me ideologically over-insistent, willed, willing — an effort to institutionalise the future.

Paulin, in condemning Ulster Protestants, aspires to redeem history, to start again from 1798 'with a pure narrative before him' ('L'Envie de Commencement'). Derek Mahon's deeper condemnation begets a recurrent imaginative hankering to abolish history ('daylong/twilights of misery'), to cut short its universally disastrous course. If Paulin's sense of history is partly religious — Calvinistic denunciation of Unionism as sin, Republicanism seen as salvation — Mahon's imagination more radically transposes the evangelist *alter ego* he satirises in 'Ecclesiastes', 'Another Sunday Morning' in *The Hunt by Night* (1982) calls poetry 'A sort of winged sandwich board / El-Grecoed to receive the Lord'. This makes him in one sense a son of his fathers. Mahon's fundamentalist view of Ulster Protestants as 'a lost tribe', rather than the elect, extends to the whole human race, and its lack of truly human or spiritual qualities. His poetry's grand prophetic sweep embraces 'civilisations', the beginning and the end, 'the biblical span'; contracts history into a Beckettian 'instant'. 'Another Sunday Morning' casts the poet as 'A chiliastic prig', i.e. a millenarian. John Wilson Foster, discussing millenarian aspects of W. R. Rodgers's vision, cites millenarianism as a tradition which looks for 'sudden divine intervention to destroy the existing order'.[40] Mahon's less 'enthusiastic' version dispenses with divine agency and ecstatic revelation, but equally adumbrates spiritual renewal through destruction (compare *Women in Love*). However, man is not among the worthy permitted to survive. In 'The Antigone Riddle'[41]

> Shy minerals contract at the sound of his voice,
> Cod point in silence when his bombers pass,
> And the windfall waits
> In silence for his departure
> Before it drops in
> Silence to the long grass.

Mahon's catch-phrase 'through with history' (and favourite adjective 'terminal') signals an artistic strategy as much as content. The less patient abolitionist scenario of 'Matthew V. 29-30'[42] preaches an absurdist but logical sermon on the text 'Lord, mine eye offended, / So I plucked it out'. Here the poet intervenes to destroy the 'offending' world himself, including 'Evaporation of all seas, / The extinction of heavenly bodies'. With equal if more humorous imaginative cheek, Mahon inverts Yeats's *creative* declaration: 'Death and life were not / Till man made up the whole . . .'. Nature more usually outlasts man in Mahon's poetry, or models 'the ideal society' (another catch-phrase, always ironic, never Paulin's 'sweet/equal republic'). In 'A Disused Shed in Co. Wexford'[43] the patient, peaceable mushrooms who have survived against the odds 'since civil war days' represent the compost of true renewal, and the first line gives history a last chance:

Even now there are places where a thought might grow —

Mahon's historical consciousness not only turns biblical Protestantism inside out, but contradicts Whig history and Belfast's industrial history. His poetry denies progress, views the rise of the bourgeoisie as a descent into 'barbarism', cries woe to a houseproud 'civilisation':

on
stormy nights our strong
double glazing groans with
foreknowledge of death,
the fridge with a great wound . . .   ('Gipsies')[44]

Michael Longley's perception of history, lacking Paulin's and Mahon's prophetic colouring, concentrates on the empirical issue of whether different histories can be accommodated, either imaginatively or communally, in a context symbolised by the last line of 'Letter to Seamus Heaney'[45] as 'A wind-encircled burial mound' — another cemetery. 'On Slieve Gullion'[46] specifically musters such histories:

On Slieve Gullion 'men and mountain meet',
O'Hanlon's territory, the rapparee,
Home of gods, backdrop for a cattle raid,
The Lake of Cailleach Beara at the top
That slaked the severed head of Conor Mor . . .

One figure in the landscape is 'A paratrooper on reconnaissance' who 'sweats up the slopes of Slieve Gullion / With forty pounds of history on his back'. In Seamus Heaney's poem 'The Toome Road',[47] a similar encounter with camouflaged armoured cars opposes to their intrusive presence 'The invisible, untoppled omphalos' — i.e. the 'indigenous territorial numen'. In 'On Slieve Gullion' Longley registers his own English connections in the phrase 'Both strangers here', and leaves the poem's mythic and historical ingredients in a state of suspension on the mountain. This implies the contemporary scarcity of such balm as 'slaked the severed head of Conor Mor'. As in 'Wounds', Longley's version of decline and fall differs from Paulin's.

But if 'On Slieve Gullion' finds no answers to the weight of the past, to 'forty pounds of history', it does not approach the determinism which characterises John Montague's vision. Montague's determinism derives from his historical awareness of both Ulster communities, 'two crazed peoples'[48] — an emphasis which contrasts with Friel's concentration on the Catholic communal psyche. Montague favours the word 'again': 'Again that note!', 'Once again, it happens', 'Again, the unwinding road'.[49] An artistic hazard of perceiving events as cyclical, is that style too can develop habits of repetition. 'Pattern' and 'ritual', also favourite words, sometimes apply to Montague's own technique, stiffening poems into a species of heraldry which excludes or precludes the active verb, rhythmical dynamic. The only process attributed to history concerns what is 'lost' or 'gone' (another favourite word), with loss itself a pattern — familial in the poem called 'Process':[50] 'time's gullet devouring / parents whose children / are swallowed in turn.' History repeats itself in Montague's imagination, presents itself as pre-processed, or perhaps as an impasse between the perspectives of 'mortality' and 'continuum'.

However, Ulster novelists too find it difficult to evade deterministic structures. Martin's *The Ceremony of Innocence* and *The Road to Ballyshannon*, MacLaverty's *Lamb* and *Cal*, all centre on characters whose options narrow to a single historical necessity. The conclusion of *Stamping Ground* falls into a similar mould; despite Leitch's gesture towards the positive, whereby a girl raped by three young men implausibly feels 'sorry for them now more than anything'.[15] Hetty essentially shares in the socio-sexual fatality, emanating from 'closed places of the spirit',[52] which has already engulfed the Valley's older generation. Her post-coital *joie de vivre* does not outweigh the past, any more than does an illusory vision near the end of *The Road to Ballyshannon*:

'I see it,' the sergeant said. 'I see it.' Through the mist and the broken
cloud a dolphin swam among the stars. 'I see it. It's a dolphin, isn't it?
And it's free.' It was then the sergeant realised that the boy's right hand
was held up by a tree root and the eyes that glistened to the night sky
were dead.[53]

Relentlessly deterministic, Martin's fictional techniques shoot
home, with loud clangs, the bolts which circumscribe existence.
His epigraphs pre-condition the reader as well: from Marx in *The
Ceremony of Innocence:*

Men make their own history, but they do not make it just as they please;
they do not make it under circumstances chosen by themselves, but
under circumstances directly encountered, given and transmitted from
the past. The tradition of all the dead generations weighs like a nightmare
on the brain of the living.

And from Nietzsche in *The Road to Ballyshannon:* '[Man] wonders
. . . about himself — that he cannot learn to forget, but hangs on
the past: however far or fast he runs, that chain runs with him.'
The Ceremony of Innocence incorporates quite a rich historical and
social panorama of Belfast since the Second World War; but all
this gives birth to a boy's destiny as 'a small black cross among
the thousand and more crosses that line the lawns of the City Hall
when the peacemarchers keep their silent, lonely vigil . . .'[54] A
leaner, less rhetorical work, set in 1922, *The Road to Ballyshannon*
follows two Republican fugitives and their RIC sergeant hostage
to an inevitable rendezvous. Although only the latter escapes
with his life, his son has earlier been killed by the Republicans.
The sergeant is additionally doomed to remain 'a hostage of the
dead',[55] because during the enforced journey he has become a
surrogate father to the younger of his captors.

   MacLaverty's *Lamb* also turns on surrogate fatherhood, this
time not derived from the literal and symbolic mixed marriages
that fascinate Martin, but an altruistic substitute for the
authoritarianism of a boys' borstal run by the Christian Brothers.
Brother Sebastian (Michael Lamb) takes rebellious Owen on an
escape-journey. Its time, money, and spirit inexorably run out:

He had started with a pure loving simple ideal but it had gone foul on
him, turned inevitably into something evil. It had been like this all his
life, with the Brothers, with the very country he came from. The beautiful
fly with the hook embedded . . . Owen was dead. He had killed him to
save him, although he loved him more than anyone else in his life.[56]

The sentimental tinge here, a counterpart to the melodrama informing Martin's doomed odysseys, also weakens the impact of Cal's fate. Cal's guilt-ridden love affair with the widow of an RUC reservist, to whose murder by the IRA he has been accessory, ends thus: 'he stood in a dead man's Y-fronts listening to the charge, grateful that at last someone was going to beat him to within an inch of his life.'[57] What in the case of poetry causes predictable cadences, in the case of fiction causes predictable plots, predictable emotional conformations, even a masochism under history's iron crushers which the novelist's sensibility shares with a passive victim-hero.

But the novelist must work with society as it is. The poet has perhaps less excuse if he fails to maintain the tension between creative dynamic and historical stasis, to detect hairfine tremors or locate chinks in determinism's defences. Perhaps Paulin's idealism weighs too hard on the dynamic scale-pan, Montague's determinism too hard on the static. Both also, unlike Mahon, write very explicitly about Irish history, which given half a chance will write the poems itself, turn idealism or aspiration back into determinism again, book the text in advance like Coulter's graves.

Seamus Heaney's 'Bogland'[58] famously does its own digging, conceives the past as a dimension to be explored dynamically rather than received statically: 'Our pioneers keep striking / Inwards and downwards', and so do the poem's rhythms. This conflates historical enquiry with psychic investigation, and Heaney's subsequent poetic soundings acquire the healing qualities of Jungian therapy, rather than Friel's implied prescription of electro-convulsion. Heaney's methods affirm the presence of depths and layers whereby the past imprints individual and community, a 'script indelibly written into the nervous system'.[59] Hence 'Broagh, / its low tattoo / among the windy boortrees.'[60] History in a word. But if the place-name poems in Wintering Out richly interleave personal and local-history associations, the procedures of North approximate more to recovery (Heaney's own term is 'retrieval') than gradual discovery. A speeded-up archaeological quest, for the bottom line of history, disinters the body of the past instead of excavating or enacting historical layers:

> now he lies
> perfected in my memory
> down to the red horn
> of his nails . . .   ('The Grabaulle Man')

Technically, the poems often repeat rhythmic syntactical and verbal structures; a patterning akin to Montague's. Perhaps the concept of the 'Bog People', symbolising, stylising, summing up history in a single 'icon', 'an archetypal pattern', was bound to have such an effect.[61] Again, the two fathers of Heaney's poetry merge into generalised ancestor-worship. 'Pinioned by ghosts / and affections' ('Viking Dublin'), the poet now elevates his farmer-father into 'god of the waggon, / the hearth-feeder' ('Kinship').

The iconography and rituals of *North* (which I have discussed elsewhere)[62] also freeze the fluid religious element which has always permeated Heaney's imaginative relation to the past. This — very different from Mahon's and Paulin's theologising — began with the natural magic of Heaney's childhood landscape (captured in *Death of a Naturalist*) when the 'pump marked an original descent into earth . . . centred and staked the imagination, made its foundation the foundation of the *omphalos* itself'.[63] In a lecture significantly entitled 'The *Sense* of the Past' (my italics), Heaney traces a progression from the child's 'intimate, almost animal response' to 'the mystery and claims of time past . . . the sense of belonging to a family and a place', to 'those images which widen this domestic past into a community or national past'.[64] In the latter connection he describes the enduring mystique within his imagination of a mass-rock picture with its 'emotional drama',[65] and of Wolfe Tone's profile offering 'a dream of the past against which all further learning took place'.[66] It might be asked whether these two ways of apprehending the past, as the second accrues political implications, are indeed progressive or concentric. Do the ripples widen evenly from the pump in the yard to the historical nation? Are the two fathers *really* one? How far does the 'common emotional ground of memory and belonging' extend? Similar questions arise from Heaney's religious sense of landscape as the primal source, the amniotic fluid. His recurrent landscaped female figure represents origins: the eternal mythic presence of the past, as opposed to the father who participates in historical process. Sexism apart, can the poet's immediate, local mother-earth stretch to abstract Mother Ireland, the 'indigenous territorial numen'? Does the synedoche work poetically, let alone historically and politically?

> Our mother ground
> is sour with the blood
> of her faithful . . .   ('Kinship')

lacks the specificity (and subtler political symbolism) of:

>All year the flax-dam festered in the heart
>Of the townland . . .   ('Death of a Naturalist')

'Kinship' enlarges the flax-dam and its frogs, 'great slime kings', into 'slime kingdoms'. In *North* Heaney sometimes rewrites his earlier poems in the light of history to whose actual pulse they seem closer.

Heaney's omphalos in his own backyard attempts a winning throw in the poetic, as well as political, game of claiming religio-historical origins. Others, like Montague, have gambled on the dolmen as symbolic touchstone. (Navan Fort poems wait in the wings.) Louis MacNeice reached back to the early Christian era when his aspiration to belong achieved its apotheosis at the end of 'The Once-in-Passing':[67]

>As though the window opened
>And the ancient cross on the hillside meant myself.

But beyond all monuments, the land itself remains 'the stable element' in poetry too, often appealed to over the head of unstable history. In 'Rocks' (after Guillevic)[68] Mahon uses geology, the long history of rocks ('Their dream of holding fast / In the elemental flux') to dwarf the human episode 'Lying in their shadows / In the last traces of time'. More broadly, the (non-human) animal, vegetable and mineral harbour 'The Banished Gods',[69] who

>sit out the centuries
>In stone, water
>And the hearts of trees,
>Lost in a reverie of their own natures . . .

Longley partly integrates natural and human history; partly sees Nature as improving on man's record of environmental accommodation, 'rinsing' the burial-mound as does poetry itself:

>The spring tide circles and excavates
>A shrunken ramshackle pyramid
>Rinsing cleaner scapulae, tibias,
>Loose teeth, cowrie and nautilus shells
>Before seeping after sun and moon
>To pour cupfuls into the lark's nests
>To break a mirror on the grazing
>And lift minnows over the low bridge.[70]   ('Spring Tide')

The Southern Irish poet Paul Durcan, in 'Before the Celtic Yoke'[71] gets rid of the past by imagining a platonic country innocent of history's invasion. Pre-human, not post-human like Mahon's millenarian dream, Genesis rather than Revelation, this land-scape's 'primal tongue' similarly sets a challenging goal for history-ridden poets: 'speak like me — like the mighty sun through the clouds.'

IV

Paul Muldoon's poetry does not overthrow the tyranny of the past by any such bold strokes as 'Before the Celtic Yoke'. Instead, it suffers death by a thousand cuts. (This contrast may reflect social and political differences between the Republic and Northern Ireland.) Most fundamentally, Muldoon enquires into the whole business of the writer, or anyone, looking to history at all.

To begin with a digression: Muldoon's points of departure are thrown into relief by the contrary methods of Heaney's long poem 'Station Island', and Brian Moore's fiction. The scenario of 'Station Island' not only builds in religio-historical pietas, but an appeal to (or for) higher authority. Heaney's theme of following or 'trailing' returns on a larger scale as his pilgrim seeks spiritual and artistic guidance by conversing with ghosts: various *male* voices from and of the past, surrogate fathers or 'fosterers' in the guise of priests, schoolmasters, mentors, master-writers, including Joyce invoked as 'Old father, mother's son'.[72] Although that last voice urges 'swim / out on your own' the poem itself enacts an entrapment, not least in its thraldom to literary history. ('Exemplary' is a favourite critical term of Heaney's.) Seamus Deane salutes what seems more like a critical than a creative agenda, a dependency rather than freedom, when he says: 'Heaney has begun to consider his literary heritage more carefully, to interrogate it in relation to his Northern and violent experience, to elicit from it a style of survival as a poet.'[73] Moore's *Fergus* (1971), perhaps also seeking a style of literary survival, revisits the past within a secular scenario very like that of *Station Island*. Fergus Fadden, serious novelist hoping to strike gold as a Hollywood script-writer, is literally haunted in his Californian beach-house by ghosts from his Irish family past. He too holds 'conversations with the dead'[74] (and younger versions of the living). His dead father, a socially and religiously conservative authority-figure who resembles Gavin's father in *The Emperor of*

Ice-Cream heads the haunters or hunters of a less securely liberated
psyche than Gavin's becomes. Moore's resurrection of a 'father's
world' bears very explicitly on the theme John Wilson Foster sees
as first surfacing in *An Answer from Limbo* (1962): 'primitivism and
provincialism become virtues, bulwarks against the erosive
hypocrisies of modern cosmopolitan life.'[75] Fergus articulates a
crisis close to the novelist's own sensibility:

He stood . . . hardly able to believe that a few moments ago, far from
fleeing his ghosts, he had pursued them with questions . . . Until now,
he had thought that, like everyone else, he exorcised his past by living it.
But he was not like everyone else. His past had risen up this morning,
vivid and uncontrollable, shouldering into his present.[76]

However, Moore's externalisation of interior or unconscious
dialogue involves fairly stock characters and responses. The
father's anticlimactic last words are: 'If you have not found a
meaning, then your life is meaningless.'[77] Moore's fiction after
Fergus oscillates within the terms of this over-neat antithesis. His
protagonists find or lose some kind of faith, with the supernatural
underlining the issue in *Catholics* (1972), *The Great Victorian Collection* (1975), *Cold Heaven* (1983) and *Black Robe* (1985). *The Mangan
Inheritance* (1979) pursues, antithetically to *Fergus*, the question of
faith in the past itself. Keeping the faith, whether religiously or
historically, draws on the same pool of Irish feeling. James Mangan,
a Canadian not an expatriate Irishman, becomes obsessed with
proving his kinship to James Clarence Mangan. His quest for
genealogical ratification of his character and talents ends in tears,
in 'hated self-images',[78] in the shattering of a talismanic ancestral
daguerrotype, in a return home to healthier emotion about his
father's death. Moore's dialectic between Irish total recall and
Californian amnesia derives — like excessive determinism or
idealism — from Ulster experience, but may be too much of a
swinging pendulum to redeem it artistically. Foster calls *Fergus*
'more of a re-hash than an advance'.[79] Despite his variations on
a theme, Moore's consciousness in some respects stands still
between a futureless Ireland (doubly so since it belongs to his
past) and a pastless North America.

Thirty years younger than Moore, Muldoon shows no signs of
augmenting Foster's 'wry irony in the sight of yesterday's apos-
tates becoming today's nostalgics'.[80] Without dramatic apostasy,
his poetry consistently queries addiction to precedent, preceptor
and pedigree (especially in the direct line). For instance in *Quoof*
(1983) his long poem 'The More a Man Has the More a Man Wants'

implies the distant absurdity of historical bloodlines by attaching unIrish-American ancestry to the Ulster crisis:

> On the Staten Island Ferry
> two men are dickering
> over the price
> of a shipment of Armalites,
> as Henry Thoreau was wont to quibble
> with Ralph Waldo Emerson.

The scene then moves to the Algonquin where, in a parody of Young Ireland's heroic genealogies, the protagonist encounters 'a flurry / of sprites, / the assorted shades of Wolfe Tone, Napper Tandy . . . Then, Thomas Meagher / darts up from the Missouri / on a ray / of the morning star, / to fiercely ask / what has become of Irish hurling?' (This poem is no respecter of ghosts.) 'The Frog'[81] attacks from a different angle the notion that 'images of the past' hold lessons, can be made 'exemplary':

> The entire population of Ireland
> springs from a pair left to stand
> overnight in a pond
> in the gardens of Trinity College,
> two bottles of wine left there to chill
> after the Act of Union
>
> There is, surely in this story
> a moral. A moral for our times . . .

This anti-Aesop fable plays down 1801 as much as Paulin plays up 1798. It also suggests that for art to hitch a lift on history might be not only portentously futile, but an aesthetic dabbling in violent waters: 'What if I put him to my head / and squeezed it out of him, / like the juice of freshly squeezed limes, / or a lemon sorbet?' However, historians get off no more lightly than poets. 'History'[82] embarks on historical research: 'Where and when exactly did we first have sex?' A series of questions having elicited no answers, the poem concludes that only *imaginative* truth can be trusted since a possible location is 'the room where MacNeice wrote "Snow", / Or the room where they say he wrote "Snow".' MacNeice's poem emerges as the only sure thing in a world of shaky facts. Similarly, the uncommitted poet in 'Lunch with Pancho Villa'[83] undermines a whole industry of publication on Northern Ireland when he states: 'there's no such book, so far as I know, / As *How it Happened Here*, / Though there may be. There may.'

Muldoon's poetry, then, attempts to loosen the grip of the past on both life and literature, perhaps as epitomised by a habituated pump attendant: 'grown so used / to hold-ups he calls after them, / *Beannacht Dé ar on obair.*'[84] He 'interrogates history' in a more genuine sense than many who flaunt this formula. His techniques sabotage all kinds of certainty about how 'far' we 'know' into the past or future. Hence the subjunctives, conditionals, qualifications, syntactical ambiguities, refusals of historic tenses, abundance of the present continuous, riddling questions, and the pervasive revitalised cliché which violates tombs of thought and language:

> How often have I carried our family word
> for the hot water bottle
> to a strange bed . . .   (*Quoof*)

To defamiliarise is also to defamilialise. Throughout Muldoon's poetry the father is a persistent metaphysical shadow. Behind, rather than both behind and in front like Heaney's father-figure, he represents 'what is . . . immediately over my shoulder'. Two poems in *Why Brownlee Left*, 'October 1950' and 'Immrama' complicate that vista. The former presents conception not as determined or determining but as 'chance' which leads to 'Anything wild or wonderful'. The speaker of the latter at first seems eager to join the poetic paternity suite: 'I, too, have trailed my father's spirit', but orthodox Irish biography ('mud-walled cabin', 'farm where he was first hired out', 'building-site') has an unorthodox South American finale: 'That's him on the verandah, drinking Rum / With a man who might be a Nazi . . .' This impugns not only any mythologised purity of family stock, but doctrines of such purity. Earlier the father's authority and factuality were revoked by the very dedication of Muldoon's first collection *New Weather* (1973): 'For my Fathers and Mothers.' This instantaneous historical pluralism generated other pluralities and mixtures in the poetry, subtler versions of those surrogacies or difficult mixed parentages in fiction: mongrels, mutations, doubles, androgyny and sexual ambivalence ('The Bearded Woman, by Ribera'[85] with her 'Willowy, and clean-shaven' consort), mergers, alter egos, alternative lives, promiscuity of cultural reference, as with this ironically international Northern Irish Muse:

> For Beatrice, whose fathers
> Knew Louis Quinze,
> to have come to this, her perruque
> of tar and feathers.   ('The More a Man Has')

Even Muldoon's puns endow words with multiple identities, and his poems unfold not just through metaphor but through metamorphosis. 'The More a Man Has', its imagery of 'mind-expanding' drugs shared by other poems in *Quoof*, only intensifies the Lewis Carroll transitions found everywhere. And just as its 'hero', a victim of violent history, metamorphoses ('Gallogly, or Gollogly, / otherwise known as Golightly, / otherwise known as Ingoldsby, / otherwise known as English'), so does its metre. That most rigidly traditional of forms, the sonnet, becomes an unpredictable kaleidoscope which dwindles at one point to single-word lines like the mouse's tail in *Alice*.

The title-poem of Muldoon's second collection, *Mules* (1977) presents a son witnessing a father witnessing an awkward birth:

> We had loosed them into one field.
> I watched Sam Parsons and my quick father
> Tense for the punch below their belts,
> For what was neither one thing or the other.

Among other things, this feared hybrid symbolises all offspring of the two traditions in Ulster, including Muldoon's poetry itself. But fathers' breeding too, as 'Immrama' suggests, can be suspect. The longer poem 'Immram'[86] takes shape as a search for the father, for an explanation of some dirty business in the past which implicates the son:

> I was fairly and squarely behind the eight
> That morning in Foster's pool-hall
> When it came to me out of the blue
> In the shape of a sixteen-ounce billiard cue
> That lent what he said some little weight.
> 'Your old man was an ass-hole.
> That makes an ass-hole out of you.'
> My grandfather hailed from New York State.
> My grandmother was part Cree.
> This must be some new strain in my pedigree . . .
>
> I suppose that I should have called the cops
> Or called it a day and gone home
> And done myself, and you, a favour.
> But I wanted to know more about my father.

But shifty and shifting, the father eludes pursuit: 'He would flee, to La Paz, then to Buenos Aires, / From alias to alias.' The son does not set out to avenge an innocent father, as he does in

'Immram Mael Duin', the medieval voyage tale on which Muldoon's 'Immram' is loosely, if not licentiously, based. However, at the end of the poem he is released like Mael Duin from thraldom to the past, and 'happily' rejoining the 'flow' of the living, returns to 'Foster's pool-room' (a pun on the fostering of Mael Duin). In 'Gathering Mushrooms'[87] we glimpse the father as a familiarly solid rural figure: 'He'll glance back from under his peaked cap / without breaking rhythm'. Muldoon may partly allude to Heaney's father-figure, and, as elsewhere, to Heaney as a literary father-figure ('rhythm' in Heaney's poems fuses poetry and rural work). Such fathers are now perceived as sadly obsolescent: 'one of those ancient warriors / before the rising tide' — a helpless Cuchulain. Set 'fifteen years on', and thus straddling *recent* history, 'Gathering Mushrooms' presents the 'tide' of violence as psychedelic transformation. The substitution of magic mushrooms for the ordinary variety symbolises a grotesque mutation of tradition. A reversed aisling, the poem is also a slow-motion reprise of 'Easter, 1916' ('changed utterly') in which nothing — or a changeling — gets born. The speaker, his head 'grown into the head of a horse', finds in his mouth the words of a Republican dirty-protestor instructing: '*If sing you must, let your song / tell of treading your own dung.*' The speaker implicitly resists imperatives delivered by the past ('dung') in the name of the future ('*the day we leap / into our true domain*'), history's attempt to dictate to the poet.

If Mahon demolishes Whig history, you might say that Muldoon dismantles its opposite. He exorcises the hovering 'ghost-life' of mythic history, what Oliver MacDonagh rather euphemistically terms 'an absence of a developmental or sequential view of past events'.[88] But his poetry does not simply or simplistically walk away from atavism into agnostic daylight. Nor does it weigh too heavily on either side of any antithesis, but resembles Brownlee's abandoned horses

> Shifting their weight from foot to
> Foot, and gazing into the future.[89]

Muldoon negotiates that small space, that inch, between necessity and possibility, with an integrity faithful above all to the present. 'Cherish the Ladies',[90] like other Muldoon poems, takes place in the present tense and is aware of itself as a tiny piece of historical process if not progress:

> In this, my last poem about my father,
> there may be time enough
> for him to fill their drinking-trough
> and run his eye over
>
> his three mooley heifers.
> Such a well-worn path,
> I know, from here to the galvanized bath.

The phrase 'my last poem' could mean either final or most recent, thus suggesting work-in-progress. 'Cherish the Ladies' (like 'Immram') braves the reader's imagined boredom with father-poems: 'Such a well-worn path / I know.' And it restores for the space of the poem the rural archetype of the father by insisting on the actuality of his opening 'the stand-pipe' — an image for begetting. Like 'Gathering Mushrooms', 'Cherish the Ladies' incorporates an italicised alternative poem, alternative history, alternative future controlled by the past:

> I know, too, you would rather
>
> *I saw behind the hedge to where the pride*
> *of the herd, though not an Irish*
> *bull, would cherish*
> *the ladies with his electric cattle-prod.*
>
> As it is, in my last poem about my father
> he opens the stand-pipe
> and the water scurries along the hose
> till it's curled
>
> in the bath — One heifer
> may look up
> and make a mental note, then put her nose
> back to the salt-lick of the world.

What might be going on, or written up, behind the hedge smacks of violence, rape, the denaturing of tradition (in the references to folk-songs). As ever, Muldoon discriminates between dead and living tradition, between apparent and real breaks with the past, between the oppressively progenitive 'pride of the herd' and the true father who really 'cherishes' the future, who makes available 'the salt-lick of the world'.

YEATS, JOYCE AND THE CURRENT IRISH CRITICAL DEBATE

TERENCE BROWN

The nascent nationalism of the early twentieth century in Ireland generated the movement known as Irish Ireland — a movement earnest to celebrate the authentic life of a nation long subjected to alien suppression. It saw as one of its enemies the Anglo-Irish ascendancy which had been, so Irish Ireland reckoned, the chief agent of anglicisation in the country, that anglicisation which had eclipsed the Gaelic world. The literature it identified with that caste, Anglo-Irish literature, was received with the profoundest suspicion. For critics like D. P. Moran, Eoin MacNeil and Daniel Corkery the question of Anglo-Irish literature posed an issue which in fact generated a critical discourse which was more sustained and coherent than anything produced by any person or group sympathetic to the achievement that literature represented.[1] And the ways in which Irish Ireland reflected on Anglo-Irish literature have proved remarkably long-lived in the country, contemporary critical debate often being conducted in terms that Irish Ireland would have found congenial. So powerful indeed has been the influence of the Revival that sixty years after Irish Ireland's first assaults upon Anglo-Irish literature the question of that literature's relationship with Irish life remains contentious and vexed, around which the nearest thing to a contemporary body of Irish criticism revolves.

The central thrust of Irish Ireland's critique of Anglo-Irish literature was that it lacked national authenticity, was not truly indigenous. A second, subsidiary element in Irish Ireland's polemical assault upon Anglo-Irish literature was that it was inauthentic because it failed to appreciate the deeply European nature of Ireland's local life. In *The Hidden Ireland* (1924) Corkery evokes the indigenous life of peasant Ireland as one that has escaped the universalising forces of the Enlightenment, retaining in its customs and beliefs a link with the medieval world of Catholic Europe. Furthermore, in his celebration of the Gaelic big

113

houses of the eighteenth century it is their European awareness
and that of their poets which he particularly esteems: 'To these,
Paris was nearer than Dublin, and Vienna than London'[2] and
'contact with Europe, then, was one of the notes that distinguished
the culture of the Catholic Gaels from that of the Planters'.[3]

Irish Ireland's critique was a powerful and pugnacious polemic
vitiated by a major weakness most evident in the work of its
principal advocate, Corkery himself. It lacked an exemplary
contemporary figure to set against the exotic, inauthentic and
non-European literature of the Revival, to confirm the analysis by
an evident national authenticity and continental imaginative
range. In the 1920s a number of literary commentators in Ireland
began to identify James Joyce in such terms, finding that his career
and work more closely approximated to Irish Ireland's cultural
map than the John Synge whom Corkery himself tried to incorporate into his own analysis as an exemplary and explanatory figure.
An early and amusing instance of this cultural strategy was
provided indeed by Joyce's friend, and subsequently Ireland's
Registrar of the Supreme Court, C. P. Curran. Reflecting in AE's
Irish Statesman on that most profound of Irish polarities, the North
and South side of the Hibernian Metropolis, he asserted 'the North
side is the Gael's, the South the Pale's'. And it is in the Gaelic
North side that the city's most vibrant cultural energies are located:

I suggest geographically that the Northern frontier of the South side
stretches from the Brewery to Trinity College. I do not deny that breweries
and colleges produce literature of a sort, nor do I fail to recognise the
existence of many admirable suburban and austral poets. But they seem
to me to lack some toughness of fibre, the intensity, the austerity, the
virile, sometimes astringent quality that makes good North side literature.
Aungier Street could write sweet verses about Bendemeer's stream,
and Merrion Square poets may write about salley gardens and more
obscurely about cats and the moon. What is all their praise to them who
tread in the footsteps of the Nameless One dreeing his weird between
the river and the famous back-parlour in North Charles Street where he
consorted worthily with his peers, Petrie, O'Donovan, O'Curry, O'Langan,
and the rest who made the lower end of the North Circular Road the
bright focus of Irish literature . . . Nor does the way-worn, travel-stained
Ulysses himself ever stray far or long from this consecrated ground.[4]

Here, in jocose fashion, Curran proposes Joyce, in a manner
that was to become conventional in Irish cultural debate, as an
adversary to his great contemporary, Yeats. Joyce in the person of
his hero Bloom is associated with the virile energies of the Gael,

with Mangan and the exploits of Gaelic scholarship, Yeats with effete Celticism and the exotic otherworldliness of the occult.

In addition, by the 1920s Joyce's achievement began to be identified as a European phenomenon by Irish critics earnest to discover in an indisputably indigenous writer evidence of Ireland's continental patrimony which set it apart from the neighbouring island and from the cultural hegemony of the Anglo-Saxon world. In 1929 the poet Thomas McGreevy (who had already contributed to *Our Exaymination round his Factification for Incumination of Work in Progress* in Paris) took Sean O'Faolain sternly to task for his unfavourable response to *Anna Livia Plurabelle*. McGreevy berated O'Faoláin for adding his voice to 'the prim and priggish university intelligences of England and America'. He continued:

These two countries, which reek with Puritanical hypocrisy, have both banned Mr Joyce's most important work, and it seems to me a pitiable thing to see a young Irish critic of some education helping, however disinterestedly or unconsciously, to find aesthetic justification for their moral cowardice.[5]

An understanding of the European significance and Catholic nature of Joyce's achievement, McGreevy asserts, allows his work to be properly apprehended. The clear inference is that the Anglo-Saxon world is incapable of such a reading which Ireland and Europe can provide: 'The conception of *Ulysses* as a modern equivalent of the *Inferno* of Dante did not strike a great many of the people who thought it infernal. They all screamed "pornography" and attributed evil motives to the author, though no single one of the eternal moral values is altered in the book.'[6] So situated in the context of European intellectual and religious tradition 'Work in Progress' can readily be understood, in McGreevy's view:

The new work regarded as a Purgatorio falls into place at once. A Catholic imaginative writer like Mr Joyce may well seize on aspects of the purgatorial ideas that were not treated by Dante, and may invent a technique suggested by some more modern writers than Dante, such as Vico, the 18th century Neapolitan philosopher, to express them. And this is to some extent what has happened.[7]

In the 1930s Irish Ireland's polemic against Yeats and revival literature became strident, even at times grotesque. A Mr James Devane (author of *Isle of Destiny*, 1936, and described by his editor as a 'dermatologist, who since his return from India has invaded Irish letters and vied with his Jesuit brother in enriching the

controversial pages of Irish journalism') took Yeats to task in
Ireland To-day. 'Why' he asked 'does Yeats . . . who has done so
much for our national culture . . . these later days, speak of the
Irish yeoman in the traditional Anglo-Irish accents of contempt.'[8]
Yeats has often been attacked for a sentimental idealisation of the
Irish peasant; rarely has he been thought inadequately appreciative
of the Irish yeoman, whoever he might be. Devane is representative, however, in his sense that Yeats's cosmopolitan eclecticism
is somehow alien to the Irish majority — his 'choice and eclectic
diet may suit the tender palate of a poet, but it will scarcely agree
with the rough digestion of a crofter, a Connemara fisherman, a
country shopkeeper, a country doctor, a lawyer, a policeman, a
soldier'.[9] In the 1930s however there was little sense of Joyce as a
radical alternative to the Yeatsian model of an artistic relationship
with society. At one level that is hardly surprising. To many, in a
decade of aggressive nativism Joyce's European literary aspirations
must have seemed an affront. Official Ireland in 1932 had issued
a *Hand Book* in which the litterateur Robert Lynd had restricted
himself in an article on 'Anglo-Irish Literature' to the cautious
observation: 'Critics differ in their estimates of the genius of
Mr George Moore and Mr James Joyce, but they are at least two
writers who have had an enormous influence on the English
novel of our time.'[10] And this in a survey which took for granted
the brilliant dominance of the Irish literary firmament by the
Yeatsian star. To many, such caution, however, would have
seemed only good sense in such a context in view of the moral
opprobrium Joyce had drawn upon himself on account of the
scandalous nature of his works. Indeed, L. A. G. Strong reported
seventeen years later how when 'invited to lecture to the Royal
Dublin Society', and when he had proposed to speak on Joyce he
was 'informed in tones of dignified reproach that such a subject
would not be acceptable to the members'. Strong concluded in
his study of Joyce, published in 1949:

Such views may not seem worth mentioning, when Joyce's status is so
generally admitted, but his case remains to be argued in his native land,
and an Irish writer must sometimes argue it — even though an attempt
to rebut the false case which Irishmen have hatched up against Joyce be
foredoomed before it is made.[11]

At another level it *is* surprising that Joyce's developing international
reputation in the 1930s did not challenge younger Irish writers to
assess his achievement as a counterweight to Yeats's august and
intimidating magnificence. In fact *Ireland To-day*, the one periodical

in the 1930s which sought to reflect on Irish social and cultural, as well as literary, matters contained no reference to Joyce whatsoever, apart from a few cursory reviews of new and republished works.

It was the short story writers Sean O'Faolain and Frank O'Connor who in the 1940s reformulated the Yeats/Joyce polarity which had achieved embryonic form in the 1920s. They did not deny Yeats's grandeur, nor even the European dimension of his imaginative synthesis but considered their own work a realistic exploration of aspects of Irish life more in the tradition of Joyce than Yeats. O'Connor makes the matter plain:

When O'Faolain and I began to write it was with some idea of replacing the subjective, idealistic, romantic literature of Yeats, Lady Gregory and Synge by one modelled on the Russian novelists.[12]

In so doing O'Connor almost unconsciously associates the enter-prise with the writings of Joyce: 'it is time that the literature of Catholic Ireland (and one needn't go beyond Joyce to prove it) is dominated by its material in a way in which the work of Synge and Yeats rarely was'[13] setting the key for what O'Faolain was to declare twenty years later:

There is no longer any question of dishing up local colour (The Noble Peasant is as dead as the Noble Savage. Poems about fairies and leprechauns, about misted lakes, old symbols of national longing, are over and done with). We need to explore Irish life with an objectivity never hitherto applied to it — and in this Joyce rather than Yeats is our inspiration.[14]

For O'Connor and O'Faolain Joyce is a more appropriate inspira-tion for an Irish writer because a post-revolutionary phase in Irish history demands a realism, in O'Faolain's words, 'knitted with common life'.[15] Yeats is not deemed to lack national authenticity, as Irish Ireland had insisted he did. He is merely a magnificent anachronism.

The O'Connor/O'Faolain critique of Yeats and Joyce took the poet's greatness for granted but assumed that his imaginative idealism could not greatly affect writers in a more prosaic age. In recent decades Irish critical thought has sought to reassess Yeats in ways that owe more to Irish Ireland's original assault upon the poet. Such reassessments do not of course indulge in the crude nationalism of the earlier movement in denying Yeats his national authenticity. They do nevertheless challenge his imaginative procedures, fearing indeed that these may have a baneful influence

on contemporary Ireland. For Yeats in these critics' view was
guilty of a highly damaging imaginative evasion. And Joyce in
their writings is comparatively adduced as the truly enabling
presence.

It was the poet Thomas Kinsella who first put this argument in
a powerful lecture in 1966.[16] His brooding reflection on 'The Irish
Writer' brings him up immediately against his sense of the Irish
tradition as gapped, discontinuous, terrifyingly disabling. The
loss of the language is felt as a crippling wound. Corkery's
analysis of the effects of this catastrophe is fully endorsed — the
effect is one of fundamental deprivation, the modern Irish world
almost completely unrealised in the country's literature. Yeats, in
Kinsella's view of things, accepted the isolation such a state of
things necessarily created, making a brilliant if fundamentally
dubious virtue of it. Yeats created his own tradition in isolation
and 'it is still a coherent entity, at a graceful elegiac height above
the filthy modern tide'.[17] The consequence of this act is that Yeats
'refused to come to terms with the real shaping vitality of Ireland'.[18]
And a further consequence is that Yeats, so masterful and energetic
a presence in the Irish world, who might have brought healing to
the Irish tradition, in fact irritated the wound:

Yeats bestrides the categories. He had a greatness capable, perhaps, of
integrating a modern Anglo-Irish culture, and which chose to make this
impossible by separating out a special Anglo-Irish culture from the main
unwashed body.[19]

There is a harshness about this argument, bred of pained regret
and a sense of national requirement which recalls Corkery. For
it seems unduly judgmental to assume that Yeats deliberately
chose to make an integrated culture impossible. At this point in
Kinsella's thesis Corkery indeed is once more directly invoked. In
Synge and Anglo-Irish Literature (1931) that critic had identified
three forces which give 'Irish national being its Irishness' and
which must be expressed in any truly national literature: (1) the
Religious Consciousness of the People, (2) Irish Nationalism,
(3) the Land. Kinsella observes that Joyce's Stephen Dedalus is
conscious of two of these forces and although he rejects them
he does not evade them. Joyce, by extension from Stephen, is
introduced to the argument as the exemplary alternative to Yeats:

His stomach, unlike Yeats's, is not turned by what he sees shaping the
new Ireland: the shamrock lumpen proletariat, the eloquent and conniving
and mean-spirited tribe of Dan. Daniel O'Connell or De Valera or Paudeen

do not deter him from his work; they are his subjects. He is the first major Irish voice to speak for Irish reality since the death of the Irish language.[20]

So Irish Ireland's main polemical threat is reaffirmed (Yeats although a major voice does not truly speak for 'Irish reality') and the force of that earlier cultural analysis is augmented by the incorporation of Joyce into the dialectics:

So, the Irish writer, if he cares who he is and where he comes from, finds that Joyce and Yeats are the two main objects in view; and I think that he finds that Joyce is the true father. I will risk putting it diagrammatically and say that Yeats stands for the Irish tradition as broken; Joyce stands for it as continuous or healed — or healing — from its mutilation.[21]

A further strain of Irish Ireland's cultural critique is re-affirmed in Kinsella's lecture, though in modulated key. For Irish Ireland indigenous Irish life was essentially European, which set it apart from the provincialism of Anglo-Saxon culture. Kinsella allows Joyce a similarly synthetic cultural comprehensiveness beside which Yeats must appear curiously parochial in his basic archaism. Joyce's is an urban and therefore modern imagination:

The filthy modern tide does not only run in Ireland, of course, and Joyce's art of continuity is done with a difference: he simultaneously revives the Irish tradition and admits the modern world. It is symptomatic that for Corkery's third force, the Land, Joyce substitutes the City. He makes up all the arrears at once.[22]

Subsequent Irish critics have endorsed Kinsella's stern view censuring Yeats for his Anglo-Irish elitism and finding in Joyce an exemplary and inspirational democrat of the imagination. A number of critics associated with the Dublin edited periodical *The Crane Bag* (which began publishing in 1977) and the Derry inspired and published Field Day Pamphlets (which began publication in 1983) have indeed mounted what has almost seemed a kind of cultural crusade in these adversarial terms. Declan Kiberd in an essay in the series *Ireland: Dependence and Independence* had this to say of Yeats in the rhetoric of the debating chamber:

Having dazzled himself with this Ireland of stolen children and fairy forts, of serene towers and violent highways, of big houses and cosy cottages, Yeats then employed his immense rhetorical powers to enrapture everybody else. The result is that Irish people no longer live in a country of their own making, but in a kind of tourist's filmset.[23]

It seems hard to blame Yeats for the vulgarisation of his symbolic imagination but the forensic trajectory of this kind of writing needs a villain beside whose misdeeds the radically innovative quality of James Joyce can appear all the more compelling. Joyce is reckoned a socialist and his socialism is a product of his European sensibility (the European is now socialist, not Catholic as it was for Corkery):

There was, however, a second form of Irish revival, an alternative to the one led by Yeats and de Valera. It was pioneered by men like Connolly and James Joyce, men who began with the courageous admission that there is no such thing as an Irish identity, ready-made and fixed, to be carried as a passport into eternity.[24]

Similarly Richard Kearney in his Field Day Pamphlet, *Myth and Motherland*, proposes Yeats and Joyce as representatives in literary terms of a tendency in Irish life to reflect a tension between mythic and anti-mythic forms of discourse. Less polemically assured than Kiberd, Kearney nevertheless sponsors the Joycean alternative to Yeatsian myth-making. Joyce, in Kearney's view, indicates how Irish identity can be re-formulated not in nationalistic fashion but in European and indeed universal modes which can liberate from myth conceived of in absolute terms, and from provincial stereotyping.

Finnegans Wake teaches us that Dublin is 'Doublin' — itself and not itself. It teaches us that our sense of tradition is not some pre-ordained continuity which makes us all the same. Myth is revealed as history and history as myth. Joyce thus shows that our narrative of cultural self-identity is itself a fiction — an epical forged cheque — and that each one of us has the freedom to re-invent our past.[25]

Yeats, it seems, passed the Irish nation a dud local cheque; Joyce can draw on the inexhaustible credit of the European and world banks.

This is why Joyce presents Anna Livia Plurabelle as a model of *unity in plurality*, a 'bringer of plurabilities' who is 'every person, place and thing in the chaosmos of alle . . . moving and changing every part of the time.'[26]

It has been Seamus Deane who has developed the most sustained and exacting critique of Yeats in recent years in Ireland.

Since 1973 when he delivered a lecture in Montreal on 'The Literary Myths of the Revival' he has subjected Yeats's historiography to an icily angered analysis. In that lecture (recently republished in revised form) he is manifestly incensed that Yeats should have bestowed a retrospective dignity by a piece of historical sleight of hand on a discredited social caste, the Anglo-Irish. So great is this offence that Deane finds it difficult to arrive at any unambiguous estimate of Yeats's artistic achievement, though his indignation is blended with admiration at the poet's 'almost inexhaustible resourcefulness'.[27] That imaginative resourcefulness expressed itself on the stage and Deane in an essay of 1978 did extend Yeats the recognition (even if at the expense of Sean O'Casey) that in his experimental theatre 'despite its esoteric ambitions, its aristocratic gestures and its select audience'[28] he does discover 'the tragic possibilities of political action and the contemplative alternative to it'.[29] The year before Deane had indeed sought to reckon with Yeats as a colonial poet whose *oeuvre* nevertheless challenges both Ireland and the contemporary world in useful ways. 'To describe Yeats's politics, and to a large extent his achievement, as colonial is not at all to diminish it',[30] Deane avers, identifying in Yeats's form of traditionalism a radical rebuke to the spiritual impoverishment of modern capitalism. But even here the critic can only allow the poet a negative virtue. By the time he wrote his Field Day Pamphlet, *Heroic Styles: the Tradition of an Idea*, (1984) qualification was overtaken by condemnation. Yeats is subsumed in a general sentence passed with magisterial distaste on the cultural manoeuvring of a fading class — the Anglo-Irish Ascendancy:

Irish culture became the new property of those who were losing their grip on Irish land. The effect of these re-writings was to transfer the blame for the drastic condition of the country from the Ascendancy to the Catholic middle classes or to their English counterparts. It was in essence a strategic retreat from political to cultural supremacy. From Lecky to Yeats and forward to F. S. L. Lyons we witness the conversion of Irish history into a tragic theatre in which the great Anglo-Irish protagonists — Swift, Burke, Parnell — are destroyed in their heroic attempts to unite culture of intellect with the emotion of the multitude, or in political terms, constitutional politics with the forces of revolution.[31]

The judge's distaste for the prisoners in the dock is here all too evident; Yeats does not escape the general indictment. He is indeed seen to exhibit 'the pathology of literary unionism'[32] and must, it seems, pay the price before the bar of history.

The main thrust of Irish Ireland's critique of Yeats and of the Literary Revival as a whole was augmented, as I have argued, by the recruitment of Joyce to the dialectical polemics as an exemplary democrat. Surprisingly in Deane's criticism, which must remind of Corkery in its ideological rigour, its severe certitudes, Joyce too must abide our question. In his essay of 1982 'Joyce and Nationalism' Yeats and Joyce are, familiarly, present as contrasting figures (though they are also seen to share a conviction that 'the supreme action was writing').[33] But it is not clear that the critic unreservedly approves the way, he discerns, that 'Ireland as an entity, cultural or political, was incorporated in all its mutations within Joyce's work as a model of the world and, more importantly, as a model of the fictive'.[34] In *Heroic Styles* this sense of judgement reserved is overtaken by one of a critical summing up in which Joyce as well as Yeats must endure an austere scrutiny:

The pluralism of his styles and languages, the absorbent nature of his controlling myths and systems, finally gives a certain harmony to varied experience. But, it could be argued, it is the harmony of indifference, one in which everything is a version of something else, where sameness rules over diversity, where contradiction is finally and disquietingly written out. In achieving this in literature, Joyce anticipated the capacity of modern society to integrate almost all antagonistic elements by transforming them into fashions, fads — styles, in short. Yet it is true that in this regard, Joyce is, if you like, our most astonishing 'modernist' author and Yeats is his 'anachronistic' counterpart. The great twins of the Revival play out in posterity the roles assigned to them and to their readers by their inherited history.[35]

What this says is that Irish Ireland may have been right about Yeats and the Revival in some crude senses but that the Irish reality it so took for granted as an unqualified good, which the artist must celebrate, is deeply flawed. And it is flawed not only because it is a reality that includes the horror of incipient civil war ('contradiction') but one which allows the superficial styles of modern capitalism to delude the unwary into an egregious complacency. Certain readings of Joyce, Deane implies, encourage such evasive complacency as Yeats, read as he intended he should be, might encourage patrician and futile individual heroics. What makes this essay by Deane important, it seems to me, is that it could provide a *terminus ad quem* to a debate Irish Ireland inaugurated at the beginning of the century and clears the way for new readings of both Yeats and Joyce which would not see them in the starkly adversarial poses in which they have recently been presented. It might allow a less reductive estimate of Yeats's achievement if the case against him could be taken as resting (it has rarely been so starkly stated) and permit a more searching Irish analysis of Joyce to proceed if it were recognised that his celebration of a fictively open, polysemic European consciousness, in Ireland's and Europe's contemporary circumstances, might itself lack full enabling significance.

THE TREASURE OF HUNGRY HILL: THE IRISH WRITER AND THE IRISH LANGUAGE

COLBERT KEARNEY

In 1939 Longmans of London published *At Swim-Two-Birds* by Flann O'Brien, the pseudonym of Brian O'Nolan. By then the author had come to have doubts about the title, considering it uncommercial and more suited for 'a slim book of poems' and suggesting that the book be called *Sweeny in the Trees*.[1] It is unlikely that the title was responsible for the fate of the book which seemed to sink without trace except among a tiny coterie. With hindsight we see the initial flop as due to the accidents of publication but it is most unlikely that O'Nolan was capable of such detachment when in 1940 Longmans decided not to publish his next novel, *The Third Policeman*. The future must have seemed grim for a novelist who had lost London and who had to remain at home in neutral Ireland while the rest of the English-speaking world concerned itself with matters more pressing than the antics of the Irish imagination. But things were about to look up for O'Nolan and within a year he was a success, even if only in Ireland: in 1940 he began his bilingual column in the *Irish Times* and in 1940 he published *An Béal Bocht* which was a huge success among the minority of Irish readers who read Irish. (Those without Irish had to wait until 1973 when a translation, *The Poor Mouth*, appeared as part of the canonisation of O'Nolan.)

An Béal Bocht is in many ways an epitome of the Gaelic prose tradition as we perceive it today — a fantastic, grotesque and parodic satire, darkly and wildly comic, a linguistic *tour de force*. The target for all this energy was the kind of book which dominated writing in Irish in the early twentieth century, books which were really transcriptions of first person reminiscences and which, typically, described the primitive poverty of the narrator's native glen/village/island in an incongruously rich style replete with formulaic phrases and reverence for all things past. *An béal bocht* is the traditional term for the mean and whingeing discourse of those who work the land.

O'Nolan was particularly well qualified to write such a book. He had been brought up bi-lingually: Irish was the first language of the family but they also spoke English to relations and neighbours. Educated in Dublin, the centre of Anglicised Ireland, O'Nolan visited the *Gaeltacht* or Irish-speaking area of Donegal in order to improve his knowledge of Irish language and culture. He studied Irish in the Germanically philological atmosphere of University College Dublin, won a scholarship to Germany and returned to write an MA thesis on Irish poetry. He seems to have spent at least as much of his student days writing — in Irish and in English — comic material with a strong element of parodic satire for various college magazines. If he was as well able as anybody to appreciate such minor classics as *An tOileánach*, *Peig* and the best of Séamus Ó Grianna, he was unlikely to be overawed by them.

When O'Nolan decided to be a novelist he chose to write in English, presumably because it offered him direct contact with the wide world which had been conquered by Yeats and Joyce and others. It was only, again one is presuming, when rejected by the English-reading public that he thought in terms of a novel in Irish. But he was not the only one to do so around 1940.

In future when people try to establish when the development of modern Irish poetry began, they will probably settle for 1939. In that year, Conradh na Gaeilge [The Gaelic League] revived the Oireachtas competitions in Dublin; at the same time the Second World War began. It would be difficult to decide if those events had a greater influence than the founding of the universities' magazine, *Comhar*, three years later. . .[2]

It was not a simple coincidence that a burgeoning of writing in Irish and of a system of patronage and publication happened as World War II began. There was a strong possibility that Ireland, an island of some strategic value, would be invaded by either the Allies or the Axis. Against the threat of take-over the infant state asserted and prepared to defend its independence; the sudden flourish of writing in the *national* language was probably a form of psychic defence against a threatened loss of national identity.

Given the success of *An Béal Bocht* and of the Irish element in his *Irish Times* column, given the sense of energetic commitment that characterised Irish writing in the early '40s, given the family and his own cultivation of Irish literature, is it not a little remarkable that O'Nolan abandoned his career as a writer of fiction in

Irish? And yet, of course, just as he chose to write in English, so too would almost all the Irish writers who were faced with the same dilemma in the years that followed. Why?

Perhaps something may be gleaned from *An Béal Bocht*.

The very title is fascinating in this context. The phrase normally connotes the whine of the suspicious peasant; but in Irish, where the word *béal* can mean 'speech' or 'language', the phrase could also suggest an impoverished or inadequate language. It is interesting to note the references to the Irish language within the novel. It is the vernacular of those benighted primitives who dwell in the rainsoaked squalor of Corca Dorcha and the cultivated 'native' language of those English-speakers who come from the cities on cultural pilgrimages but it is absolutely useless, a positive disadvantage, outside Corca Dorcha. The fact that the language has survived in Corca Dorcha is no coincidence because 'It was always said that people achieve mastery of Irish (just like sanctity of soul) in inverse proportion to their material wealth'.[3] Education is through the medium of English, a language which the natives do not understand, and consists of being beaten for speaking Irish and of being told that, irrespective of one's Irish name, 'Yer nam is Jams O'Donnell'.

The ingenuously idiotic narrator, Bónapárt Ó Cúnasa, meets his fate because of his linguistic limitations. From his grandfather he learns the Irish version of the Flood. Only one man survived and did so in a manner reminiscent of Noah: Maoldún Ó Pónasa — named after the famous Irish navigator — anticipated the great flood and not only did he make the first boat in Corca Dorcha, he also 'saved' all the wealth of the community.

He slipped safely away on the high tide, bringing with him all the things which had been left behind them by those people who had bidden farewell to this life — the best of potatoes freshly pulled from the soil by the torrent, little domestic articles, small quantities of spirits and valuable gold coins which had lain hidden for ages. I can promise you that when he escaped from Corca Dorcha he was rich and well satisfied and no doubt about it.[4]

Bónapárt, with uncharacteristic energy, recovers this treasure from where Maoldún came to rest, on the top of Hungry Hill, but the treasure is no use to him: his imprisonment within the Irish confines of Corca Dorcha means that he cannot use the wealth to buy anything more beautiful, more luxurious, more life-enhancing than boots. And these boots are his downfall. He pays for them with one of his gold coins and this brings him to the attention of the police who are investigating a recent case in which a Galway man was murdered for his gold. Unable to defend himself in court because he doesn't understand a word of what is happening — in fact he doesn't know what a court of law is — he is sentenced to twenty-nine years in gaol.[5]

The sudden darkening of tone from the gregariousness of clever parody to the discomfort of bleak farce leads one to wonder what lay behind such a savage backlash. Could it be that O'Nolan realised that, like his idiot hero, he had recovered the Irish language and literature — the lost treasure of the community — but that, far from enhancing his own world, it made him even more of a prisoner in the wide world of English? Could it be that O'Nolan, who had tried to address the world with two novels in English, resented the constrictions of Irish? He had not continued to write in Irish the kind of work he had written in English and this suggests that he felt the Irish language to be in some way incapable of absorbing the likes of *At Swim-Two-Birds* and *The Third Policeman*. In that case, the national tongue was for him an inadequate language, a *béal bocht*, and the world of Corca Dorcha an image of a cultural nightmare.

It was commonly believed that the remnants of a Gaelic civilisation — the treasure of Hungry Hill — had been of enormous value to those Irish writers who had flourished in the early decades of the century — to Yeats and Lady Gregory who had studied Hiberno-English dialect, to Synge who had steeped himself in Irish, to Joyce who had described himself on the 1901 census as acquainted with Irish, to O'Casey who was a fluent Irish speaker, to O'Faolain and O'Connor who had studied and published in Irish, and to many others. O'Nolan, who for complex reasons seldom had a good word to say for any Irish writer, wrote to O'Casey who had praised *An Béal Bocht*:

I cannot see any real prospect of reviving Irish at the present rate of going and way of working. I agree absolutely with you when you say it is essential, particularly for any sort of a literary worker. It supplies that unknown quantity in us that enables us to transform the English language and this seems to hold of people who know little or no Irish, like Joyce. It seems to be an inbred thing.[6]

That was in April 1942, at a time when Brendan Behan, a young Dubliner who was also embroiled in the Irish tradition, was too busy for letter-writing.

On April 5th Brendan Behan fired several shots at the forces of Irish law and order and was sentenced to fourteen years.[7] He used his years in prison to study Irish literature and to write in Irish. He was encouraged by some of his fellow-prisoners, several of whom were native speakers of Irish, who saw the creation of a national literature as part of the objective of the IRA. One of his fellow-prisoners was Máirtín Ó Cadhain who was developing his own kind of modern Irish short story dealing with the characters and character of his native Connemara.

The people he presents are survivors, remnants of a Celtic civilisation that had been pushed ever farther towards the western seabord by succeeding waves of English-speaking peoples. They have lost everything, forgotten by history, and still sunk in a serf-like medieval economy, they are barely clinging to life on bog, stony garth, mountain pasture and shore. But they have preserved almost intact the riches of an ancient language which had been subject to centuries of literary development in fiction, poetry, satire, social and metaphysical thinking.[8]

Here is another perception of the Treasure of Hungry Hill but Behan, an expert on imprisonment, saw writing in Irish as an escape from his own confusions. Behan translated one of his own early dramatic efforts, *The Landlady,* a play set in English-speaking Dublin, into Irish, wrote a new prison play called *Casadh Súgáin Eile* which would eventually become *The Quare Fellow,* and began a short but successful career as a poet in Irish. How strongly Behan was drawn to the idea of himself as a writer in Irish may be gauged from his willingness in March 1957 to write a play in Irish for Gael-Linn, an organisation which had published his Irish poetry and prose and which ran a tiny theatre in Dublin, the Damer Hall. By 1957 Behan was an international celebrity, famous as the author of *The Quare Fellow* and *Borstal Boy* and notorious as the ultimate Broth-of-an-Oirish-Bhoyo — the *huer* with the heart of gold. Some very powerful force pulled him away from the cameras and towards the Damer Hall.

I have argued elsewhere that it is useful to distinguish between the influence which the Irish literary tradition had on Behan's career as a writer and the influence it had on his individual writings.[9] The first should not be underestimated: for Behan, and especially during the productive part of his life, the act of writing was political. He began to write for radical periodicals, his main theme was the tragedy of political conflict, and his final effort in life was to repudiate his surrender to the amorality of the publicity machines and to return to the people and places he associated with his earlier, purely political allegiances. Among fellow-republicans in prison he would have felt that writing in Irish enabled him to avoid the complex question of identity and voice which haunts the Irish person who writes in the shadow of a domineering culture — then English, later on American. Behan sought to become a writer in Irish — and had some success — but though he was willing to risk his life for a free and Gaelic Ireland and though he never lost an opportunity to communicate in Irish, he did not persevere as a writer in Irish. In a 1948 poem on the desertion of the Irish-speaking Blasket Island, *Jackeen ag Caoineadh na mBlascaod*, he had glimpsed not only the ruin of the Irish-speaking community but also the cold isolation in which he would write in Irish. Two years later in *Guí an Rannaire* he lambasted the unworthies who were using the cause of the Irish language to settle themselves in steady jobs but, in the final couplet, he implies that he is not the great poet who will restore the fortunes of the Irish language. Shortly afterwards he abandoned poetry in Irish and concentrated on *Borstal Boy*. There was always the chance that the success of *An Giall* would tempt him to continue in Irish and it did — but too late and in a questionable manner. *The Hostage* — that prelude to the Sixties — was, literally, an overwhelming hit and Behan, sick and confused, was terrified by the fear that he would never be able to repeat such a success. Perhaps his last desperate effort was to draft *Lá Breá san Roilg* with the hope of repeating the *An Giall/The Hostage* formula: opening in Irish in the Damer, translating to London and from there to New York and the world at large. Here again is the belief in the Treasure of Hungry Hill, the belief that the Irish writer had what O'Nolan called 'that unknown quantity that enables us to transform the English language'.

O'Nolan had gone on to suggest that this ability was not dependent on a knowledge of the Irish language but was inbred. The implication must be that it was transmitted through the medium of Hiberno-English and this seems likely. To say that Behan abandoned Irish for English is obviously inadequate. The language of *Borstal Boy* occupies a position on the linguistic scale between English and Irish: it is an extreme form of Hiberno-English, that dialect of English so coloured by the structure and style of Irish as to be in many ways closer to Máirtín Ó Cadhain than, say, to Evelyn Waugh. Behan — and he was not alone among Irish writers in this — grew up in a community where there was almost no Irish spoken and where the influence of such non-Irish institutions as the British Army and the music hall was strong but, as Behan must have noticed later on, this community was closer in spirit to a Gaeltacht community than it was to any

non-Irish community. For example, Behan's people were possessed
of a strong oral tradition not unlike that into which Máirtín
Ó Cadhain was born:

[They] had retained the habit of taking pleasure in language. Speech was
one of their pastimes. Many of them, men and women, were artists in
words, delighting in making fresh combinations and minting fresh
images from sea, sky, mountain, legend, and the details of craft and daily
work. They transcended the drudgery of daily life in song, verse, sharp
saying, and 'the wild oats of speech'.[10]

('Sea, sky and mountain' did not figure quite so prominently in
the worldview of Russell Street as they did on the coast of
Connemara where Máirtín Ó Cadhain grew up.) The superbly
modulated prose of *Borstal Boy* reflects such an oral tradition and
it is obvious that the narrative technique derives, at least partly,
from the art of the Irish *scéalaí* or storyteller, an art that has crossed
the barrier between Irish and Hiberno-English. The oral origins
of Behan's style are nowhere more patent than when it becomes
almost a string of formulae which, while making no literal or
rational sense, articulate perfectly the passions of young Brendan
in a way which would not have sounded out of place in the world
of the *Táin* or before the walls of Troy:

I was no ordinary country Paddy from the middle of the Bog of Allen to
be frightened to death by a lot of Liverpool seldom-fed bastards, nor was
I one of your wrap-the-green-flag-round-me junior Civil Servants that
came into the IRA from the Gaelic League, and well ready to die for their
country any day of the week, purity in their hearts, truth in their lips, for
the glory of God and the honour of Ireland. No, be Jesus, I was from
Russell Street, North Circular Road, Dublin, from the Northside, where,
be Jesus, the likes of Dale wouldn't make a dinner for them, where the
whole of this pack of Limeys would be scruff-hounds, would be et, bet
and threw up again — et without salt, I'll James you, you bastard.[11]

Translate that into the language of your choice!
   Synge was the first major talent to explore the nature of Irish
speech and he presides over a host of dramatists — such as
O'Casey, Behan and Hugh Leonard of Dublin, Fitzmaurice and
John B. Keane of Kerry, Brian Friel of Derry — who have learned
to build dialogue on the rich colour of Irish dialect. Soon a writer
like Behan will require explanatory notes — even in Dublin. As
the Irish language has waned under the imperialism of Anglo-
American — and especially since the arrival of television and the
growing urbanisation of Irish society — the English of Ireland

has tended to lose its Gaelic character and join the drift towards Standard Mid-Atlantic. Consequently it has become a less obvious feature of Irish writing, even in the drama.

In 1960 Eugene Watters (1919-1982) published his first book, *Murder in Three Moves*, a novel of detection set in the Connemara Gaeltacht and featuring an Anglo-Irish composer of problems.[12] It is a fascinating novel despite a rather unconvincing narrator — a minor BBC-type poet with a disproportionate talent for intuition — and some structural features which would strike the *afficionado* of detective fiction as somewhat stale. The really interesting character is Blake, the chess problemist who spent his childhood in a Big House in Connemara and learned the Irish language before being evacuated during the Black and Tan War. Towards the conclusion he comes to dominate the narrative. Chapter eighteen is his account of his key move — playing twentyfive through the medium of Irish, alcohol and the murk of a shebeen. The style features Blake's formal English, his flamboyant Irish (in translation) and, best of all, a blending of both which enables him to give this superb account of a *lash* at twentyfive:

It was my turn then, I flipped the cards out at conjuring speed, robbed the trump ace, took my dealing trick with a deuce, struck hard with the ace and collected half-a-dozen trumps on the round including a hesitant queen, struck with the knave and collected a chagrined ace of hearts from the hesitant man, and won the last two tricks with the king and the ten of clubs. The whole thing took less than ten seconds and I was a game up.[13]

And of course he also discovers the key to the mystery — that the English painter murdered in Connemara was the same man who, all those years ago, had commanded the Black and Tans in Galway and Mayo and raped the local girl to whom the young Blake had once addressed a poem in Irish.

Lurking behind the Holmes/Watson *genre* is a version of the Anglo-Irish complex, the dilemma of the modern Irish writer pulled between two languages, a dilemma which Watters often referred to as a form of split personality and which he himself epitomised. To some he was Eugene Watters, novelist and poet in English, while to others he was Eoghan Ó Tuairisc, novelist, poet, dramatist, editor and critic. He was prolific in both languages and his large output has yet to be properly evaluated. It could be argued — and not unreasonably — that in the context of Ireland in the twentieth century, he has written the finest long poem in English, *The Week-End of Dermot and Grace* (1964), and the finest long poem in Irish, *Aifreann na Marbh* (1964). Such a claim is only possible because of the critical neglect of Watters, a neglect which may be due to his position in the cleft stick of Irish writing. However, there are some signs that he will receive after his death the attention he could well have done with during his career.[14] He also wrote two fine historical novels in Irish, *L'Attaque* (1962) and *Dé Luain* (1966), which one hopes will soon be translated competently into English. It would take at least a thesis to consider the cross-fertilisation between his two languages and even then it would become immediately obvious that Watters writes both Irish and English as a European, deeply indebted to the classics of Greek, Latin and English. Something of his range of orchestration may be glimpsed in the opening lines of the *Week-End*:

> Amiens Street. I tipped the porter a shilling
> And walked the length of the platform twinned
> In the reflective windows of the carriages,
> The I and the I shall be.
> I was the sunrise and its shadow the evening,
> I was the spring field and the stooked corn,
> The alphabet and the Iliad,
> First kiss on a bench at startime,
> The last gag when candles are lit to sweeten the air.
> The engine wagged its grey beard and said,
> Vah! Himself he cannot save.[15]

A variety of circumstantial pressures led to Watters deciding to settle for being Ó Tuairisc and concentrating on Irish. (His 1981 volume, *Sidelines*, a collection of poems in English most of which were written in the '50s and '60s, was published over the Irish form of his name.) His life had been fractured in 1965 when his first wife died and he felt increasingly alienated from the person he had been till then; in 1972 he married again and sought a *vita nuova*, a new place, a new language. In the preface to *Dialann sa Diseart* [Desert Diary] (1981), a collection of short poems which he and his second wife, Rita Kelly, wrote in the new place, he explained:

We need a new language. That is the major advantage of Irish: an ancient language that comes to us as a new language. For us it is something of an alien language; excellent, because we are dealing today with an alien planet.[16]

It was an extreme strategy but not unique. In 1975 Michael Hartnett, a young poet of some reputation, had turned his back on the

English-speaking town and sought contact with his own past
and people by writing in Irish.

The economic and social boom of the '60s was welcome in Ireland
after the drab '50s. John Kennedy was living proof of what Irish
people could achieve. The republic took its place among the
United Nations, sending soldiers to die in Africa and telling
the Soviet Premier to shut up. At home there was the arrival of
television, economic expansion and efforts at political dialogue
between North and South. Cultural inferiority was felt to be a
thing of the past: Anglo-Irish literature was being studied all
over the world, everybody else made a fuss about Irish writers
and so why not the Irish? A new generation of writers promised
not to lower the traditional standard — the intensely modernist
Kinsella (*Another September*, 1958), the refreshingly feminine Edna
O'Brien (*The Country Girls*, 1960), the deliciously direct Seamus
Heaney (*Death of a Naturalist*, 1966). The production of books in
Irish increased, thanks largely to state sponsorship and the
energy of *An Club Leabhar* (The Book Club). There was even the
whiff of the idea that, with modern techniques and growing
national pride, the Irish language could be revived in some vague
way without, of course, displacing English. One man epitomised
all that national resurgence more than any politician or writer,
Seán Ó Riada. Even today, when so much that emerged in the '60s
seems to have been dissipated by the cold winds of recession, the
influence of Ó Riada is still pervasive.

Ó Riada had impressed people as a potential composer even
while still a student at University College Cork. He became
something of a household name as the composer of the music for
two films, *Mise Éire* (I am Ireland) (1959) and *Saoirse?* (Freedom?)
(1961), music which consisted of modern orchestration of traditional Irish tunes in the manner of, say, Kodaly. The *Róisín Dubh*
crescendo of *Mise Éire* captured the national aspiration that the
old style, the *sean-nós*, should be the leaven of a modern Irish
culture. Ó Riada was to go much further when producing the
music for a film of *The Playboy of the Western World*.

The high individualism of the Irish musical tradition is preserved in
performance: there are no written parts, each player making his personal
contribution to the texture of the music according to a design pre-
arranged in discussion with the director: an *impromptu à loisir*, in fact!
The instruments used are flute, uillean pipes, and tin whistle; two double-
row button accordions; two fiddles; bone-castanets and *bodhran* or
goatskin drum. These instruments are used for playing this kind of

music in different parts of the country: the music itself is of course to be heard in every corner of Ireland.[17]

Ó Riada caught a wave which was about to sweep the western world — the folk boom, every man his own guitarist, the dominance of the singer-songwriter in popular music — and by the time of his death he had inspired a huge resurgence of traditional music in Ireland and a general acceptance of the kind of ensemble he had brought together for the *Playboy* music; even today, although his creative drive is palpably missing, the impetus of his efforts has carried Irish traditional music around the world from Cúil Aodha to China by way of Carnegie Hall.

Ó Riada's achievement was an example of what writers — and especially, perhaps, Irish writers — often dream about: a new integration of ancient and modern, of national and international, of 'high' and popular culture. The Irish musician has distinct advantages over the writer: traditional music survived where the traditional language died and music is not limited by national or linguistic considerations. Most Irish writers wished to emulate Ó Riada but were unwilling — the few who would have been able — to live in the Gaeltacht and adopt the Irish language. Thomas Kinsella, to take an interesting example, longed to make contact with the ancient Irish poets but would not commit himself to Irish because

that would mean loss of contact with my own present — abandonment of the language I was bred in for one which I believe to be dying. It would also mean forfeiting a certain possible scope of language: English has a greater scope, if I can make use of it, than an Irish which is not able to handle all the affairs of my life.[18]

Kinsella was one of many poets who were drawn to Ó Riada and who lamented his early death. Though he does not write in Irish he writes out of a deep study of and affection for the language and literature, as is reflected in his work as a translator of *The Táin* (1969) and of *An Duanaire: Poems of the Dispossessed* (1981) which he produced in collaboration with Seán Ó Tuama.

Since 1968 most Ulster writers have been forced to consider the Irish language as part of their confused inheritance. In his *Faber Book of Irish Verse* John Montague offered 'versions' of early Irish poetry while *The Rough Field* considered the grafting of tongues in the history of Ulster; he continues to find energy in his study of the Irish past, in his bardic stance and, for example, his pointed inclusion of the *dinnsheanchas* or place-lore element in his 1984 volume on the death of his mother, *The Dead Kingdom*. The best known play of Ulster's best known playwright is an explicit exploration of what happens when one language invades another. Underpinning much of Brian Friel's work is the sort of traditional/pastoral *v* modern/urban polarity which has long been a feature of Irish writing and whether it be Ballybeg *v* Philadelphia or Derry demonstrators *v* British troops the linguistic encounter is always prominent: it becomes the informing metaphor of *Translations* (first produced in 1981), a study of the Anglo-Irish complex. The play imagines what happened when British Army Engineers, making an anglicised map of Ireland, come to translate An Baile Beag to Ballybeg in 1833. Hearts are broken and blood is shed just as in 1983 and, it is implied, for the same basic reasons: the Irish and the English cannot or will not understand each other. The Irish peasants are obsessed with Greek and Latin, pathetically apt for those whose language will soon be similarly 'dead'; the English engineers, on the other hand, are so barbarian as to be unable to distinguish between Irish and the classic tongues. The Irish language is seen — rather romantically — in the circumstances — as the language which can cure the speechless Sarah and unite the local girl Maire with Lieutenant Yolland; militant English undoes both miracles. Of course the audience following this English-language play knows what happened before it happens. The elderly scholar rambles on about exogamy with Pallas Athene while the schoolmaster begins to forget his Virgil. The particular passage is the celebrated *Urbs antiqua fuit* which contains an analogy with the old Irish polity and the new English imperialism which would be its downfall. The new language will rule all — apart from the odd western island and peninsula whither the young retreat.

Languages seldom sink without trace: even Greek and Latin were integrated by happy conjugation into acquiescent English as this drama constantly demonstrates while Irish remains rooted in most Irish placenames and, as we have seen, in the Irish dialects of English. Placenames are part of the lore of the traditional Irish poet — and of other poets as well, of course. Another Ulster writer remembered growing up in County Derry in the '40s:

In the names of its fields and townlands, in their mixture of Scots and Irish and English etymologies, this side of the country was redolent of the histories of its owners. Broagh, The Long Rigs, Bell's Hill; Brian's Field, the Round Meadow, the Demesne; each name was a kind of love made to each acre. And saying the names like this distances the places, turns them into what Wordsworth once called a prospect of the mind. They lie deep, like some script indelibly written into the nervous system.[19]

Seamus Heaney goes on to remember his lifelong love of digging down into the earth, an old family trait and one which he continues in his verse — exploring the nature of places as revealed by the layers of sectioned bog and local lore. His sense of locality has widened as he has grown and travelled and learned and yet two recent works show that the cord which linked him (even before his birth) to his Derry omphalos has been stretched but not cut.[20] *Station Island* summons him back to the ancient shrine of his Ulster Catholic people — a hard station for a sensuous and gregarious cosmopolitan. Unable to destroy the old icons, he finds relief in an antic disposition and assumes the figure of another Ulster poet perplexed by the traditional mixture of religion and violence: in 1983 he published *Sweeney Astray,* a version of the Irish medieval *Buile Shuibhne.* In his introduction he considers the various attractions the figure had for him and concludes:

I was in a country of woods and hills and remembered that the green spirit of the hedges embodied in Sweeney had first been embodied for me in the persons of a family of tinkers, also called Sweeney, who used to camp in the ditchbacks along the road to the first school I attended. One way or another, he seemed to have been with me from the start.[21]

It is likely that he made his first acquaintance with the literary figure of Sweeney in Brian O'Nolan's *At Swim-Two-Birds,* named from one of the Sweeney lyrics which were translated so expertly in the book which seemed to sink without trace when it was first published in 1939 but which survived to become one of the classics of modern Irish writing.

                              *   *   *   *   *

Neil Jordan's novel, *The Past* (1980), is an imaginative analysis of the narrator's inheritance which is more or less that of Ireland in this century. His grandparents included two figures who vaguely resemble Maud Gonne and Kevin O'Higgins. She, Una, was a flamboyantly bad actress, well suited to playing Kathleen in the approved manner of the day; typically, she only half-knew Irish but pronounced it with a winning *blas.* She is in many ways a ridiculous character but she has an enormously vital energy: it is she who turned her husband, a Redmondite who almost joined the Irish Guards to fight in the Great War, into an Irish-speaking guerilla hero and founder of the new state. Their daughter, the narrator's mother, is very much her mother's child — magnetic, histrionic, touring with a travelling company (echoes of Anew MacMaster) and acting while heavily pregnant. She too has inherited her mother's gift of Irish — even less knowledge but the same wonderful *blas* — and she teaches Irish by going through the list of words in a dictionary. Again there is something incongruous, something ridiculous about it but at the same time there is a strong implication that what formed this state and this creative family is strangely connected with the language which they prize so highly and use so badly.

LANGUAGE AND AFFECTIVE COMMUNICATION IN SOME CONTEMPORARY IRISH WRITERS

MICHAEL TOOLAN

In rehearsing the standard 'problems' felt to be attendant on the development of English in Ireland, the displacement of Gaelic, and the growth of dialect in pronunciation, vocabulary, and syntax, an over-quoted passage is that expressing Stephen's thoughts, in *A Portrait of the Artist as a Young Man*, in the wake of a humiliating exchange with the dean of studies over the word *tundish*. The dean's manner is taken to imply that *tundish* is a quaint, inferior, alien substitute for the 'truly English' word *funnel*. Stephen reflects:

How different are the words *home, Christ, ale, master,* on his lips and on mine! I cannot speak or write these words without unrest of spirit. His language, so familiar and so foreign, will always be for me an acquired speech. I have not made or accepted its words. My voice holds them at bay. My soul frets in the shadow of his language.[1]

There are so many ways of reflecting on this passage and its context that it seems unsatisfactory merely to extract from it the summarised judgement, as Edward Said has recently done, that

Joyce's work is a recapitulation of those political and racial separations, exclusions, prohibitions instituted ethnocentrically by the ascendant European culture throughout the nineteenth century.[2]

To begin with, the reflection is Stephen's, not Joyce's, and it is quite distorting to elide that author/character distance. If we are talking of Joyce, then his heterogeneity of styles, languages and cultural sources not only uncovers but is a *defiance* of nineteenth century ethnocentric exclusivity: he is the paradigm case of the modernist European writer, many-tongued, many-placed. If we are talking of Stephen, then the passage seems striking primarily for the numerous ways in which it misleads or distorts, and as the pessimist talk of an individual temporarily hesitant, perturbed and demoralised. Stephen is a gifted phrase-maker, and here all builds towards the fin-de-siècle lamentation: 'My soul frets in the shadow of his language.' At one level we know that Stephen, opting for exile and cunning, will not fret in the shadow of any individual much longer; while it is the inescapable condition of the writer to fret in the shadow of *some* language. But we should not ignore the way that the sheer fluency and memorability of this passage gives the lie to its own complaint, of the irrevocable alienability of its language.

In fact Stephen's quarrel here is not with the dean, or with English: it is with language itself, and the unavoidable sense of loss, inadequacy, alienation, that Derrida has argued is entailed in all entering into words. As the declaration 'My voice holds them [these words] at bay' makes clear, the dilemma of the language-user must be dissolved not by *rejection* of language (how can voice remain voice, if it uses no words?), but by struggling with it and re-making it. In what follows, I hope to apply this broad principle to that working-with-Irish-English which is a major rhetorical feature and theoretical concern of Brian Friel, Seamus Heaney, and others.

In relation to that topic, one or two further observations on the *Portrait* passage may be in order. In general, the passage is characterised by the controversial nature of its claims, axiomatic in ways that almost invite distrust of the axioms themselves. The very first concession, that the dean is proprietor of the English Language, that it is more legitimately his than it is Stephen's, who is some kind of latecomer, speaks to a naive myth of origins, of a purer and more authentic version of the language, to which the dean has natural access. The second sentence justly recognises the differences, not merely of pronunciation presumably but of value too, of various words as used by the dean and Stephen. But the wider implications, of multiple differences in a multitude of respects, are not faced.

Stephen's lament that the dean's language 'will always be for me an acquired speech' might prompt the rejoinder that *all* speech is, to a large degree, acquired — for the dean as much as for Stephen. Using a language entails submitting to contracts about words, the major terms of which cannot all simultaneously be re-drafted. If the dean's language is foreign to Stephen, which language is 'native'? Certainly not Gaelic, to which he seems to have had little exposure. Underlying the reflections in this passage is a native/foreign dichotomy (relatable to Said's opposition of metropolitan colonialist centre to oriental and barbarian colonised periphery). But as Stephen is intermittently aware, that dichotomy is easily inverted — in some ways, for example, it is the dean who is the outlandish foreigner, 'a humble follower in the wake of clamorous conversions, a poor Englishman in Ireland' (p. 188). What needs to be recognised is the basic inappropriateness of any such simple dichotomy in this setting. My rejection of this distorting and reductive dichotomy parallels rejections of related ones by recent critics.[3]

There is some evidence of a probing of the native/alien dichotomy, as related to English, in John Montague's *The Rough Field*. This work explores a mental space as much as the topography of Garvaghey/*garbh achaidh*, so as to see more completely 'the unhappiness of its historical destiny'.[4] Versions of such a procedure are a persistent argument of many modern Irish writers. Their conviction is that they do not write out of a merely conventional sense of place, but rather that place itself generates sense, that native places and associations are a shared or shareable economy of symbols, a sub-language for self-identification and expression. In Heaney's words, sense of place in its richest manifestation involves 'an equable marriage between the geographical country and the country of the mind'.[5]

Of *course* there is the temptation to dwell on 'the unhappiness of historical destiny', to damn the dean of studies, as Stephen does (p. 251), whether he came to Ireland 'to teach us his own language or to learn it from us'. Of *course* one might succumb to the consuming self-hatred that Yeats admitted sometimes experiencing.[6] But Joyce definitively established a different reaction: 'a willingness to accept the realities of a gapped culture, a broken tradition and the irreparableness of the loss of the old Gaelic identity.' In Thomas Kinsella's estimate Joyce is 'the first major Irish voice to speak for Irish reality since the death of the Irish language';[7] he might also be called the first (earliest and best) writer of *Irish* literature in English.

Friel, Montague and Heaney are well aware of what is lost — but not psychotically so. There is persistent reference to versions of disappearance, disinheritance, dispossession, abandonment, and severance, in their work. But their involvement is creative and therapeutic, for they are properly aware that *all* modern writers inherit, in Kinsella's phrase, 'a gapped discontinuous, polyglot tradition'.[8]

John Montague surveys 'the shards of a lost tradition' in *The*

Rough Field. Section IV, 2, titled 'A Lost Tradition' in his more recent *Selected Poems*, is at once intensely evocative and poignant:

> The whole landscape a manuscript
> We had lost the skill to read,
> A part of our past disinherited;
> But fumbled, like a blind man,
> Along the fingertips of instinct.[9]

Such is the sense of poise and control here that there is space, in its seven stanzas, to incorporate disparate references to the retreat from Ulster, to the Golden Stone, and to Carleton, as well as to relate a mournful childhood incident where Montague's 'school Irish' is prized like a holy relic by the last Gaelic speaker in the parish. But the shards are more physical yet:

> No rock or ruin, dun or dolmen
> But showed memory defying cruelty
> Through an image-encrusted name.

Perhaps this poem of Montague's — and these lines in particular — most clearly reveals his influences on and inspiration to Seamus Heaney. The work of both writers is itself a re-registration within the culture and community of that which has been shattered or neglected.

In 'A Grafted Tongue', from *The Rough Field*, Montague reflects on the particular anguish from the suppression of Gaelic, the imposition of English: 'In shame / the altered syllables / of your own name; / . . . To grow / a second tongue, as / harsh a humiliation / as twice to be born.'[10] Yet resisting the complacency of a self-pitying circling of that tragic historical period, Montague moves on to more recent times, the distinctive indigenising of English in Ireland ('Yet even English in these airts / Took a lawless turn'[11]), where even the supplanting English place names take on a nativist colouring and evocative power. Adapting Stephen's terms, the alien language was thus re-made and (provisionally) accepted.

A less admirable re-making of an alien language occupies several scenes in Brian Friel's *Translations*: the systematic Anglicisation of Irish place-names that was undertaken in the early nineteenth century. That Anglicisation was sometimes a genuine translation, an attempt at rendering the sense of the original into English; more often however there was simply an adjustment of the Gaelic name, to a form that was at least penetrable, if not quite domestic, to the English eye and ear. Such an enterprise is part of the wholesale refashioning of a colony as an inferior copy of the 'mother country'. Officers of the British ordnance survey, encamped in Donegal, are engaged in drawing a new map of the country, and in 'standardising' the barbarous place-names, so that both the places and the naming of them will be more 'manageable'.

Friel's play is resonant with a sense of socio-historical translation, of a context of other events that will visit profound changes on this community. Thus a National school with a standard, English-medium curriculum and the alleged aim — as one proponent tactlessly put it — of making its student 'a happy English child', is being established locally. It is the time of Daniel O'Connell, pragmatist advocate of English and populist champion of Catholic emancipation. And there are allusions to the sweet smell of the potato blight, a reminder of the community's present vulnerability, its future grief.

But even all this might seem rather thin material for a whole play, if Friel did not identify translation activities within the rendered community, at a variety of levels. The play is set in a hedge-school, where, in the same classroom, a brilliant self-taught classicist sits reciting his Homer in Greek and then rendering it in his native tongue, while a young woman with an acute speech defect struggles to put into words the simplest act of self-identification: 'My name is Sarah'. The schoolmaster, Hugh, has hopes of being translated from his hedge-school to the new National school. His son, Manus, acts as scribe for illiterate villagers, translating their speech into letters to relatives abroad. For a long time the mapmakers mis-hear the name of their own local assistant, the schoolmaster's other son, Owen, and persist in addressing him as Roland.

But the central translation involves the British officer named Yolland, who falls in love with Manus's intended, Maire. The first encounter between Yolland and Maire is chiefly ludicrous: with Owen as go-between or translator, they respond to each other's native-tongue declarations of incomprehension with further cries of 'What? What?', 'Sorry? Sorry?' and so on. Act 2, scene 2, however, presents the dramatically compelling spectacle of the couple, alone, addressing each other in their different languages (rendered in English), and confirming their mutual comprehension with a kiss. This is not quite communication without language, for their words here have clearly played a part; it may be more like an extreme case of what in fact occurs in most everyday interaction, where final and unresolvable uncertainty about others' meanings does not prevent us understanding one another.

Grounding all this, although Friel makes no mention of it in his stage directions, is the fact that the speech of this Gaelic-speaking community is rendered in English throughout — the most basic translation-work of all. The play is rendered in Irish English and British English (as appropriate), but verisimilitude requires us to 'understand' that Irish English as now representing Gaelic (e.g., whcn Manus talks to Maire), now representing English itself (when Hugh and Owen talk to Yolland). While clearly a necessary *modus operandi* given Friel's chosen audience, this seems also a welcomed contrivance. There is no evidence to suggest Friel would disown or regret the comedy that arises, even at the expense of characters: when, for example, the audience observes Maire and Yolland protesting their incomprehension of each others' speech even as they express themselves in perfectly comprehensible English. There is an edge to this contrived comic absurdity, which indicates Friel's preparedness to satirise the whole over-ventilated business of proclaiming profound and impassable barriers between languages and cultures. (Friel touches base, both here and in his splendid ridicule of various cherished language totems in *The Communication Cord*,[12] with the *saeva indignatio* tradition that has come down to him from Swift and Brian O'Nolan.)

Yolland is the ingenuous son of a model colonial administrator who (in his own words) lacks his father's energy, coherence, and *belief* in the colonial enterprise. In his interaction with the villagers is a nice reversal of the typical Irish-English relation, where the Irish outsider struggles to 'pass' within the English culture and language. It is Yolland who makes some efforts to learn Irish, who regrets 'I may learn the password but the language of the tribe will always elude me'.[13] Though Owen assures him 'You can learn to decode us', Owen himself is a man who has opted for self-serving accommodation to the dominant colonial administration (like Stephen's forebears?), and who as yet avoids confronting the covert violation of the community that such an administration entails.

If there is a weakness in this play of ideas, it is perhaps in the characterisation of Yolland, the innocent coloniser who becomes an equally innocent victim. Friel's apparent ambivalence towards him is understandable, but awkward edges remain. Yolland declares, on his arrival in Baile Beag, that he felt he had entered a new environment: 'I had moved into a consciousness that wasn't striving nor agitated, but at its ease and with its own conviction and assurance' (p. 40). This, I'm afraid, sounds a dead note to me, especially since the Irish English *nor* (where standard British English would have been *or*) does not help. No doubt it is partly intended to: Yolland is the retiring, naive Englishman who easily becomes confessional with those he trusts. But it is not, I think, chiefly intended as parody. Yolland is to be one of those who arrive at an enlarged awareness: of the possibility of communion without unification, of the pleasure in seeing and respecting differences, and of the way that translation itself is a double-edged sword. The attempt at sincere disclosure of genuine change simply doesn't ring true as rendered here — too rapidly arrived at, too blandly delivered in clichés. It is because earlier scenes in the hedge-school *have* suggested that here is a community 'with its own conviction and assurance' that we feel awkward at hearing this from the naive, vulnerable Yolland.

Among the positions taken up in the play, that of Hugh is particularly suggestive. The hedge-school master appears not to be instinctively ill-disposed towards English (as his son Manus perhaps is). With a nod to the forces of history, he reminds that words are 'not immortal', and that 'it can happen that a civilization can be imprisoned in a linguistic contour which no longer matches the landscape of . . . fact' (p. 43). As Yolland observes, Hugh 'knows what's happening', and is quite misunderstood by Owen, who judges him 'not to be able to adjust for survival'. Owen mocks Hugh's inflated declaration, that the villagers endure 'around truths immemorially posited' — but what Hugh has actually said is much more doubled-edged, and aware:

We like to think we endure around truths immemorially posited.
(my emphasis, p. 42)

Early in Act Two, Owen tries to show Yolland how defective the old names really are:

We call that crossroads Tobair Vree . . . Tobair means a well. But what does Vree mean? It's a corruption of Brian — (*Gaelic pronunciation.*) Brian — an erosion of Tobair Bhriain. Because a hundred-and-fifty years ago there used to be a well there, not at the crossroads, mind you — that would be too simple — but in a field close to the crossroads. And an old man called Brian, whose face was disfigured by an enormous growth, got it into his head that the water in that well was blessed; and every day for seven months he went there and bathed his face in it. But the growth didn't go away; and one morning Brian was found drowned in that well. And ever since that crossroads is known as Tobair Vree — even though that well has long since dried up. I know the story because my grandfather told it to me. But ask Doalty — or Maire — or Bridget — even my father — even Manus — why it's called Tobair Vree; and do you think they'll know? I know they don't know. So the question I put to you, Lieutenant, is this: What do we do with a name like that?   (pp. 43-44)

What Owen presents, in his story of the source and development of the name Tobair Vree, is an informal lexicological account of the word's value — to him — as a sign. The account shows how misleading it is to assume a surrogationalist 'fit' of words to things. The example also demonstrates both the unpredictable workings of reference, and how language meaning is not uniform through a speech community: only for Owen does this placename have quite this rich and wayward signification. The question then becomes: how much should what Tobair Vree means to Owen count for? Typically, language-users do not need to inspect their own prescriptive practices so openly, but in this given context — of an Adam-like supplying of names — the question cannot be evaded or consigned to the care of (supposedly) supra-human socio-historical forces. In the given situation, what Owen thinks of Tobair Vree as an appropriate name and description is of crucial importance. As Yolland points out, even though no one else remembers the story behind the name, *Owen* does, and a supplanting of that name becomes an erosion or, more truly, an excision, of the stuff of cultural memory.[14] It is also a repression, one that in its elaboration can engender psychosis. Seamus Heaney's work shows an intense awareness of this, along with the recognition that language is community memory, that a heal-ing wholeness can come from Freudian/Foucaldian 'archaeological' work on buried words and meanings.

The major point is, I believe, that there is no easy resolution to the dilemma posed whenever the prescriptiveness of our judgements about language is inspected. (Owen in fact ducks the dilemma by acceding to the choice of name of the Hibernophile outsider, Yolland — but the dilemma remains.) Typically we can proceed without troubling ourselves with such matters, but translators, lexicographers, place-namers, language planners, and literary artists must tackle these issues head-on. There is inevitably a taking of sides, an advocacy or assertion of certain uses, spellings, senses, rather than others. And it is that taking of sides which exposes the limits to the arbitrariness of signs, so widely assumed since Saussure. To all but Owen (though, after

Owen's discourse, perhaps Yolland should be included here too), Tobair Vree will remain arbitrary, even absurd, and certainly without 'natural fit', as the name for the crossroads. But for Owen, the name, though still not natural, is no longer merely arbitrary and conventional, but a motivated evocation of a piece of community history, a stone — however eroded — in the cairn of cultural memory.

As in Joyce and Heaney, so in *Translations* and *The Communication Cord*, the opposition of native and foreign is constructively collapsed. Thus one scene has Maire doing a little mapping of Yolland's native region in Norfolk. She rehearses the Anglo-Saxon names — Winfarthing, Barton Bendish, Saxingham Nethergate, and so on — and concludes (as Yolland has of Gaelic names):

Strange sounds, aren't they? But nice sounds; like Jimmy Jack reciting his Homer.   (p. 60)

And it is such ethnic openness or tolerance which dismantles the native/foreign opposition. For the opposition rests on the prejudice that the native is good and authentic, the foreign is inferior, unattractive, to be shunned or reformed. To affirm that the foreign is also pleasing, that though strange is it also beautiful, is to work free of the straitjacket of a categorical hostility and distrust. Again, a parallel in Heaney's recent work is clear: as Christopher Ricks and Blake Morrison have noted, *Field Work* is a renewal of trust — not least a reaffirmed trust in Heaney's own voice which, for good or ill, is 'A voice caught back off slug-horn and slow chanter / That might continue, hold, dispel, appease . . . .'[15]

But the forced entrance of colonial translation does not proceed without some answering violence: there are occasional references to the disruptive activities of the Donnelly twins, concluding with the disappearance and presumed killing of Yolland. As Hugh explains, Yolland has become the victim of tribal anger. The mutual comprehension and consent of Marie and Yolland, their transcending of the conventional translation barrier, is a crossing, or rather innocent *denial*, of borders which is not tolerated.[16] We are forced to reflect on how language, and other cultural touchstones, can be used not simply to express a tribe or nation, but manipulatively and coercively to delimit and regulate the tribe or nation. If one response to unwelcome change is violent suppression, another is compulsive retreat into the doomed cocoon of the world and culture one has always known — a retreat from history into myth. Even as the ruthless English retaliation for Yolland's murder faces the community, Jimmy is absorbed by his whimsical notion of marrying Athene — the celibate goddess of wisdom — while Hugh falteringly recites the *Aeneid*.

If, as I argue, there is within the logoid expressionism of Friel and Heaney a constant but fluid interplay of prescription and persuasion, it is rarely solemn: it is more typically sufficiently self-critical to foster irony, satire, and farce. It works at minor levels as well as major ones. Thus, as I read it, one of the nicest running jokes of *Translations* is the repeated use, by less educated villagers such as Doalty, of the exclamation 'Cripes!' Unless we are to question Friel's judgement in identifying this expression as part of the vulgar slang of Irish English, we are repeatedly forced to puzzle over the way a word that most of us will associate with the (fictitious) Edwardian public school world of Billy Bunter comes to be in use in Baile Beag. Ideologically the two worlds are a million miles apart, so that 'Cripes!' becomes a marvellous instance of what Bakhtin has called the double-accented word, evoking in the hearer two irreconcilably conflicting contexts or value-systems.[17]

Heaney's involvement with language, like Friel's, seems to take a Whorfian turn: a respect for the distinct cultural worlds that different languages may express.[18] In Heaney, there is in addition — like Whorf — a difficult probing of that distinct metaphysics. Again, no more than in Whorf or Friel, is this done with the conviction that cross-cultural communication is impossible: quite the reverse, as his world-wide readership would suggest. His technique is to take particular words and names and probe their associations, their phonetic identity, the possible significances of that phonetic nature, and so on. In *Wintering Out* (1972) there are many instances of this: see poems such as 'Toome', 'Broagh' and 'A New Song'. A word or name is supplied, and then its senses are un- or recovered: an exploration of a personal (but not private) lexicon. This dictionary-work persists. In 'Kinship' (*North*, 1975) Heaney contrasts the alien labels quagmire, swampland, morass ('the slime kingdoms, / domains of the cold-blooded, / of mud pads and dirtied eggs') with the indigenous word: 'But *bog* / meaning soft, / the fall of windless rain, / pupil of amber. / / Ruminant ground, digestion of mollusc / and seed-pot, / deep pollen bin' — and more.[19] The observations of M. P. Hederman, writing on Heaney's poetics, seem germane:

It does not seem to matter, in this kind of poetry, whether the poems are in English or in Irish. The words come from a guttural realm of language which is beneath the divide between one particular language form and another. 'In some senses' Heaney tells us, 'these poems are erotic mouth-music by and out of the anglo-saxon tongue', but this does not prevent either the titles from being Irish place-names or the poet from being convinced 'that one could be faithful to the nature of the English language . . . and, at the same time, be faithful to one's non-English origin'.[20]

What seems to be happening is that certain words, 'English' though of varied origins, come to the surface of consciousness and are then inspected for their significances. Again, such activity shows how the traditional linguistic distinction between the natural and the conventional doesn't always hold: somewhere between these poles, Heaney's unique wordhoard is trawled by him, articulated, put to work, so that complex meanings and impressions are derived from specific signs in a way that is neither natural nor conventional, but *motivated*. Heaney's sensitive 'working-over' of the language of (rural, peasant, Catholic) Irish English — a working-over which we motley community of his readers participate in, to the degree that we are drawn into the discourse he has fashioned — is a prominent instance of the extent to which considerable areas of our language are for us, as individuals, non-arbitrary. Words are not randomly associated with specifiable uses and meanings, but expressive of ideas in a way which, while not claiming any natural, inherent or essential connection, is fundamentally motivated.

Earlier I described the name Tobair Vree as a stone in the cairn of cultural memory. It is also, like any act of naming, an assertion of particular identities, allegiances, values, of both the namer and the named. Similarly, when Heaney inspects a name like Toome or Anahorish or Moyola or Ardee he is not merely asserting that the sound or manner of articulation *mimes* the sense — a variant of elegant onomotapoeia — but more radically that in *his* speech various details of the substantiality of the sign are integral to the *signifiances* (to use Barthes' term) that, under the pressure of intense 'arterial' digging, are uncovered. The psychological turn here in Heaney's technique is too apparent to be ignored, a burrowing into the Antaeus-oriented earthiness of his unconscious, confident of finding rich alluvial seams of sense, association, and coherence so typically repressed by that clean, well-lighted collective superego of a language, the dictionary.

And more particularly bearing on my defence of the centrality of Irish English (however anarchic, divided, Janus-faced) to Irish

Literature, Heaney has skilfully exploited that peculiar institution in his expressions of his native culture and his own relations to it. Re-working the ancient *dinnsheanchas* genre, poems which invoked old placenames and rehearsed their meanings, he has constructed a personal mythological etymology. He has written at length on the name of his childhood home, Mossbawn: *moss*, a Scots word meaning 'bog', *bawn*, an English word meaning 'fortified house', hence a mossbawn is a fortified farmhouse on the bog. But again, the trans-planted, grafted words are entwined with the native stock: Heaney reports that their pronunciation and interpretation of bawn was Gaelic — *ban* (white) — so that a quite different sense was conferred on the compound: 'the white moss, the moss of bog-cotton.'[21] There is, then, in both the sounds and the location of Mossbawn (between Castledawson and Toome), not only a rich symbol of Ulster's cultural divisions, but also an exemplum of the potential heterogeneity of contending sources: a reminder that the cairnstones of our personal and cultural inheritances are bedded down not only beside but *against* each other.

A similar double-edgedness to that involved in the maintenance of tribal loyalty arises in the use of dictionaries. Even such marvels of nineteenth century scholarship as the Oxford English Dictionary, intended primarily as a historical record and a work of reference, are rapidly adopted as definitive authorities on the language (as though they were timeless), repositories of unerring wisdom on the 'true' words of English, their senses and uses. Mere ordinary speakers of a language can very easily become victims of unquestioning 'belief in the lexicographer's word (in both senses)'.[22] To the extent that speakers do so submit, their speech is frozen in the attitudes of the dead.

It is for such reasons that I have read Tom Paulin's pamphlet, *A New Look at the Language Question*, with unease. There he reports that Irish English 'appears . . . to be in a state of near anarchy', adding that 'because no scholar has as yet compiled a *Dictionary of Irish English* many words are literally homeless. They live in the careless richness of speech, but they rarely appear in print'.[23] This impassioned plea for social justice for words — 'Decent Housing Now! A Toilet and Bath in Every Word's Home!!' — looks a bit of a cod to me, and would no doubt have suffered brilliant elaboration by the greatest writer of Anglo-Irish prose spoofs, Myles na Gopaleen.

But Paulin seems to be serious, and persists in what must be exposed as a pretty mean-spirited notion of a word-sanctuary:

housing words in a dictionary is about as generous and protective
as 'housing' people in a cemetery. And it is simply absurd to
lament that Irish English 'is a language without a lexicon, a
language without form' (p. 13).

But Paulin has a further grievance: not only does Irish English
lack an established vocabulary, supported by the gold standard of
dictionary entries, it also lacks an exemplary style. He mentions'
Beckett's zero-degree prose, which even then has 'faint, wistful
presences' from Irish English, as a purist's solution, but also
acknowledges the attractions of dialect in its local rootedness, its
expression of a group's identity, loyalty, intimacy, and separateness. Urging a 'federal concept of Irish English', he argues that
this 'would redeem many words from that too-exclusive, too-local,
usage which amounts to a kind of introverted neglect' (p. 17). But
this can only seem an ill-considered — and futile — gesture
towards linguo-cultural engineering if one does not accept that
words need 'redeeming' in the first place. If there are exclusively
local usages of words, then good luck to the locals who use them.
No Dictionary of Irish English (*DIE?*) could in itself bring them
alive to a wider community of speakers and writers. No doubt
linguists and scholars would find such a work most valuable —
but they are quite different customers.

Let me hasten to add that I'm no denouncer of scholarship. Let
us have a Dictionary of Irish English: it would be invaluable to
me and my kind, for whom Irish English is to a greater or lesser
degree a foreign dialect. Indeed there may lie its strongest
rationale: with students from Omaha to Osaka (via Oldham and
Omsk) taking courses on Irish writers, a dictionary or glossary
may assist them in reaching an insider's understanding of the
texts they read.

Paulin asserts: 'A confident concept of Irish English would
substantially increase the vocabulary and this would invigorate
the written language.' (p. 17) It would, surely. But then isn't there
one abroad (I mean, as Myles na gCopaleen would say, in Ireland)
already? And isn't the only sure way of sustaining and enriching
spoken and written Irish English that of attending to the everyday
language behaviour of Irish speakers and writers? There's no
legitimate substitute for living language, acquired through a
chink in the floor, or some other more comfortable and, preferably,
more participatory observation-point.

Certainly if *writers* were to get their hands on Paulin's dictionary
they would court the disasters that Heaney justly notes having
befallen Hugh McDiarmid. Many of McDiarmid's poems are

disfigured by grotesque conjunctions of arcane vocabulary, so that, in Heaney's words, 'we witness the amazing metamorphosis of genius into bore'.[24]

In fairness to Paulin it may be noted that the linguist Randolph Quirk, from a more detached perspective, has commented:

Frank public statements on Irish English and its status are still rare, and standardization has proceeded largely without benefit of any official establishment structure corresponding to Comhairle na Gaeilge, but the fact is that the chief national language of the Irish Republic is cultivated Irish English. Irish history, north as well as south, might well have been different if the constitution had designated *this* as 'Irish' and had proceeded from the 1920s to make explicit its standards with the full panoply of dictionary and other insignia of linguistic independence.[25]

All this may be true, but historical, political and cultural reality hindered such a move.

As if to clinch his argument, Paulin concludes:

Thus the writer who professes this language must either explain dialect words tediously in a glossary or restrict his audience at each particular 'dialectical' [sic] moment. A writer who employs a word like 'geg' or 'gulder' or Kavanagh's lovely 'gobshite', will create a form of closed, secret communication with readers who come from the same region.

(pp. 17-18)

But how impenetrable to outsiders are the words Paulin cites? Even without context I think I have a pretty clear idea what *gobshite* denotes, while the senses of *geg* and *gulder* are unlikely to remain opaque in context. Should they appear to remain so, the encumbrance of a glossary still seems a handier immediate aid than a dictionary. In the case of *gulder*, direct refutation of Paulin's claim comes in Brian Friel's recent play, *The Communication Cord*, where a German character, Barney the Banks, is repeatedly noted to be 'apt to gulder a wee bit' when he has drink taken. In context, we have no problems whatsoever in assigning a sense to *gulder* and *guldering*.

A conclusion may perhaps draw us back to Joyce's Stephen who, not long after his tussle with the dean of studies, rejects Davin's simple Gaelic nationalism:

— My ancestors threw off their language and took another, Stephen said. They allowed a handful of foreigners to subject them. Do you fancy I am going to pay in my own life and person debts they made? What for? (p. 202)

Again, there are eccentric judgements on colonialism here. But Stephen's remarks seem to contain a more provocative challenge: granted that we live in the chronological wake of colonialism, must we also, and despairingly, linger at its cultural wake? For P. F. Sheeran, Anglo-Irish Literature lingered long in such a sub-colonial phase, where writers (Swift, Yeats) sustained love-hate relationships with their portraits of both the coloniser and the colonised.[26] Stephen then proceeds to his famous dedication, to try to fly by Davin's nets of 'nationality, language, religion' (p. 203), snares which are significantly echoic of the three sorts of ignorance that Yeats identified in 1903 as plaguing the Irish theatre: the ignorance of intolerant Gaelic propagandism, that of the Catholic hierarchy's intolerance of the intellect, and that of opportunist politicians. But a generation later, almost exactly these interests are those granted privileged status in Daniel Corkery's immensely influential *Synge and Anglo-Irish Literature* (1931): Nationality, Catholicism, and the Land.[27] These tribal touchstones, when thus narrowly and intolerantly celebrated, run counter to the openness in crossing the field of one's troubled cultural homeground,[28] of merging traditions, which has come down to Friel and Heaney from Yeats and MacDonagh, Kavanagh, Montague and Kinsella.

Yeats's negative manifesto came at a crucial time not merely in his personal life, for as F. S. L. Lyons has put it, 1903 was 'a turning-point . . . in the battle of the two civilisations'.[29] The year was critical for Joyce too, being that of his mother's death, and his return to Dublin; the following year he began work on *Dubliners* and *A Portrait*, and it is of course the year in which *Ulysses* is set. What I would like to suggest is that it was at about *that* time, the early years of the century, that Irish English established itself, by virtue of the richness and compelling natural authority of its users (the only proponents who really count in the long run), as a distinctive and adequate vehicle (anarchic or otherwise) for all the verbal arts.

In his article entitled 'Writers in Quarantine', Declan Kiberd has developed the persuasive argument that Irish literature (in English or Gaelic) can be national without being narrowly nationalist. The two languages and literatures of Ireland must be recognised more effectively as often mutually supportive, a dual (not double) vision, rather than as permanently opposed in a combat to the death:

All over Europe the borders between national literatures are rapidly disappearing and this is especially true of the fake border between Irish and English — a division which was never recognised by our finest writers but which is still observed and enforced in every classroom on the island.[30]

If Kiberd's is the theory, Heaney's is the practice: his recent work includes a vivid translation, from the Irish, of the medieval Sweeney legend. It also includes *Station Island*, a collection at the centre of which is 'a sequence of dream encounters with familiar ghosts'.[31] In the last of these, Joyce's shade definitively dismisses that revelatory moment in *Portrait* which Heaney's persona dubs 'The Feast of the Holy Tundish':

>   ... 'Who cares,'
> he jeered, 'any more? The English language
> belongs to us. You are raking at dead fires,
>
> a waste of time for somebody your age.
> That subject people stuff is a cod's game ...'.   (p. 93)

POST-WAR ULSTER POETRY: A CHAPTER IN ANGLO-IRISH LITERARY RELATIONS

JOHN WILSON FOSTER

I

'Since Congreve and Sterne there has always been at least one major Irish star on the British literary scene.' It would be imprecise to say that A. Alvarez claims this in his review of Seamus Heaney's *Field Work*.[1] I think he laments it. One senses that Alvarez praises another Irish poet the more ('the gifted, underrated Thomas Kinsella') because he has, according to Alvarez, 'departed for America, disappeared into the interior, and has scarcely been heard from since'. In the light of the fact that Kinsella lives in a large American city (Philadelphia) and has published steadily, and that Alvarez presumably owns a library ticket, one wonders at first what he can mean. But what he means is that the *English* have not heard from Kinsella, and to say this while including himself is to betray the very provincialism Alvarez proceeds to attack.

For it is Alvarez' contention that the British 'are comfortable with Heaney' — the current major Irish star — 'because he himself is comfortably in a recognizable tradition'. That tradition is English, still capable of Victorian ornamentation, uneasy with Modernism, cosy and unambitious, and its prevailing vice is 'a monotony of the mundane'. Heaney's work, we are told, 'challenges no presuppositions, does not upset or scare, is mellifluous, craftsmanly, and often perfect within its chosen limits. In other words, it is beautiful minor poetry, like Philip Larkin's . . .'. Alvarez is not wrong in implying that Heaney is as British as he's Irish (I will argue something of the sort myself), but the terms in which he couches the poet's Britishness and Irishness seem contradictory. He sees in abundance in Heaney 'a gift which the English distrust in one another but expect of the Irish: a fine way with the language. What in Brendan Behan, for instance, was a brilliant, boozy gift of the gab is transformed by Heaney into rich

154

and sensuous rhetoric. He is a man besotted with words and, like all lovers, he wants to display the beauties and range and subtleties of his beloved'. To liken Heaney to Behan, via an alcoholic metaphor, is absurd, especially when Alvarez also sees Heaney as allusive, intensely literary, even at times downright pedantic. But having done so, he then turns round and accuses Heaney of being too discreet, steady and reliable, in a word, *English*. Moreover, it seems unfair that the gifted Heaney, as it transpires, is the distrustable Heaney, the trustable being the cosier and less ambitious. A difficult man, Alvarez; almost as difficult as Geoffrey Grigson, who has denied the very possibility of an Irish poetry written in English.[2]

In Alvarez' reaction to Heaney we glimpse the tangled relations between English and Irish writers, which may be as tangled as those between the English and Irish peoples. To the English, and rightly, the Irish writer is both an exotic and a familiar, as the Irish people are both British and not British, provincial citizens of the archipelago and at the same time strange, troublesome, and backward colonists. The ambivalence of the English writers towards their Irish counterparts, that odd mixture of envy and admiration, respect and condescension, can be found at least as early as Sidney's *Apologie for Poetrie* (1595) in which occurs the remark: 'In our neighbour country Ireland, where truly learning goeth very bare, yet are their poets held in a devout reverence.' Praise for the exalted position of the poet in Ireland is accompanied by the charge of cultural poverty. A compromise status for the Irish writer is that of overseas citizen: the Irish writer has a special passport entitling him to behave in ways unacceptable from holders of ordinary passports, but that special passport has of course been issued from the Colonial Office and may be revoked at any time. Alvarez rings the changes on this arrangement by revoking Heaney's special passport *and* carpeting him for travelling with an ordinary passport.

The inconsistency is not all on the one side. Irish writers want to avail themselves of the hospitality of English readers and at the same time maintain the refuge of difference against the day when the critical going gets rough. 'I have never been much considered by the English critics', Patrick Kavanagh began his 'Author's Note' to his *Collected Poems*, in a tone poised between truculence and self-pity, between anglophobia and unrequited love. Such ambivalence, on both sides of the Irish Sea, is concentrated in Northern Ireland, a province geographically Irish but constitutionally British. The career of Ulster poetry since the war, written

as it has been by those who think of themselves as primarily Irish
as well as by those who think of themselves as primarily Northern
Irish (i.e. British), is a vivid case-study in the history of Anglo-
Irish literary relations, with their mutual incursions, and their
two-way traffic in poetic reputation and critical reception. I
content myself in what follows with drawing attention to what I
believe are the high-points of that case-study; if I stress the
'English dimension' of this chapter in Anglo-Irish literary history,
it is because the 'Irish dimension' has been amply accounted for
elsewhere.[3]

II

In the 1940s, in the absence of Auden and despite the tetchy
vigilance of Grigson and *New Verse*, there was a bout of enthusiasm
in Britain for Celticism as a pseudo-geographic strain of the
dominant romanticism of the period. It was claimed that there
was a 'Welsh Renaissance' (one imagines the youthful Kingsley
Amis waiting in gleeful ambuscade) and also a 'Scottish Renaissance', but that 'the Irish, especially in *The Bell*, have been busy,
but more traditionally'.[4] *Poetry Scotland* (a regional counterforce,
though not a poetic counterforce, to *Poetry London*), encouraging
the Irish, published John Hewitt, Maurice James Craig and Donagh
MacDonagh in their second number (1944). It was, however, an
indecisive showing, especially since Hewitt, despite his presence
here and later in *A New Romantic Anthology* (1949), edited by
Stefan Schimanski and Henry Treece, was if anything closer to
the Grigson camp in which he found himself when Grigson
anthologised him in his *Poetry of the Present* (1949).

  In the words of Robert Herring, written at the end of the war,
the Celt is a romantic, endowed with a sense 'of the mystery of
Man': 'the difference between English and Celtic love-poetry, for
instance, is that between sentiment and passion and the Celtic
passion is not only personal but directed to the divinity enshrined
in the person.'[5] When Celts mobilise, Irish poets are an obvious
group to conscribe, but it appears that there was token resistance
to conscription. In 1942, the Ulster poet Robert Greacen co-edited
with Alex Comfort, *Lyra: An Anthology of New Lyric*. Of the Irish
poets represented in the volume (all of whom were from Ulster),
the editors wrote: 'The Irish-Ulster group, who are more like a
school than any of the others, includes Greacen, McFadden,
Gallen and Brook (who is English). They are evolving something

which again is new, a form of poetic realism.'[6] But the company
the Ulster poets were keeping rendered suspect such an enterprise.
The anthology was published by Wrey Gardiner, editor of *Poetry
Quarterly*, home to many of the 1940s neo-romantics, and included
such prominent members of that band as G. S. Fraser, Alex
Comfort, Nicholas Moore, Tambimuttu, Henry Treece and Vernon
Watkins, as well as Robert Herring and Gardiner himself. There
was a Preface by Herbert Read, and in 'A Word from the Editors',
Comfort and Greacen described their anthology as 'a contribution
to a new romanticism'. In fact, the Ulster poets, like their co-
anthologised, flourish a hackneyed romantic enervation that the
war seems to have encouraged in contemporary poets:

> Not world as world is, but world as wish is
> but the long suffering of 'I' at last lost, lip-puffed-by:
> dreams no doubt — there is no need of courage
>
> nor of anything but dreaming, in a dream.
> > (Gallen, 'A Little Lyricism on a New Occasion')
>
> Whin and thistle and the weeds of a wan winter
> You are fit symbols for this time of tearing war
> > (Greacen, 'Lines for Friends expecting a Baby
> > at Christmas 1941')
>
> What can we say who have said it all already?
> Who have seen the years fall
> Like leaves or tears on to a million coffins
> Returning dully to the blissful womb;
> What can we say, here, by the hardening fire,
> As the clock ticks history, and the flowers drip blood?
> > (McFadden, 'Poem for To-Day')

McFadden's is meant, of course, to be brass-tack sentiment, and
one of his three poems, 'Gaudeamus Igitur', is mock-romantic,
but realism and end-of-the-tether rhetoric are not one and the
same, and Greacen is surely in error when he suggests in a recent
and otherwise valuable reminiscence that McFadden gave up
romanticism abruptly in 1939 on Greacen's recommendation.[7]
There is no distinction in theme, matter or style to be made
between the Ulster contributions to *Lyra* and the English, Scottish
and Welsh contributions of the kind that the phrase 'poetic
realism' would seem to invite.

On the evidence of *Lyra*, Ulster poetry in the 1940s written
by the newcomers was hardly distinguishable from British

neo-romanticism at large, even though they wrote out of a discouraging wartime in Belfast. (This apparently is how the Ulster poets wanted it. According to Terence Brown, they display 'an iconoclastic irritation with the Irish mode' available to them, McFadden in particular believing that 'an emulation of contemporary English experiments is the only possible way forward for Irish poets'.)[8] In the light of this, it seems odd that *Lyra* did not include W. R. Rodgers, especially since Greacen in his reminiscence admits that he and the others were very aware of Rodgers 'and the stir made by his first collection, *Awake! and Other Poems*' (1941).[9]

Rodgers, indeed, became one of only two Irish poets of his generation to enjoy a substantial British and American reputation, the other being Louis MacNeice, another Ulsterman. In the 1940s and 1950s, Rodgers worked for the BBC in London and was friend to MacNeice and also to Dylan Thomas, whose poetry Rodgers' occasionally resembles. *Awake! and Other Poems* appeared in England and America to great acclaim, and the poet was heralded by some as the new Auden. The spendthrift and joyous use of words ('a fine way with the language'!) is the immediate quality of Rodgers' verse.

> Always the arriving winds of words
> Pour like Atlantic gales over these ears.

One poem opens, and the reader, like the poet, is an astonished host to lines both buoyed and weighted by alliteration, assonance, puns and breakneck rhythms and charged with exclamatory and imperative urgency. Such poetry unfortunately contributes to the English stereotype of the word-besotted Irish bard for whom reason is low on the totem-pole of priorities.

Although he was an Ulster Protestant (indeed, a Presbyterian minister who forsook the collar of the cleric for the collar on a pint of Guinness), Rodgers thought of himself as thoroughly Irish:

> O these lakes and all gills that live in them,
> These acres and all legs that walk on them,
> These tall winds and all wings that cling to them,
> Are part and parcel of me, bit and bundle,
> Thumb and thimble.

As for his poetry, Rodgers claimed that 'The faculty of standing words or ideas on their heads — by means of pun, epigram, bull, or what-have-you — is a singularly Irish one . . . To the English ear, which likes understatement, it is all rather excessive and therefore not quite in good taste. But to the Irish mind which likes gesture, bravado, gallivanting, and rhetoric, it is an acceptable tradition'.[10]

Perhaps Rodgers' self-advertising Irishness dismayed Greacen and the Ulster poets, even though they too were wartime neo-romantics. Yet Rodgers shares linguistic verve and dash with his contemporaries George Barker and Dylan Thomas, two poets Kenneth Rexroth thought it natural to bracket with the Ulsterman in his resourceful Introduction to *The New British Poets* (1949). Given Barker's part-Irish ancestry and Thomas' Welshness, perhaps we could say that what the three poets share is Celticness, though this is debatable. Despite the fact that the Thirties poets were his initial, acknowledged inspiration,[11] Rodgers' reliance on the unconscious (by way of association and suggestion) and his lack of political commitment mark him as a post-Auden British romantic. And the obtrusively apocalyptic theme and tone of many of the poems in *Awake! and Other Poems* associate him with Henry Treece, J. F. Hendry and the poets of the Apocalyptic anthologies, *The New Apocalypse* (1939), *The White Horseman* (1941) and *The Crown and the Sickle* (1944), which briefly, but only briefly (thankfully), lit up the sky over the English poetry scene.[12]

III

In short, Rodgers was a sitting duck for the new generation of poets (Kingsley Amis, Robert Conquest, Philip Larkin, John Wain and others) that was beginning to make its presence felt in British poetry. The year after Rodgers' second (and last) volume, *Europa and the Bull and Other Poems*, appeared in 1952, Amis tried to make ribbons of Rodgers' verse in *Essays in Criticism*. The punning title of Amis's piece struck the attitude: 'Ulster Bull: The Case of W. R. Rodgers.'[13]

Taking the opening four lines of 'Europa and the Bull' as text, Amis concluded after some elementary Empsonian analysis that whereas attention to the meaning of Rodgers' verse is disastrous, attention to the sound is in the end equally disastrous. For Amis, Rodgers' poems — and by association the poems of New Romanticism for which he let them conveniently stand — were so many 'word-salads'. In a poem entitled 'Here is Where', Amis seemed to mock Rodgers and his ilk:

> *Here, where the ragged water*
> *Is twilled and spun over*
> *Pebbles backed like beetles,*
> *Bright as beer-bottles*
> *Bits of it like snow beaten*
> *Or milk boiling in saucepan . . .*
>
> Going well so far, eh? . . .

In 'Wrong Words', possibly with Rodgers in mind, Amis rounded on poets who are 'Too fluent, drenching with confectionery/One image, one event's hard outline'.

But though in 'Ulster Bull', Amis dissociated Rodgers' verse from the first Romanticism, Amis himself acidly rewrote a chief Romantic text in 'Ode to the East-North-East-by-East Wind' in which he makes a toughminded attack on Shelley's poetic egotism. The assault on Shelley seems sincere enough, originating possibly in Leavis's downgrading of that poet, but it would be a mistake to take such a poem too seriously. Still, Amis and the other Movement poets were generally (Larkin having apparently come out of his Yeats phase) against Romanticism. In a poem of just that title, Amis expressed a desire for temperateness and realism in verse as in life. Romanticism is equated in this poem with anarchy, reminding us of the Movement's penchant for an order (masquerading as consensus) that was challenged by Rodgers' (as by Thomas's) love of duality, trinity and in the end fecund dishevelment and 'throughotherness'. (Far from believing in order, Rodgers seemed to hold a millenarian view of history not as continuity but as a series of ruptures. His world is full of prophecies, revelations, catastrophes, redemptions, resurrections, myths, dreams and mysteries.)[14] In later years, Amis and Larkin developed a sympathy for right-wing politics,[15] but we can see a disdain for the left as early as 'Against Romanticism', which concludes:

> Let the sky be clean of officious birds
> Punctiliously flying on the left;
>   Let there be a path leading out of sight,
> And at its other end a temperate zone:
>   Woods devoid of beasts, roads that please the foot.

Mention of Dylan Thomas is a reminder that Movement reaction against romanticism entailed reaction against the immensely popular Welsh poet, who died in 1953. In *Poets of the 1950s* (1955), the first anthology of Movement verse, D. J. Enright wrote of Thomas:

The rich and brilliant imagery in which his work abounds almost blinds the critic to its deficiency in intellectual conviction. Perhaps the kind of admiration which Thomas received encouraged him to leave 'thinking' to the *New Verse* poets; but poetry is like the human body in needing bones as well as flesh and blood. Poetry must possess (and honour) its own kind of logic, however elusive it may be; and Welsh rhetoric seems a deadly enemy to all varieties of logic, even the poetic.[16]

'Our new poets', claimed Enright, are 'moderate' (Amis would have said 'temperate'), both in technique and in attitude, 'and of course moderation lacks the immediate popular appeal of the extremes', i.e. of the bards, romantics, Apocalyptics and Celts. Thomas, of course, had been reproved before the Movement came into being by Grigson and also by Robert Graves. More to my point, he had also been attacked by Orwell, who was something of a hero to members of the Movement. In the Movement's assault on extremism, especially of anarchist and leftist varieties, we might detect stirrings of Orwell's anti-Stalinism and Cold War anti-communism.[17] The facts of life in postwar Britain seemed to indicate a circumspect realism. A Shelleyan romanticism was bound to be a casualty under conditions in which social order, after the recent catastrophe, was trying to reassert itself. Indeed, any romanticism was bound to be a casualty and so Rodgers' heady verse came under attack (not just for its lack of merit but also for its colouration and ideology) in the changed and sober circumstances of postwar Britain.

Much has been made, rightly, of the provincial stance of the Movement poets, their suspicion of the metropolis. The provincial stance came perhaps from a natural wish on the part of young writers to settle alternative sites for themselves away from the established centre of literary power, which was London. It came too, perhaps, from the fact that the young writers were the New University Wits, as Van O'Connor early nicknamed them, who needed university posts after graduation, most of these being in the provinces. Their provincialism was, then, both necessary and strategic, and consisted as much in the 'metropolitanization' of the provinces (though links with London via publishers, readers and critics, as well as via the BBC and journals) as in the creation of regional alternatives to London (for settings and subject-matter). Provincialism, in any case, implies, even entails, a metropolis from which is derives its values and standards.

This is a largely English perspective on the Movement. From a Scottish, Welsh and Irish perspective, the Movement was English in three vivid ways — its writers were mostly English nationals, they attended Oxford or Cambridge, and they were, at least temporarily, associated after graduation with the English academy. The Movement may have been provincial in one sense or another, but it was also anti-regionalist, the regions (Scotland, Wales and Ireland) being associated with romanticism and Celticism; in short, with Enright's 'extremes', poetic and geographic. The equation of regionalism with romantic Celticism had been established in the 1940s by the neo-romantics themselves. Neo-romanticism was even on occasions seen hopefully as a force in 'the revival and revitalisation of nationalist and regional cultures'.[18] In this light, the Movement can be viewed as much as a reaction as a revolution, an English, centralist reaction against a brief, regional interregnum, a Commonwealth between kingships (in which Dylan Thomas played a benign Cromwell). Critics have already drawn attention to the Little Englandism of the Movement, and Morrison has correctly linked it in its international context to the Movement's provincialism in an English context.[19] Anti-regionalism may have been as much an aspect of post-imperial (as well as post-war) tristesse as provincialism and xenophobia.[20] We see an aggressive insularity at work in an interview with Larkin, who may himself have been unaware of it at that precise moment. 'So you don't ever feel the need to be at the centre of things?' he was asked. 'You don't want to see the latest play, for instance?' 'Oh no', he replied,

I very much feel the need to be on the periphery of things. I suppose when one was young one liked to be up to date. But I very soon got tired of the theatre. I count it as one of the great moments of my life when I first realized one could actually walk out of a theatre. I don't mean offensively — but go to the bar at the interval and not come back. I did it first at Oxford: I was watching *Playboy of the Western World* and when the bell rang at the interval I asked myself: 'Am I enjoying myself? No, I've never watched such stupid balls.' So I just had another drink and walked out into the evening sunshine.[21]

Is it a coincidence that the play he was watching when his great moment occurred was an internationally acclaimed, extravagantly *Irish* play?

This might help to explain Kavanagh's neglect by the English at the time of the Movement. Alvarez to the contrary, there was no English desire for an Irish star in their firmament between Behan and Heaney, between, say, 1955 and 1975. For his part, Kavanagh knew the poetry of the Movement was hostile to his own work. His impatience with Movement verse anticipated Alvarez' strictures in his Preface to his 1962 anthology, *The New Poetry:*

> I say to hell
> With all reasonable
> Poems in particular
> We want no secular
> Wisdom plodded together
> By concerned fools.[22]

It might also help to explain — since the Movement held sway for some time — the later neglect of Kinsella and John Montague. True, Kinsella and Montague write a verse responsive to Modernism and therefore more welcome in America, where they have sought their largest audience outside Ireland, than in England. But the naturalness of their choice of America may be as culturally (even racially) explicable as it is poetically explicable. If Kinsella and Montague were (as far as an English readership is concerned) victims of the Movement, they have been victims too of partition, being, as they are, too unambiguously Irish. Since the Movement, with its implicit redefinition of Britishness as a cultural nationality radiating from its English core, there has been little English interest in southern Irish writers.[23] (Exceptions such as Edna O'Brien and William Trevor are fiction writers who do not threaten English political sensibilities in the manner of a Montague or English aesthetic sensibilities in the manner of a Kinsella.) Certainly the Irish poets most highly regarded in England today are from Northern Ireland.

IV

If what I have said is true, it is all the more hilarious to stumble upon, in Iain Fletcher and G. S. Fraser's Introduction to their 1953 anthology, *Springtime: An Anthology of Young Poets*, this inspired inaccuracy: 'Irish poets, like Mr. Larkin, though writing in Standard English, reflect another regional value, that of rootedness.'[24] This about the future and firmly English author of 'The Importance of Elsewhere', a poem which begins, 'Lonely in Ireland, since it was not home'! For rooted and regionalist are precisely what Larkin is not, even if we decide to label England as a region. In his work there is no Wordsworthian attachment to place: 'Nothing, like something, happens anywhere', as he ends the ironically titled 'I Remember, I Remember', a line that also disavows revelation. In Larkin there is no romantic memory of beginnings or fond recalls of boyhood. Coventry is 'only where my childhood was unspent', he says in the same poem.[25]

It is not easy to picture Larkin in Belfast (the city whose post-mark his poems to Fraser and Fletcher would have borne), but he spent five years there as a librarian at Queen's University (failing to overlap with the student Heaney by only two years). The city's lack of those romantic and literary associations clinging to Dublin would have gratified him, as would its awkward poise of relationship with England and Ireland, but most of all, it seems its foreignness appealed. Belfast lay on the far side of that mere provincialism Amis exploited in Swansea. Larkin being Larkin, he found the city's strangeness familiar, its difference congenial. Belfast, whose fifties sights, sounds and smells I can corroborate.

> Their draughty streets, end-on to hills, the faint
> Archaic smell of dockland, like a stable,
> The herring-hawker's cry, dwindling . . .

became one of the several 'elsewheres' that have underwritten Larkin's poetic, and, he would no doubt claim, his real existence.

'After finishing my first books', Larkin has said, 'say by 1945, I thought I had come to an end. I couldn't write another novel, I published nothing. My personal life was rather harassing. Then in 1950 I went to Belfast, and things reawoke somehow. I wrote some poems, and thought, These aren't bad, and had that little pamphlet *XX Poems* printed privately. I felt for the first time I was speaking for myself. Thoughts, feelings, language cohered and jumped.'[26] Thirteen of *XX Poems*, printed in Belfast, reappeared in *The Less Deceived* (1955). The seminal collection of post-war English poetry, the volume that changed the direction of British poetry, was, then, largely written in Belfast. It was this city's undeceived, unromantic, unEnglish (and yet unIrish) provincialism, its negative identity (unavailable as it is to any English perspective on Ireland or England), that was the poetry's inspiration.

Another English poet arrived at Queen's University to teach English in the early 1960s. Along with Edward Lucie-Smith, Peter Redgrove and others, Philip Hobsbaum was a leading light in The Group, Cambridge's delayed answer to Oxford's Movement. Movement and Group poetry seem to me indistinguishable except by merit. The title poem of Hobsbaum's first volume of verse, *The Place's Fault and Other Poems* (1964), in which he recalls, unlike Larkin, his childhood (and with distaste), reverses Larkin's judgement in 'I Remember, I Remember' that his unspent childhood was not 'the place's fault'. The reversal is nevertheless a salute to Larkin. Hobsbaum was aware of following in Larkin's footsteps to Belfast, and he offered as epigraph to his second volume (*In Retreat and Other Poems*, 1966) the opening line of 'The Importance of Elsewhere': 'Lonely in Ireland, since it was not home'.

Hobsbaum played a large part in the galvanising of Ulster poetry; unlike Larkin, Hobsbaum was pedagogical, proselytic and convivial, and his role as catalyst has been by now fully acknowledged.[27] Through Hobsbaum, rather than Larkin, the values of the Movement were carried to Belfast (if I may risk a vector theory of literary influence), putting paid to any romantic residue in Ulster poetry of the time.[28] Perhaps it was more like a devolution of poetical power. Like Alvarez after him, Hobsbaum has tried to appropriate the work of Heaney (one of Hobsbaum's Belfast Group) in the name of an essentially English tradition. Hobsbaum claimed the wedding sequence of *Wintering Out* (1972) as the best of Heaney thus far, and placed it firmly within 'the central line of English poetry', a line allegedly extended by the Group poet, Redgrove.[29] We can, of course, bridle at the confident sweep of the claim, the blindness to Heaney's Irishness, but that is not to deny that Ulster poetry since and including Heaney's carries the imprint of Movement and Group verse.

V

We discover it, for example, in Derek Mahon's unease with the academy and its familiars, the critic-as-sutler and the writer-in-residence. Larkin's 'Posterity' finds its equivalent in Mahon's 'I Am Raftery'. Mahon and Larkin share an almost pedantic nurturing of ignorance, a versed bravado leading in each case to pervasive, even reflex paradox of tone and attitude. Larkin's purely assumed philistinism in 'A Study of Reading Habits' — 'Get stewed: / Books are a load of crap' — has its fellow in Mahon's excellent 'Rock Music' (*The Hunt by Night*):

> The ocean glittered quietly in the moonlight
> While heavy metal rocked the discotheques;
> Space-age Hondas farted half the night,
> Fired by the prospect of fortuitous sex.
> I sat late at the window, bland with rage,
> And listened to the tumult down below,
> Trying to concentrate on the printed page
> As if such obsolete bumf could save us now.

Like Larkin, the Ulster poets, Mahon, Ormsby and Muldoon, specialise in versifying sentiments to which every bosom returns an echo.

The Movement influence I would define broadly as the studied concern for the techniques of poetry behind the pretence (possibly at times a genuine fear or conviction) that poetry in these times and in the real world doesn't matter. Mahon's lines

> And all the time I have my doubts
> About this verse-making . . .
> All farts in a biscuit tin, in truth —
> Faint cries, sententious or uncouth.[30]

and his fear that the Ulster poets, ostensibly concerned about the Troubles, are really 'middle-class cunts', strike the attitude vividly. The refusal of bardism, then, with a concomitant dedication to the craft of verse. Indeed, the refusal of bardism may be a rearguard action of regret, pique and self-pity against society's disregard for poets, which is how we might read 'I Am Raftery' and 'Rock Music'.[31] If that disregard is a postwar phenomenon, we might care to allow no essential difference between the Movement reaction and that of a writer who preceded the Movement, Samuel Beckett. Mahon, who admires Beckett, especially the Beckett of the trilogy, may be the mediating figure here rather than solely being a provincial post-Movementeer. Mahon's picture of himself as 'Scribbling on the off-chance, / Darkening the page' is an unacknowledged image from *Molloy*.[32] Beckett as much as Larkin has encouraged in Mahon what the Ulster poet calls 'the love-play of the ironic conscience'. To complicate things still further, what Geoffrey Thurley observes in Larkin — 'a residual self-distrust, leavened by wit' — and about Larkin — 'eliminating the bogus is in fact Larkin's chosen profession' — are equally true for Mahon.[33] But Thurley would explain this in terms of what he claims is the poetic harvest of the English intellectualist tradition begun by Eliot, Richards and Empson — irony, scepticism, doubt, failure of nerve, loss of faith in literature itself.

Moreover, even if Mahon, Ormsby and Muldoon have learned from the Movement, there is a specifically Ulster context for their irony and scepticism, for the eloquent displacements their nervousness has caused. The Ulster poets are mostly from the urban working-class or lower middle-class or from their rural equivalents, and are not to the literary manner born, and this bears some resemblance to the class situation of the Movement writers.[34]

But some are Catholics in a Protestant archipelago and all are triply provincial — self-conscious (like all British provincials) before London, but self-conscious too (as colonials) before the mainland, as well as self-conscious (as literary men) before Dublin. They are, then, going to be uneasy about their role as poets and about their readership. However, that unease has probably been reinforced by their inheritance of Movement values. Likewise, their refusal of a too evident Irishness, indicated by their Ulsterness, was stiffened no doubt by the Movement refusal of bardism. This refusal suggests some discomfiture with place, even a kind of rootlessness, though in the Ulster poets it doesn't have Larkin's succinctness of expression.

As luck would have it, the kind of unease I am talking about has mingled in the Ulster poets with their political unease over the progress of the Troubles in Northern Ireland. For many observers, this has been a happy conjunction, for it has put a welcome brake on any reflex, extreme or ancestral response to a difficult situation. The Movement quality of moderation, rooted in a rejection of 1940s romanticism and romantic nationalism as well as in Orwell's 'advocacy of quietism',[35] even the Movement failure of nerve, if that was what it was, have permitted or encouraged a poetry in Ulster angularly at odds with the brutal facts of life and history there.[36] (On the other hand, there is no trace of Movement anti-leftism in Ulster poetry, but then 'right' and 'left' hold little meaning in Northern Ireland.) One senses conscience at work in an almost Nonconformist way; John Holloway once referred to the Nonconformist background of many of the Movement writers,[37] and while this might account in small part, and in Arnoldian terms, for the philistinism of the Movement (largely affected), it might also suggest an anglicising or protestantising of Catholic writers in Northern Ireland (to match the hibernicisation in other regards of Ulster Protestant writers).[38]

This is not the whole story, of course. Some of the Ulster writers, from James Simmons on, have struck a blunt, no-nonsense attitude to life and literature in Ulster. It puts to work, half-ironically, the stereotype of the 'honest Ulsterman' (the Northern equivalent of Myles na gCopaleen's plain people of Ireland). It crosses this stereotype with the stereotype of the American tough guy. Simmons, Michael Foley, Ormsby and Muldoon are all enamoured of Americanism that reaches them second-hand or is turned by them into the second-hand by parody or imitation. One recalls, of course, the well-publicised liking of Amis and Larkin for American jazz, which goes hand in hand with their refusal to be deceived by mandarin flummery. Yet *The Honest Ulsterman*, a highly successful and long-lived magazine, begun by Simmons and for which Foley has written, may owe more of its no-nonsense literary posture to the English magazine, *The Review*, edited by Ian Hamilton, both magazines carrying blunt reviews and on occasions pseudonymous satires and parodies.[39] Hamilton and Alvarez were enemies of the Movement, but the chief influence on the first volume of poetry by the present editor of *The Honest Ulsterman*, Frank Ormsby, would seem to have been Larkin. Larkin's droll self-deprecation lightens *A Store of Candles* (1977), as well as his humorous and precise observation of the mundane, his awareness of the strength of absence and elsewhere. Like Larkin, Ormsby has several poems that offer a jocularly detailed description or narrative capped by an irony that is apparently accepted but conceals a blank misgiving, a sense of loss. Larkin's 'Sunny Prestatyn' suggests the formula and it is put to good use in Ormsby's 'Spot the Ball' and 'Ornaments'.

VI

The Movement was famously repudiated by Alvarez in his anthology, *The New Poetry*, which brought its poets before their readers for a public caning and to benefit from the example of two American visitors to the school, Berryman and Lowell. Although he had been associated with it in earlier years, Alvarez considered the Movement tame, monotonous and fearful of the heart of darkness.[40] We might have thought that Heaney would have satisfied Alvarez. After all, Alvarez is an admirer of Ted Hughes, and Heaney's notion of poetry as a raid into the dark is actually Hughes's, as is Heaney's location of meaning deep underfoot accessible in some sense through wells, ponds, divining-rods, burial-chambers, bog-holes.[41] However, Alvarez has chosen to stress the Movement rather than Hughesian side of Heaney, and I cannot quarrel with him for doing so, since I preceded him in his choice.[42] Let me just supplement my earlier observation by suggesting that Heaney's early affinities with Larkin, though more surprising than Larkin's affinities with the more filtered personalities of Mahon and Ormsby, are there, despite the presence in his verse of the violence from which Larkin would run a mile. Like Larkin, Heaney has cultivated his 'elsewhere', and Heaney's being lost, unhappy and at home in Denmark (see 'The Tollund Man') puts me in mind of Larkin's being lost, unhappy and at home in Belfast. Read Larkin's 'MCMXIV', a poem that captures with the dim precision of an old photograph a turning-point in his country's history (the line of volunteers outside the recruiting offices in August 1914), and you might well think of Heaney's Irish equivalent, 'Linen Town', which captures an afternoon in Belfast before the 1798 rebellion in the same way and to the same end. Perhaps this is to say no more than this: that Larkin injected post-war British poetry with the now pervasive feelings of regret, nostalgia, loss, unease and reticence, that he established as expected practice in poetry, a public but guarded self-inquisition.

If Alvarez has spurned Heaney, the new men in England, Blake Morrison, Andrew Motion and Craig Raine, are much taken with him. In 1982, Motion and Morrison promoted Heaney to father-figure in their anthology, *The Penguin Book of Contemporary British Poetry*. This compilation is meant to register 'a reformation of poetic taste' and a decisive break with the Movement and its ageing members. The Ulster poets constitute a vanguard fleet: six out of the twenty poets represented in the anthology are from a province of a million and a half people. However, the connections I have tried to establish between Ulster and Movement poetry throw the enterprise in some doubt, apart from the fact that the anthology is actually duller than the one it is meant to replace, Alvarez' *The New Poetry*, itself a perverse demonstration of dullness enlivened by its editor's polemical Preface. In their rather laboured and term-paperish Introduction, Motion and Morrison, needing a break with the Movement, invent a geologic fault. The new poets, it seems, are not inhabitants of their own lives so much as intrigued observers, 'inner emigrés' (Heaney's phrase). But if this does not fit Larkin, it fits no one. It seems odd that Morrison does not see to what extent he has re-imported into English Poetry — Ulsterised certainly — many of the values, standards and postures of a poetry he earlier chronicled.

Nevertheless, for the post-Movement poets and critics, Ulster poetry has rehabilitated the regionalism that the Movement scorned (but not the romantic regionalism of the 1940s), and does so in a way that is both model and inspiration for mainland verse: Tony Harrison, for example, has extended Heaney's probings of dialect and language-place connections. Through a cursory, even reflex reading of the Northern Irish political situation, Ulster poetry also permits for the post-Movement writers reinstatement of the leftist, working-class and anti-authoritarian perspectives to which the Movement was in reality hostile. Above all, then, Ulster poetry is *useful* to the English writers, helping them to turn English provincialism (in the honorific sense of indicating a lower-class background in the North or Midlands) into an authentic regionalism in the way that the Liverpool poets of the sixties might have done but in the event could not do. No doubt for a very brief time, Belfast is in some sense for these writers the British capital (as Liverpool was twenty years ago). Motion has made his obligatory pilgrimage there and commemorates it in verse; his 'Leaving Belfast' (in *The Pleasure Steamers*, 1978, and dedicated to Raine) can be set beside Raine's 'Flying to Belfast, 1977' (included in the Penguin collection). The 'Belfast poem' is now a small tradition among English poets, for different reasons to those which prompted Larkin's 'The Importance of Elsewhere'. For all, Belfast is strange and unfamiliar, but whereas the Motion and Raine poems are to-ings and fro-ings and wine-tastings of fear between flights, Larkin thrived on his separateness in Belfast, for it productively cleft his life into *here* and *there*.

It is a nice irony that in the service of homage as well as the principles of regionalism and anti-authoritarianism, the English poets have culturally bound Ulster more firmly to a Britain that will always be the dominant country in the enforced partnership of English-Irish contiguity. Perhaps this realisation (if it wasn't that Alvarez touched a nerve) prompted Heaney — Motion and Morrison's captain — to stage a one-man mutiny. Suddenly he has seen *The Penguin Book of Contemporary British Poetry* as a colonialist venture. (The effect of their captain's mutiny on the morale of the other Irish crew-members, Muldoon, Paulin, McGuckian, Mahon and Longley, I don't know.) In *An Open Letter* (1983, Field Day Pamphlet Number 2), Heaney politely but firmly refuses the adjective 'British':

> As empire rings its curtain down
>   This 'British' word
> Sticks deep in native and *colon*
>   Like Arthur's sword.

He admits that he has spoken out only after what he regards in himself as typical dithering, and he is characteristically aware of the irony in his stance:

> Yet doubts, admittedly, arise
> When somebody who publishes
> In LRB and TLS,
>   *The Listener* —

In other words, whose audience is,
Via Faber,

A British one, is characterized
As British.

But he is nonetheless defiant:

be advised
My passport's green.
No glass of ours was ever raised
To toast *The Queen*.

Permission to reprint Heaney's poems having been sought and granted, permission fees presumably having been paid, Heaney's demurral cannot be seen as a case of his usual reticence and circumspection. One senses instead political pressure unrelated to the original literary decision to appear in the anthology. *An Open Letter* must be seen in the context of increased polarisation of postures in Northern Ireland, and of the reversion to origins and heritages of which this polarisation is cause or effect. Behind the understandable ambivalence towards Britain felt by all the Irish, one suspects the specific pressures on Heaney from his own tribe. He is talking in this pamphlet not so much to Motion and Morrison as to his own, and he is making appropriate anti-colonialist noises, but noises which are not only comfortless but also unHeaney-like, poetically as well as politically.[43] More than some influential others in Ireland, Heaney knows how tangled are the literary as well as political relations between Ireland and Britain, how unavailable they are to the simplicities of doggerel, as the past forty years, especially in Ulster, have once more shown.

THE GO-BETWEEN OF RECENT IRISH POETRY

DILLON JOHNSTON

For purposes of contrast let me recall the responses of Yeats and Joyce to the Easter Rising of 1916 and to Ireland's war for independence, respectively. Yeats concludes his elegaic paean to the executed leaders of the rising, which he dates September 25th, 1916, with these celebrated lines:

> I write it out in verse —
> MacDonagh and MacBride
> And Connolly and Pearse
> Now and in time to be,
> Wherever green is worn,
> Are changed, changed utterly:
> A terrible beauty is born.[1]

These leaders of the rising, who once seemed to Yeats familiar and comic, have been translated into a tragic permanence through their self-sacrifices 'in the name of God and of the dead generations', and through the force of the poet's style. Although all of us in the poet's Irish audience are asked to accept uncritically this matyrdom — 'We know their dream; enough / To know they dreamed and are dead' — it is the poet himself who will enrol them in the eternity of beauty: 'I write it out in verse . . . a terrible beauty is born.'

It is just this uncritical complicitness of poetry and song with politics and national image-making that Joyce satirises in the Cyclops episode of *Ulysses*, which seems particularly savage if we recognise that it was written during the opening years of Ireland's war with England. Mocking formulaic responses of all kinds, but specifically, in this one passage, ballads such as 'The Croppy Boy' that eulogise martyred patriots, Joyce writes:

The *nec* and *non plus ultra* of emotion were reached when the blushing bride elect burst her way through the serried ranks of the bystanders and

172

flung herself upon the muscular bosom of him who was about to be launched into eternity for her sake. The hero folded her willowy form in a loving embrace murmuring fondly *Sheila, my own*. Encouraged by this use of her christian name she kissed passionately all the various suitable areas of his person which the decencies of prison garb permitted her ardor to reach.[2]

Joyce's passage would undercut that suasive disposition of the narrator or poet towards his audience that Yeats cultivated, and it would substitute for Yeats's one timbre or style a democratising multiplicity of voices.

Seamus Deane has extended the contrast between Yeats's and Joyce's attitudes toward tradition in the fourth of the Field Day pamphlets:

There have been for us two dominant ways of reading both our literature and our history. One is 'Romantic', a mode of reading which takes pleasure in the notion that Ireland is a culture enriched by the ambiguity of its relationship to an anachronistic and a modernised present. The other is a mode of reading which denies the glamour of this ambiguity and seeks to escape from it into a pluralism of the present. The authors who represent these modes most powerfully are Yeats and Joyce respectively.[3]

Evidently, it is the objective of the Field Day essays — especially those by Deane, Richard Kearney, and Declan Kiberd — to raze the monumental myths of the literary and nationalistic revival (perhaps I should say 'the so-called revival') in an appeal for a revisionary politics and literature which would be 'unblemished by Irishness', as Deane says, 'but securely Irish'.[4]

Actually the Joycean effort to escape from anachronistic myths and attitudes 'into a pluralism of the present', which Field Day endorses, has been made intermittently in the last forty years — by Sean O'Faolain in founding *The Bell*, by Patrick Kavanagh, and most significantly by the current generation of poets. When Deane says that 'everything, including our politics and our literature, has to be rewritten', he might add that this process of deconstruction and revision has already begun in the poetry of Thomas Kinsella and Paul Muldoon, and to a lesser degree in the poetry of Heaney, Montague, and Mahon.

The revisionary aspect of this poetry comes into focus when we gaze, as we did with the passage from Yeats, at the poetic speaker's relation to his audience. In the increasingly dramatic nature of Irish poetry, the multiplicity of poetic speakers, and the substitution of demotic voices for a lyric timbre, Joyce's influence is manifest in recent poetry, as most of these five poets have confessed. However, because Ireland's major writers are too complex to serve as types, let me characterise the relation of the speaker to his audience in recent Irish poetry not in the name of Joyce and Yeats but in terms of a more ancient type borrowed from syncretic myth, the type of Hermes.

Hermes survives most currently in the word *hermetic* — sealed or impenetrable — which some readers might apply to certain elliptical poems by Austin Clarke, Denis Devlin, or Brian Coffey or to recent work of Kinsella and Muldoon, the Irish poetry most resistant to hermeneutics. However, the older attributes of Hermes convey richer and more revealing associations with Irish poetry. Although inventor of alphabets, music, and the musical instrument the lyre, Hermes gave away the lyre to his rival and friend, Apollo, who became the god of poets and singers. Hermes himself preferred to patronise messengers, thieves, and magicians, but he was also a god of revelation.[5] God of the roads, he conducted souls to and from the underworld. As father of Hermaphrodite and Priapus, he also mediated between the sexes. In his appearance to mortals, he often assumed disguises. Whereas Hermes was the intermediary between heaven and earth, gods and mortals, heroes and their adversaries, and dream and waking, he remained the neutral messenger, siding with neither one state nor the other. In fact, he was amoral, concerned less with goodness and beauty than with delivering his message.

The signature of Hermetic poetry is this neutral, amoral tone, which baffles and even affronts the reader. It enters Irish poetry probably at the publication of Kinsella's *Nightwalker*,[6] with its Joycean interlocutor, persists in Kinsella's subsequent publications, and becomes most audible in *A Technical Supplement*, where the narrator William Skullbullet guides us through the most pathological of the twenty-five poems with a gentle scientific tone so detached it becomes affrontive: 'You will note firstly that there is no containing skin / as we understand it, but "contained" muscle.'[7] He opens another poem apologetically: 'How to put it . . . without offence / even though it is an offence, / monstrous, in itself. / / A living thing swallowing another. / / Lizards:' (KPP, 83). Because the tone of the Hermetic speaker is so noncommittal about the message he brings, the reader is drawn into the moral vacuum.

Insofar as the reader resists this book's encyclopaedic evidence that the life-force in man is worm-blind and ephemeral, to that degree the reader fills the affirmative role of the narrator in conventional poetry. In the nineteenth poem of *A Technical*

Supplement, the Hermetic narrator describes the reader's dynamic role in what he calls 'a serious read':

> getting settled down comfortably for the night
> with a demanding book on your knee
> and your head intent over it,
> eyes bridging the gap, closing a circuit.
>
> Except that it is not a closed circuit,
> more a mingling of lives, worlds simmering
> in the entranced interval: all that you are
> and have come to be
> — or as much as can be brought to bear —
> 'putting on' the fixed outcome of another's
> encounter with what he was
> and had come to be
> impelled him to stop in flux, living,
> and hold that encounter out from
> the streaming away of lifeblood, timeblood,
> a nexus a nexus
> wriggling with life not of our kind.   (KPP, 92)

Whatever or whomever Hermes leads back from the underworld or the land of the dead must reside in the living moment of the poem. Although Kinsella makes frequent reference to the traditional matter of Ireland, material from *The Book of Invasions* or his father's past is clothed in a contemporary dramatic idiom. As Joyce does, the Hermetic poet fulfills Saussure's definition of synchronic literature, as restated by Hugh Kenner: 'all that exists exists only now, and the past is really only as I imagine it.'[8] The seventeenth poem of *A Technical Supplement* illustrates this present tense:

> A smell of hot home-made loaves
> came from the kitchen downstairs.
>
> A sheet of yellowish Victorian thick paper,
> a few spearheads depicted in crusty brown ink
> — Viking remains at Islandbridge —
> added their shiny-stale smell to the baked air
> like dried meat.
>
>   Man-meat, spitted.
> Corpses scattered on the river mud
> in suds of blood, a few here and there
> with broken-off spears buried in them,
> buried with them, preserving the points
> unweathered for a period.

For, let me see . . .
a few years — say a lifetime —
(That bread smells delicious!)
over the even thousand years.   (KPP, 90)

Nothing in Kinsella's language 'whitewashes ugliness' or
'saccharines' the dead, as in *Station Island* Heaney accuses himself
of doing.[9] The elliptical moment of reflection, the intrusive paren-
thetical comment, the adjective 'shiny-stale', which manacles
oxymoronic and synesthetic modifiers with a hyphen, the three
revisions, all contribute to the fugitive quality of the Hermetic
poem.

The gentle tone of our guide through *A Technical Supplement* —
'How to put it . . . without offence', 'Is it all right to do this?'
— with a note of the fastidious anatomist is echoed in Paul
Muldoon's recent volume *Quoof*. Here, the hushed and gentle
first-person conveys shocking or bizarre confessions, as if we
heard over folded hands, Yes Father, 'More and more, I make / do
with her umlaut / / as, more and more, she / turns her back on me
/ / to fumble with / the true Orion's belt'.[11] or, Yes Father, 'Not that
I care who's sleeping with whom / now she's had her womb /
removed, now it lies in its own glar / like the last beetroot in the
pickle jar' (Q, 31). The most disturbing confessions are offered as
generalised warnings of a very specific future to a 'you' or 'we':
'They will seem shy / as they help you with your wrap, / though
their palms are spread / across your breasts. They hail a cab'
(Q, 36). In most of *Quoof's* poems this first-person is a disguise, a
way of rendering specific and dramatic some general expectation
off which the poem plays.

As with its buzz-form 'ludic', 'plays' could misleadingly geld
Muldoon's poetry of serious intention. We need to recognise
how often in this poetry the disruption of habitual modes of
reading introduces us to some new poetic experience. Muldoon
accomplishes this by establishing a decorum of gentle diction
which he will then curdle with an obscene or colloquial phrase.
Often he will begin a poem by plucking the note of rhyme which
he will then abandon as he trades his lyre for the snaky caduceus.
He often teases our formal expectations with spectral sonnets —
conventionally our love poem and autonomous lyric — which are
as tainted as modern love and which, as Geoffrey Stokes has said,
'open and open and open'.[10] For example, in 'Why Brownlee Left'
the final couplet, conventionally a clincher, transforms the sonnet
to a preface:

> By noon Brownlee was famous;
> They had found all abandoned, with
> The last rig unbroken, his pair of black
> Horses, like man and wife,
> Shifting their weight from foot to
> Foot, and gazing into the future.[12]

By rhyming 'foot to' with 'future', he not only translates the word 'enjambment' but also enacts the poem's thrust into uncertainty. As with Kinsella, rarely does Muldoon slam the door on his poem ('The More A Man Has . . .' concludes with 'Huh.').

Muldoon also depends on the reader recognising and reacting to broader generic and social conventions. This becomes most evident in the poem 'Aisling', whose title evokes a visionary poetry about Ireland's political future. Yet, in place of the beautiful personification of Ireland who raised the nationalist hopes, and flesh, of the poets Aogán Ó Rathaille and Eoghan Rua Ó Súilleabháin, the speaker recalls a meeting that promised an erotic harvest: 'Her eyes spoke of a sloe-year, / her mouth a year of haws.' Identified only by the conventional series of anonyms (which includes the unconventional 'Anorexia'), the girl yields the speaker 'a lemon stain on my flannel sheet'. The image repels the reader by confounding the appetites, a frequent nasty practice of Muldoon's, so that in place of fruits we have the symptoms of a venereal disorder, which drives the speaker to the ironic thanksgiving, 'It's all much of a muchness', and to the hospital for a urine test. By metonym rather than overt metaphor the poem draws in a hunger-striker, recovering in a Belfast hospital ward:

> In Belfast's Royal Victoria Hospital
> a kidney machine
> supports the latest hunger-striker
> to have called off his fast, a saline
> drip into his bag of brine.
>
> A lick and a promise. Cuckoo spittle.
> I hand my sample to Doctor Maw.
> She gives me back a confident *All clear.*   (Q, 39)

The Royal Victoria actually employs a Dr. Maw, but the physician's gender has been altered to align her with the visionary woman and to evoke the voracious female principle — Nerthus, the sea-goddess, Cathleen Ni Houlihan — in the work of Heaney, Montague, and earlier Irish poets. Echoing the tannoy's *All Clear,* the last line declares that the speaker and the hunger-striker have survived another 'close call' from the vision of great promise.

The messenger of 'Aisling' becomes more mysterious as he revises our expectations. As with the mysterious narrator in the guise of William Skullbullet (William Shakespeare?), the variable unidentified persona, the neutral tone, the insistence on confronting us with a stark message, the depressed lyricism, and the present tense, all suggest the appropriateness of the Hermes type in characterising the poetry of Kinsella and Muldoon.

A useful category, however, must also exclude, and we may wonder by what means we distinguish the dramatic poetry and depressed lyricism of John Montague and, recently, of Seamus Heaney from the Hermetic poetry of Kinsella and Muldoon. In his two volumes *Field Work* and *Station Island*, Heaney has introduced dramatic voices and a dialogue with past writers so that his poems offer the reader less lyric uniformity and a more dramatic or Joycean or Hermetic disposition. For example, among the dramatic cantos of 'Station Island', the ghost of Kavanagh, who once also wrote of this Lough Derg pilgrimage, croaks these lines: 'Sure I might have known / once I had made the pad, you'd be after me / sooner or later. Forty-two years on / and you've got no farther!' (SI, p. 73). Neither Heaney's nor Kavanagh's most lyrical utterance, the passage demonstrates that Heaney can successfully admit other voices into his poem.

Montague also dramatises his poetry by varying the poetic forms and points of view, as other voices speak through epigraphs, translations, or dramatic monologues. In *The Great Cloak* his other speakers mouth the worn phrases of love which he then can turn and renew. For example, the volume opens with a passage in French from Stendhal of twenty-eight words which is followed by the poet's version of the same idea, rendered in eleven words. Later, a translation of André Frenaud's general statement about love-making is followed by the poet's improved version of the same poem set in a contemporary urban setting. In another poem, he has an abandoned wife say, 'But I have lost both faith and hope, and live on sufferance, an old tower crumbling by the water's edge'.[13] Again, Montague renews the tired image of the tower by transforming it to a lighthouse or signal tower:

> Upstairs my wife & daughter sleep.
> Our two lives have separated now
> But I would send my voice to yours
> Cutting through the shrouding mist
> Like some friendly signal in distress.   (MGC, p. 61)

Ultimately, the volume dramatises the play between sympathy and the limits of language in expressing another's emotions. The wife's plea in the beautiful poem 'Herbert Street Revisited' — 'don't betray our truth' (MGC, 41) — contains a double irony. In one sense the entire volume attempts this betrayal, but ultimately it honours the silence at the emotional centre of the former wife's story. Montague once praised John Berryman's attempt at emotional biography in *Homage of Mistress Bradstreet*, admiring especially the book's 'relentless seriousness which drives it towards the limits of communication. One cannot', he continued, 'penetrate the secret and total meaning of another's life . . .'.[14] This gesturing toward silence, of Berryman and Montague, is an Hermetic function.

Less overtly than in *The Great Cloak*, Montague dramatises his account of the Northern crisis in *The Rough Field* where the poet's spare, beautiful commentary is interrupted by voices from historical documents, old periodicals, Protestant propaganda, and the journal of an uncle, Thomas Montague, S.J. As we adjust to the various speakers and identify the shifting tones, we develop the illusion that the book has said much more than the poet himself has said. In praising Montague's mixture of voices in *The Rough Field*, Thomas Dillon Redshaw has recognised its American influences: 'Montague's ten cantos and epilogue surely adapt to an Irish setting the poetic means of the American epic devised by Whitman and refined in William Carlos Williams's *Paterson*.'[15] Montague himself has acknowledged Williams's impact in words rather like those of Kinsella when he explained that finally 'hearing the American voice in Williams' was 'the single most helpful thing . . . It's been a sort of leverage out of a rather clamped tradition — with very few exits for poetry — into a state of thinking, and attitude where anything is possible'.[16] It seems likely that the example of Williams's dramatic speakers and suppressed lyricism were as helpful as Kavanagh's example in liberating Montague and Kinsella from the hieratic tone and logocentric statements of Yeats's verse.

In the light of these acknowledgements, what we have labelled Hermetic — poetry that employs a mysterious persona or various dramatic speakers rather than a recognisable and consistent narrator, that suppresses the persuasive force of music and rhetoric, and that tends to be synchronic rather than diachronic — may be seen merely as an Americanised reaction to Yeats. Whereas Yeats proclaimed his loyalty 'To gradual Time's last gift, a written speech / Wrought of high laughter, loveliness and ease',

Williams advertised America as 'the place where one might reasonably expect to find the instability in the language where innovation would be at home',[17] in words that phrase positively Stephen Dedalus's concern in *A Portrait* that the Irish writer must labour fretfully in the shadow of an acquired speech.[18] Williams's statement also clarifies Kinsella's praise of Williams and reminds us that occasional flat diction and broken rhythms of Kinsella and Montague, which earn their place in a larger context of a sequence of poems, may also follow an American strategy recommended by Robert Duncan:

Were all in harmony to our ears, we would dwell in the dreadful smugness in which our mere human rationality relegates what it cannot cope with to the 'irrational', as if the totality of creation were without ratios. Praise then the interruption of our composure, the image that comes to fit we cannot account for, the juncture in the music that appears discordant.[19]

American influences have even added a pewtery patina to Heaney's silver verse, although his models — Frost, Lowell, and Bishop — mediate between the polarities of Williams's and Eliot's dictions. The opening of Heaney's 'Elegy' to Robert Lowell — 'The way we are living, / timorous or bold, / will have been our life. / Robert Lowell',[20] — pays the ultimate tribute of imitation to Heaney's American fosterer by setting aside Heaney's habitual rich poetic texture. In some of the relatively spare lyrics of *Field Work,* we sense also the influence of Elizabeth Bishop's laconic line.

However, although the suppressed lyricism and dramatised narration distinguishes the verse of Montague and, more recently, Heaney from that of Yeats, Higgins, and early Heaney, it is not as bridled as Williams's verse or as horsepowerless as that of some of Williams's American descendants, nor is it, finally, Hermetic. Regardless of how often we are diverted by lyric understatement and dramatic speakers, at the heart of Montague's and Heaney's volume is the lyric poet, our Orphic guide through the rough field or the purgatorial stations. For example, even in Heaney's most dramatic volume, *Station Island*, we take comfort from the resurfacing of a recognisable narrator: 'I came as Hansel came on the moonlit stones / Retracing the path back, lifting the buttons / . . . / . . . the wet track / Bared and tensed as I am, all attention / For your step following and damned if I look back' ('The Underground', SI, 13). Such an Orphic voice we follow with confidence, just the sort of confidence undermined by the sinister gentility of Kinsella's narrator — 'How to put it . . . without offence' — or of Muldoon's — 'His head, when we come to examine the head / we would never allow ourselves to touch' (Q, 21). Yet, questions of comfort in art, the requirements that art provide solace (entertainment) and sententia (moral instruction) seem less compelling in a world of unstable moral footing than the requirement that the poem put us in contact with the truth of that real world. We may recall that, when Orpheus failed to save his beloved Eurydice, it was the psychopomp Hermes who drew her to the light.

As if to confirm the utility of the type of Hermes, both Kinsella and Muldoon overtly invoke him in long poems. Kinsella's *The Messenger* employs a speaker who seems, at first reading, too optimistic and committed to qualify as the amoral Hermes. I once suggested to Kinsella himself that this volume might mollify such critics as Calvin Bedient and Helen Vendler who find Kinsella's work too bitter. Dedicated to Kinsella's father, who died in 1976, the book recounts five episodes in his father's life which, if arranged chronologically from youthful expectation to embittered old age, might recount the plot of any ironic bildungsroman such as *L'Education Sentimentale* or *The Way Of All Flesh*. Rather, *The Messenger* devolves from morbid reflections about John Kinsella's corpse back through the stages of his life to arrive at the image of his first day of his first employment as a telegraph delivery boy:

> A new messenger boy
> stands there in uniform, with shining belt!
>
> He is all excitement: arms akimbo,
> a thumb crooked by the telegram pouch,
> shoes polished, and a way to make in the world.   (KPP, 133)

By reversing chronology, Kinsella frees his father from both burial plot and the plot of his failed life to stand as the type of fresh beginning, reborn in the grandchildren who gather about his coffin at his funeral. Literally, he is the messenger and first reference of the title.

At my praise of his long poem as a palliative, Kinsella smiled and reminded me that it was only this poetic form that had recovered his father's youthful hopefulness from annihilation. Kinsella, then, would see the tone as a dramatic adaptation to the 'what if' fiction of his poem. Consequently, on another level, the poet becomes the messenger, leading the soul up from the land of the dead and preserving it within the intermediacy of the poem. This idea is reinforced on the original cover of this volume by the substitution of Mercury or Hermes for the Christian icon that graced the cover of the Catholic journal *The Messenger*, poetry replacing religion as conductor of the dead.

   Within the long poem, certain images that suddenly shift the poem from one level of consciousness to another, which I have called in my own book 'hinged images', may be seen as hermetic intermediaries between states. For example, the volume opens with the poet passing from sleep to waking, as he does at the opening of a previous volume *One*, with 'Deeper. A suspicion in the bones / as though they too could melt in filth' and with disturbing images of his father's corpse:

> A moist movement within.
> A worm winds on its hoard.
> A rim of hide lifts like a lip.
>
> A dead egg glimmers — a peal in muck
> glimpsed only as the muck settles.
> The belly settles and crawls tighter.   (KPP, 119)

The maggot egg suggests the pearl buried with bodies in Laos to encourage rebirth. It also represents the concentrated residue of the father's youthful aspirations —

> (a cyst, in effect, of the subject's aspirations
> painful with his many disappointments)
> absorbs into the psyche, where it sleeps.   (KPP, 124)

— and therefore the 'eggseed Goodness'.

   Midway through the long poem, at the moment of the poet's conception the egg image metamorphoses, becoming a dragon-fly, a spermatozoon, and, by implication, the messenger:

> A gossamer ghost arrows and hesitates
>
> out of the reeds, and stands in the air above them
> insect-shimmering, and settles on a bright
> inner upturn of her dress. The wings
>
> close up like palms. The body, a glass worm,
> is pulsing. The tail-tip winces and quivers:
>
> I think this is where I come in . . .   (KPP, 129)

Into the present moment of the synchronic poem, the dragonfly brings its 'saw-jawed multiple past' of cocoon, larva, and imago, the genetic code by which the past enters the present. The dragonfly image provides the reader with instant transport between the romantic riverbank idyll and a complex world of evolutionary history and therefore may itself be a version of Hermes as psychopomp, whom Karl Kerenyi describes as 'the messenger and mediator, . . . the hoverer-between-worlds who dwells in a world of his own'.[21]

The spirit of Hermes also hovers above Paul Muldoon's long narrative 'The More A Man Has the More A Man Wants', which concludes *Quoof*. First, a human shape-changer is the protagonist of his poem, comprising forty-nine sections, whose fourteen-liners play all of the changes on the sonnet-form. Gallogly — a.k.a. Golightly, Ingoldsby, English, gallowglass, the Green Knight, and Sweeney — shares the central role with a Sioux or Apache who is his dope-dealer, contact man, assassin, or, if we track the pronoun-references from the second to third stanzas or see a shadowy anagram in the tribal name Oglala, a version of himself. Gallogly's actions are set in contemporary Belfast, the orchards of Armagh (near Muldoon's childhood home), and, transported by drugs and art, or, as Muldoon would have it, by an aisling,[22] to New York and Boston — in other words, the theatre of the Troubles or stages of a universal condition of violence.

So confident is the narrative of 'The More A Man Has . . .' so instant and confidential the transitions, as if we are all in on the joke (it's our choice to be or not), so clear the imagery and fragments of scenes, and so rapid the cinemagraphic jump-cuts that we experience delight and anxiety before enlightenment. An allusion to Frost in 'a pebble of quartz' with which the poem opens and closes teases us with the possibility that any truth we may see in the poem is merely a reflection of ourselves. However, the poem does convey meaning. As Adrian Frazier has wisely stated, 'We have been given the whole texture of a political world and an implicit judgment of it. We have been denied a simple answer but we have been granted an understanding'.[23]

We recover some of Muldoon's intention, nevertheless, from Faber & Faber's jacket blurb, which relates the poet's assertion that his narrative has parallels to the Winnebago Indians' Trickster cycle. Certain of Gallogly's actions duplicate those of the 'Foolish One, Trickster',[24] who is called 'the oldest of all figures in American Indian mythology, probably in all mythologies'.[25] Just as Trickster wars with his own body, handwrestling with himself or burning his own offending anus, so Gallogly 'seizes his own wrist' and 'stares in disbelief / at an Aspirin-white spot he pressed / into his own palm' (Q, 45) or advances into shotgun range 'led by his own wet nose' (Q, 45). What reviewers have seen as Gallogly's masturbation in section 18, where he takes cock in hand 'and then, with a birl and a skirl, / tosses it off like a caber' (Q, 48), more closely approximates Trickster's courtship of an Indian princess by fly-casting his penis across a pond.[26] That Gallogly accompanies a woman in her Winnebago camper further aligns him with Trickster. Other shape-changers are evoked. The epigraph extends the source to a shamanistic legend of the Netselik Eskimos in which a female shaman transmogrifies snow into a dog and herself into a man.

Trickster has been unmasked as the Indian form of Hermes by anthropologists and mythographers such as Karl Kerenyi and Carl Jung. Kerenyi's identification — 'In the playful cruelties which the little god practised . . . which conferred no benefit on mankind . . ., we see the sly fact of the trickster grinning at us'[27] — might easily be extended to Gallogly. Yet, Gallogly hardly serves as a messenger or go-between, functions of Hermes we might assign to the Indian Mangas Jones or, more appropriately, to the metaphorical and narrative techniques of this poem. For example, when Gallogly fails to aspirate the Heaneyish dialectical word *sheugh*, the narration shifts into a parody of Heaney's *Sweeney* which is interrupted by a tale from Ovid in which the goddess Leto metamorphoses some stingy reed-cutters into bullfrogs. Although Leto's feat is formidable, the principal shape-changer and psychopomp must be the poetic narrator who can quickly transport us from city to city, country to country, or text to text (we also enter the worlds of Hawthorne, Gertrude Stein, Lewis Carroll, Robert Louis Stevenson, Castaneda, and others).

The narrator's Hermetic agents are the metaphor and simile which may hasten a transition (e.g. 'three miles west as the crow flies' [Q41] not only shifts the scene but insinuates also Ted Hughes's Trickster) or, more often, 'go between' a pastoral or artistic setting and the arena for guerrilla warfare. For example, a bomb-blast victim's dismembered foot is compared to 'a severely pruned-back shrub'; arterial blood spouts 'like an overturned paraffin lamp'; Gallogly's site of ambush is an Edward Hopper rendering of gas station; and Gallogly enters the U.S. by stepping through the carnage of Picasso's 'Guernica'. Because through metaphor the benign and the bloody are yoked by violence together, our habitual and comfortable disposition toward the domestic and everyday, which is evoked by precise images, is continually violated. In this Hermetic poem, the benign face of the world seems only a disguise.

In an essay in the *London Review of Books*, John Kerrigan placed Muldoon's poetry in the forefront of what he called 'the New Narrative' which he defined in the following terms: 'Reflexive, aleatory, and cornucopian, the New Narrative deploys its fragmented and ramifying fictions to image the unpredictability of life, and its continuous shadowing of What Might Be.'[28] Kerrigan's terms seem to duplicate those of Kerenyi when he describes the function of the Trickster myth:

Disorder belongs to the totality of life, and the spirit of this disorder is the trickster . . . The function of his mythology, of the tales told about him, is to add disorder to order and so make a whole, to render possible, within the fixed bounds of what is permitted, an experience of what is not permitted.[29]

By defying our lyrical, formal, and contextual expectations, Muldoon expresses 'what is not permitted': he conveys the randomness of political and sexual violence without invoking their binary rationalisations, without ratifying, in Seamus Heaney's words, 'the sectarian categories which had us where we were'.[30]

Beyond the overextended colonial troubles in Ireland, ontological considerations also contribute to the tone of Hermetic poetry. When Kerenyi speaks of the transformation of chance and mischance into 'hermetic art . . . love, poetry, and all the ways of escape from the narrow confines of law, custom, circumstance, fate',[31] he also reminds us that the Hermetic poet, such as Muldoon and Kinsella, acknowledges the limitations of language to convey our reality and answers the overstated appeals of deconstructionist critics for a demolition and restructuring of our very terms of reference. In so far as the Hermetic poets are answering, as well, the appeals of Deane for everything in Irish literature to be rewritten and reread, to that extent we suspect also that the father of the Derry-based Field Day is Derrida.

It may be that the destruction and revision of Irish literature is a creative rather than a critical act and that the radical deconstructionists have always been Hermetic writers such as Villon, Rabelais, Donne, Swift, Sterne, Blake, Baudelaire, Muldoon, Kinsella, and, to return to our beginning, Joyce. When in *Ulysses* Stephen Dedalus reflects on 'Thoth, God of libraries, a birdgod, moonycrowned. And I heard the voice of that Egyptian highpriest', whom in *Finnegans Wake* Joyce calls 'my shemblable! My freer!',[32] he invokes the Egyptian alias of that god of shape-changers, the truthful go-between Hermes.

A QUESTION OF IMAGINATION — POETRY IN IRELAND TODAY

GERALD DAWE

I

In this essay my main concern is with the public face of poetry in Ireland rather than with a specific analysis of this poet or that poem. It is doubtful whether one can ever really separate the two, so that in discussing their relatedness I hope to show how a poet's identity *as a poet* is influenced by several literary, cultural and social assumptions about what poetry is and what 'being a poet' means.

I am mindful of the dangers in approaching my subject in this way — the poem can evaporate into an abstract Poetry, and there is also the pitfall to which the Russian poet and critic, Osip Mandelstam referred in his essay of 1922, 'On the Nature of the Word':

If one listens to literary historians who defend evolutionism, it would appear that writers think only about how to clear the road for their successors, but never about how to accomplish their own tasks; or it would appear that they are all participants in an inventors competition for the improvement of some literary machine, although none of them knows the whereabouts of the judges or what purposes the machine serves.[1]

As someone who writes poems and also writes about poetry, I hope I am sufficiently wary of this 'theory' which Mandelstam justifiably calls 'the crudest, most repugnant form of academic ignorance'. He describes its failure in the following terms:

In literature nothing is ever 'better', no progress can be made simply because there is no literary machine and no finish line toward which everyone must race as rapidly as possible. This meaningless theory of improvement is not even applicable to the style and form of individual writers, for here as well, each gain is accompanied by a loss or forfeit.

186

So while there is, as Mandelstam maintains, no inevitable progress in literature, it is fair to say that various conventions and pressures can get in the way, restricting and weakening the integrity of poets and poetry to accomplish their fullest potential. I would like to concentrate upon one of these factors, the thematic bias of much contemporary poetry in Ireland.

I mean by thematic bias those *clichés* of history through which poetry is both written and read in Ireland. The persistent concern with 'Identity', for instance, strikes me as being most characteristic of the recent period; of brooding upon what 'Irishness' means and what it is not. Poetry is taken as a central means towards negotiating this definition in, for example, its celebration of Irish landscape, or in the conveyancing of that landscape through the Irish language into the poetic forms of English. Uniting both points is the pervasive assumption that History is a terrible home for all Irish poets, the nightmare from which they must escape, like the archetypal artist-figure Stephen Dedalus. Feeding into this convention are various influences, one of the most important of which is that we have a *naturally* poetic language because of the once central influence of the Irish language upon English as it is spoken in the country. While this may well be true in regard to common speech, it is essential to state the obvious here, that whatever benefits a poet can make out of this rich linguistic resource, they will not amount to much unless the poet possesses the necessarily imaginative rigour to use them effectively.

One thinks of Flannery O'Connor's remarks when addressing a Southern American Writers Conference on 'the gifts of the region', by which she meant speech, contrast, irony and contradiction:

... you [may] have seen these gifts abused so often that you have become self-conscious about using them. There is nothing worse than the writer who doesn't *use* the gifts of the region, but wallows in them.[2]

In Ireland it is possible to relate this question to the way in which 'poetic' language is itself seen as a natural refuge, or homeplace, for the poet. Language becomes a message from History which the poet receives and transcribes through the medium of vowel, consonant and assonance:

> The tawny guttural water
> spells itself: Moyola
> is its own score and consort,

> bedding the locale,
> in the utterance,
> reed music, an old chanter
>
> breathing its mists
> through vowels and history.
> A swollen river,
>
> a mating call of sound
> rises to pleasure me, Dives,
> hoarder of common ground.[3]

The colloquialism of idiom and image becomes an eloquent defining point of the poetry and not the other way around. The pivotal metaphorical figure is in a place-name (Moyola) and clustered around it the images gather from Nature (the river), its voice (reed music) and the traditional Irish musical instrument (the Uilean pipes) into a summarising of 'vowels and history' and the completion of 'pleasure' for the rich man, Dives, 'hoarder of common ground'. These cyphers of meaning become rhetorical and the sentiment conventional in the hands of lesser poets than Seamus Heaney.

Literary precedence can be found, as Daniel Hoffman has remarked, in Yeats and latter-day Romanticism where

> . . . local-color writing celebrated the individualities of particular places, and gloried in whatever dialectical speech or surviving antiquities of custom or belief could be offered to prove the uniqueness of life in a given locality. Such a course, while risking quaintness, could put into a writer's hands ancient traditions as yet untouched by the mechanical forces of change since the Industrial Revolution. But in Ireland the impetus toward the literary uses of such material was not only from Romantic nostalgia. From the beginnings, the local-color movement had an overt political significance.[4]

The contemporary risk is thematic predictability, with the result that the poetry loses out to a liturgical nostalgia which serves 'political significance' in the end.[5] Men and their physical environments recede into the folklore of locale and placenames.[6] Or to paraphrase the German poet Heine, poetry is lost in 'green lies', susceptible to the 'fake greenishness' of landscape poetry.[7]

II

In a very useful review of new poetry in *Stand Magazine*, Terry Eagleton referred to the 'paradigm poem' and, giving an example from Paul Muldoon's *Quoof*, went on to say:

. . . the poem trades entirely on the intrinsic interest of its materials rather than on any imaginative transformation it submits them to . . . It is sentimentalism to believe that memories are valuable in themselves . . . To write of regional memories . . . is often enough a way of evading struggle with meaning, for such lovingly preserved experiences seem deceptively meaningful in themselves, and the act of narrating them assumes an auratic significance for which it has not sufficiently paid.[8]

The significance which Eagleton is scrutinising here comes from, in his estimation, an assumption that 'the close rendering of an experience is somehow *inherently* meaningful; and this assumption survives only because the urban English reader will tend to collude with it, believing that an experience remote from him/ herself — milking a cow, confronting the B-specials — is somehow more inherently significant than one more routinely familiar'. Eagleton approaches this relationship between experience and language from another angle when he writes in *Literary Theory: An Introduction* that if we

. . . understand the 'intentions' of a piece of language, we interpret it as being in some sense *oriented*, structured to achieve certain effects; and none of this can be grasped apart from the practical conditions in which the language operates. It is to see language as practice rather than as object; and there are of course no practices without human subjects.[9]

I think this is a most convincing argument and when applied to Irish poetry it is interesting to note that one of the more discernible trends is away from the use of language as practice towards viewing language in a static sense, as a sacred object. The poet communes with and through language to form an abstract and rhetorical recognition out of his/her own poetic consciousness. It is in Tom Paulin's 'voicing the word *nation*':

> I'm tense now: talk of sharing power,
> prophecies of civil war,
> new reasons for a secular
> mode of voicing the word *nation*
> set us on edge, this generation,
> and force the poet to play traitor
> or act the half-sure legislator.[10]

It is in John Montague's naming of places:

> . . . we leave, waving
> a plume of black smoke
> over the rushy meadows,
> small hills & hidden villages —
> Beragh, Carrickmore,
> Pomeroy, Fintona —
> placenames that sigh
> like a pressed melodeon
> across this forgotten
> Northern landscape.[11]

Seamus Heaney's work is generally acknowledged for the exemplary nature of precisely this kind of poetic consciousness. Take 'Anahorish' for example:

> My 'place of clear water',
> the first hill in the world
> where springs washed into
> shiny grass
>
> and darkened cobbles
> in the bed of the lane.
> *Anahorish*, soft gradient
> of consonant, vowel-meadow,
>
> after-image of lamps
> swung through the yards
> on winter evenings.
> With pails and barrows
>
> those mound-dwellers
> go waist-deep in mist
> to break the light ice
> at wells and dunghills.[12]

This is a perfect illustration of the way *one* central theme in Heaney's poetry marks out language as an object and of how the poet defines his self and his past in that special pastoral awareness of his own place through a metaphorical appropriation of its idiom.[13] Heaney's *Station Island*[14] shifts this preoccupation on to those occasions, real and imagined, when the poet succumbs to the poetry-making, as he states in 'The Loaning', 'I knew/I was in the limbo of lost words', or in 'Making Strange':

> I found myself driving the stranger
>
> through my own country, *adept*
> *at dialect*, reciting my pride
> in all that I knew, that began to make strange
> at that same recitation.[15]

Heaney's poems consolidate this process of treating language as an object in that he considers his relation to the very experiences he is writing about *as a poet*. The sequence 'Station Island' seeks to sort out an appropriate place for the poet, one that is adequate to both the world he presently inhabits and the world of his past. My own reading of *Station Island* is that the book represents this particular poetic self-consciousness as confining. It makes Heaney concentrate much more upon the fact that he is writing, rather than upon what he is actually writing about. Perhaps this is the likely result if we bear in mind again the perspective that Terry Eagleton offers in the above quotations. For if language becomes an object in the poet's hands, the occasion of his writing will be viewed with equal importance and by its very literariness this focuses on the poet and the personality of his or her own artistic self in relaying the poem to us:

> Then I sat there writing, imagining in silence
> sounds like love sounds after long abstinence,
> eager and absorbed and capable
> under the sign of a snowshoe on a wall.
>
> The loop of the snowshoe, like an old-time kite,
> lifts away in a wind and is lost to sight.
> Now I sit blank as gradual morning brightens
> its distancing, inviolate expanse.[16]

It is on these three themes that much of the attention given to Irish poetry is centred. The critical perspectives converge upon where the poet fits into public debate (Paulin's 'prophecies of civil war'), the delineation of nostalgic landscapes of home (Montague's 'small hills & hidden villages') and the sense of being a poet in the first place (Heaney's 'I sat there writing, imagining in silence').

In Ireland, too, there is the widely-held perception of the poet as some kind of public figure who, in regards to both his social life and beliefs, voices on behalf of 'The People' an accessible articulation of their spiritual and cultural beliefs. This stereotypical image of the Poet as a public figure is possibly derived from the populist context in which Irish poetry in English first developed, from the mid-19th to the early part of the 20th century. However, the fact there are now dramatically changed social and cultural conditions, wherein complex and contradictory ideals conflict, does not seem to have substantially altered this perception of the Poet. It may well be another remnant of that Romantic idealism to which Daniel Hoffman refers; in this instance, of seeing the poet as a sensitive soul, damaged at birth by a fragmented inheritance, bearing artistically the scars of an inadequate Irish cultural milieu. A failure, in other words, not of our own making, but of England's; their language, imposed on ours; their culture forced upon us.

This conventional and normative view still obtains in Ireland and poetry internalises the vision, transforming it into an acceptable myth which sustains the generally accepted cultural and politico-religious dogmas of modern Ireland.[17] As Sean O'Faolain remarked in his book *The Irish*, Irish writers from about '1890 to about 1940'

. . . saw Irish life, in the main, romantically. It was as a poetic people that they first introduced themselves to the world, and it is as a poetic people that they are still mainly known abroad.[18]

Poetry itself continues to be seen in this light, both in Ireland and elsewhere, as having a place not so much imaginatively *questioning* reality, but rather in *naturalising* the traditional and inherited ways of reading it. An attitude, I am sure, which comes from the political nature of Irish life where a homogeneous cultural nationalism holds sway and is mediated through the established images and modes of writing.

It is noticeable then that, given the crisis-prone history of contemporary Ireland, with its proverbial emphasis on 'Identity', traditional roles have asserted themselves in the poet's own work and the audience's expectations of that work. This conformity is an illustration of how generally acceptable that tradition is to poets. An artistic need to challenge it often occurs in poets who endeavour to examine those areas of freedom (personal as much as social) which are available to them in the context of the literary and historical conditions of modern Ireland.

III

Thomas Kinsella's 'Nightwalker' (1986), for example, retains its sharp critical edge and relevance as a major exploration of modern Irish experience and feeling:

> The officials on the corridors or in their rooms
> Work, or overwork, with mixed motives
> Or none. We dwell together in urgency;
> Dominate, entering middle age; subserve,

> Aborting vague tendencies with buttery smiles.
> Among us, behind locked doors, the ministers
> Are working, with a sureness of touch found early
> In the nation's birth — the blood of enemies
> And brothers dried on their hide long ago.
> Dragon old men, upright and stately and blind,
> Or shuffling in the corridor finding a key,
> Their youth cannot die in them; it will be found
> Beating with violence when their bodies rot.[19]

Kinsella's solitary anticipation of the issue of 'Identity', that governs so much of the current discussion about literature and Ireland, well repays attention today. In his 1966 address to the Modern Language Association in New York, for instance, he states:

It is not as though literature, or national life, were a corporate, national investigation of a corporate national experience — as though the nation were a single animal, with one complex artistic feeler.[20]

In stating this basic fact, Kinsella also picked out the essential condition of any poet writing today:

... every writer in the modern world — since he can't be in all the literary traditions at once — is the inheritor of a gapped, discontinuous, polyglot tradition ... Nevertheless, if the function of tradition is to link us living with the significant past, this is done as well by a broken tradition as by a whole one ...

It is the imaginative exploration of this condition that distinguishes the best of Kinsella's poems, as it is with the poetry of Derek Mahon. His poetry, it can be said, composes that 'gapped, discontinuous, polyglot tradition' to which Kinsella alludes. For Mahon brings into creative alignment with our own time a whole range of writers from Brecht and Pasternak to Gerard de Nerval, and his particular accomplishment has been the way he has discovered a *poetic* voice to achieve these new imaginative perspectives. It is a poetry of manner highly-tense yet balanced, and formally set within the conditions of definite times and places, but ineluctably leading out of these to wider questions, thoughts and feelings. By its very composure, Mahon's austerity of language rebukes sentimentality and denies any appeal to rhetoric. This incontrovertible restraint energises the poetry, drawing its forcefulness from the poet speaking his mind;

When I returned one year ago
I felt like Tonio Kroger — slow
To come to terms with my own past
Yet knowing I could never cast
Aside the things that made me what,
For better or worse, I am. The upshot?
Chaos and instability,
The cool gaze of the RUC.[21]

Feelings here are held in reserve, as a private matter mostly, but the actual world, which is being scrutinised in a dynamic way, includes the poet's sense of himself. This form of imaginative address can, in turn, be contrasted with the substantive formal disintegration one finds in the poetry of Padraic Fiacc.[22] Ironically, at a time when extensive discussion surrounds Irish literature, of how it relates to History and of how the present crisis has challenged the poet's imagination, Fiacc is rarely mentioned. Questions should be asked why this is so since his work, on every conceivable artistic level of style and content, records the collapse of a society, its past and the nature of its contradictory ideals. Perhaps one reason for this failure of criticism relates to the kind of traditional relationship which exists between an Irish (or British) poet and his audience. Fiacc's poetry mocks this relationship and brings seriously into question the poet's place as regards a society (like Northern Ireland's) which lurches from crisis to crisis. It is a poetry that has little in common with the well-intentioned decorum that underlies the following comment from the introduction to *The Penguin Book of Contemporary British Poetry*:

It is interesting to speculate on the relationship between the resurgence of Northern Irish writing and the Troubles. The poets have all experienced a sense of 'living in important places' and have been under considerable pressure to 'respond'. They have been brought hard up against questions about the relationship between art and politics, between conscious 'making' and intuitive 'inspiration'. But on the whole they have avoided a poetry of directly documentary reportage.[23]

Speculations apart, Fiacc's poems have, for the past three decades, carried the marks of disaffection, prejudice and hope that are embedded in ordinary Northern Irish speech and idiom, and have formally and experimentally balanced the conscious 'making', the intuitive 'inspiration' *with* a poetry of 'directly documentary reportage'. Perhaps Fiacc's position is explainable in similar terms to Raymond Williams's remark about Thomas Hardy being 'very disturbing for someone trying to rationalize refined, civilized, balancing judgment. Hardy exposes so much that cannot be displaced from its social situation, particularly in the later books'.[24] Indeed Fiacc's later work, in particular, sympathetically and critically explores the social, cultural and religious situation and the illusions fostered by both sides in the Northern conflict. This makes an exceptional witness out of his poetry rather than making it a testament to 'living in important places'.[25] His poetry is important precisely because it *revokes* those very notions and assumptions that I have looked at earlier in this essay by subverting them and leaving in their place little by way of *traditional* aesthetic consolation. Instead we find a harrowing act of imaginative redemption or an image bordering on what is grotesquely, comically human. Fiacc's poem 'The Wearing of the Black', for instance, mediates between the formal family scene of himself as a boy, 'like the Prince of Wales' listening to his mother playing the piano, and the knowledgeable background of his father *'gone to America for / He is on the bloody run!'* The recollected music of 'See the Conquering Hero Comes' and 'Blue Bell of Scotland' gives way as the awkward young boy drops a porcelain teacup:

Now

Near half a century after, why
Can I recall that flash of fire
On the tile floor as I scalded my bare
Knees when I pray to care even

That this rotting self-dinner-jack
-eted hero's grave, tonight in black
Cuff links (sparkle like hand cuffs)

At least has the wit to dress for death.[26]

The clash between these two worlds of the past and present is characteristic of Fiacc's poetry, as is the culminating wry portrait that links both worlds together in a new and disturbing perspective. It is as if nothing ever changes, only the ways and our ability to remember. The 'political situation', as Milan Kundera reminds us, 'has brutally illuminated the ordinary metaphysical problem of forgetting that we face all the time, every day, without paying any attention. Politics unmasks the metaphysics of private life, private life unmasks the metaphysics of politics'.[27] Possibly another reason for Fiacc's neglect is that his poetry unceasingly reasserts the unpalatable truthfulness of Kundera's statement.

Indeed there is a 'political' consciousness in Fiacc's poetry, an appropriate rhetoric, which brings his work much closer to European and American models than it is to English poetry. This only further underlies his comparative isolation as a strangely modernistic voice while he completes his work-in-progress, 'Missa Terribilis', in the form of a traditional Mass.[28]

I see, however, in the poetry of Padraic Fiacc, Thomas Kinsella and Derek Mahon, as well as in some of their younger contemporaries such as Paul Durcan, a relative freedom from the kind of public conformations and conventions that I have briefly noted as significant in the poetry of John Montague, Seamus Heaney and Tom Paulin. The poetic fruits of this freedom are found in the poet's own ironic, *critical* and questioning relationship with the details of his individual experience, feelings and ideas, and of how rigorously these are probed in and through his poetry. This is a valuable, if sometimes obscured, development: an imaginative negotiation that takes into account the Ireland we actually live in and the image poetry presents of it, along with all the other things that a poet needs to imagine.

HEARTH AND HISTORY: POETRY BY CONTEMPORARY IRISH WOMEN

ARTHUR E. McGUINNESS

If one were to judge the importance of poetry by Irish women from any of the standard anthologies such as *The Faber Book of Irish Verse* (1974), *Irish Poetry After Yeats* (1979), or *Poets From the North of Ireland* (1979), one would have to conclude that the contribution of women to twentieth-century Irish poetry has been meagre. In the recent McHugh and Harmon *Short History of Anglo-Irish Literature* (1982), poetry by contemporary Irish women is virtually ignored. In the last paragraph of a lengthy discussion of recent Irish poets, McHugh and Harmon mention 'Eilean Ní Chuilleánain's natural metaphysics' and 'Eavan Boland's notations of feminine concerns'. Poetry by contemporary Irish women deserves more substantial treatment.

Three Irish poets, Eithne Strong, Eavan Boland, and Medbh McGuckian, explore the complex question of being a woman and a poet. Each of these poets has had a significant poetic career to date. Strong, born in 1923, published *Songs of Living* in 1961, and *Sarah, In Passing* in 1974. Boland, born in 1944, published her first volume of poetry, *New Territory*, in 1967, followed by *The War Horse* (1975), *In Her Own Image* (1980), and *Night Feed* (1982). McGuckian, born in 1950, first published in a collection of poems in *Trio Poetry 2* (1981). This was followed by *The Flower Master* (1982), and *Venus and the Rain* (1984).

Hearth and history provide a context for these poets. Strong and Boland are inspired by both subjects, by the domestic and by the cultural. Their poetry typically has an Irish quality, whether this quality be the Celtic landscape which still manifests the ancient culture, the alienating suburban places which encourage one to forget one's cultural roots, their children who have traditional Irish names, demystified horses in city streets that can still evoke the old glories from time to time, or the old stories themselves which may at times still be vivid and evocative, and at other times mere nostalgia. Medbh McGuckian has a very different

197

orientation from Strong and Boland, so different in fact that one would be hard-pressed to identify her as an 'Irish' poet were it not for the fact she was born and lives in Ulster. One does find 'history' in her poems, but not the history of Irish battles, Celtic heroes, Risings against the British. Her poems probe the psyche, the depths of the unconscious, the sources of creativity.

All three poets have distinctly feminine perspectives. Eavan Boland has written several poems about painting which note the dominance of male painters in the history of art from the Renaissance to the Impressionists, painters such as Van Eyck, Degas, Ingres, Renoir. Women were painted by these artists in traditional domestic or agrarian postures. Boland herself perceives woman as far less sanitised and submissive. Her collection *In Her Own Image* (1980) introduces such shocking and taboo subjects as anorexia, mastectomy, masturbation, and menstruation. Several of the poems have accompanying line drawings which effectively support these candid poems. The drawings are by a woman. Both poems and drawings subvert the romantic conventions. Eithne Strong also has a startling candour as a poet. She writes about one of her children who is retarded, about her own continued battle with being overweight, and about the dismaying physical symptoms of ageing and dying. Medbh McGuckian's poetry is the most consistently 'domestic' of the three. Most of her poems are set in houses or gardens and have such titles as 'Flower Master', 'Mr. McGregor's Garden', 'The Sofa', 'For the Previous Owner'. McGuckian perceives the mythic in woman, house, and garden. 'Venus and the Rain', the title poem of her second volume, suggests this mythic vision.

Looking at typical poems by these three poets will give the reader a better sense of each poet's view of 'woman'. For Eithne Strong one can consider the following poems from her first volume *Songs of Living*: 'Synthesis: Achill 1958', 'A Woman Unleashed', 'When Men Don't Love', and 'Woman'; and from *Sarah, In Passing*: 'Hater's Hymn' and 'Credo'. For Eavan Boland, representative poems would be 'Night Feed', 'Domestic Interior', 'It's a Woman's World', and 'New Pastoral', (*Night Feed*), and the entire volume *In Her Own Image*, because it is conceived of as a single long poem. Medbh McGuckian's views about female identity can be grasped by looking at groups of poems which deal with three aspects of womanhood: first, the analogy to the cosmos (the Venus poems — 'Venus and the Sun', 'A Day With Her', 'Venus and the Rain'); second, the relation of art and life ('The Rising Out', 'Ode to a Poetess', 'Painter and Poet'); third, a woman's instinctive relation to domestic places ('The Flower Master', 'Collusion', 'The Mast Year', 'Sabbath Park').

In his introduction to Eithne Strong's first volume *Song of Living*, Padraic Colum expresses admiration for what he calls the 'Spae-Woman' quality in the poems, the runic character of these short lyrics which seem to be uttered more by priestess, druidess, or sybil than by a mortal woman.

I find it hard to describe the effect that these runes have on me. At its strongest the effect comes from a sense of solitariness: the voice has the tone of one who lives outside companies. The solitariness of voice as of one speaking from herself and for no other one, makes these poems remarkable. The speech is from the Maiden, the Wife, the Crone.[2]

Colum senses here Strong's ties to the archetypal, her awareness of profound truths which can be experienced only by keeping one's ear close to the ground.

Two poems in *Songs of Living*, 'Woman' and 'A Woman Unleashed', approach woman in contrasting ways. 'Woman' affirms romantic woman, the object of male fantasy; 'A Woman Unleashed' suggests in its title its opposite view, an unromantic view of woman. A more genuine woman is 'unleashed' from the idealisation of romantic myth. Strong presents the idealised view extremely well in 'Woman':

> Grace about the hips
> and liquid lines flowing down the limbs:
> the round breast and the flower-glow of the body: . . .
>
> Woman:
> seductive out of the heart of the earth
> the brooding of the aeons all about her . . .
>
> And there is no ache like unto that final ecstacy
>   when the man yields in the soul-quest.   (64)

The 'woman' presented here reminds one of the aisling poems, which deal with men questing for ideal beauty. Irish poets from Yeats to Heaney have described such romantic quests. But Eithne Strong offers the reader another sort of 'woman' in the second poem, 'A Woman Unleashed'. Here one finds no such idealisation, but rather an intense, gnomic assertion of the menacing aspect of woman. The poems together allude to Irish Catholicism's schizophrenic view of woman which holds that a woman is either Virgin or Whore. Because of Original Sin, the physical body has been corrupted and the soul seeks throughout each person's life to escape from that tainted body. Final escape occurs only after death. In terms of a woman's identity in this theology, she manifests either the soul or the body. If the former, she is worshipped as Virgin Most Pure; if the latter, shunnèd as Whore Most Foul. Strong's poem, 'A Woman Unleashed' runs through a litany of curses which fall upon the head of the Woman who centres on her body. Images of blood, sin, fire, and witchcraft occur in the poem: 'Swift breed of sin', 'a witch's sabbath', 'cauldron of gluttony and lust', 'the savage carnaging of blood', 'Queen of blood' (p. 10).

Strong herself abhors this separation of woman into two distinct entities, one looking heavenward, the other looking earthward. Instead, she stresses that the truly united female self has profound ties to nature and to the spirit-of-earth. Two poems in *Songs of Living* particularly affirm woman's tie to the forces of the natural world, 'When Men Don't Love' and 'Synthesis: Achill 1958'. The first of these begins on the level of social chat, but soon reveals its deep-rootedness.

> All in a room about a table
> the women gossip.
> Idle gabble . . .
> Dances, men,
> again again —
> in never-ending hen-cackle
> cat-spitting, snake-hissing —
> and the quiet pulse of life
> beneath
> but for the pausing
> the silent knowing.   (30)

The final phrase, 'silent knowing', indicates the quiet confidence women have of connection. The images in this poem come from nature, as do those in 'A Woman Unleashed', but the two poems differ in tone. One finds nothing negative or menacing here for a woman (though it might be for a man). The 'Queen of blood' in the previous poem becomes in this poem 'the quiet pulse of life'.

'Synthesis: Achill 1958' has an integrated view of woman which perceives abiding ties to Irish landscape, Irish mythology, and arguably even to Irish Catholicism. The witch's sabbath and cauldron of gluttony and lust in 'A Woman Unleashed' here become a 'mystic time', a 'midnight tryst', indeed a 'tryst with

with God'. The menacing flow of blood in the earlier poem here becomes the 'inner pulse'. The speaker puts her ear to the earth to hear its soundings, and what she hears is Druid-lore.

> But I must go alone
> and put my head low upon the heather
> to find my strength.
> Old druid hills
> gird black the sunset sky.
> Old, old strength of immemorial earth
> lies quiet beneath my tangled heart.   (66)

One notes in this passage other aspects of Eithne Strong's druidic vision, namely, the night-time setting, the presence of the moon, and especially the images of 'darkness' and 'blackness' which run through 'Synthesis'. Strong returns to these symbolic images in other poems.

Eithne Strong's vision of woman is further defined in her second volume, *Sarah, In Passing* (1974), particularly in two poems, 'Credo' and 'The Hater's Hymn'. 'Credo' insists on the poet's distance from political subjects. Her subject is the individual person and the family: 'Large happenings / in the state wear secondary / coverings. My bent is primary. / . . . the human composition / person to private person / is my sphere. . . . fathers, brothers, lovers, / rivals, mistresses, mothers, wives.'[3] Her imaginative centre is the self, the 'demand of predatory devouring "Me" '. In 'The Hater's Hymn' that demanding ego takes on a more specific, more menacing character, as one can see from the first line, 'A hill of stone and a black tree'. These images remind one of Beckett's bleak landscapes. The reader senses a divided personality in the poem, hears the voice of the 'hater', but learns as well of the 'lover' against whose ameliorating voice the hater's diatribe is directed. The voice of the hater scorns the suburban pleasures experienced by her alter-ego, whom the hater addresses as 'fat-lady'. The hater unequivocally rejects the things which preoccupy the 'lady', 'goods and shoes and babydoos'. 'I cannot cry glory to the colour / of lampshade and plastic'. The hater's territory, a much darker and more violent place ('A hill of stone and a black tree'), resists the destructive efforts of the 'lady': 'I turn my side and your soft / collapsible knife has screwed my belly, / ripped my bony strength of hate / in a flow of odorous love.' The conflict between opposing elements of the self resembles Freud's warring superego and id, the one oriented towards meeting the demands of those outside the self, the other expressing the self's uncensored desires. The word 'hymn' in the poem's title alerts the reader to a religious dimension. Religious language is associated with the 'lover'. The poem's final line, 'Tonight you crucify me', focuses this religious level. The 'hater' knows that orthodox Roman Catholicism discourages outbursts of inner personality, of 'predatory devouring "Me" '. The voice of the 'hater' vows not to be silenced. Unpleasant aspects of the personality must be allowed to exist. Eithne Strong enlarges upon these unorthodox aspects of female personality in other poems such as 'Strip Tease', 'Statement to Offspring', 'Measuring', 'Retarded Child', 'Response to Munch's "Scream" ', and 'Now the Cold Eye'.

Eavan Boland's two most recent volumes *In Her Own Image* (1980) and *Night Feed* (1982) deal exclusively with the subject of woman. The volumes remind one of Eithne Strong's defining poems 'A Woman Unleashed' and 'Woman' because they present sharply different views of woman. *Night Feed* for the most part treats suburban woman and chronicles the daily routines of a Dublin housewife in a quite positive way. The book has poems about baby's diapers, about washing machines, about feeding babies. The cover has a very idyllic drawing of a mother feeding a child. But the other volume *In Her Own Image*, published two years before *Night Feed*, seems written by a different person. Its candid and detailed treatment of such taboo subjects as menstruation, anorexia, and masturbation contrasts sharply with the idyllic world of *Night Feed*. Boland's ability to present both worlds testifies to her poetic maturity.

Like Eithne Strong, Boland often makes 'connection' the subject of major poems. But the poets differ greatly in their attitude towards this theme. As Padraic Colum notes in his introduction to Strong's first volume, her poems are instinctively tied to the land and to Irish mythology. They read like runic pronouncements of an Irish oracle. Eavan Boland appreciates the needs for ties such as these, but she does not experience these ties herself. Aware of traditional connection both in Irish and in classical mythology, she longs for an earlier period when such connection came instinctively. Her sense of loss with respect to these traditional connections extends beyond mythology to Irish history as well, even to Irish history in this century. Modern-day Dubliners have been cut off from the sustaining power of myth and history. Their lives, therefore, seem empty and superficial. Surrounded with shards of a lost culture, they cannot piece together these shards into a coherent system.

The alienation of the modern urban Irish from their cultural roots is the subject of Boland's poem 'The New Pastoral'. She considers alienation from a woman's perspective. Aware of the myths which have traditionally sustained males, Boland desires equivalent myths for females. The speaker longs for a 'new pastoral' which will celebrate women's ideals, but finds none. She encounters many domestic 'signs', but they do not 'signify' for her. She has a vague sense of once having participated in a coherent ritual, of having 'danced once / on a frieze'. But now she has no access to the myth. Men seem to have easier access to their cultural roots than women do. The legends of the cave-men contain flint, fire, and wheel which allow man 'to read his world'.[4] Later in history, men had pastoral poems to define and celebrate their place in the world. But a woman has no similar defining and consoling rituals and possesses no equivalent cultural signs. She seems a 'displaced person / in a pastoral chaos', unable to create a 'new pastoral'. Surrounded with domestic signs, 'lamb's knuckle', 'the washer', 'a stink / of nappies', 'the greasy / bacon flitch', she still has no access to myth. Hints of connection do not provide a unified myth. 'I feel / there was a past, / there was a pastoral / and these / chance sights — / what are they all / but late / amnesias / of a rite / I danced once / on a frieze?' (p. 45). The final image of the dancer on the frieze echoes both Keats's Grecian urn and Yeats's dancers and golden bird. But the contemporary poet has lost contact. Paradoxically, the poem constitutes the 'new pastoral' which it claims beyond its reach. The final allusion to the dancer on the frieze transforms the mundane objects of domestic life into something more significant, indeed something sacred.

Boland seems conflicted over whether woman should simply conform to male stereotypes for women or should resist these pressures to lead 'lesser lives', to attend to 'hearth not history'. Many poems in *Night Feed* accept this lesser destiny, poems such as 'Night Feed', 'Hymn' and 'In the Garden'. The several poems in this volume which deal with paintings, 'Domestic Interior', 'Fruit on a Straight-Sided Tray', 'Degas's Laundresses', 'Woman Posing (After Ingres)', 'On Renoir's "The Grape-Pickers" ', all deal with paintings by male painters which portray women in traditional domestic or rural roles. The women in these paintings appear content with their 'lesser lives'. But poems like 'It's a Woman's World' seem less accepting, more in the spirit of *In Her Own Image* which vigorously rejects basing one's identity on male stereotypes. 'It's a Woman's World' complements 'The New Pastoral' in its desire for a balance between hearth and history.

as far as history goes
we were never
on the scene of the crime . . .
And still no page
scores the low music
of our outrage.   (41-42)

Women have had no important roles in history, Boland asserts.
They produce 'low music' rather than heroic music. Nevertheless,
woman can have an intuitive connection with their own 'starry
mystery', their own cosmic identity. The women in those paintings
apparently pursuing their 'lesser lives', may have a sense of
'greater lives'. The male world (including male artists) must be
kept in the dark about this, must keep believing that nothing
mythic is being experienced.

That woman there,
craned to the starry mystery
is merely getting a breath
of evening air,
while this one here —
her mouth
a burning plume —
she's no fire-eater,
just my frosty neighbour
coming home.   (42)

The 'woman's world' and the 'starry mysteries' are presented
far less romantically in Boland's volume *In Her Own Image* (1980).
The poems in this volume refuse to conform to male stereotypes
of woman as happy domestic partner. They explore male/female
conflicts in the deepest and most intimate psychic places. The
title *In Her Own Image* indicates the volume's concern with the
problem of 'identity'. The persona in many of the poems wishes
to be an individual, free to determine her own life, but other forces
seek to control her, to make her conform to female stereotypes. A
woman should be perfect, unchanging, youthful, pure, in short,
should be ideal. Male-dominated society does not wish women
to explore their own deepest desires. Women transform these
social messages into the voice of their own consciences, or in
Freud's terms their own super-egos: 'Thou shalt not get fat!'
'Thou shalt not get old!' 'Thou shalt not get curious.'
    These nay-saying inner voices dominate the first three poems
of *In Her Own Image*: 'Tirade For the Mimic Muse', 'In Her Own
Image', and 'In His Own Image'. The 'mimic muse' in the first

poem urges the speaker to 'make up', to conceal ageing with cosmetics. The illustration for this poem shows a chunky and unkempt woman gazing into a mirror and seeing a perfect vision of herself, thin, unwrinkled, physically fit. The phrase 'her own image' in the second poem refers to another idealisation, the 'image' of perfection which the speaker carries around inside herself. She finally frees herself of this psychic burden by planting it outside in the garden. The illustration shows a naked woman bending over a small coffin. The third poem, 'In His Own Image', considers the pressures of a husband's expectations on a wife's sense of self. The speaker in this third poem does not try to reshape her features with make-up. She is battered into a new shape by a drunken husband. No illustration appears with this poem.

The speaker's 'tirade' in 'Tirade for the Mimic Muse' begins at once, and establishes the intensely hostile tone of much of *In Her Own Image*. 'I've caught you out. You slut. You fat trout.'[5] She despises the impulse in herself to conform to a stereotype, to disguise the physical signs of time passing: 'the lizarding of eyelids', 'the whiskering of nipples', 'the slow betrayals of our bedroom mirrors'. In the final section of the poem, the authentic self has suppressed those conforming impulses: 'I, who mazed my way to womanhood / Through all your halls of mirrors, making faces.' Now the mirror's glass is cracked. The speaker promises a true vision of the world, but the vision will not be idyllic: 'I will show you true reflections, terrors.' Terrors preoccupy Boland for much of this book.

'In Her Own Image' and 'In His Own Image' deal with different aspects of the 'perfect woman'. The first poem has a much less hostile tone than 'Tirade'. The speaker seems less threatened by the self-image from which she wishes to distance herself. Images of gold and amethyst and jasmine run through the poem. Despite the less hostile tone, Boland regards this 'image' as a burdensome idealisation which must be purged for psychic health: 'She is not myself / anymore' (p. 13). The speaker plants this 'image' in the garden outside: 'I will bed her, / She will bloom there', safely removed from consciousness. The poem 'In His Own Image' is full of anxiety. The speaker cannot find her centre, her identity. Potential signs of identity lie all around her, but she cannot interpret them: 'Celery feather, . . . / bacon flitch, . . . / kettle's paunch, . . . / these were all I had to go on, . . . / meagre proofs of myself' (14). A drunken husband responds to his wife's identity crisis by pounding her into his own desired 'shape'.

He splits my lip with his fist,
shadows my eye with a blow,
knuckles my neck to its proper angle.
What a perfectionist!
His are a sculptor's hands:
they summon
form from the void,
they bring
me to myself again.
I am a new woman.   (14-15)

How different are these two methods of coping with psychic
conflict. In the former the speaker plants her old self lovingly in
the garden. In the latter the drunken husband reshapes his wife's
features with violent hands. The wife in the second poem says
she is now a 'new woman'. If one reads this volume as a single
poem, as Boland evidently intends that one should (all the illust-
rations have the same person as their subject), one understands
that the desperate tone of other poems in the book derives from
the suffering of this reshaped 'new woman', victim of male
exploitation.

The next four poems of *In Her Own Image* deal with very private
subjects familiar to women, but not often treated in published
poems: anorexia, mastectomy surgery, masturbation, and menstruation. Both the poems and Constance Short's drawings are
startlingly frank. The poet wants readers to experience 'woman'
in a more complete way, to realise the dark side of being female.
The poems further illustrate Boland's sense of alienation from
cultural myths or myths of identity. She desires connections, but
she knows she is unlikely to have them. She is therefore left with
images which signify chaos rather than coherence, absence
rather than presence, emptiness rather than fullness.

Two of the four poems, 'Anorexia' and 'Mastectomy', read like
field reports from the battle of the sexes. The other two poems,
'Solitary' and 'Menses', have a female perspective, but are also
full of conflict. In the illustration for 'Anorexia', a very determined,
extremely thin, naked woman, arms folded, looks disapprovingly
at a fat woman lolling on a couch. An anorexic woman continues
to believe that she is fat, despite the fact that she is a virtual
skeleton. Boland introduces a religious level in the first three
lines: 'Flesh is heretic. / My body is a witch. / I am burning it' (17).
The speaker's conviction that her body is a witch runs through
the whole poem. Here in an extreme form is the traditional
Roman Catholic view that soul and body are separate. The body

must be punished because, since the Fall, it has been the dwelling place of the devil. The soul must suppress the body in order for the soul to be saved. This tradition provides the anorexic with a religious reason for starving herself. In this poem, she revels in the opportunity to 'torch' her body: 'Now the bitch is burning'. An unnamed presence even more disturbing than the witch is introduced in the second half of the poem, a ghostly male figure whom the anorexic speaker desires to please. To do so, however, the speaker must become thin enough that she can somehow return to the womb, imagined here paradoxically as male: 'I will slip / back into him again / as if I had never been away' (18). Such a transformation will atone for the sin of being born a woman, with 'hips and breasts / and lips and heat / and sweat and fat and greed'.

In 'Mastectomy', male-female conflict predominates. Male surgeons, envious of a woman's breasts (an effective transformation of the male-centred Freudian paradigm) cut off a breast and carry it away with them. The shocking drawing shows one gowned male surgeon passing the breast on a serving dish to another gowned male surgeon. The woman who has experienced this physical and psychological violation cries despairingly 'I flatten / to their looting' (21). The sympathetic words of the surgeon before the operation belie the sinister act of removing the breast. It can now become part of male fantasy, as a symbol of primal nourishment and primal home: 'So they have taken off / what slaked them first, / what they have hated since: / blue-veined / white-domed / home / of wonder / and the wetness / of their dreams.' (21)

The next two poems, 'Solitary' and 'Menses', deal with equally private aspects of a woman's life, auto-eroticism and menstruation. 'Solitary' has a celebratory attitude towards self-arousal. The drawing shows a relaxed naked female figure lying on her stomach. Religious imagery is used in this poem as it is in 'Anorexia', but here the body is worshipped rather than feared. The only negative aspect of 'Solitary' is its solitude. The female speaker is unconnected with another person. Solitary pleasures are intense, but less so than the pleasures of intercourse. The reader is taken on a journey from arousal to orgasm to post-orgasmic tranquillity. The religious language at first seems gratuitous, but then perfectly appropriate. The speaker affirms the holiness of her body: 'An oratory of dark, / A chapel of unreason' (23). She has a few moments of panic as the old words of warning flash into her mind: 'You could die for this. / The gods could make you blind.' But these warnings do not deter her from this sacred rite:

how my cry
blasphemes
light and dark,
screams
land from sea,
makes word flesh
that now makes me
animal.   (24)

During this period of arousal and climax, her 'flesh summers',
but then it returns again to winter: 'I winter / into sleep.' 'Menses'
deals with the private act of menstruation. A cosmic female voice
addresses the speaker as menstruation begins, attempting to
focus her attention solely on the natural powers working in her
body. The speaker resists this effort. She feels simultaneously
'sick of it' (25) and drawn to this process. She struggles to retain
her freedom. 'Only my mind is free', she says. Her body is taken
over by tidal forces. 'I am bloated with her waters. / I am barren
with her blood.' At the end of the poem the speaker seems more
accepting of this natural cycle. She reflects on two other cycles
which she has experienced, childbirth and intercourse. All three
cycles, she begins to see, make her a new person: 'I am bright and
original.'

The final three poems of *In Her Own Image*, 'Witching',
'Exhibitionist', and 'Making-up', return to the theme that 'Myths
/ are made by men' ('Making-up'). Much of a woman's life is
spent reacting to male stereotypes. In 'Witching', Boland further
explores the idea of woman-as-witch which was introduced in
'Anorexia'. Historically women accused by men of being witches
were doomed. The charges were usually either trumped-up or
trivial. Boland's witch fantasises turning the table on her male
persecutors and burning them first: 'I will / reverse / their arson,
/ make / a pyre / of my haunch / . . . the stench / of my crotch'
(29-30). A grim, but fitting fate for these male witch-burners!
Another male stereotype, woman-as-stripper, is treated in the
poem 'Exhibitionist'. This poem has the last accompanying drawing, a vulnerable young woman pulling her dress up over her
head and naked to those watching her, perhaps as Boland feels
naked toward those who have read through this volume. The
male observers in 'Exhibitionist' have in mind only gratifying
their lusts. The speaker detests this exploitation and hopes to
have a deeper impact on these leering males, hopes to touch them
spiritually with her shining flesh: 'my dark plan: / Into the gutter
/ of their lusts / I burn / the shine / of my flesh' (34). The final

poem, 'Making-up', returns to the theme of 'Tirade for the Mimic Muse', that women must alter their appearances to please males, but that men have no such demands. The poem rehearses a litany of transformations of the speaker's 'naked face'. 'Myths / are made by men', this poem asserts. The goddesses men imagine can never be completely captured by that 'naked face'. A woman's natural appearance inevitably has flaws, is not perfect like a goddess. Women are encouraged by men to disguise these flaws to make themselves look perfect. From these 'rouge pots', a goddess comes forth, at least in men's eyes. Women should really know better.

> Mine are the rouge pots,
> the hot pinks, . . .
> out of which
> I dawn.   (38)

The idea of woman-as-goddess also fascinates Medbh McGuckian, the final poet to be considered in this essay. But McGuckian generally has a more positive view of 'woman-goddess', as one can infer from the title of her most recent book *Venus and the Rain*. Whereas Boland is alienated from myth, McGuckian feels very much bound up with it. Boland's anxious females use cosmetics to look more like goddesses. But the effort fails and one feels the gap existing between myth and reality. In McGuckian's poems one is far less conscious of such a gap. Many of her major poems imply connection, ties between the phenomenal and noumenal. But the context of myth that one finds in McGuckian's poems differs significantly from the contexts of Boland and Strong. The specifically Irish dimension is missing in McGuckian.

McGuckian's poetry seems almost obsessively domestic. In terms of the two viewpoints suggested by the title of this essay, 'hearth and history', McGuckian is clearly drawn much more towards the former than towards the latter. Few of her poems deal specifically with Irish history or Irish myth. One does not find in McGuckian's poems either the druids on the black hills which have much significance for Eithne Strong, or the stories of Lir and Etain which have deeply moved Eavan Boland. This is not to deny range and depth to Medbh McGuckian's poetry, but merely to state that its focus and boundaries are extremely different from these other Irish poets. Her poetry has a density which immediately distinguishes it from the much more circumstantial poetry of Strong and Boland. These poets wish to communicate with readers. McGuckian seems far less concerned with being accessible. Her poetry is much more private, disjointed, obscure. She alludes to the 'mad river' of her father's brain: 'his brain simmered so fast.'[6] Her own poetry also seems to 'simmer', to fly on from point to point often without conventional signs to help readers.

The obscure ambience of the painting reproduced on the cover of *Venus and the Rain* (1984), is suggestive of her poetic vision. Unlike the simple line drawings which one finds in Strong and Boland's volumes, this cover illustration (McGuckian's note identifies it as a portion of a painting by Jan Toorop called 'The Younger Generation', painted in 1892) has a pre-Raphaelite quality, rather like Rossetti or Burne-Jones. (Toorop is also considered an Impressionist painter and a Symbolist painter.[7]) The entire painting is full of images, the focal centre of which is difficult to establish. There are no male presences in this wild tangle of plants and trees. A child sits in a chair happily playing in the garden. A ghostly female figure, obviously the child's mother, peers in at the child in the garden through the house-door which she has just opened. As is frequently the case with McGuckian's poems, here also signs abound, but do not immediately signify.

Since she does not regularly use familiar Irish places or cultural traditions, McGuckian typically focuses on husband, children, mother and father, grandmother, and especially the self. Her poetry is concerned with identity and value. Eithne Strong has her ear to the Irish ground and can commune with a female Irish Earth Spirit. Eavan Boland does not sense such connection herself, but she writes nostalgically about earlier times in Ireland which did experience it. Medbh McGuckian seems intensely 'tuned in', but not to any force specifically Irish. She uses 'Venus' in her most recent volume to represent her own intuition or 'tuning-in' to the cosmos. She senses cosmic forces all about her, and so her 'house and garden' poetry can, like Emily Dickinson's, range far beyond its domestic origins. McGuckian's poems contain planetary forces (sun, moon, planets, stars) which impinge on human lives. Unlike other poets who look downward for inspiration into the earth, McGuckian typically looks upward to the sky, and especially to the evening sky. Her sense of value derives from this intuition of cosmic forces rather than from any Catholic or Irish traditions. Her poems disorient the reader looking for familiar places, for a typical or normal world. Unlike those of Strong and Boland, McGuckian's settings often seem like places one has really never visited before. And so her poems do resemble that painting on the cover of *Venus and the Rain*, full of images but not offering the audience easy entry or easy understanding.

Because her poems are so self-referential, one can begin a study of womanhood almost anywhere in McGuckian's work. Whereas Strong and Boland deal with experiences that might readily be associated with the average woman, McGuckian's persona is very much an individual, one who, attracted to the confessional mode, often reveals herself as seemingly on the edge of breakdown. One finds confessional poetry in Strong and Boland, the former's poems about her retarded child, the latter's poems about menstruation and masturbation. But these do not have the psychological intensity of McGuckian's poems. McGuckian's understanding of womanhood emerges clearly in the title poems of two of her volumes, 'The Flower Master' and 'Venus in the Rain'.[8] Forces of all kinds interest the poet, the force of passion which keeps people together or drives them apart, planetary forces which silently influence this sublunary world, forces in nature which can bind together, forces in the psyche which can disturb or comfort. The title 'The Flower Master' immediately suggests power. The female speaker addresses the reader from her garden, a place crowded with different types of flowers, very much like the garden illustrated on the cover of *Venus and the Rain*. (The cover of *The Flower Master* also has a garden subject, a single trumpet flower in detail from 'The White Trumpet Flower' by Georgia O'Keeffe.) At the beginning of the poem, the garden has no other person in it, but at the end another person (a man?) is expected. The speaker feels quite peaceful in the garden, where she knows the names and needs of all the plants: foxgloves, daffodils, violets, hibiscus, feverfew, bluebells, sloes, sweet sultan, nipplewort. The speaker knows how to tend these plants, which ones need special care. She knows how to straighten and prune flowers. The gardening tasks are being done for a 'special guest' soon to arrive, a visitor who, in entering the garden, will have to yield to the speaker's power, will have to 'stoop to our low doorway'. The tone of 'The Flower Master' is peaceful, untroubled: 'we come to terms with shade, with the principle / of enfolding space.' (35)

The title poem 'Venus and the Rain' does not have the serenity of 'The Flower Master'. It deals with forces in the world, but not with balanced, benevolent forces. This poem embraces the cosmos rather than the enclosed and manageable garden. The cosmos seems menacing rather than protective. The hot, dry planet Venus has a troubling influence on the Earth. Venus needs water, but can never produce water, because of its dryness. The title 'Venus and the Rain' contains a paradox, since it does not rain on Venus. McGuckian personifies Venus as a female presence who hovers over the landscape obsessed with thoughts of water. This sort of hovering presence appears again and again in McGuckian's poems, the voice of imagination in a dry or depressing place, depending on whether the poem describes the external world or the internal world of the psyche. In an alienating place, the imagination can still function; it can create images of water in a dry place, images of a garden in a wilderness. In 'Venus and the Rain', Venus imagines water where it does not exist. The poem concludes with the lines 'a waterfall / Unstitching itself down the front stairs' (p. 31). The waterfall cannot literally exist on the dry planet, but the artist imagines a waterfall which does not flow, but 'unstitches' itself, a brilliantly convincing metaphor.

McGuckian devotes three poems in *Venus and the Rain* to this personified female figure: 'Venus and the Sun' (the first poem in the volume), 'A Day With Her', and 'Venus and the Rain'. 'Venus and the Sun' explores cosmic forces very inventively. Natural laws require that a planet orbit around the sun. Venus expresses displeasure at this restriction to her freedom. She envies the stars which have no orbit and thus are freer than she is. At the point in her orbit when she is furthest from the sun, Venus feels more freedom. The sun is described as a seducer who uses fragrance to woo Venus into his power: 'The scented flames of the sun throw me, / Telling me how to move.' McGuckian relates this sun/Venus conflict to more general male/female conflict:

> I am the sun's toy — because I go against
> The grain I feel the brush of my authority,
> Its ripples straying from a star's collapse.
> If I travel far enough, and fast enough, I seem
> To be at rest, I see my closed life expanding
> Through the crimson shells of time.

All objects in the universe, including the stars, are subject to controlling forces. But the stars seem freer, subject not to a law of gravity, only to the more general force of that first explosion which sent all matter moving outward. 'But the stars are still at large, they fly apart / From each other to a more soulful beginning.' McGuckian here observes one of the fundamental paradoxes about the universe, according to some physicists.

In the second Venus poem, 'Venus and the Rain', the freedom and power of the planet are radically diminished. She can barely be seen or felt. Her light is absorbed by the stronger light of other heavenly bodies: 'White on white, I can never be viewed / Against a heavy sky.' Her influence is reduced to making faint impressions on earth's leaves: 'my gibbous voice / Passes from leaf to leaf.' The word 'gibbous' perfectly captures the diminished power of the planet. Venus has phases like the phases of the moon. At times her entire disc is visible, but at other times only a thin silver rim is visible, and at still other times, this period referred to as 'gibbous', just a 'hump' is visible, just half of her disc. In this phase the planet's power is diminished. One gets a generally negative impression of Venus from 'Venus and the Rain'. Under cover of cloud, she is not a garden, but a desert place where no water flows, a place of 'fractures', 'torn edges', 'sagging sea', and 'rocks'. She speaks constantly of water, but always accompanied by dryness: 'rivers sawed their present lairs', 'cruising moonships find / Those icy domes relaxing', 'a waterfall / Unstitching itself down the front stairs'. This attenuated place symbolises for McGuckian the contemporary artist who must create even in a dry and barren world. Imagination becomes the solace in such barren places.

In the final Venus poem, 'A Day With Her', the point-of-view shifts to the poet-painter who feels a kinship with her 'sister planet'. Venus has both positive and negative qualities. The planet is an ugly desert, but Venus continues to cloud the vision and persuade her admirers she is a queen after all, a paradise rather than a wasteland. The poet-painter empathises with these two aspects of Venus. She herself is torn between truth and love. Her aesthetic sense tells her that a particular combination of colours would ruin her painting, but her lover insists on the change and she prefers companionship to beauty: 'I suffered / A yellow paper to remain I knew would be hurtful / To my pictures' (48). The male friend believes the change is magical, and signifies permanence in their relation: 'We must stay here, stay here forever.' McGuckian is very suspicious of such absolutes. She has a keen sense of mutability in the world. The imagination offers perhaps the only aversion to permanence. McGuckian's attitude here is a Romantic one. Art offers an escape from mutability, albeit a problematic escape.

The relation of painting and poetry to woman's identity has recently become a more prominent theme for McGuckian. Six poems in *Venus and the Rain* explore this theme: 'Ode to a Poetess',

214 Cultural Contexts and Literary Idioms

'The Sitting', 'Painter and Poet', 'Rowing', 'The Rising Out', and 'Catching Geese'. Conflict occurs in each poem, inner conflict with forces which resist the imagination or with forces which insist upon the imagination, external conflict with lover or with family. In 'The Rising Out', the speaker encounters a 'dream sister', an inner voice which challenges the freedom of the imagination and urges conformity to traditional cultural values. In 'Ode to a Poetess', the situation is reversed. A bewildered speaker is troubled by the insistent visitation of the poetic muse: 'this onset of a poetess and her / Persuasive bones sending me and my life away' (11). Conflict with her lover has an impact on poetry and art in several poems. In 'Catching Geese', the speaker wishes she could transform the fractiousness of their love affair into the perfection of art: 'All I had to do to hold the sentence still / Was paint it on the circumference of a plate' (50). The poem 'Rowing' deals with the lovers' conflict as the conflict of two artistic styles, the feminine circle and the masculine line; and as a conflict of types of light in paintings, one of which McGuckian calls 'perfect' and 'classical', the other 'artless': 'these circles call / Towards each other' (33). In 'Painter and Poet', the conflict with her lover is imagined as a struggle between two interior decorators who live in the same house: 'I choked the crimson flock / Wallpaper with sheets of mimosa. / . . . he scratched out / Regiments of flowers.' (20) Finally, 'The Sitting' describes the conflict with a relative who has been asked to sit for a portrait: 'She is posing furtively, / . . . she prefers / My sea-studies, and will not sit for me / Again' (15).

In 'The Rising Out', two inner voices conflict, the imaginative and the maternal. The poet's voice speaks of another 'Venus-project', this one a poem called 'Venus Trying the Wings of Love'. But the conventional voice of a 'dream sister' insists that such pagan enterprises be abandoned and that the speaker return to orthodoxy. This unnamed 'dream sister' represents the maternal instinct. The poem's title has a significant ambiguity. It refers to the 'rising out' of a woman's body during pregnancy. Describing this 'dream sister', the voice of the poet writes: 'her dream / Is the same seed that lifted me out of my clothes / And carried me till it saw itself as fruit' (p. 35). 'The Rising Out' also has a Christian meaning in the poem in terms of Easter and 'rising out' of Christ. The 'dream sister' is determined to suppress these alien, pagan forces in the speaker before Easter: 'My dream sister has gone into my blood / To kill the poet in me before Easter.' The voice of imagination does not feel threatened by this visit of the 'dream sister', and indeed speaks of it as a 'tender visit', and later says 'She gentles me'.

This inner conflict between the imagination and traditional attitudes is also the subject of 'Ode to a Poetess', but here the viewpoint has shifted. Instead of the poet's voice speaking, as in 'The Rising Out', the 'dream sister' speaks about the disturbing and potentially disabling presence of the poet in the psyche. McGuckian defines the two opposing perspectives with opposing images. In 'The Rising Out' the inner-directed poet sees only idealised forms: 'For any that I loved, it was for their hair / That never really belonged to them.' But the speaker in 'Ode to a Poetess' is clearly tied to the imperfect external world: 'The rain has left a scare across the countryside; / . . . What survives of our garden is held together / By the influence of water' (p. 11). In no way an ideal setting, this place has obvious flaws: 'Like a window not made to open, or a house / That has been too long to let.' The 'onset of a poetess' threatens the conventional speaker: 'this onset of a poetess and her / Persuasive bones sending me and my life away. / / I will not write her name although I know it.' The 'name' which the speaker resists saying may well be 'Venus', because Venus is the inspiring muse of this volume. The conclud-ing lines strongly suggest Venus, a cosmic power which moves over the earth, a power associated with the dawn and with the moon rather than the sun:

> I am thinking of those
> Eyes of yours, as of something just alighted
> On the earth, the why that had to be in them.
> What they ask of women is less their bed,
> Or an hour between two trains, than to be almost gone,
> Like the moon that turns her pages day by day,
> Letting the sunrise weigh up, not what they have seen,
> But the light in which the garden, pressing out into
> The landscape, drew it all the more into its heart.

(pp. 11-12)

The 'dream sister' understands the price of entering into Venus's influence, namely, loss of identity, loss of contact with the external world. The real garden will no longer matter, but only the light it reflects into the inner landscape of the imagination.

The theme of art versus life is explored through the conflict of lovers in 'Catching Geese', 'Rowing', and 'Painter and Poet'. In 'Catching Geese', the speaker addresses her lover, telling him that her creativity matters more than their love. She mentions even

leaving lover and children, to keep her imagination unshackled.
Her lover can care for the children. 'If I disappear, it's only to
worry you / Into getting the children on their feet' (p. 50). The
atmosphere in her house is tense and 'unhappy', with all of this
territorial in-fighting. But the speaker hopes that her art will
transform this restlessness into beauty. The poem 'Rowing'
reverses the situation in 'Catching Geese', where art prevails over
love. In 'Rowing', the lover prevails. The first half of this poem
describes how painting is done. In the second half, the male lover
challenges art and bests it. The speaker describes painting in
terms of two 'circles of light', one the inner light which the artist
projects onto the subject, the other the light which comes from
the subject and enters the painter's eyes. She calls the first sort of
light 'perfect', the second sort 'artless':

> There are two kinds of light, one perfect
> Inside, pear-coloured, shedding that cool
> Classical remorse over the angered field,
> The other gifted with an artlessness too
> Painful to live with, like a spur
> Eloping from the room below, its nurtured
> Discipline of dark tobacco golds. . . .
>   how these circles call
> Towards each other.   (p. 33)

Despite the power of these 'circles of light', the lover possesses
and 'remakes' his beloved: 'Your body renovates me like an
artisan, / A goldsmith, none too delicate, despite / Its strength of
loving.' Being lured back to the domestic world does not please
the speaker; she uses terms like 'pain', 'sour honey', 'sutures',
and 'thickening' to describe her feelings at the end of the poem.

   The conflict between art and love takes on an almost surreal
form in 'Painter and Poet'. The boundary between reality and
illusion is hard to place in this battle of the sexes. The combatants
attack one another by transforming their house: 'I turned his
room into a shell' (20). House and text merge here, as do painter
and poet. At one point, the speaker is talking about wallpaper
and then about changing a ceiling into the chapter of a book.
The speaker hates the house's wallpaper: 'I choked the crimson
flock / Wallpaper with sheets of mimosa'; 'I mushroomed / The
hills of his ceiling into a kind of chapter / Of hats and walking
shoes'. The lover also attacks the wallpaper (or perhaps a painting,
or perhaps the garden): 'he scratched out / Regiments of flowers.'
The battle ends indecisively in this poem. The exhausted warriors
head out of the house for neutral territory.

In her poems about house and garden, McGuckian further develops her understanding of womanhood. As noted earlier, the cover illustration for *Venus and the Rain*, Toorop's 'The Younger Generation', contains these two places which bound McGuckian's imaginative world. The two human subjects in the painting, young woman and child, clearly are at ease in these places. The title poem of her first volume, 'The Flower Master', makes woman master of the garden. The poem just discussed, 'Painter and Poet', is set in a house. McGuckian's understanding of woman seems always to involve woman in relation to an enclosed space, either house or garden: woman in garden and house, woman as garden, woman as house, house as nest, lover as house, garden as plenitude, house and marriage, house and child, house and garden in times of loss.

The poems which conclude each of McGuckian's three published volumes affirm this central theme of woman in relation to enclosed spaces. These poems are 'Collusion', the final poem in *Trio*;[9] 'The Mast Year', concluding poem in *The Flower Master*, and 'Sabbath Park', final poem in *Venus and the Rain*. 'Collusion' celebrates the mutually enriching powers of woman and garden. 'The Mast Year' has trees for its subject. 'Sabbath Park', the final poem in McGuckian's most recent volume, places the poet in the nest of her house, which does not desert her even in trying times. 'Collusion' has a Wordsworthian ambience. The speaker tends her flower and the flower connects the speaker to the elemental powers of nature; hence the 'collusion':

> The begonia's soil is rich and wet
> I tuck it around her
> As I would pat my hair,
> Straightening her tubered root.
>
> We keep our sources secret — she
> Swells with lymph and electricity,
> Her fibres transparently taped up, and I
> Sprout willowy as any sweet begonia.   (p. 44)

Here garden and person begin with separate identities, but merge into a single entity by the end of the poem. Tone and vision are positive and idyllic.

'The Mast Year' has trees rather than flowers as its subject. The title alludes to the fact that Irish trees were for many years used by Britain to construct the ships of its empire. Ireland became deforested as a result. Few ancient trees remain outside Ascendancy demesne walls. McGuckian prefers to experience trees growing rather than trees cut down for masts; the domestic world rather than the social and political world is her natural habitat. In 'The Mast Year' the speaker describes the many trees that are now once again found in Ireland: oak, pine, beech, birch, alder, sycamore, yew. Certain trees in Ireland have ties to Celtic mythology, for example, the oak tree's association with the Druids. Though she does not develop this aspect of her theme at great length in 'The Mast Year', one finds an allusion to this tradition in the poem's final lines: 'as winded oaks / Lay store upon their Lammas growth, / The thickening of their dreams' (51). Lammas Day, the first day of August, is important in the ancient Celtic calendar as the day when the first harvested grain is made into loaves of bread.

A more problematic view of poet, house, and garden is found in the final poem of Medbh McGuckian's most recent volume, 'Sabbath Park'. This far less optimistic poem acknowledges the contingencies of life. Sabbath Park is the name of the house, and the word 'sabbath' would seem to suggest the day of completion and rest. But the poem begins in the 'Paradise Lost rooms', suggesting a post-lapsarian world where one is daily reminded of one's fallen state. Lower creatures have not lost their Edenic powers; the bird can build the 'perfect nest'. But fallen humans have lost this gift and are conscious of their loss. After the suffering which is found throughout *Venus and the Rain*, the speaker is willing to settle for a flawed house and garden:

> Now, after a year misspent on the ragged
> Garden side of the door, I put faith
> In a less official entrance, the accidental
> Oblongs of the windows that I find
> Have neither catch nor pulley.   (p. 54)

McGuckian questions the easy romanticism of poems like 'Collusion' and 'The Mast Year'. But when her spirits are low, the poetic persona is presented as needing house and garden to feel complete. At the end of 'Sabbath Park', she can feel a new poem beginning to stir within her: 'I feel the swaggering beginnings / Of a new poem flaring up, because the house / Is dragging me into its age.' She does not need a man to be creative.

McGuckian uses houses to explore the beginning and the ending of a sexual relation in 'The Soil Map' and 'The Villain'. 'The Soil Map' guides the male who can interpret its code to the deepest truths about a woman. These truths are symbolised by the house. As suggested by its title, 'The Villain' deals with ending rather than beginning. A house symbolises the deteriorating affair. The speaker in 'The Soil Map' describes an idealised 'House' whose parts manifest the essential female: 'the swinging of your two-leaf door', 'the petalled steps to your porch', 'your splendid fenestration, / Your moulded sills, your slender purlins, / The secret woes of your gutters' (*The Flower Master*, p. 29). McGuckian develops the symbolism of house-as-woman in the following passage:

> I have found the places on the soil-map,
> Proving it possible once more to call
> Houses by their names, Annsgift or Mavisbank,
> Mount Juliet or Bettysgrove: . . .
>   I drink to you as Hymenstown,
> (My touch of fantasy) or First Fruits,
> Impatient for my power as a bride.   (p. 30)

The 'soil-map' leads those who can 'read' its signs to a place ruled by women. Houses in this country have women's names and offer abiding shelter to males who can find their way. The second poem, 'The Villain', has as its subject a failed marriage. A house symbolises the breakup of the relation: 'This house is the shell of a perfect marriage / Someone has dug out completely' (*Venus and the Rain*, p. 19). The failed marriage seems even sadder, as a loss of 'The Soil Map'. The male partner has lost his nest, the female partner someone to cherish. The unity of the house has been destroyed; its parts no longer intersect: 'its mind / Is somewhere above its body, and its body / Stumbles after its voice.'

McGuckian's mapping of female identity includes two poems about adolescence, 'That Year' and 'Chain Sleeper'. She considers 'That Year' important enough to make it the only poem which appears in two volumes (*Trio*, and *The Flower Master*); it is the opening poem of *The Flower Master*. Both poems have an eccentricity about them which one often finds in McGuckian. Each poem presents a very individual adolescent; but the experiences of these adolescents seem typical as well. The speaker in 'That Year' recalls the awkwardness associated with the sudden consciousness of growing up:

> That year it was something to do with your hands
> To play about with rings, to harness rhythm
> In staging bleach or henna on the hair,
> Or shackling, unshackling the breasts.   (p. 32)

The effort to stop the rhythms of life flowing within one is familiar, as is coping with breasts. The speaker has a dim awareness of and desire for her mature sexuality: 'I wanted curtainings, and cushionings; / The grass is no bed after dark.' The title 'The Chain Sleeper' refers to the adolescent's need to sleep for extended periods because of physiological changes. The young girl described in this poem clearly is experiencing 'That Year'. 'Unshameable this leggy girl who sleeps and sleeps / In china duck-down, one breast bigger than the other' (12). She desperately wants 'to be usual', but cannot cope with the strange thing her body has become. At one moment she thinks of herself as a 'goddess', but at the next moment her 'semi-precious stones' are transformed into 'costume jewellery' fit less for the palace than for the garbage can. These conflicting feelings capture effectively the traumas of adolescence.

This essay began by offering hearth and history as guiding principles in the search for identity which has preoccupied three Irish poets, Eithne Strong, Eavan Boland, and Medbh McGuckian. In the case of Boland, these terms have been considered mutually exclusive. Hearth cannot contain history, nor history hearth. Boland's poems are generally pessimistic about woman's place in the world. She senses gaps between woman and society, and between then and now. Her poetry has more nostalgia than the poetry of the other two women. She longs for the past and dreads the future. For Strong and McGuckian, the terms hearth and history are not mutually exclusive. Their poetry explores 'hearth-history' rather than 'hearth vs. history'. Both of these poets have faith in a mythology of the hearth. Strong's mythology has clear Irish roots, while McGuckian's comes from the cosmos. Both believe that attentiveness to familiar places can often provide access to the deepest sort of history, to cultural and psychological structures.

IRELAND'S *ANTIGONES*:
TRAGEDY NORTH AND SOUTH

ANTHONY ROCHE

There continues to be a fruitful interaction between the scholarly polymath George Steiner and contemporary Irish playwriting. In 1980, Brian Friel's play *Translations* acknowledged the influence of Steiner's *After Babel* and its study of the complex relations between language and the consciousness of a culture.[1] In 1984, Steiner published *Antigones*, which addresses the recursion of the Greek dramatic myth in nineteenth and twentieth century thinking and speculates on the reason for its persistence.[2] That same year, without prior knowledge of Steiner's magisterial survey or — they claim — of each other, three Irish poets independently moved into the theatrical medium by writing versions of Sophocles' *Antigone*. In reviewing Steiner's book, Oliver Taplin remarked that during the years 1962-5 'there [were] at least four productions of *Antigone* in Poland' and asked why.[3] Similarly, having noted that three versions of the *Antigone* emerged in Ireland during the same twelve months, this paper would like to explore the phenomenon by looking at aspects of the myth foregrounded by different writers, especially as they reflect on the contemporary direction of Ireland's politics.

Surprisingly, only one of the three versions issues from a Northern Irish perspective, Tom Paulin's *The Riot Act*, first presented by the Field Day Theatre Company at the Guildhall, Derry, in September 1984.[4] Paulin himself does not slot conveniently into the dividing categories so favoured in the North. He was born in England and teaches at the University of Nottingham; he was raised in the North as a Protestant Unionist when his parents returned there; and in the late 1970s he changed sides, switching allegiances from his Unionist heritage, not so much to its Catholic counter-image as to a utopian vision of nationalist identity that would reconcile Protestant Dissenter and Catholic Republican. The zig-zag movement Paulin deliberately traces and the mixed heritage he embodies enlarge the perspective of the 'Northern problem' to set it in the dual context of the Republic of Ireland (the 'South') and Britain ('Westminster'). The two other versions of the play, by poets Aidan Carl Mathews and Brendan Kennelly, proceed from and bear upon the Irish Republic, the neglected half of the equation in recent critical studies, not only taking the measure of the pressure exerted on that state by events in the North but also the longer entanglement of Britain in Ireland's affairs. The emphasis in my title — on north and south — is equal.

On the political and social occasions which irresistibly attract the energies of the *Antigone* myth, Steiner writes:

Whenever, wherever, in the western legacy, we have found ourselves engaged in the confrontation of justice and of law, of the aura of the dead and the claims of the living, whenever, wherever, the hungry dreams of the young have collided with the 'realism' of the ageing, we have found ourselves turning to words, images, sinews of argument, synecdoches, tropes, metaphors, out of the grammar of Antigone and of Creon.[5]

The first person to draw the comparison between events in the North of Ireland and Sophocles' *Antigone* was diplomat-critic, Conor Cruise O'Brien. He did so very early on, in October 1968, within the same month as a Civil Rights march was set upon by the Ulster police. In *The Listener*'s reprinting of his Belfast lecture, O'Brien defined the action of Sophocles' heroine as 'non-violent civil disobedience',[6] terms deliberately meant to echo the Civil Rights movement in the U.S., especially Martin Luther King's doctrine of passive resistance and his argument that civil laws are just or unjust when viewed in the light of a divine or higher law. In his very next sentence, however, O'Brien lays the blame for all of the deaths in the play — Haemon, Eurydice, and her own — squarely on Antigone and her provocative defiance of legitimate civil authority. But what of the play's final judgement (via the chorus and the prophet Tiresias) that Creon is to blame for unleashing this cycle of death by denying the dead Polyneices to the earth and by forcing the living Antigone into the grave? O'Brien concedes that Creon's

decision to forbid the burial of Polyneices was rash, but it was also rash to disobey his decision . . . Creon's authority, after all, was legitimate, *even if he had abused it* [italics mine], and the life of the city would become intolerable if citizens should disobey any law that irked their conscience.

Increasingly throughout the piece, O'Brien becomes the apologist for Creon and his practices. In so doing, he ignores his own finer perception that 'Creon and Antigone are both part of our nature, inaccessible to advice, and incapable of living at peace in the city'. This occurs in a paragraph beginning 'the play is still performed', which suggests the intimate connection between theatre and politics by wittily transferring the play and its cast from the stage to the realm of political action. Translated into the local conditions of Northern Ireland in 1968, Antigone collectively represents the Catholics marching to protest the inequities of a state which has consistently discriminated against them; individually, Bernadette Devlin (as she then was) steps into a role which could have been written for her, a strikingly young and impassioned woman standing up against the oppressive, patriarchal institutions of Stormont and Westminster. If in O'Brien's overall argument Creon wavers between being an individual ruler in whom power is vested or an institution which preserves the fabric of the status quo, then in the political allegory he embodies both the local power of Stormont and the longer arm of the Westminster law which took over direct rule in 1972 but which had never entirely relaxed its grip. At the close of his piece, O'Brien rounds again on his rational pragmatism to weigh the gaining of peace against 'the price of [the] soul', an unintentional anticipation (as he later noted)[7] of the title of Bernadette Devlin's autobiography, *The Price of my Soul*.

In 1980, Tom Paulin displayed his first interest in the *Antigone* when he used the occasion of a *TLS* review to focus on the writings of Conor Cruise O'Brien.[8] In particular, he notes the revisions *The Listener* lecture underwent when reprinted in O'Brien's 1972 book, *States of Ireland*, and the increasing shift its revision registers 'from the instinctive and intuitive [stance of an Antigone] towards the rational [Creon]'.[9] Four years later, O'Brien himself declared:

I find myself no longer in sympathy with the conclusion. Antigone is very fine on the stage, or in retrospect or a long way off, or even in real life for a single, splendid epiphany. But after four years of Antigone and her under-studies and all those funerals . . . you begin to feel that Ismene's commonsense and feeling for the living

are preferable.[10] The final issue for O'Brien is one of obedience to authority, allegiance to the body politic, the rationally codified and transmitted civic law. But if O'Brien is denying the Antigone within him, Paulin in his essay is denying the Creon he once was, attempting to exorcise and castigate the earlier affiliations:

Until about 1980 . . . [I] reacted like most members of the Unionist middle class and believed that Conor Cruise O'Brien was putting 'our case'. But there was something different in the air as the decade ended. I started reading Irish history again and found myself drawn to John Hume's eloquence, his humane and constitutional politics. As a result, O'Brien's articles in the *Observer* began to seem sloppy and unconvincing and I felt angered by them.[11]

Tom Paulin takes his argument a crucial, transformative step further when he writes a version of the Sophoclean tragedy that has figured so largely as a mythic paradigm for politics in the North. The debate with O'Brien was clearly an incentive; and Paulin's dramatic articulation of the issues gives them a range that transcends mere personal polemic. Where the figure of Creon in the prose debate was subordinated to a gloss on the development of O'Brien's conservatism, the dramatic persona now absorbs O'Brien as only one of several partial and incomplete reflections. Cruise O'Brien can be heard most clearly through those lines of Creon where he aligns his own motives with the pragmatic defence of the state. But when Paulin's Creon speaks in more distinctive tones, we hear accents that come from the mouths of Northern, not Southern politicians. More precisely, we hear a verbal medley of the two reigning powers in Northern Ireland, Westminster and Unionism. Creon comes on stage shortly after assuming power and his remarks are very much those of the new man on the job. His 'I shall be doing a very great deal of listening' (10) sounds, as Fintan O'Toole of the *Sunday Tribune* remarked, like a 'parody of a Northern Ireland Office political functionary appealing for public support'[12] and Mitchell Harris finds the sentence itself echoing 'the opening remarks of Northern Ireland's incoming Secretary of State', Douglas Hurd, in the summer of 1984.[13] Hurd has already been replaced by Tom King; but the mouthpiece is irrelevant, since the abstract locutions and essential political message remain the same.

But if Paulin's Creon starts out by sounding like a Westminster functionary, other identifications soon emerge. He is introduced by the chorus as 'The big man', an unmistakeable reference to the Reverend Ian Paisley, the demagogue of the Democratic Unionist Party. Creon's speech, therefore, is not only that of the practised public official from 'the mainland' but also of someone from Ulster, a Unionist anxious to reassure those he represents by sounding the code words of the tribe, 'law', 'order' and 'loyalty'. Creon's speech progressively mutates into distinctively Ulster, rather than Oxbridge, tones and dialect, as in his reference to Ismene: 'And this one here — / the sneaky, sleaked one — / she

lived in my house too' (30). In Sophocles' play, the character of
Creon under the pressure of events abandons his appeal to the
larger forces of stability and civilisation in whose name he acts
and soon has no higher argument than the brute assertion of will
and violence; similarly, Paulin's Creon ends up sounding like
nothing more than the hard man of violence, self-appointed
leader of a gang of bullyboys deciding who shall live or die: 'Go
on boys . . . Bring out the dirty bitch / and let's be rid of her' (42).

All three of the Irish playwrights take least liberties in presenting Antigone herself and are all the more taxed to have her make
a distinct dramatic impression. Paulin finds his means by concentrating on her speech and the larger issues of language
thereby raised. Since he is looking for a distinctive Anglo-Irish
usage in all his writings, the issue of speech is as central to
Paulin's translation of Sophocles as it was to Friel's *Translations*, the
begetter of the Field Day enterprise. Drawing on Richard Jebb's
nineteenth-century translation,[14] Paulin pares away the florid
Victorian embellishments to arrive at a short verse line, lean,
terse, understated. The play is written in a pared, minimal style,
conversational yet urgent, whose Anglo-Irish speech and syntax
find a home and context for such lexical outcasts as 'screggy',
'sleg', 'pobby'. The characterising epithet of his Antigone is
sounded in the first scene by Ismene when she responds to her
sister's declaration of filial allegiance by calling her, or more
precisely her manner of speaking, 'wild':

Antigone.	He's my own brother, and he's yours too. I can't betray him.
Ismene.	You're talking wild — it's Creon's order. (11)

This brings us back to Paulin's debate with Cruise O'Brien. The
closest point of rapprochement between them is reached when
Paulin seizes on a play by O'Brien, *Salome and the Wild Man*, and
Salome's admission to the sophist, Philo, that they are both
'lonely for the wild man'.[15] Paulin goes on to define 'wild' as 'a
word with a distinctive usage in Ireland' and to cite as a characteristic example 'Yeats remembering the pre-revolutionary Constance
Gore-Booth "With all youth's lonely wildness stirred"'. This wildness is not a barbarism to be set over against civilisation since the
terms of these polarities have been too long co-opted by the
British, casting themselves in the light of the bearers of civilisation,

order, rule, and moderation, and the Irish as the unkempt barba-
rians who will not be tamed but Caliban-like insist on wallowing
in the mud. The 'wildness' may be transvalued as exuberance,
primitive earthiness, an integrity of body and soul that resists
social integration or confinement within limits. This lonely
'wildness' is something Antigone claims and it is something
Creon will have to share or understand to some degree, as Paulin
uses it to find unlikely agreement with W. B. Yeats and Conor
Cruise O'Brien.

From the perspective of Creon and the state, Antigone's
behaviour is 'wild' only in the sense that it is unruly, potentially
anarchic, threatening the stability of civic order and the rational
principle it incorporates. But Antigone, in Paulin as in Sophocles,
claims she is acting in accordance with another set of laws, one
that is not officially inscribed in the edicts of the state. Her loyalty
is to her own, kith, kin, family, tribe, and in insisting on proper
burial rites for her brother, she insists she is exonerating herself
before another court of appeal than the state's tribunals.
Although Paulin has cut back on Antigone's references to the
gods, and resisted giving them a Christian gloss, those he retains
are the references in Sophocles where the gods are not on high
but located down among the dead, the instinctual aboriginal
forces to whose submission Antigone owes her 'wildness':

> Antigone.   It was never Zeus
> made that law.
> Down in the dark earth
> there's no law says,
> 'Break with your own kin,
> go lick the state.'
> We're bound to the dead:
> we must be loyal to them.
> I had to bury him.   (27)

This notion in the Greek original of two sets of laws at variance
with one another transfers best to those contemporary societies
where some inequity or variance is widely perceived to exist in
the man-made laws, where a portion of its people suffer under
such inequities that a gap is opened into which other laws may
be summoned. It is no surprise, therefore, to learn of productions
of *Antigone* in Poland or to find two black prisoners in South
Africa's Robben Island coerced into performing the play in Athol
Fugard's *The Island*. The long interposition of Westminster in the
making of Irish laws north and south has encouraged an equivocal,

ambivalent adherence, to a body of laws widely perceived as externally imposed and alien. A revolutionary opposition emerges that derives its own laws from a sense of extended family, the sibling relations of brotherhood. It is just such a 'familial' political gesture that Antigone offers to Ismene at the beginning of the play: 'Will you go in with me or not?' (10). When Ismene rejects the offer, she effectively rejects this pact of sister-hood and is no longer regarded as such by Antigone. As she goes to face her own death, Antigone addresses in turn each of the members of the House of Laius who has preceded her — Oedipus, Jocasta, Eteocles and Polyneices — and in so doing, invokes their invisible presences as more palpable than those on stage. Implicit in the play's mythos, Antigone's dual allegiance to the dead and to her family also resonates off the recent Hunger Strike. Richard Kearney writes of this tradition of sacrificial martyrdom:

In 1980, a Maze prisoner reiterated this sentiment when he wrote on the wall of his cell: 'I am one of many who die for my country . . . if death is the only way I am prepared to die.' The *many* here refers to a long litany of martyrs whose sacrificial death for Ireland has been translated into the 'sacred debt' of the 'freedom struggle'.[16]

Finding no point of sustained identification with the formal body of laws encoded in the North, Republican prisoners apprehended under those laws turn in a self-consciously ritualised and dramatic way to the extended family of those who have preceded them. The only mediators the baffled faculties of the state can turn to in such an impasse are members of the immediate family (most powerfully and persuasively, the mother) and a priest, the two chthonic forces released by such a supra-rational gesture.

Kearney continues by remarking that 'one of the most popular responses to this sacrificial attitude has been the emergence of ballads, snatches or rhymes which, like myths, are often authored by nobody yet known to everybody'. Before she is led away, Paulin's Antigone sings her own dirge with snatches of an anonymous folk-song:

Antigone. (*Sings to herself*)

> I heard her cry
> as I climbed the track —
> my friends are cold
> though my bairns are dead.   (46)

This touches upon Antigone's declaration in Sophocles just before she is led off that she is condemned to have 'no part in the bridal-song, the bridal-bed, / denied all joy of marriage, raising children'.[17] What is dramatically so surprising about this final wrenched admission is the lack of emotion previously displayed. Nowhere prior to this does she refer to the fact that she is affianced to Haemon; Ismene brings it up. Antigone's subordination of her own personal life to the cause that compels her is so absolute that Anouilh softened it by offsetting the unflinching martyr-to-be with a nervous, romantic schoolgirl. Paulin only makes several brief additions, not to sentimentalise his tragic heroine, but to show the 'excess of love' from which her actions spring: when she breaks off her repudiation of Ismene to admit 'it tears my heart, though' (32), and when the term 'love' is added to both her sister's and fiance's names in the direct address of intimate endearment. 'Excess of love' comes, of course, from Yeats's 'Easter 1916': 'And what if excess of love / Bewildered them till they died?'[18] My reference is not gratuitous; for Paulin himself has Creon react to the transformed perspective that the death of wife and son have wrought in him with the same poem's most famous line:

Chorus.	It was too late
	you changed your mind.
Creon.	I changed it, but.
	Aye, changed it utterly. (60)

Yeats's 'Easter 1916' is part of Paulin's design, therefore, in its fusion of personal sacrifice and political event. His Creon undergoes a profound change of mind, unlike the annihilation of Sophocles' ruler to a state of nothingness. Both Creons are denied what they most seek, to follow after wife and son, barred access to the realms of the dead they have all along denied. Paulin makes clear that what Creon suffers, under pressure from the concentrated catastrophe he has just borne, is a living re-enactment of Antigone's fate. What registers the transformation is, once more, the language. Creon now speaks Antigone's tongue, addressing his (dead) son for the first time in terms of loving kinship as 'my own wee man' and 'bairn'. The penultimate choral ode places this individual transformation in a larger context by locating the gods neither in Olympus or in Hades but 'in the quick of tongues plunging' (55), conferring the power to heal wounds not only on speech but on such other rites of celebration as dancing, music, prayer and poetry. Creon 'shared power with no man' and, in setting his face against power sharing, has paid a bloody price. When he finally capitulates and performs the burial rites of Polyneices, he takes 'olive branches / and green laurel leaves / to crown and lap him in' (58), the 'green' deftly highlighted among the classical emblems of peace. In Paulin's poem 'Under Creon', the questing narrator responds to 'a free voice [singing] / dissenting green';[19] he has written elsewhere that he and his work assume the existence 'of a non-sectarian, republican state which comprises the whole island of Ireland'.[20]

Though green of hue, this state would seek to absorb the traditions on both sides which have been driven underground. For Paulin repeatedly points, not just to a proscribed Catholic Republicanism, but to a genuinely Protestant 'dissenting tradition in Ulster [which] created a distinctive and notable culture in the closing decades of the eighteenth century, [but which] went underground after the Act of Union and has still not been given the attention it deserves'.[21] In 'Under Creon' it is this alternate dissenting tradition which the speaker searches for in the gaps in the imperial shrub:

> The daylight gods were never in this place
> and I had pressed beyond my usual dusk
> to find a cadence for the dead: McCracken,
> Hope, the northern starlight, a death mask
> and the levelled grave that Biggar traced;
>
> like an epic arming in an olive grove
> this was a stringent grief and form of love.
> Maybe one day I'll get the hang of it
> and find joy, not justice, in a snapped connection
> that Jacobin oath on the black mountain.[22]

When Creon at the close turns his back on the daylight gods by which he has lived his life and says 'All I want's the dark' (62), he is not only seeking annihilation (as in Sophocles) but acknowledging the instinctual forces he has all along denied. This places him in the company of Beckett's Krapp, who turns from seeking illumination in the light to embrace the dark; politically, it belatedly recognises the claims of the dead; and culturally, it at least marks out an open space through the Field Day Theatre Company on which two dissenting traditions can begin to find common holy ground.

*   *   *   *   *

When Aidan Carl Mathews's version of *Antigone* was first produced at Dublin's Project Arts Centre during the summer of 1984,
copies of the Criminal Justice Bill were handed out to members of
the audience as they entered. The Bill, which was then passing
through the Irish Parliament on its way to becoming law, encountered widespread opposition because of its further enlargement
of the powers of the police to seize and detain suspects and a consequent erosion of the rights of the individual in such a situation.
Though Mathews calls this a directorial decision[23] (by Michael
Scott) and shrinks from so overt an agitprop gesture, the Criminal
Justice Bill is nevertheless one of the key subtexts of his own
version or, rather, subversion of the *Antigone*.[24] When a tape
Creon has been recording throughout Act One is played back, the
stage directions indicate that 'we are listening to a reading of the
Criminal Justice Bill, though this should never be obvious.
Instead one has the impression of arid legalese, of an unimpas-
sioned gobbledygook' (26). The tape continues as the act ends
and the actors leave the stage: 'the tape of speech continues to
play through the auditorium during the interval. It is always
audible, never intrusive.' Such a staging represents the Bill, not
as a discrete coherent text to be scrutinised on a handout, but as
the scarcely intelligible soundtrack to our lives, a threatening
ever-present undertone to which the audience hardly attends, a
slow erosion of the ground of individual liberty from under its
feet. The playing of the tape, initially within the diegetic structure
of the play but then persisting while the other withdraws, bridges
the gap between stage and auditorium. The strict comforting
division of then and now collapses into then-as-now in the
perpetual present of the theatre.

This metadramatic dimension is one of the most striking and
persistent features of Mathews's reading of Sophocles. In a piece
on the play published in *Theatre Ireland*, he writes: 'it seemed
an excellent idea to collapse the stage-space, blur the line of
demarcation between actor and audience, and thereby achieve a
moment of deconstruction, of reciprocal leakage from one
sanitised area to another.'[25] This effect is even more fully realised
in the one-man chorus Mathews devises, utilising the streetwise
Dubliner's compulsion to comment, to assume a knowing tone
whatever the topic and rhetorically to direct his exasperated,
cynical comments to an invisible audience. This chorus as
Dublinese *vox pop* would have been enhanced by the casting in
the original production of Mannix Flynn, a Brendan Behan for
the 1980s:

I'll come in here, I'll traipse around, I'll say my lines — I got the most
fuckin' difficult lines in the whole thing — I'll do my party piece, scrub
down, and fuck off home again, O.K.?   (1)

The chorus informs us by way of the programme that 'The
dream is set in Ireland in the 1980s B.C., soon after Sparta has
entered the war on the German side'. The classical Greek allusion
points to one, but only one, of the play's several frames of temporal,
spatial and cultural reference. What Mathews hopes to restore to
the Sophoclean original is a sense of immediacy and of the
frantic, disordered nature of events within a play from which
time and familiarity have distanced us:

The play is rushed, riotous, askew; the shorthand minutes of a crisis,
dispatches from the front . . . Psychological conflict is central to it, but
political chaos is crucial to it; the first is only a symbolic encapsulation
of the second. From first to last, one has the sense of frantic individuals
shouting at and to each other across the hubbub of catastrophe, the
storm-centre of emergency. Creon is 'torn', the chorus is 'split' . . .[26]

Antigone, even in its original, then, barely resembles what we
take to be the model of classical form, lucid, ordered, serene; its
very form calls into question such a concept by provoking its
opposite. Mathews takes license from his reading of the Greek
original to embody in the structure of his *Antigone* the splits,
fissures, fragmenting and deconstruction that afflict the characters
psychologically.

As we piece together the play, the scene emerges as, if not quite
post-nuclear, bearing many of its features. The urban landscape
is pulverised, there are shootings in the street, mass executions,
all the signs of a military takeover. The scene is one of devastation
and deprivation, with much talk of food rationing and searching
among the ruins for firewood. The few items of technology that
still function — a traffic light, a coke machine — are as close as
the society gets to furnishing miracles. If the setting conforms to
the composite mental picture we have formed of fascist regimes,
certain of the details — especially the herding in camps and
the mass executions — deliberately evoke the Second World War,
the play's second frame of reference as the chorus's talk of 'the
German side' makes clear. That war has thrust the *Antigone* back
into consciousness, into the place dominated by Oedipus as read
by Freud since the turn of the century; the holocaust in particular
appears to have set off endless replications of the play's central act
of the unburied dead and has brought a renewed number of

Antigones to the stage in the wake of Jean Anouilh and Bertolt
Brecht's immediate response to its civilised barbarity.[27]

Mathews' play, at a certain level of abstraction which its futuris-
tic setting enables it to maintain, is about all societies that endure
such political upheaval. But three more specific sites are consistently obtruded: Greece in the period B.C., Germany in the Second
World War, and Ireland in or near the present. As the chorus
indicates, the drama *is* 'set in Ireland', something the sound of
his own scabrous and unrelenting speech won't allow us to
forget. But it is not an Ireland that is immediately recognisable. If
the time is the 1980s, it's a projection several years hence to the
decade's end. For by the play's insistence that the setting is
Ireland in the 1980s, the playwright is reflecting imaginatively on
a society radically at odds with itself, torn between the challenge
of individual freedom, a more than nominal independence, and
a longing for the old paternal securities which formerly gave it
direction, the British Empire to oppose and the Catholic church
to espouse. A merry-go-round of governments in the early 1980s
significantly increased the disillusionment with democratically
elected governments and has given rise to privately voiced
longings for a strong man to take control and rule by absolute fiat.
Mathews has taken these under-currents in the Republic's polity
and projected them into the surrealistic scenario of his play. The
clinching demonstration that these *are* the issues, and that they
have a specific grounding in Dublin, is provided by the fate of the
chorus. During Act Two, in the course of a scene where three of
the characters go to a parody of Catholic confession, the chorus's
request when in the box is:

I was hoping you might be kind enough to relieve me of my freedom.
(*Starts to weep.*) It's a terrible responsibility. I keep making moral decisions.
It's ruining my health.

Throughout the play, the chorus's cowed relations with both
Creon and Heman issue in a verbal and visual image of the
master-slave relationship that directly echoes the representation
of Pozzo and Lucky in Beckett's *Waiting For Godot*. Of the many
textual allusions that litter Mathews's play, *Godot* is the most
crucial, recurrent and deeply embedded: as the seminal text of
postmodernist drama; as a play specifically deriving from the
conditions of the Second World War; and as the work of the
foremost living Irish writer. The role of Pozzo is occupied by
Heman. His effect is immediately apparent when, upon his

entering, the chorus switches from private, confidential abuse to public praise: 'Our president . . . The kind of man who finds a cure for cancer. I mean, really brilliant. A visionary.' (3). The scene that follows also recalls Beckett in its deliberate playing of the drama and its protagonists with conventional expectations, theirs and the audience's: 'And let the expectation mount. The expectation is half the pleasure.' But Heman is also playing a psychological game with the chorus, enforcing a sense of superiority by seeking to dominate a subject, and make it an object. In the world of diminished expectations and possibilities which Samuel Beckett more than anyone else has realized dramatically for us, the sign of this tyranny is a cigarette, as in *Godot* it is the bones that Pozzo throws to Vladimir and Estragon. There, one succumbs, the other doesn't. Here, the chorus emulates Estragon and capitulates rapidly, falling to his knees to beg and weep. When Heman says 'Get up, there's a good fellow' (4), we hear Pozzo's exaggerated politeness mingle with the act of degradation and cruelty we have just witnessed.

The play in its early stages might best acknowledge its debt to Beckett by being retitled *Waiting for Antigone*. This phrase describes the action not only in terms of the on-stage characters waiting for the belated entrance of the eponymous heroine. But it also describes the play itself and its conscripted players awaiting the arrival of the Sophoclean classic text of *Antigone*, the ostensible occasion for the gathering together of actors and audience. Nothing closely resembling that accepted shape or verbal content ever arrives, a point underscored by the opening of Act Two where a critic rises from the audience to protest what he sees as a travesty of the original 'tremendous play' (27), as an attack on official culture. The character of Antigone eventually rewards expectations to the extent that she shows up on stage. But she does so with full, self-conscious knowledge of her theatrical lineage, of all the many times she has played the role and with a reluctance to assay it once again. Her heroism is also redefined in terms not of doing but of a Beckettian waiting, now keyed in feminist terms:

I represent ordinariness . . . tens of thousands of faceless women. Women who stand in queues, and wait. And their waiting is more busy, more concentrated, than all the bustle of men. (35)

This Antigone also acts, not by burying a brother but by inscribing the letter 'P' on a wall. Her revolutionary gesture fits the context of the overall action, which is one of inscription, erasure, and counter-inscription in a play of contending signs. The chorus' primary activity is literally whitewashing; he carries around a brush and a bucket of paint, covering what is written on the walls with slogans that read: 'Hear no evil, see no evil, speak no evil', 'Loose talk costs lives', 'Strength and patience', 'Think yes'. (1) This erasure of names anticipates the treatment of Polyneices. The dramatic emphasis no longer falls on the fate of the corporeal remains; the political action of Creon and his party now consists of a systematic effort to destroy all evidence of Polyneices' identity, erase all signs of his former existence. Antigone looks at a group photograph that included her brother, and finds him missing: 'They air-brushed him out of the photo taken at the stadium . . . [he's] been painted out. Even his shadow' (18). When Ismene makes the plausible suggestion that their brother may not have been in the photo, Antigone responds by pointing to the synecdochal remains of Polyneices' presence at the original event: 'But, you know, they did it so quickly, they forgot something. Because he had an arm around Petey. And his right hand was lying on Petey's right shoulder . . . And then it strikes you. Just lying there, on his shoulder. The whole hand.' (18)

The bond of true fraternity proves equally difficult to erase in Antigone's case. Her final gesture on her brother's behalf is described as follows:

Antigone is now seen at left of stage, chalk or paintbrush in hand. She waits a moment, lifts the chalk/paintbrush, and writes the letter P on the wall. Then she goes out.   (43)

The gesture is more arbitrary and equivocal than might at first appear. For in his version Aidan Carl Mathews has renamed Eteocles as Peteocles (or Petey) with the result that both brothers now share the same first initial 'P'. And when Creon wishes rhetorically to assert the absolute difference between the brothers Polyneices and Peteocles from a political point of view, the visual evidence contradicts or undercuts him, since the photograph flashed on the wall for each brother is absolutely identical. Creon and his government are determined to control interpretation within the play; at one point, he defines his authority as 'the difference that makes order possible' (52). The threat posed by Antigone is to deny this difference, to assert identity where politics and culture insist on difference. This assertion bears closely on the issue of violence. For, as Mathews' Stanford mentor René Girard has argued, violence effaces the differences between opponents to the point of absolute identification.[28] But for political reasons this equation, this root resemblance, must and will be denied by each side in a cause, official and unofficial, Irish and English, Republican Catholic and Unionist Protestant, IRA and UDA. Antigone, in this reading, exposes the violence on which the state is inescapably founded, but which it consciously mystifies, and so she must be scapegoated. Her painting of the letter 'P' will cost her life. When Creon questions Antigone's action, she replies that she isn't throwing her life away but 'throwing it out. As a suggestion'. (8) By making a gesture, a sign, of this kind she is countering the play's pervasive erasure and the government's control of authorised interpretation (including the universities and their canon of classics) by reinserting a token, like the disembodied, surrealistic hand of her brother in the revised stadium photo, whose very arbitrariness is politically threatening and disruptive, as likely to recall one brother as the other.

The final point about this Antigone, character and play, is how she resists the pervasive self-conscious theatricality. Not only is she absent at the beginning and end of each act, but those beginnings and endings are each marked by a strong metadramatic gesture: the chorus coming on to address the audience in the tones and terms of the Dublin streets they have just left; the Criminal Justice Bill continuing beyond the close of the act; the teacher-critic at the opening of Act Two standing up to make an academic protest; and the winding down of the play with the players, still on stage, taking off their make-up and engaging in small talk. And each of the major characters continues to indulge in theatrics: Ismene consciously sees herself as under-study to big sister and declares herself ready to take on the title part at a moment's notice; Creon's speech and gestures are exaggeratedly theatrical and his actions play up the intimate connections between politics and theatre since many of them have to do with preparing a speech and seeking or making comments about its effectiveness; he makes the most onstage use of a tape recorder since Krapp in Beckett's play. But Antigone is the one figure who stands out against and deliberately resists this process of theatricalisation. She is, as Mathews points out elsewhere, living up to her name, which is 'anti-agon', not only 'the personal embodiment of an abstract principle of pacifism, non-retaliation, non-violence. Antigone means more than this, however; for "agon" also denominates "play", "theatre-piece", "drama", etc. . . . So Antigone is herself violent in at least this respect: she opposes dramatic form, she stands against the ritual of violence which a dramatic performance re-enacts, she de-means drama . . . [and] seeks to deny the very ground of theatre.'[29] In this, as in all versions, she says least. Her taciturnity helps to discredit the elaborate rhetorical procedures of those who address her, especially Creon, a Cordelia-like gesture in the face of a fatally compromised language. In her key speech quoted earlier, when she denies heroic status by saying she represents 'ordinariness', she is also denying herself any markedly individual qualities that would make her personally or theatrically memorable. Instead, by claiming to represent 'tens of thousands of faceless women', she reverses the trend of those like Ismene who aspire to her public persona by relinquishing it in her statement that she is herself merely a stand-in, not for some prominent personage but for the anonymous figures offstage who claim her allegiance.

This reversal of direction which Antigone initiates, away from the compromised practices of the political and theatrical stages toward the street, the society, the world, is continued and concluded by the way she fares at play's end. Antigone's exit has a significantly different quality from that of the other members of the cast. For they reappear toward the close and are seen to take off their makeup, change costume, etc., shedding their roles to reassume their everyday selves. But Antigone does not. One reason is that her exit is the modernist sign for her death as a character. But an exit on stage, as Stoppard and before him Sartre observed, is an entrance somewhere else. When a member of the cast inquires whether anyone has seen Antigone, the chorus answers: 'Nobody's seen her. Nobody. Just . . . vanished. Gone.' (64) But his reply is denied by Heman, who claims she was 'seen in Karkhov only last year'. This exchange clarifies the point that Antigone has exited the theatrical domain which her presence has called in question to seek the more open possibilities of the world of history, to do there what Steiner argues the poet and dramatist do in translating the Sophoclean play: 'call upon, compact, the disseminated energies and authority of myth in order to give a current, circumstantially bounded event or social conflict the "visibility", the compelling dimensions, the inexorable logic and extremity of the mythical.'[30] Yeats did something similar in *Cathleen ni Houlihan*, where the dramatic movement of the play is away from an increasingly discredited existence in the peasant cottage toward a fuller imaginative life made possible by the fusing of her mythic energies with the world of Irish history, revolution, and change. Mathews in his version is also seeking to bring the past-ness of the classic text of *Antigone* very much into the present and make it present to the audience. Antigone's last words to them urge the connection:

Antigone: (To audience.) Do any of you know Polyneices? Polyneices? Please. Please tell them. Please stop them doing this. (Chorus attempts to muffle her mouth with his hand. She bites it, he strikes her.) Jesus, my nose is bleeding. Stop it please. Tell them. Tell them. They'll come for the woman down the street. Will you tell them then? They'll come for your next door neighbour. Will you tell them then? They'll come for you. And after that, when there's nobody left, they'll come for themselves.

The audience is further urged to relate onstage and offstage practices, to study the play's deconstruction of prevailing ideologies and react accordingly, by the closing words ironically and provocatively directed at them: ' "Go home. Go home. You can do nothing." (Final instructions from Creon picked up on loudspeaker and repeated at intervals as audience files out.)' (p. 65)[31]

*   *   *   *   *

The third version of Sophocles' *Antigone*, by southern Irish poet Brendan Kennelly, is the least obviously Hibernicised. It is, in his own words, 'a straight translation',[32] the most straightforward of the three. But it does not take a theory of translation as implicit invention/creation to see that Kennelly's stance of apparent objectivity, of self-effacement in the face of the pre-existent text, cannot be long sustained. He describes his working method as follows: 'I worked from late nineteenth-century translations, six or seven of them, then put them away and wrote it out of my head.' Those who have read Kennelly's poems over the last twenty years or so will not read his version for long before encountering familiar images and realising the extent to which the themes of the *Antigone* have cross-pollinated with the most abiding concerns of the poet's imagination. His Antigone projects the indignity her brother's corpse will suffer through the image of children throwing stones at its exposed skeleton.[33] In one of Kennelly's earliest poems, entitled 'The Stones', children pelt an old woman with stones as they improvise a nursery rhyme around her name, Nellie Mulcahy. The image is cognate to but not identical with the Yeatsian trope of calcified hearts; with Kennelly, the issue is not one of protracted, petrifying sacrifice but of the negative forces in Irish society which pervert loving relations into acts of cruelty, verbal and physical. In Sophocles and in Kennelly, the fate for infringing the word of Creon is literally the

same: 'Whoever disobeys the word of Creon / Will be stoned to
death before the people' (2). But with his metaphoric elaboration
of the stoning image, Kennelly gives voice to one of his recurrent
concerns in showing how the institutionalised forces of repression
embodied by the leaders of a society are replicated in even its
youngest members, witlessly mimed as child's play.

Kennelly dates his version of *Antigone* 'July 1984' (47), as did
Mathews. What adds to the interest of his version, particularly as
it reflects however wittingly on the contemporary state of Ireland,
is the proximity of its writing to the major work of his career, the
long poem *Cromwell*, written and published in 1983, 146 pages of
mainly short poems, occasionally interrupted by longer meditations.[34] Kennelly's *Cromwell* is no more restricted to being a
historical poem about the Puritan leader's sanguinary trek through
seventeenth century Ireland than *The Great Hunger* in Patrick
Kavanagh's long poem or Thomas MacIntyre's stage version is a
documentary account of potato blight in the 1850s. Rather, all
three works are situated in the present or immediate past and have
less to do with literal historic events than a symbolic rendering of
the continuing effects of these events on the Irish psyche. What
Kennelly writes in another context applies equally to his own
poetic procedures in *Cromwell*: 'Many Irish poets are deeply
concerned with the past, finding in Ireland's turbulent history
images and personalities that, when dramatised and charged
with imagination, help to shed light on current problems.'[35] And
so Kennelly's overall design is to shuttle remorselessly between
past and present, alternating poems in which we are as likely to
encounter Oliver Cromwell running Drogheda's football club as
putting the town to the sword; more often, he engages the narrator
Buffún in debates on contemporary Ireland. Kennelly does not go
as far as such recent Field Day pamphlets as Declan Kiberd's
Anglo-Irish Attitudes in denying the dimension of historical reality
to the tangled relations between Ireland and England — several of
the most vivid poems dramatise at close hand the bloody justice
for which Cromwell's name is still a byword — but he is as
concerned as they are with the interiorised mutilation of which
such obsessiveness speaks.

In Kennelly's reading, if Oliver Cromwell had not existed, the
Irish would have found it necessary to invent him, since he
serves so amply as the bogeyman by which their behaviour can
be justified. In 'Therefore, I Smile' Cromwell prophetically sees
how they will 'make me an excuse for what they / Would fail
to do, to be, being themselves' (136). 'Vintage' shows the Irish

reincarnating his presence through shedding blood, eating his flesh and drinking his blood in a parody of the Mass. The narrator then turns to reflect that Cromwell's blood is 'not wine' but rather 'much the same as yours or mine' (133). This line characterises the poem's overall strategy of confrontation with and attempted exorcism of Cromwell as the ghost repeatedly evoked to 'people [our] emptiness'. Finally, it asks the Irish reader to acknowledge not the baneful otherness of an Oliver Cromwell but the complicit intimacy in which we have used his image to engender and act out our worst nightmares. *Cromwell* is a remarkable work, arguably the most important volume from an Irish poet since Seamus Heaney's *North* ten years earlier.

If the poem continues to reverberate in the minds of those who have read it, then it can do no less in the head of the man who generated it. And in going on to write a version of Sophocles' *Antigone*, Kennelly implicitly encourages his readers to look for continuity and connection between the two endeavours. The most striking is the resemblance between Cromwell's speech and actions in the poem and those of Creon in the *Antigone*. As with Paulin's Creon and Conor Cruise O'Brien, the harsh alliteration urges the consonance. Kennelly's Cromwell and his Creon are the source of a terrifying power in their respective fictional domains, operating as absolute and unquestioned incarnations of political authority. Creon announces as he enters that he now occupies 'the throne' of Thebes; Cromwell is not only the agent of English imperialism in Ireland but the Lord Protector. They derive their authority, however, not from orderly succession in a stable institution of civil rule, but from an act of carnage, a military exchange in which they proved their superiority by force of arms. Cromwell justifies his actions on the battlefield by appeal to God's judgement: 'God ordained they be avenged. / At Drogheda, I saw his judgement executed / Upon these barbarous wretches . . .' (55). Kennelly's Creon expresses the absolute distinction between Eteocles and Polyneices, the two sides of the civil/ fratricidal strife, in the same Biblical terms: 'The wicked are not the just / And must not be treated as if they were' (8). Creon's refusal to temporise in the matter of Polyneices springs from the contradiction at the heart of his rule: the need to separate himself as much as possible from the acts of blood through which he came to power. Accordingly, he speaks of Theban law as something immutable and unchanging in order to conceal the violent and disruptive methods by which his authority was established. Similarly, in the case of Cromwell, the absoluteness of God's rule

which he proclaims may be verbally self-evident but requires
repeated demonstration at the end of a sword. The contradiction
lies at the heart of all countries that emerge as republics through
an act of violent revolution, as Ireland did, and subsequently
require frequent and bloody reprisals to distance the affinities
between those maintaining the new state and those still committed
to attacking it:

> Eteocles, who died fighting for our city,
> Will be buried in full dignity
> And rest among the noble dead.
> Polyneices, his brother, who came back from exile
> And tried to destroy by fire
> The city of his fathers
> And the shrines of his fathers' gods,
> To murder his own brother
> And lead our people into slavery,
> Polyneices will not be buried.
> His corpse must corrupt in the open air,
> His corruption must be seen by all . . .
> We have a city to maintain.
> It will be maintained by rule, by law,
> By men who understand that truth.   (8)

When Creon asserts that this is his 'word', the Chorus is forced to
admit: 'You have the power to turn your word to action.' This
same 'power' is attributed to Cromwell in Kennelly's poem. Over
and over, he makes good his 'word' sheathed in the sword of
action. To this, Kennelly opposes (and criticises) the Irish addiction
to talk for its own sake, undercutting 'the rhetorical man / In the
pulpit who roared' (126) by providing a 'welcome' for 'one who
knows his own thinking, / A man for whom a word is a deed come
true'. If Creon and Cromwell must use the threat of violence to
back up their sole authority, there is a more authentic dimension
to their agency. They speak and act out of an idealist conviction,
a visionary sense of things, and so pose the same dilemma as the
men of 1916 do to the Irish Republic which followed them: how
to reconcile the idealism with the apparently endless cycle of
reciprocal bloodletting that succeeds it? Kennelly, therefore,
draws on his poem and portrayal of Cromwell to realise the
puritanical and prophetic aspects of Creon's character. Both inherit
a situation poised on the brink of social anarchy; by sheer force
not alone of physical might but even more of messianic will, they
struggle to realise a dream of order. Cromwell holds to his bloody
purpose; Creon recants when, as the Chorus moans, it is too late,

too late (45). They share an avidity and ability to translate their word into deed that speaks not only to their centralised position within the depicted society but even more to their compelling mythic dimensions as figures for poetry and drama. Steiner quotes Holderlin's definition of the key to Greek tragic discourse, which maintains that 'the Greek-tragic word is factually deadly. It seizes upon the human body and kills it. In Greek-tragic drama there occurs . . . "real murder through words" . . . the "athletic, plastic" (Holderlin's adjectives) immediacy of physical destruction through an act of speech'.[36] Creon and Cromwell are the most radical of poets, restoring to words their bloody immediacy. This makes of Kennelly's Creon an especially powerful presence when his words are incarnated through a living actor in the 'athletic, plastic' medium of theatre.

What is true of Creon, however, in his power to translate word into deed precisely defines the nature of the threat that Antigone poses, since she herself not only makes but vindicates the same claim: 'I sought to bury my brother. / That is my word, my deed. / Word and deed are one in me' (19). The single greatest shock to Creon and the Chorus up to that point is caused by the revelation that the antagonist is not male, as they have assumed, but female. This discovery provokes a whole new area of concern, the confrontation between man and woman, and the related concepts of the masculine and feminine. Steiner posits this most intimate and complex of encounters as the essence of dramatic dialogism: 'the absolute purity of collision, the blank space of the irreconcilable between a man and a woman . . . act out the finalities of human confrontation (the mortal "affront" of our intimacy with otherness).'[37] The affront that Antigone offers to Creon is a challenge not only to the institutional power he claims to represent but to the inescapably patriarchal character of that power and those institutions. Creon makes it clear that, when he discovers the subversive agent is female, he is punishing her for usurping the prerogatives of his sex: 'I would be no man, / She would be the man / If I let her go unpunished.' (18) The sexist nature of his discourse reaches a higher pitch when he talks with his son, alternately appealing to Haemon on the basis of their shared maleness and deriding him for his weakness in joining the other side. What starts as a speech on the emotions, aims and desires of fatherhood modulates rapidly into a defence of patriarchy, with Creon stressing reason as masculine, strong, hard, pleasure as feminine, weak, deceptive. The logical conclusion is that woman is the foe, that the threat Antigone poses is not so much that of a

single citizen to the stability of the state but that of a woman
to the opposed world of male values. Haemon's response, his
espousal of Antigone and her cause — 'The world is full of
different words, different voices. / Listen to the words, the voices'
(28) becomes in Kennelly's version an appeal to the doctrine of
pluralism. That appeal has an increasingly ironic resonance in
the Ireland of the 1980s, given the advocacy of a pluralist state on
which Garrett Fitzgerald based his rise to leadership and the
recurrent setbacks suffered through referenda prohibiting abortion
and divorce. These indicate to the Northern communities that
the South has rejected not only pluralism but also the idea that
a woman has the right to biological control of her own body and
destiny.

For Antigone's threat to patriarchy is twofold: not only encroach-
ment on or usurpation of traditional male areas of action but
advocacy of a radically different way of being and set of values
centred on the feminine. What the play, in both its Greek original
and these modernist versions, does is show Antigone 'acting for
and, in the perspective of prevailing conventions of society and
of politics, as a man'[38] in taking over the vacated male role in the
House of Laius (which leaves the traditional and marginal role of
helpless, suffering femininity to Ismene). But she also takes
initially uncertain but increasingly confident steps towards an
advocacy and enactment of the feminist. The first issue in such a
progress is that of speech versus silence. Disturbed as she is by
the nature of what her sister is about to do, Ismene is even more
disturbed by Antigone's lack of traditional feminine reticence,
her determination publicly to articulate and take possession of
her actions:

> Ismene.   At least, tell no-one what you plan to do.
>   Be secret. So will I.
>
> Antigone. Go shout it from the roof-tops, Ismene.
>   Forget your despicable silence.
>   Your silence will bring more contempt on you
>   In the end. Be true, not silent.   (5)

His version is, as Kennelly himself says, a feminist 'declaration
of independence'. And that declaration emerges in full in the
key exchanges with Creon. The first scene between the sisters
establishes a sense of woman not only taking over a moral vacuum
left vacant by men but transforming the image of heroism from
violent self-assertiveness to ministering self-sacrifice. That image

is developed in the Guard's account of the prohibited act when he describes how Antigone 'gave a sharp cry / Like a wounded bird or a mother / Brutally stripped of her children' (17). The language makes of Antigone's gesture something maternal in her treatment of her brother's corpse, the dual nature of the relationship that she thereby establishes as sister and mother serving to provide a healing counterpart to the cursed double relationship her father Oedipus bore her. But hers is also the voice of primordial sound breaking the silence in which her brother is shrouded. 'She cried a cry beyond all bounds of words', raising a howl of protest against an unspeakable act. She is without words at this point as Creon never is, a point to which I will return.

Antigone's verbal encounter with Creon immediately engages the sexual dialectic. He addresses her, not by name but by gender, as *girl*, with overtones of contempt, objectification, and denial of their kinship. She retaliates by addressing him in turn as *man*, thereby appropriating the sexist terminology and using it against him. In what she says, she stresses her obligations to her dead brother but also makes the vitally related point that the obligations she follows, the values to which her act refers, are outside the accepted norms and conventions of established political exchange and so incomprehensible to patriarchy. 'If I seem foolish to you, this may be / Because you are a foolish man, a foolish judge' (18). Creon's response — 'I would be no man, She would be the man / If I let her go unpunished' — confirms in its stychomythia the extent to which Antigone has rightly disclosed the double nature of the discourse, the fundamental threat she poses not so much to the status quo of stable rule (judges, kings) but to the masculine appropriation of power which its apparently disinterested objectivity scarcely veils. Steiner points out the reciprocal logic by which, if Antigone prevails, 'a twofold inversion of the natural order will ensue. Creon will no longer be a man and, in perfect expression of the logic of reciprocal definition, Antigone will have become one. . . . The masculinity of Antigone's deed, the masculinity of the risks which she has incurred, a masculinity postulated *a priori* and, in consequence, perceived as self-evident by the ruler of the city no less than by his sentinels and councillors, fundamentally impugns the manhood of Creon'.[39] But it does more than that, especially in Kennelly's skilful development of those areas of the text in which a feminist subtext is latent. For already, by this stage in his version, the counter-assertion of non-patriarchal values by Antigone is well advanced. The primordial cry and maternal gestures over the corpse of

Polyneices cannot simply be interpreted as traditional womanly traits. They are coupled with an assertive and provocative act and the effect of that conjunction is to undercut both established masculine and feminine norms through this enlarged synthesis of speech and act.

The Kennelly text goes on to assert the more threatening principle of difference which Antigone's stance embodies and which is not susceptible to Creon's attempt to address it in traditional terms:

> Creon: Are you not ashamed to act
>   Differently
>   From all these other people?
>
> Antigone: No . . . never forget the possible difference
>   Of that other world of the gods.
>   Thinking of difference there
>   May make us different here.   (19-20)

The difference between the living and the dead is analogous to that between the areas of male and female experience. Antigone's talk of 'the gods', even in the original, is never pitched consistently in terms of organised religion but serves rather as the sign for a series of personal imperatives to which only she has the key.

The last section initiates a series of contrasting images, a cluster of associations, defining the zone in which these personal prerogatives can best be articulated. In the play's terms these are the regions of the dead and not the living, the dark rather than the light, the hitherto unexplored regions of her own being. For Antigone is not simply put to death; she is led away to a place of confinement, a dark space where she is to sustain a minimal existence: 'When you have placed her / In that black hole among the rocks, / Leave here there, alone. / Banished from the world of men, / This girl will never see the light again' (36). Not only her movement but that of the play as a whole is away from the garish light of Creon's *realpolitik*, from the discredited life and activities of the daylight world, towards the dark, physically circumscribed but in many ways open possibilities of a personal, feminist space.

Antigone's last rejoinder to Creon — 'You chose to live for fear. / I chose to die for love' — reminds us of their equal status in the play as what Steiner terms *autonomists*, 'human beings who have taken the law into their own keeping'.[40] They make the same claim in insisting on their power to translate their words into deeds, to make good a verbal promise through the integrity of action. Antigone's retort to Creon makes a superior claim for the values on whose behalf she acts, the principle of love and not fear, and what makes her claim the more compelling is the choice she outlines before entering her tomb: 'Because I have given my life to the dead / I have never stretched in the marriage-bed' (33). Her choice to forego the possibilities of procreation is no mere rhetorical gesture but one that is enacted through the language of her body and so can forego the medium of words altogether. For the male Creon as for Oliver Cromwell, his power to translate his words into deeds has a crucial reliance on external agency, on the deferral of an edict on to the instruments of sword, servants or words required to convey and enact that command. But there is no such deferral or displacement in the woman's claim; it is absolute and made good on and through her body. This is the sense in which Antigone is finally unassailable and before her all words, those of Creon or the male Chorus, must fall. The inevitable gap or lack in the male theatrical version of carnal immediacy reaches vanishing point in the enacted presence of the female body. No wonder the Greeks and the Elizabethans wished to keep actual women from performing these roles.

The Chorus' belated tribute, praising her isolation, her aloneness, does so in feminist terms. In being a law unto herself, Kennelly's Antigone evades the self-entrapping stratagems to which her sex is usually reduced:

> Chorus: You are mistress of your own fate
>   Unlike these women
>   Who have to prowl among men
>   Or other women
>   For their little pleasures.
>   You have created your own solitude.   (33)

But Antigone rejects their apparent turn in her favour as belated and condescending, insincere and insufficiently radical, as she has earlier rejected her sister Ismene's apparent change of heart:

> Antigone: You are used to flattering men.
>   But I am a woman
>   And must go my way alone.
>   You know all about men,
>   You know all about power,
>   You know all about money.

> But you know nothing of women.
>
> What man
> Knows anything of woman?
> If he did
> He would change from being a man
> As men recognize a man.   (34)

The Chorus is here identified with the unholy triple alliance of 'men', 'power' and 'money' Antigone has dared to confront and by her action call in question. This speech to the Chorus broadens in its rhetorical range to include the audience, collectively indicting them for their paternalism and urging the males to work free of the limitations of gender, the acquired attributes of maleness on which so much of society operates (not least Ireland with its rituals of all-male drinking, etc.). One male in particular, Creon, has said accusingly: 'I want Antigone to think of her life / As she lies in that black hole / Among the rocks' (32). But he changes his tune when the roles are reversed and he is the one marginalised, dispossessed, by the deaths of his son and wife. This is even more the case in his rejection by death and his being left to wander on stage bereft not only of his kindred but of all the ego-sustaining props of male rule. Creon finally has no place left to go, no inner refuge. That dark space to which Antigone withdraws is one which she implicitly calls each man and woman to follow — but which the play itself does not follow her into. Having brought us to the edge, Kennelly can go no further, both because his literary source does not and because that 'black hole' is a woman-centred space towards which none of the three male writers, Paulin, Mathews, and Kennelly, can do more than gesture.

Each version, in the order in which this essay has considered them, has gone further in that feminist direction. Paulin, as one would expect of the heavily male preserve of the Field Day enterprise, has least to say on that score; the rhetoric in which his use of 'wild' could be situated shows little desire to disturb the prevailing male/female categories as part of its agenda of contradiction. Mathews' *Antigone* has a discernible feminist edge, in her claim (quoted earlier) to speak for women denied voices and in some sharp satiric counterpointing of Antigone's grandstanding with Ismene's quietly heroic struggles with the travails of domesticity and motherhood. And Kennelly develops the feminist subtext into a full-scale exposure of the bonded forces of patriarchy as oppressing not only women but men, of the classifications of gender as self-deceiving and self-entrapping. But the three versions still leave the nagging sense that Ireland lacks a truly feminist *Antigone*. Or at least so I thought until realising that not three but four *Antigones* emerged in response to the social, political and cultural conditions prevailing in Ireland circa 1984. This version did not explicitly identify itself as such, was not realised in theatre but through the related medium of cinema, was authored by a woman (Pat Murphy) rather than a man, and goes further than any of the other three both in embedding a feminist discourse in a specifically Irish historical setting and in dramatically following Antigone into that 'black hole' where her goal is not repentance but redefinition.

The film is Pat Murphy's *Anne Devlin* (1984), based on the life-narrative of a woman consistently sentimentalised in Irish history as the housekeeper of Robert Emmet, his faithful servant in the abortive rebellion of 1803. Murphy draws on Devlin's own journals to offer a counter-narrative to the traditional image of the woman overlooked by official written history and misrepresented in the popular oral accounts.[41] With Anne Devlin's consciousness as the central focus of the film, the historic events of the rebellion by the United Irishmen and its breaking by the British forces under Major Sirr are displaced to the margins of the narrative. Instead, the camera and the framing stress the isolation of Anne Devlin (Brid Brennan), moving with her through the empty rooms and dark spaces that first we merely take to be her exclusion from the world of men's affairs, overheard in an adjoining room. Increasingly, she not only fills the frame with her presence but defines it as an authentic, woman-centred space, especially in the 'third act'[42] where she is incarcerated in prison.

The connection with the *Antigone* is established in the opening sequence. Pat Murphy's rereading of woman's place in Irish history and society opens with an image of exhumation, a woman's hands brushing clay from the features of a dead male. The corpse is taken from its grave and placed on a cart drawn by a company of women. When armed British redcoats intervene, Anne Devlin stands challengingly before them and, without offering a word of rational explanation or apology, proceeds on her way — to offer this body of a United Irishman she has taken from an unmarked grave a proper burial, not only with Catholic rites but among the community that has fostered him. One of the film's final images is of Devlin, during her imprisonment, suffering the death of her younger brother and holding his body in her arms in a pieta-like pose. These authoritative framing images

function at least as much as 'quotations' (in my reading) of the
Antigone than as integral elements of the narrative.

The latter image, of Devlin holding her brother's body, is kept
from mere passivity by its integration in a series of actions throughout the film where, following on from her stance before the British
army, Devlin's passivity is not to be read as acquiescence but as
resistance. The same is true of the series of interrogations midway
through between the silent prisoner and the Creon-like figure of
Major Sirr. Devlin holds information on the whereabouts of the
dispersed rebels that he would dearly like to know and so her
refusal to speak, to divulge what she knows, can be seen as heroic
in something resembling traditional terms. But when even the
subsequently imprisoned Robert Emmet counsels her to confess
and Anne Devlin replies, 'I'll not swear one word against you —
it's not for you I did it', the film's displacement of the male-
ordered discourse of power is complete. Initially aligning itself
with Republican ideals, *Anne Devlin* uses its heroine's equivocal
status to call those ideals in question. The traditional rhetoric
and imagery employed by the Irish Republicans, especially the
mirroring implicit in their countering the red uniforms with
green ones, become increasingly irrelevant to an individual act of
rebellion which will move beyond such self-serving and deluded
theatricalisation.[43] Where earlier Anne Devlin was marginal to
the approaching revolution, the film's centring on her builds to a
full validation when the patriarchal practices of the rebels (who
persist in treating Devlin *as* a housemaid) are discredited by
being seen through and hence defeated. In this feminist context,
the literal overthrow of the rebellion is no longer relevant (besides
being, in the context of Irish history, a foregone conclusion) and
is scarcely adverted to in the narrative. When he approaches her
in prison, Robert Emmet is now as marginal as Major Sirr to Anne
Devlin's concerns and registers as one more male voice urging her
not to disrupt the patriarchal hegemony by her silence.

It is in this third and final act that *Anne Devlin* functions not
only as a feminist version of *Antigone* in an Irish context but as a
sequel to it. The film develops beyond the point where the earlier
versions of necessity stopped short (in their male adherence to
the original's boundaries) by entering and dramatising the 'black
hole' into which Antigone vanishes — out of the play. Murphy
has said of this final section: 'the climax of the film is the whole
third act, because this is where her energy, which has been
gathering over the two previous acts, is released. It's released very
slowly, and the music plays an important role here. I'm very

interested in the strength that Anne Devlin had — it wasn't explosive like the rebellion, it was released very slowly and that was what defeated her opponents.'[44] Murphy achieves this effect by deliberately revising and rewriting all the requirements of what a traditional third act should offer. The plot of the narrative, if we have misread the signs and presumed its alignment with the narrative curve of the rebellion itself, does not come to a phallocratic climax of bullet, powder and rifle. Indeed, in following Anne Devlin into her place of confinement, the film abandons both plots (hers and the uprising's) simultaneously; or rather it replaces them with a new plot whose bearings are internal rather than external, whose energy is borne by and incarnated in Anne Devlin's persona and presence, and whose release is slow and multiple rather than fast, singular and incendiary.

The third act also offers redefinitions of time and space. The dialogue at one point makes the suggestion that time has stopped. Without any clocks and because of the unrelenting darkness, without news from the outside world to establish chronology, all external aids to measuring time are absent. Instead, as Devlin herself says, the only guide she has to measuring the passage of time is the monthly menstrual change her body undergoes. And outer place no longer has meaning in the succession of dark, claustrophobic, isolated cells in which she is set. The gestural movements, the expressive face of Brid Brennan, the music, and the deliberate visual stylisation all enable the viewer to follow Anne Devlin-as-Antigone into the black hole. In so doing, we come to see the process as the logical and natural culmination of her gradual disengagement from the traditional roles to which her sister and the other women in the film are consigned. It is even more a disengagement from the fatally compromised, tainted speech of male power in which the Irish and British sides have both engaged and to which her actions, questions, and final refusal to speak have been a consistent challenge. When the historical Anne Devlin (in 1806) and the viewer of the film (in the closing moments) are released from this enlightening darkness, the response is one of a blinking, unblinkered stare back at the outside world and a realisation that there is no return to the old ways, either of political action which would deny women a meaningful role or of the stereotypical narrative images in which not only they but so much of Irish experience continue to be articulated, the colonial legacy of sentimentality and abject victimage.

That legacy is what all four versions of the *Antigone* are responding to — the difficult balance between the claims of the

status quo and the urge to revolution, between the need to build
stable political structures and maintain tribal loyalties. This
balance, difficult in any society, is particularly fraught and
precarious in the Irish context. Without a continuous centuries-
old tradition of unified political process, any political leader
inherits a situation close to Creon's, who takes over power straight
from the battlefield and has to build a credible structure even as
he continues to defend it rhetorically. Hence, at least in part, the
particularly histrionic nature of Irish politicians and the appeal
of drama in the first place, its ineluctable intersection in Ireland
with moments of key political crisis (cf. the Abbey riots). And
Antigone restores the centrality of woman to the culture, in a
society so largely based upon and derived from a sense of extended
family, but also with the legacy of a Gaelic past in which their
own sexuality and the Brehon laws granted them something
closer to autonomy and power within the political sphere. The
appeal of an Antigone who makes her claims in terms of her own
extended lineage and personal obligations, who retains her spirit
formidably intact even while her body and person are abused
and violated, offers a less questionable (because more open to
question) version of Ireland's dilemma, internal and external,
than the image of rape (of Ireland by England) in Heaney's *North*
or, to go further back, the ravening blood-queen Cathleen ni
Houlihan. What George Steiner says in his conclusion would seem
to be particularly true of Ireland: 'New "Antigones" are being
imagined, thought, lived now; and will be tomorrow.'[45] They
were never more needed than at present, when every statement
from political and church leaders carries with it the implicit
injunction: 'Antigones, lie down.'

THE MARTYR-WISH IN CONTEMPORARY IRISH DRAMATIC LITERATURE

CLAUDIA W. HARRIS

Contrary to the prevalent critical emphasis on the divisiveness in Irish society as reflected in culture generally and literature in particular, theatre can be seen as an effort towards at-one-ment, as an art form which by its very nature can create harmony through shared experience. Theatre has been called the most democratic of the arts because of its ability to bring together disparate individuals and groups for a common, although brief, encounter. Certainly theatre enjoys a dynamic relationship with its audience. The ritual inherent in the repeated re-enactments of stories important to the participants, actor and audience alike, creates a communal experience comparable to other ritual occasions, such as religious events or political pageants. And in addition to possibly changing its audience's attitudes, theatre has the capacity both to change events and be changed by them.

The theme of a play itself can also help create this at-one-ment or harmony as an adjunct to the phenomenon of the shared theatrical experience. Contemporary Irish playwrights from diverse backgrounds explore alike the need for reconciliation and compromise. Usually not content to simply show life as it is, they expose the audience to issues which highlight the similar needs of the seemingly dissimilar groups. One recurring, dominant theme which does this effectively is martyrdom and the concomitant violence which often adds to the dire consequences of the sacrifice. This theme of sacrifice and martyrdom, of expiation and atonement, causes the *content* of Irish theatre to follow the *form* of the theatrical event. At-one-ment becomes atonement; form follows function.

Martyrdom has always been and continues to be a pervasive theme of Irish playwrights, despite political statements that modern Irishmen have 'risen above' that behaviour. Whether the plays focus on historical or contemporary figures, political or non-political subjects, most demonstrate some aspect of the theme.

The point of view the playwrights display towards martyrdom might range from sympathy to irony, and the tone of the plays can vary from tragedy to comedy. And yet, nearly all Irish plays explore the theme either explicitly or implicitly, and some plays present it as a problem, needing solution.

In Daniel Magee's play *Horseman Pass By*, Brendan, the revolutionary, says:

> The only crown we were brought up to respect was a crown of thorns.
> Now if the big flashy gold crown symbolises wealth, success and victory
> is it not reasonable to ask if the crown of thorns might lead people who
> use *it* to symbolise their aspirations into poverty, failure and defeat.
> Have you ever noticed, it's only us Irish taigs who seem to think that a
> martyre is a real plus. Wait 'till you read the English papers about Harry
> Samson's death. If they use the word 'martyre' at all it'll be as a jibe. That
> word used nowadays in relation to the Irish struggle is a sneer, a total
> and compleate perversion of the word. For 'martyre' read 'gobshite', and
> that's the message.[1]

Sacrifice or 'victimage' is a pervasive element in Irish political life as well as in Irish theatre. 'Victimage' is the term Hugh D. Duncan uses in *Symbols in Society* to explore this theme of violence and the community's need for expiation in order to maintain itself. He claims that 'the basic function of atonement, in religious as well as social drama, is the re-establishment of communication with authorities who are believed to sustain social order'.[2] This statement is reminiscent of what Henri Hubert and Marcel Mauss say in *Sacrifice: Its Nature and Function* where they define the social function of sacrifice as 'a means of communication between the sacred and profane worlds through the mediation of a victim'.[3] In *Violence and the Sacred*, René Girard asserts that there is 'hardly any form of violence that cannot be described in terms of sacrifice'. He states the case even more strongly by claiming that 'violence and the sacred are inseparable' and by defining sacrifice as 'an instrument of prevention in the struggle against violence', in the struggle against 'bad' violence. Girard declares that sacrifice is designed to suppress internal violence: 'The purpose of sacrifice is to restore harmony to the community, to reinforce the social fabric.'[4]

The stated purpose of Bobby Sands's hunger strike was to communicate with the British authorities about prison reform. A hunger strike can be seen as a classic case of victimage. It has all of the requirements Victor Turner outlines for social drama in *From Ritual to Theatre*: a conflict or breach which has become a crisis; a sacrificial victim (self-chosen, in this case, yet ratified by the group); a performance or sacrifice which is an attempt to heal the breach; and finally, a reconciliation or agreement to differ. Bobby Sands was unsuccessful, ostensibly, in his attempts to communicate with British authority; however, he did communicate successfully with Irishmen and others in the world who believed him to be part of an oppressed minority. Harmony was enhanced in certain parts of the community. But the hunger strikes left the British even more adamant, and that outcome has further radicalised the Irish. Although the result has been greater polarisation overall, the increased unanimity among discrete groups of the population is evidence that the hunger strikes apparently met their sacrificial purpose. They did not heal the Irish-British breach, but they did unite the Irish and also united the British in their opposition.

The hunger strike is an ancient practice used by the Irish to shame and obligate their enemy; the practice has been treated repeatedly in dramatic literature and re-enacted frequently as social drama. What then is the relationship between stage dramas and the actual hunger strikes? Terence MacSwiney's death in 1920 in Brixton prison after seventy-five days of fasting spurred the Anglo-Irish Treaty of 1921 which created the Irish Free State. Yeats rewrote the end of *The King's Threshold* after MacSwiney's death so that now the fasting poet dies on that threshold. Is this a case of life imitating art, then art imitating life? And what of the recent hunger strikes? What has been their significance both *for* theatre and *as* theatre?

If Jesus Christ is our model for atonement, and a strong case could be made for Christ being the archetypical, sacrificial victim in Ireland, then that model requires certain qualities of its victims — that they be pure, beautiful, wise, loving, heroic, and all powerful, and yet willing to sacrifice everything for some greater good. As Hubert and Mauss point out, the victim does not come to the sacrifice with these qualities already perfected or clearly defined; 'it is the sacrifice itself that confers this upon it.'[5] And often in contemporary Irish society it is the play, the continual re-enactment of the story, that confers these qualities upon the victim.

Tomás MacAnna of the Abbey Theatre has directed several of the pageants held in Dublin commemorating the 1981 hunger strikes. When discussing Bobby Sands and his companions with me, he said:

In Northern Ireland the hunger strikers were attacked by the media, they were attacked by the church. The hunger strikers were up against the most virulent and vehement opposition. They were condemned outright. They were told they were committing suicide. All this was hurled against them. They steadfastly stayed the course. Ten of them died. Now, what followed on that, and rather like in 1916, was a change of opinion, a realisation that there had been a sacrifice. A realisation among most people that criminals, because that's what it was all about their being labelled as criminals, criminals do not go on hunger strike. Criminals are a different type all together. To have carried through the hunger strike to the final sacrifice was something which was shattering in its impact.[6]

The repeated Irish uprisings are designed not so much for *victory* as to develop *community*, to develop a desire for a distinct Irish nation. The ritual of repeated uprisings moves participants toward a stronger community and a greater desire to be free of the ritual oppressor. To take up arms against a supposedly invincible enemy is seen as a duty, not folly; the show of resistance is the important concern. And theatre often becomes a powerful celebration of this superficially futile resistance, of this martyrdom theme. Irish theatre then creates cohesiveness not just through the nature of its communal experience but through its content as well.

But the reworking of this theme in the theatre or in life is not necessarily a conscious preoccupation. Girard explains that 'the sacrificial process requires a certain degree of *misunderstanding*. The celebrants do not and must not comprehend the true role of the sacrificial act'.[7] Although sacrifice is often the central theme in Irish plays, it is just as often treated subtly or as a counterpoint in other plays. Therefore the pervasiveness of the theme is recognised only when all plays are considered with this theme in mind. Furthermore, the universality of martyrdom as a social metaphor in Ireland can only be assessed when sacrifice is isolated from other possible motivations for the behaviour in question and when the need for a degree of 'misunderstanding' of sacrificial behaviour is allowed for. Only then can sacrifice be recognised as the potent metaphor it is in both Irish theatre and life.[8]

Turner discusses how particular genres, such as drama, become paradigms for political action, freezing the principals into a specific course. Definitions become blurred as emotions take precedence; consciousness gives way subtly to allusion and metaphor. The unconscious sensing of axiomatic values leads to irreducible life and death stances.[9] Turner's analysis helps explain the power of sacrifice for the Irish. Cloaked in allusiveness, charged with emotion, martyrdom passes beneath Irish consciousness to that cultural value of a type of death which gives meaning to life. Martyrdom has become an Irish 'cultural root paradigm', to use Turner's vocabulary. Nevertheless, recognising the pervasiveness of martyrdom as a social metaphor is not saying that the Irish worship death — a frequent accusation — but rather that they celebrate committed, meaningful life — noble death being just one aspect of that life.[10]

Girard speaks of a sacrificial crisis which he links to a tragic crisis such as that found in Greek drama. 'The more a tragic conflict is prolonged, the more likely it is to culminate in a violent mimesis; the resemblance between the combatants grows even stronger until each presents a mirror image of the other.' He could be describing the situation in Northern Ireland when he defines the crisis as one where distinctions disappear, where it is no longer possible to tell 'the difference between impure violence and purifying violence'. In this situation vengeance becomes the style, and each violent act calls up another violent act. In a sacrificial crisis there is then no control; sacrifice loses its power to limit violence. The violent reciprocity creates 'a crisis of distinctions'.[11]

Frank Wright, a lecturer in Political Science at Queen's University of Belfast, used the term 'mirror image' when he discussed the extreme factions with me:

If you look at the way that both the Paisleyites and Provisional Sinn Fein behave nowadays, to put it simply, they're both extremely effective community work organisations; they both make a point of advocating grievances of people . . . And in the case of the Provisionals, the British government gets nothing except duress . . . Any successes they might have in the field of securing better social conditions of any kind would obviously not tend to legitimise the British state but to legitimise themselves. I think, perhaps, more surprising is that the same observation can be made about Paisleyites, too, that their successes do not legitimise the British state but the Paisley party. Both organisations are, in fact, operating what are Nationalist policies, which is obvious in the case of the Provisionals and less obvious in the case of the Paisleyites. But in fact, the technique is the same; it involves attacking and increasing the disgrace or distance of the central state . . . So that there's a mirror image there of sorts; it's not perfectly symmetrical but it's something like a mirror image. And one day if Britain does remove itself, these lines, these forms of political activity would just collide and there would be an explosion because there's no method of accommodation between Paisleyites and Provisionals. And one can't imagine one being devised in our crisis situation with any speed.[12]

Wright echoes Girard. What he describes suggests that this tragic crisis in Northern Ireland with its long-sustained violence

might be approaching a violent outcome — that violent mimesis
which Girard claims is the predictable outcome when sacrifice
loses its power to limit violence. Wright is active in Corrymeela,
the interdenominational community centre at Ballycastle, Co.
Antrim. The centre promotes reconciliation by bringing diverse
people from the different communities together. After reading
Girard's analysis in *Violence and the Sacred*, Wright no longer struggles for the meaning of the place but now asks a new question:
'Why isn't every place like Northern Ireland?' He believes Girard's
analysis of violence explains Northern Ireland and perhaps all
society. Nonetheless, my application of the term theatre to life
events puzzled him. If the Orange marches are theatre as I claim
they are, he said: 'If that is theatre, it's theatre which is threatening
to leave the stage or the time and the audience. I suppose we
consider chorus for this purpose; we are very conscious in any of
those Euripidean sagas of the danger of actually becoming
involved in the plot.' This is an apt definition of the term theatre
as I use it in this discussion. Theatre need not be bound by stage
conventions although it is informed by them. I describe here
theatre not only threatening to leave the stage but having already
involved the audience to the extent that the conventional interpretation of stage no longer applies. The stage can now be
defined as any arena where actors and audience are involved in
a performance.

Desmond Fennell, an Irish historian and political analyst, movingly shared his experience at Bobby Sands's funeral with me,
demonstrating by his description that the stage area of this
particular performance involved much of West Belfast and, by
extension, included TV screens throughout the world. Fennell
described in detail the church and the roadway, the throngs of
people, the crowd stewards, the journalists, even the Protestants
watching from their neighbourhoods, and then the procession,
including the four hundred women carrying wreaths of flowers.
Finally, he said: 'There was absolutely no disorder — 70,000
people. It was amazing. What makes the difference between a
mob and a crowd of conscious people doing a particular conscious
thing! They were totally in control. Not downcast, just quietly
dignified. You felt a sort of resolution.'[13] When Fennell began
his account he was simply doing me, a fellow researcher and
writer, a favour by describing something which I had not witnessed. But as he proceeded, his matter-of-fact delivery changed
to one filled with emotion as he became caught up again in the
event. When he concluded, his eyes were filled with tears. Often,

a sacrificial performance can be repeated in the retelling and the resolution renewed.

Theatre is not just a simulation; it is an exaggerated performance of those interactions which create the most trouble for a society and which would benefit most from the clarity that might come through practice. According to Richard Schechner, 'drama is not a model of all human action, not even most of it measured by time spent, but only the problematical, taboo, difficult, liminal and dangerous.'[14] Drama develops where clarity is needed most and links two actions — a misunderstanding and violence, especially political violence and rebellion. Theatre therefore becomes the link between crisis and sacrifice, as Schechner echoes Girard. The martyrdom theme then is not only central to Irish theatre but is also a paradigm for all theatre.

Nowhere is this link clearer than in *Antigone*, a play repeatedly revived in Ireland. One such revival was Tom Paulin's *The Riot Act* performed by Field Day Theatre Company in 1984. Set in modern Ireland with the cast in street clothes, the play is a colloquial retelling of this 'crisis of distinctions'. The King, Creon, insists upon treating the warring brothers differently and accuses Antigone of levelling the hero Eteocles with the state traitor Polyneices when she buries Polyneices despite Creon's decree. When Antigone insists she can't distinguish between them because she loves them both, Creon declares that she can join them then, 'I'll not be bested by a woman'.[15] He does not relent when Ismene, Antigone's sister, asks, 'You'd slay the girl / your son would wed?' Creon's crude answer is a good example of Paulin's sparse language: 'There's plenty more / that he can poke' (23). Creon does not relent even when his son, Haemon, pleads with him in a speech that echoes the pleas to Margaret Thatcher that she soften toward Bobby Sands:

> We make mistakes, get lucky,
> by learning from them.
> It's madness, though,
> to go so far far out
> you'll hark to no man.
> Be firm sometimes,
> then give a bit — that's wise.
> You don't back down,
> just go with the tide,
> then ride it tight.   (27)

Not even Teiresias can bend him: 'Creon, you were too tough; /
the state is dead. . . . Now so much blood's been spilt / there's none
can call a halt / to those thrawn and jaggy hates / deep-rooted in
your state' (39, 42). The crisis is now full blown and the play ends in
that violent mimesis Girard outlines. Haemon kills himself when
he discovers that Antigone has hung herself in the cave where
Creon has sent her to die. Hearing this, Eurydice stabs herself by
the altar, cursing her husband, Creon. The messenger blames
Creon: 'He could neither bend nor listen. He held firm just that
shade too long. There was no joy nor give in him ever' (44). The
Chorus then denies Creon the death he seeks: 'Pray no more,
Creon. / For you must bide / by what the gods have set' (50).

From the first introduction of Creon as 'the big man' (6), the
audience is led to make parallels between ancient Thebes and
modern Ireland. 'The big man' is a well-known appellation for
Ian Paisley. Creon's first speech to the people relates him directly
to the then new Secretary of State for Northern Ireland, Douglas
Hurd. Creon echoes Hurd's early statements and even utters some
of his own words: 'I have always held that one of the soundest
maxims of good government is — *always listen to the very best
advice*. And in the coming months I shall be doing a very great
deal of listening' (7). Fintan O'Toole in the Dublin *Sunday Tribune*
called this first speech 'a brilliant parody of a Northern Ireland
Office political functionary'.[16] In fact, of the ten reviews of the
play which I read, only Keith Jeffery, writing for the London *Times
Literary Supplement*, mentions another possible model for Creon's
abuse of power: Richard Nixon.

O'Toole claims, as do other reviewers, that Paulin's recasting of
the story is flawed because there is not enough sympathy for
Creon: '*Antigone* works as a play because we are also interested in
Creon as a man, concerned with his dilemma and the way he tries
to cope with it. Sophocles' Creon is a tragic hero as well as a
villain. By satirising him from the start, the drama of his conflict
with Antigone is rendered impossible.' But Jeffery sees it quite
differently; he calls Antigone 'somewhat colourless': 'Stubborn,
bitter and unbending in defence of individual human decency
and the laws of the Gods, the heroine, as perhaps she should,
deflects our attention back to the more sympathetically portrayed
Creon. The king, after all, suffers most in the play, and does not
even have the sanctimonious satisfaction of pious self-sacrifice to
ease his soul or his conscience.'[17]

I do not believe sacrifice would be characterised in this manner
in an Irish newspaper. In Ireland its 'terrible beauty' is recognised.

But the differing perceptions of O'Toole and Jeffery about the roles of Creon and sacrifice in this play expose the Irish-British divide over this subject. Nowhere were these different cultural viewpoints more in evidence than in the 1982 production of Peter Sheridan's *Diary of a Hunger Strike*. The Hull Truck theatre company in Hull, England, commissioned the play and then performed it for English and Irish audiences in a four-month tour. As written by Sheridan, an Irish playwright, the play was a sympathetic retelling of the 1980/1981 hunger strikes in Northern Ireland. As produced and changed by Pam Brighton, an English director, the play developed into a more balanced account, presenting all sides of the issue. And it is this shift in emphasis, which Sheridan insists was politically motivated and Brighton insists was a dramatic necessity, that caused Sheridan to repudiate the production and ended a long friendship between the writer and director. The cast, containing both Irish and English actors with Protestants playing Catholic roles, became increasingly polarised during the course of the tour. Involvement in the play actually seemed to make some members of the cast less sympathetic to the other cultural point of view.

John Keegan, an actor who comes from a Northern Irish Protestant background, was nonetheless quite republican in sympathy when he was in the play and had no difficulty playing a Catholic hunger striker. Others in the cast were not likeminded. John believes:

The politics of the people involved in the play eventually totally changed the whole shape of it as well as the way we responded to each other. The guy who played the other hunger striker was the son of a loyalist, one of the founders of the Vanguard movement which was Bill Craig's right-wing group. We had this rosary to say in Gaelic and he wouldn't say it. He had all these arguments the whole time.[18]

Frances Quinn, an actress who disavows labels but admits to a Northern Irish Catholic background, expressed surprise at the narrowness of many of the cast members. She described the late night political arguments and the rewriting which involved the cast in a haphazard way. Cast members made suggestions for changes which were then written down and not reworked by the author or even the director. She is amused by the criticism from critics that the play was too balanced because she believes that the cast members, excluding John Keegan, thought the play was very republican and had qualms about performing in it because of that:

Because it was a tour and you're with people for a considerable amount of time, a lot of tensions came out, political tensions in the company. And when we were doing the rewrites, I can remember saying something for the rewrite and there was an outcry of 'Oh, this is all turning quite republican' or Catholic or something which really amazed me because I was playing a Catholic character in the play. And there was this sort of sudden paranoia set in. To me it was a bit of a revelation. All the tensions that came out and people playing parts that were against their political viewpoint maybe and finding that difficult. Or doing it for work because work is scarce for actors. But it created problems for them, I think.[19]

During the course of the run, new scenes were added, others were dropped, speeches were changed, and the play shifted subtly from a focus on the human drama to a focus on the issues. Keegan asserts that before the changes the play was balanced because it dealt with human beings dealing with an extreme situation, but afterward explanation took the place of emotion, issues superceded the human condition. 'See it was very flawed when it was in Edinburgh and when it first went out on tour but extremely powerful and riveting.' Keegan believes that the cast and director ruined the play with their suggestions and changes:

In all there were five new scenes put in. Just before we opened in London, I was just handed this speech that was written by a friend of the director, an English socialist, just before going on in London. And I just had to learn that one. When I was being taken from my cell to the hospital bed, I had to turn around and tell what trouble the country's in. They might as well have given me an orange box that I could have stood up on and made the speech. . . . It was her very brilliance as a director really. I think she just worked it too much and ruined it.

One of the scenes Keegan is referring to was a pivotal scene (Act II, scene two), which was originally a powerful dialogue between the two prisoners as Pat, the leader, decides to begin a new hunger strike since the agreement with the government for concessions following the earlier hunger strike has collapsed. Pat says: 'There'll be no medical intervention this time. This time it'll be all the way.'[20] His cellmate, Sean, worries that he doesn't have Pat's determination. Sean is tearful when he says: 'I just wanted to tell you I love you . . . and what you're doing, well . . . I'd lay down my life for you, Pat, you know that . . . I'm just not sure I could do it this way, that's all' (48). They speculate about when the craving for food stops and refute the idea that anyone has been coerced into fasting. The scene ends with Pat reciting to the warder the standard hunger strike declaration. This original scene is full of pathos and humour and real feeling. But substituting for it in the production script is a scene between the two warders, a scene which reflects the good cop, bad cop stereotype. It begins with the sympathetic warder repeating Pat's hunger strike declaration to the other, whose response is 'Bastards, fucking bastards, the bastards. Billy, if they want to, let them, let them die — it's their choice. Now we'll hear Westminster over negotiating — pandering to them, feeling sorry for them. The newspapers feeling sorry — the television — everyone' (43). This short scene does deal with the issues and could naturally follow the original scene. But when it supercedes it, I can understand the loss and frustration Keegan expresses.

Sheridan insists that Act II problems were the fault of the director not the script. Certainly, Act I changes, which were apparently made by Sheridan, do seem to be for dramatic purposes and simplify the staging of the play. But Act II changes, which Sheridan rejects, do not only change staging but characterisation, focus, and emphasis, as well. Brighton certainly tried to present the issue as she saw it. In fact, Keegan believes the problem was that the play 'tried too hard to confront the issue. It became quite unemotional. It became really just that, just a discussion of issues'.

But comparing the two scripts gives a strange sense of the relative truth of the two approaches. In some ways, the production script seems to show more clearly how things really are. The cabinet minister's response to the hunger strike demands even foreshadows Thatcher's 'out, out, out' response to the New Ireland Forum report. Sheridan's version is much more hopeful; it is a dramatic unfolding rather than an historical retelling. In the original script, you sense that at any moment there's a possibility of agreement, that the terrible deaths can be avoided, that the inevitable need not happen. In the rewriting, the play switches from Sheridan's present tense to a type of past-tense inevitability, from the wishful subjunctive mood to the factual indicative, from Irish credulity to English scepticism.

And these two approaches to the subject were confirmed by the varying audience reactions to the play. Both Keegan and Quinn believe Irish audiences reacted differently than English ones. As Quinn explains:

Irish audiences were moved; they were very, very moved, and emotional, crying, all sorts of things. When you had an English audience in, sometimes they were impressed by it, and depressed by it, the odd, sensitive person. But generally speaking, they found it very interesting on an intellectual level. There wasn't an emotional response, at all. None whatsoever. And you've got people coming out saying, 'It's very interesting seeing sides of the problem, but, you know, it was so ridiculous those men starving themselves to death'. Very, very detached. And a lack of comprehension of the culture or attitudes.

Perhaps because script changes seemed to encourage a thoughtful response to an issue which for the Irish requires only a gut-level reaction, the emotional responses of the participants became heightened and hardened. But the experience of this production was really quite contrary to expectations of anyone involved with the theatre. Usually working on such a rigorous project helps develop group cohesiveness. The longer people work together and the more hardships they survive the more it seems to cement relationships. And I sense bewilderment and disappointment on the part of the director and the writer and the two actors I spoke to that this production could not somehow rise above the divisive situation it portrayed. Usually we hope that theatre teaches and changes its audience for the better. Here is a case where even those involved in producing the play were somehow caught in attitudes and life stances which ultimately caused disjunction and disharmony not empathy and understanding. No at-one-ment here.

But possibly this in itself is an indication of the power of the play and of the production process. The fact that individuals were not able politely to gloss over feelings and behave in the expected, polite manner no doubt means the play successfully confronted those deep and sometimes hidden emotional responses to this explosive issue. After all, the hunger strike event itself polarised people. Sheridan told me how shocked he was when he went north just after the hunger strikes were over to begin preparing to write this play. Everyone was now radicalised. People he had known before who had taken moderate positions were now expressing quite extreme views. And apparently a play about such an event can have the same power to polarise, at least a play about a subject that is so deeply a part of the fabric of a society, a subject that so clearly marks the dividing line between cultural understanding if you're a part of the culture and cultural misunderstanding if you're not.

But it is not only these plays where sacrifice is a central issue which demonstrate the pervasiveness of martyrdom as a cultural root metaphor in Ireland. Whether the play deals with historical figures or social issues some aspect of sacrifice is present. At times central to the development and at other times only part of some startling denouement, this theme of sacrifice and martyrdom, of expiation and atonement underlies much of what is written in Ireland for the stage. In a play about Robert Emmet, martyrdom is not a surprising theme, but it is surprising that in Conor Farrington's *Aaron Thy Brother*, John Philpot Curran who was to defend Emmet turns out to be a martyr as well. Curran is manoeuvred into a position where in order to protect his daughter whom Emmet loved, he must turn over the defence to McNally who is less able. The silenced Curran, a failed Aaron, becomes another martyr to the cause because his daughter is afraid of prison, of being sustained only by 'the bread / Of price, the water of fidelity?'[21] She refuses the sacrificial role, the chance to stand by Emmet, out of fear, so her father protects her by his own downfall.

Fidelity, divided loyalties, betrayal are all concomitant themes. Set in 1920, Jennifer Johnston's *Indian Summer*[22] ends with a knock at the door, the knock Cathal has been waiting for. He has betrayed his cause in order to save the Protestant friend of his youth whom his paramilitary friends rightly believe is an English spy. In essence, Cathal has traded his friend's life for his own; his ultimate motives are good ones. But Eric, in Graham Reid's *Hidden Curriculum*,[23] is a cunning traitor who betrays even his own son. As Reid originally wrote the ending, Eric leaves on the Liverpool boat thus escaping the immediate effects of his behaviour. But Lynda Henderson, editor of *Theatre Ireland*, criticised the ending of the play because it offered no message.

They had already gone to print when he read what I'd written. I noticed when the books came out that all they'd been able to do is cut the ending of the text. The play suddenly stops, it doesn't even say 'the end' or 'fade' which is the way Graham usually gives lighting directions to indicate the end of scenes. They had just simply managed to cut out the last six lines from the text that was published. In both productions, the Abbey and the Lyric, they actually got on the boat. The play as it's published now stops with Eric saying 'I can't go'.[24]

Interestingly, this change turns Eric into an unintended martyr rather than someone concerned only for his own safety. The implication is now that he stays and risks his own life rather than never see his imprisoned son again. Perhaps this also means that Reid has written a different play than he originally intended.

The martyr, however, is usually the best character in the play, the one who can see beyond himself with an innocent goodness.

This is certainly true in Brian Friel's *Translations*[25] which takes place in August 1833. The Englishman, Lieutenant Yolland, loves Ireland, its language and its people, but he is the one who is sacrificed in the bitter battle over the usurped land. In *The Flats*, John Boyd describes his sacrificial victim, Monica Moore, as 'a wisp of a girl. A beautiful face but somehow unawakened'.[26] A true innocent, she is shot trying to help her mother when Protestants marched on their Belfast neighbourhood during the summer of 1969.

The innocent in Martin Lynch's *The Interrogation of Ambrose Fogarty*[27] is crazy Willie Lagan, who is obviously harmless, yet the police keep him in custody when Fogarty resists their brutal urging to confess and is released after the seventy-two hours. In *We Do It For Love*, Patrick Galvin explores even the interrogator Hammond's point of view: 'It's funny how they come in — full of wind and bounce. They don't go out that way. I see to that. They talk. Give statements. Make lists. That's the joy of the Irish. Way down, deep in the gut, they all want to talk. I read history. A long line of rebellions — and always the betrayal.'[28] And so here is revealed another concomitant theme: confession.

Implied also is the inevitability of history repeating itself. In his radio play *Grey Eye*, Conor Farrington has Saint Columba wander as a pilgrim trying to prevent other young men from following his path of seeking justice through killing: 'We are *all* as unclean things and our righteousnesses are as filthy rags! . . . The innocent are out of my care; my flock, that I stand among, are the guilty. . . . The road you're on was my road and I went that road to the end.'[29] Columba prevents these two young men from killing this particular policeman as partial atonement for his own deeds in battle. But the script makes clear that it is only a temporary resolution and does not successfully stem the tide that 'left the grass red-wet' (27).

Sometimes it is the Ulster-British soldier who is sacrificed for tradition or patriotism or a cause. A notable example of this treatment dramatically is *Observe the Sons of Ulster Marching Towards the Somme* by Frank McGuinness. To Pyper who yearns for victory and for home, Craig answers: 'We know where we are. We know what we've to do. . . . We joined up willingly for that reason. . . . This is the last battle. We're going out to die. . . . Whoever comes back alive, if any of us do, will have died as well. He'll never be the same.'[30] Christina Reid also deals with this subject peripherally in *Tea in a China Cup*,[31] but, unlike McGuinness who explores the Protestant sensibility where the battle of the

Somme is concerned, Reid repeatedly undercuts the idea that dying in war is a noble death. From her female viewpoint, Reid shows the sacrifice to be a barren one rather than full of glory. However, the overall horror at the useless waste conveyed by McGuinness's play has a similar effect. What all of these playwrights have in common, besides the fact that they are using an Irish setting for their plays, is that they question martyrdom as a useful life goal.

Patrick Galvin's *Nightfall to Belfast* is peopled with victims; from the paramilitary, whose dying is coldly monitored by three representatives of the church, law, and business as they play cards, to the sixteen-year old barman Tommy:

You might wonder how a lad like Tommy could get himself killed. . . . He went out on the pavement to give that a sweep. He was standing there when a car drew up. The window was lowered. And Tommy was shot. A mistake? Probably. Last week, a gunman burst into a house. Opened the bedroom door and fired six shots at someone lying in the bed. It was a fourteen year old boy. That was a mistake. . . . Last month, a bomb went off in the local bus station. I heard the explosion and went down to see if I could help. The soldiers were shoveling the remains into plastic bags. That was a mistake? Two minutes later, a bomb went off in almost every other part of the city. Eleven people were killed and nearly two hundred were injured. Maybe that was a mistake too. I don't know.[32]

So another related theme is accidental martyrdom including the irony inherent in that possibility. The character who has set up the sacrifice in Victor Power's *Who Needs Enemies* says, as he drapes the blood-stained flag across his unintended victim, 'The blood of martyrs is the seed of Christians . . . and patriots . . . even martyrs by accident'.[33]

Accident of birth is a theme related to sacrifice in many of these plays and outlines a different kind of war — a sociological war. Several playwrights, socialist and otherwise, deal with the theme of sacrifice as related to oppressive social problems. In *Castles in the Air*,[34] Martin Lynch dramatises the true story of a woman who desperately wanted a new flat and hung herself when the quest seemed hopeless. And the mother in Thomas Murphy's *Famine* goads the father into killing her and the children rather than let them continue to struggle among themselves for a crust of bread meant for him: 'Jesus Christ above, what's wrong at all, all the clever persons in the world? Biteens of bread are needed only. Life blood of my heart: hunger, children, pain and disease! — What are we going through it for?'[35]

This cry, 'What are we going through it for', could have been voiced by many of the characters in these plays as they struggle to make sense of their suffering. However, in plays with strongly socialist viewpoints, the martyrs seem to recognise that their sacrifice is for the greater good, and they approach their role with courage and fortitude. This is certainly the case in *Over the Bridge*, Sam Thompson's play about sectarian violence on the docks. Although Davy Mitchell is respected by the older hands at the shipyards, his efforts are unappreciated by the young men who have not suffered the same hardships: 'There's not one of you knows what a sacrifice for a principle means. . . . Davy never wanted to be a martyr. He was made one by Fox and them bunch of corner boys he calls gaffers, and by people like you who thought he was made because he insisted on carrying out his duties as a staunch trade unionist against the odds.'[36] And those odds are overwhelming. Davy Mitchell is killed by the very men he has helped when he supports a Catholic's right to work at his job without intimidation.

Martin Lynch's *Dockers* offers a reprise on Thompson's play. Now it is Catholic unionmen who are using unfair tactics on one another. Bigotry still exists. Yet John Graham is not beaten as Davy was because he supports a Catholic but because he sings a song on International Workers' Day that the others label as Communist. Despite the beating he continues to sing. Even when he's beaten unconscious by his labour leaders his wife promises: 'He'll be back on Monday mornin'. I'll make sure of it. Should I have to carry him myself.'[37] The heroes in these plays are undaunted.

Although this discussion might give the impression that these plays are unrelentingly serious, most of them are funny as well as sad, entertaining as well as disturbing. In fact, some playwrights treat the theme of sacrifice humorously, almost sacrilegiously. And apparently, this humour among the pathos is not without good reason. *The Communication Cord*,[38] Field Day Theatre Company's offering for 1982, is an uproarious departure for Brian Friel from his usual more serious style. Poor Senator Donovan, in worshipping the past rather than progress, becomes the mock sacrifice in this play as he inadvertently becomes chained where cows were once tethered in this traditional Irish cottage. Friel literally brings the house down upon its incoherent inhabitants. This play, set in the present, overturns the romanticism of *Translations*, and both plays should be considered to assess more fully Friel's view of Irish culture. In the programme notes, Seamus Deane explains Friel's new direction:

The Communication Cord is an antidote to *Translations*. It reminds us that farce repeats itself as history and that the bogus, the fixed, and the chaotic are features of our daily lives in the social and political world. Tragedy gives us perspective and ennobles our feelings by rendering them subject to forces we can recognise but never define. Farce shows everything in close-up; it is concerned to reduce, to expose, to humiliate, and at the same time, to rescue us, via laughter, from the heroics of failure.[39]

Perhaps Friel offers the play not only as an antidote to *Translations* but as an antidote to the myths and symbols of sacrifice, which have brought Ireland a perpetual line of dead heroes but very little change.

This catalogue of plays does not answer the question why these and other playwrights use the theme. Are they desiring reconciliation as much of Irish society does? Are they trying to debunk the myth of glorious sacrifice? Is the theme unconscious on their part, or do they choose it in a calculated way because they recognise its success on the stage? And what of the para-militaries? Are they caught in their culture and act as martyrs because they must, or do they choose this behaviour because of its destabilising effect, as a way to bring down the old order to make room for a new one of their choosing? These questions may be unanswerable even by the participants. No, this listing of plays from playwrights of all persuasions can only identify sacrifice as a theme endemic to the theatre as well as to the culture.

In *Horseman Pass By*, Dan Magee not only explores the theme but brings together all of its concomitant aspects, as well. He deals with the issues of fidelity, divided loyalties, betrayal, and the need to confess. He shows history painfully repeating itself. Blind adherence to tradition, nationalism or patriotism, and even martyrdom are shown to be at least questionable if not barren goals. The power of the sacrifice itself is accentuated by the innocence of its victims and the arbitrary and accidental nature of its execution. And no hero could be more disillusioned than Brendan. Magee's ironic play certainly questions that there is anything glorious about sacrifice. In fact, only the socialist struggle is left as offering any modicum of hope.

The Quinn family, Magee's focus, are being torn apart by the struggle and are symbolic of a large segment of the northern population. One son, Brendan, is in a paramilitary group; another, Patrick, is in college studying film-making on a British grant. Their conflict over the relative value of being committed or uninvolved sets the tone for the play. When Brendan expresses an interest in his film-making, Patrick rejects any involvement in the revolution 'beyond trying to make sure a little bit of it, like a dialectical bit of lead doesn't lodge itself between my eyes. What I'm doing, I'm doing for me, not so that it can be of some use to somebody else, now, or in the future' (17).

Despite Brendan's realistic view of the value of martyrdom — 'It's only us Irish taigs who seem to think that a martyr is a real plus' (70) — a martyr is just what he is setting himself up to be. In order to prove to his angry, rejecting father that he does not just send others out to die, Brendan plans a lone ambush designed to lead to his death. The scheme backfires, however, and, through no fault of Brendan's, Bobby, one of his recruits, is killed instead. Hearing about Bobby's death from British soldiers searching the house, Brendan's incensed father starts to tell them where Brendan is hiding. But, out of sheer reflex, the mother shoots the father with Brendan's gun, which she is hiding from the soldiers in her apron, and a British soldier shoots her. The play has resolutely proceeded to this violent mimesis and now ends with bodies piled up on the stage and with Patrick, who has carefully stayed clear of the 'revolution' to this point, hauled off to the police station for questioning. Apparently, in a place like Northern Ireland, rejecting a role in the struggle gives someone like Patrick no protection because martyrdom can still be thrust upon him. Brendan is left waiting alone at the end of the play, unaware of how his activities have affected others, waiting for his death which does not come.

Magee may have the final word on the subject. In one of their many arguments, Brendan says to his brother: 'If I went out there tonight and got shot by a Brit, that's not what would make me a martyr. It would be some "artist", if he chose to, who'd do that. Sure the pubs are full of them, piss artists, up to their eyes in martyrs, crying into their pints for them' (48). Is this then what all this theatre is about — perpetuating the myth, reinforcing the cultural root paradigm, renewing the ritual by the continual re-enactments, assuring a goodly number of martyrs from each generation? Or is this only a side effect because neither the writers nor the actors can help themselves, can keep from using the metaphor that characterises their culture? So form does follow function. But at-one-ment leads to a type of atonement that these playwrights, at least, expose as questionable — a perverted atonement that brings only violence and death rather than reconciliation, renewal, and rebirth.

THE HISTORY PLAY TODAY

Christopher Murray

I

'If only confusion could be used as a weapon. It's the only thing we're good as spreadin'.' The line is from a play by, of all people, Andy Tyrie, Chairman of the Ulster Defence Association. *This Is It!* (1984) is not a history play, nor much of any kind of play for that matter, but it is useful for two reasons. It gives the lie to the frequent assertion that the Irish must forget the past if a solution to their problems is to be found. Mr Tyrie's quaint subscription to the 'culture and anarchy' argument is that the Ulster Protestant stock actually predated the Celts, who drove them out of the country to Scotland, whence they returned as planters. Thus the Ulster Protestants need to rediscover their true identity before they can live in peace with the Catholics. The second point is that confusion reigns in the minds of the Ulster people to the point where a sense of direction is all but lost. I would argue that virtually the same points can be made with respect to society in the republic of Ireland. The collapse of the history play is one way of demonstrating this, or, looking at it the other way, the fate of the history play reflects the contemporary paralysis of history itself in Ireland as a whole.

II

The history play has always been concerned with power, identity and the national consciousness. Shakespeare's histories have been interpreted by Philip Edwards in *Threshold of a Nation* (1979) as attempts to create a sense of national identity in Elizabethan England, and Edwards interestingly relates this interplay of drama and nationalism to a similar one in Ireland three hundred years later. The role of the history play in Ireland, as in England, has always been politico-cultural. All through the seventeenth

269

and eighteenth centuries, from the opening of the first professional theatre in Dublin in 1637, such Irish historical plays as were staged interpreted some national crisis in an unequivocal way. Saint Patrick's defeat of the Druids was interpreted as the conquest of reason over superstition, auguring the triumph of British civilisation over native barbarism. Brian Boru's defeat of the Danes was seen in the light of 'colonial nationalism', the triumph of Anglo-Irish government over invading pirates. The Ascendancy point of view was invariably asserted at the end of such plays. In the nineteenth century, however, a different emphasis appeared. Following the Act of Union and the emergence internationally of a romantic, quasi-revolutionary drama, the history play tended rather to attack than to reinforce establishment beliefs. Censorship, which in Ireland was operated by the Lord Lieutenant and not, as in England, by the agents of the 1737 Licensing Act (the Lord Chamberlain and the Licenser of Plays), kept the amount of political feeling generated by the theatre at a minimum, however. Only a harmless, colourful and somewhat childish form of historical melodrama was therefore allowed. The Irish plays of Boucicault contain very little solid history, and rather more geography (equally picturesque). When Boucicault tried to introduce a more adult and more topical note with reference to the nationalist question he ran into trouble in Dublin: 'The Wearing of the Green' was not allowed to be sung in *Arrah-na-Pogue*. So long as melodramas remained patently melodramas they could tell the stories of Patrick Sarsfield, Michael Dwyer, Robert Emmet and all the rest, for such plays entertained the crowds at a theatre significantly called the Queen's Royal.

Yeats had a deep suspicion of Irish nineteenth-century political poetry and its 'apologetics'. In the theatre too he was suspicious of propaganda, but one of his major problems in sustaining the Irish Dramatic Movement was somehow to reconcile the claims of art and of nation. Once he had written *Cathleen ni Houlihan* (1902),* set in the year of the uprising of 1798, he was caught in the middle, between art and politics. Deflect as he might the imputation that his play was propaganda it was only by asserting himself as the author of *Cathleen ni Houlihan* that he could get a hearing during the *Playboy* riots.[2] Whether it did or did not 'send out certain men the English shot', *Cathleen ni Houlihan* summed up in an intense way the zeal for freedom which lay behind the 1916 rebellion. Conor Cruise O'Brien may deplore this fact as

* Dates cited for plays are for first production.

evidence of an 'unhealthy intersection' of literature and politics,[3] but it may be well to recall what another Irish playwright has said also, 'the birth of a nation is no immaculate conception'.[4] And it is well too to remember that Yeats, whom too many critics regard as merely an esoteric playwright, said that 'the drama has always been a disturber'.[5] It is in this context that *Cathleen ni Houlihan* may be regarded as the archetypal Irish history play. It was at once a critique of pusillanimity and an advocate of ultimate self-sacrifice for the sake of the *patria*.

In the summer of 1984 four Yeats plays were staged at the Peacock Theatre, the annex to the Abbey. These were *At the Hawk's Well*, *The Cat and the Moon*, *The Dreaming of the Bones*, and *Cathleen ni Houlihan*. It was a production which one might call allegorical of the contemporary Irish theatre, daring in style and method, uncertain in theme or statement. Three women musicians appeared as chorus to three of the four plays and were absent from the last, *Cathleen ni Houlihan*. Some of the speeches of the Old Woman came over on speakers before and after the other plays, threading together mythology and history. In interview the director said: 'Cathleen is the link with the musicians because she's the ultimate matriarch' (*Sunday Tribune*, 17 June 1984). Yet when *Cathleen ni Houlihan* was staged the style of production changed radically from representation to narration. There was no cottage setting. On a darkened, bare stage several black-cloaked actors held out white masks to one side of them and spoke the dialogue as if for puppets. The Old Woman was herself masked. The young man abandoned his mask before joining her. The effect of this stylisation was severely to undercut the play's fervour. The audience could only view the action ironically and with detachment. The history play had been dissolved into pure theatre.

III

To understand what befell the history play in recent times it is necessary to go back in time for a wider context than I have so far provided. As is well known, one of the main aims of the original Irish Literary Theatre was 'to bring upon the stage the deeper thoughts and emotions of Ireland'.[6] One of the deeper thoughts and emotions — it is hard to say which — in Ireland is politics. And Daniel Corkery noted (for not all of Corkery is bunk) that one of the major determinants or defining characteristics of

Anglo-Irish literature is the theme of national consciousness.[7] It
follows that Irish drama after the founding of the Irish Literary
Theatre necessarily had a political dimension. Plays submitted to
the Abbey Theatre, Yeats said later in 'Advice to Playwrights' ought
to contain some criticism of life (a phrase obviously borrowed
from Matthew Arnold, for all that Yeats was a symbolist), but
ought not to be propagandist, 'nor plays written mainly to serve
some obvious moral purpose'.[8] How this was to be done, within
the parameters of a national theatre, Yeats never did clarify, with
the result that there were some very strange rejections during his
term as director of the Abbey. One need mention only *The Silver
Tassie* (1928) and *The Old Lady Says 'No!'* (1929) to suggest Yeats's
arbitrariness in this area.

In general, the history plays in the Abbey repertory fell into
three categories, all of them related to the fate of Ireland at the
hands of the English, a narrower scope than that spanned by the
modern history play in other countries. The first category might
be called inspirational or educational and it is best represented
by some of the plays of Lady Gregory. Speaking of *Kincora* (1905),
a play on Brian Boru, Lady Gregory said: 'I had had from the
beginning a vision of historical plays being sent by us through all
the counties of Ireland. For to have a real success and to come into
the life of the country, one must touch a real and eternal emotion,
and history comes only next to religion in our country' (*Our Irish
Theatre*, pp. 57-8). What interested her was the version of history
held by the people and embedded in tradition, as is plain from
the pictures offered of King James and Sarsfield in *The White
Cockade* (1905), and consequently her history plays are really folk
plays, emanating from the racial memory like dramatised ballads. It
has recently been argued that a number of Lady Gregory's plays
covertly refer to the tragedy of Parnell,[9] but she did not and
probably could not deal directly with recent Irish history.

The second category is the biographical, a form somewhat
neglected in the early years of the Abbey, probably because the
Queen's was still very actively turning out melodramas on Irish
patriots and competition was not in question. Lennox Robinson's
play about Robert Emmet, *The Dreamers* (1915) has no fellow at this
period of the Abbey's history, which makes it archetypal perhaps
and explains why the painting by James Sleator of the actor Fred
O'Donovan as Emmet dominates the top of the staircase of the
new Abbey. A mild republicanism pervades Robinson's romantic
tale, and politics inevitably was to be a subdivision of this
category of history play. Robinson was a very clever writer, too

skilled to descend to propaganda, but it is revealing how, in the foreword to the printed text he can make the theme seem allegorical: 'Dreams are the only permanent things in life, the only heritage that can be hoarded or spent and yet handed down intact from generation to generation. Robert Emmet's dream came down to him through — how many? — generations. He passed it on undimmed. It is being dreamed to-day, as vivid as ever and — they say — as unpractical.'[10] One member of the original cast, Sean Connolly, was to die in action in 1916. In *The Lost Leader* (1918) Robinson went on to write a play about Parnell, but it is less a history play than an exploration of belief that Parnell had not in fact died at all, a belief Lady Gregory had referred to in her note on *The Deliverer* (1911).

The third category is myth, the culmination of the other two modes of history play. In Ireland history tends always towards myth, for what shapes political attitudes are the versions and images of the past standing as symbols rather than as factual records of experience. Once again Yeats was the initiator here, for whereas as a lyrical poet he struggled to forge a mythology symbolic of his own feelings and experiences, he sought also to combine this mythology with the fate of his country. *The King's Threshold* (1903) gives a fair idea of what this means, for it is a tale which at once records the value of the poet to society and asserts the political power of self-sacrifice, a point made more strongly in the revised version of 1922, after Terence MacSwiney's death on hunger strike. The heroic ideal was fundamental to Yeats's mythology, and his greatest expression of it was in his Cuchulain plays. It is significant that in his last play, *The Death of Cuchulain*, completed just before he died, he saw his own achievement as national image-maker in relation to the insurgents of 1916, as commemorated by the statue of Cuchulain in the General Post Office. The question 'Who thought Cuchulain till it seemed / He stood where they had stood?'[11] implies the involvement of his whole enterprise as a poet with the historic moment of national self-realisation which was 1916. Myth and history fuse like a moment of beauty in a Noh play.

In the period after Yeats the three categories of history play just sketched persisted but with gradually changing emphases. The first or folk type history play made little headway, largely, no doubt because its naïve consciousness raising was a redundant factor in an Ireland freed, however controversially, from British rule. The only playwright of recent times to occupy himself with such material is M. J. Molloy. *Petticoat Loose* (1979) was set in 1822 and told a tale of changelings, superstitions and a powerful Fairy Doctor opposed by a defrocked priest. Molloy's purpose would appear to be to enlighten a modern audience (the play was staged at the new Abbey) on the ways of its ancestors. Referring to his work in general Molloy has said: 'I found myself dramatising aspects of rural life, which city people knew very little about and refused to believe.'[12] Thus *The King of Friday's Men* (1948), set in the eighteenth century, informed one of the nature of faction fighting and of the landlord's *droit du seigneur* in those times. When it was revived at the Abbey in 1973 it was hard to believe that this play had once made it on to Broadway. Nowadays *Siamsa Tíre* probably do more straightforwardly what Molloy had in mind. *Petticoat Loose*, at any rate, is antiquarianism rather than history. Molloy's best work is *The Wood of the Whispering* (1953), revived in a magnificent production by the Druid Company from Galway at the Dublin Theatre Festival in 1983: here the life style, the manners, customs and dialect of the impoverished people of county Galway were presented not as in a glass case in a museum but tragically related to the history of Ireland since 1922. As Molloy said in the preface: 'For forty years Ireland has been free, and for forty years it has wandered in the desert under the leadership of men who freed their nation, but who could never free their own souls and minds from the ill-effects of having been born in slavery.'[13] Thus a contemporary folk play can have a sharp historical edge.

Molloy works in this field alone, for although John B. Keane has a similar concern for the values of rural life Keane writes always in the present tense about the tyranny (rather than the charm) of customs and conventions. The second category, the biographical history play, did better after 1922 than before. There were copious plays on Parnell, Casement, Pearse, and Collins right up to 1966, the fiftieth anniversary of the rising, which was a watershed. The scope of such plays was narrow, in contrast with the universality of Shaw's *Saint Joan* (1923) or Brecht's *Galileo* (1947), for example. They were not plays of ideas. What they achieved was a popular rendition of controversial figures, so that the controversial aspects seemed less troublesome. They were not dramatically belligerent but cosily realistic in the well-made style. One of the most successful writers of the history play in modern times has been G. P. Gallivan, whose *Decision at Easter* (1959), *Mourn the Ivy Leaf* (1960), and *Dev* (1977) are probably as good of their kind as can be found. They attempt to fit into the three-act realistic form the dilemmas of great men presented as the sort of people one might meet at close of day coming from counter or desk: the effect is less political than to elicit a sense of familiarity. But from 1966 on a different, harder, more intellectual line is discernible in this kind of history play, as authors set themselves the task of assessing and re-evaluating the achievements of the leaders of Ireland's fight for freedom. Eugene McCabe's *Pull Down a Horseman* (1966) offered a straightforward debate between Pearse and Connolly over the political course to be taken in 1916. Gallivan's first act of *Decision at Easter* had covered similar ground but an ideological battle was not there allowed. McCabe made dialectics the essence of his play, as in this exchange:

PEARSE   I am nothing so new fangled as a Socialist, I am an old fashioned Catholic, and Nationalist, I am at peace with my fellow slaves, Capitalist and worker, rich and poor, fed and hungry. We have no Christless cities here.

CONNOLLY   The Church preaches pity for the poor, they admit the injustice of the social system, and they offer pity, ever counselling humility, but sitting in the seats of the mighty. But she is coming to recognise now, that if she does not move with the people, the people will move without her.[14]

The differences of the two men are not reconciled, but they nevertheless find common ground in the need for revolution, the moral basis for which is the real subject of the play.

   In a later play, *Gale Day* (1979), McCabe held Pearse's character up to greater scrutiny than he did in *Pull Down a Horseman*. In the printed text he quotes from Ruth Dudley Edward's biography of Pearse, *The Triumph of Failure* (1977): 'There were no observers of Patrick Pearse's last days; his solitary confinement left him fittingly remote from his friends.' McCabe adds: 'This sentence prompted "Gale Day".'[15] The playwright is now firmly engaged with the historian whereas in Lennox Robinson's day he took licence to invent a great deal of his material. *Gale Day* is, necessarily, invention, but it takes its stand on an imaginative interpretation of character as supplied by a specific historian. Pearse is put on trial. The prosecutor says: 'We require to know who and what you are that without mandate from the Irish people you should declare yourself President of a non-existent Republic' (pp. 56-7). By means of flashbacks to Pearse's childhood and early manhood we glean his mystical dedication to self-sacrifice. But in turn this is taken by the prosecution as evidence of perversion, and Pearse is accused of homosexuality: 'In twentieth century Ireland pederasty is clearly the first refuge of a patriot.' (p. 68) Pearse's defence is calm, neatly combining the 'slander' with the political wrong done to Ireland for centuries. The simplicity and directness of the style here operate in Pearse's favour and the charge is rendered grotesque, not because facts are adduced but because personality is established. Pearse's execution, which follows immediately, seems to ratify his own defence. The historian is answered by the playwright.

The court in *Gale Day* is a dream court, rather like the court in John Osborne's *Inadmissible Evidence* (1964) which implies that the contemporary history play is by no means confined to conventional realism as heretofore. Far more experimental than this, however, was *The Non-Stop Connolly Show* (1975), by Margaretta D'Arcy and John Arden. This six-part (and five volume) depiction of the life, times, and death of James Connolly took two days to perform (at the Liberty Hall, Dublin), since it is really a medieval cycle of plays with a modern theme. In clarifying the genesis and aims of the cycle, in an essay entitled 'A Socialist Hero on the Stage', D'Arcy and Arden indicate that Hindu folk drama or mystery plays supplied a modern counterpart to the medieval form which they adopted. The features involved they describe as follows:

Extreme formality mixed with unexpectedly coarse realism; highly decorative costumes, make-up and/or masks, with small relation to everyday naturalism; the regular use of music and dance as part of the dramatic structure; strongly rhythmical verse-narrative to link passages of action; very little in the way of Aristotelian *climax*; and, perhaps above all, a feeling between actors and audience that the persons and events of the drama were something more than the 'historical fictions' we are accustomed to in the western theatre — that they *had been*, still *were*, and *would be* in the future.[16]

The quality and the formal richness of *The Non-Stop Connolly Show* are suggested by this quotation. If one can speak of the cycle as a single play, it stands out as simply the greatest achievement in the Irish history play in modern times.

Politically, the cycle has a Brechtian clarity. Every aspect of Connolly's life received careful research before each of the discrete but continuous parts was written, and the published texts supply a bibliography. In *To Present the Pretence* the authors said that if the plays were shown in Ireland the aim was to demonstrate the internationalism of Connolly, 'in contrast to his traditional image of a national martyr' (p.113), but if staged in England 'we were more concerned to convey the complexities of Britain's imperial

legacy across the water'. The aim as regards Ireland became
sharpened in the printed text, 'to counteract what one might term
the "Conor Cruise O'Brien historical revisionism", currently
much in vogue in Irish intellectual circles'.[17] The ideological basis
to the cycle is not only firm but essential, lending coherence to
the whole thing. Yet there is much humour in the manner in
which the various portraits of political types are drawn, as in this
speech of the Second Employer, a stage-Irish opportunist, a
candidate in an election campaign in Edinburgh (staged as a
wrestling bout):

> Who is to stop me — the bould O'Toole — ?
> I'm as Irish as the Cross of Cong:
> I invoke the Pope the whole day long!
> It is a sin to be a socialist:
> The very word of the parish priest.
> Stand firm for the faith and the ould Irish sod:
> A vote for James Connolly is a vote against God![18]

What brings Connolly finally to join with Pearse — and the
authors deal with the same problem here as had Gallivan and
McCabe in their plays on Pearse — is shown to have its background
in Connolly's long years of experience in Scotland, America, and
Ireland as fighter for the rights and freedom of the working class.
After the rebellion Connolly refers to criticism by international
socialists: 'They'll never understand why I am here. They all
forget I am an Irishman.'[19] But so wide has been the scope of the
material prior to this point and so full the analyses of exploitation
and the limits of reform that the audience or reader *does* understand
and this is perhaps the greatest merit of the cycle.

One would have to agree with the authors' own description of
the cycle, in the essay already quoted from in *To Present the Pretence*
(p. 137): 'It is not so much "propagandist" as exploratory and
educational. But it *is* propagandist in that it finally brings the
authors, and consequently the audience, to some "partisan" conclusion.' Which is to say, of course, that it is in a direct line from
Cathleen ni Houlihan. It is rather significant, therefore, that the
Abbey Theatre showed no interest in *The Non-Stop Connolly Show*.

IV

The third category, history as myth, underwent a major change of
emphasis after 1922. Yeats's heroic ideal disappeared from Irish

drama, and with it, almost entirely, his poetic form. Perhaps one would have to mention by way of exception some of the efforts of Austin Clarke, Padraic Colum, and Ulick O'Connor, where the Yeatsian form without the Yeatsian power is on display. Clarke's plays on Celtic themes, such as *Black Fast* (1942) or *The Son of Learning* (1945) did attempt to fuse history and myth, but with no political implications. History for Clarke was a psychological landscape, a clearing in an early Christian wood where Saint Patrick and Oisin, emblematic of ascetic and sexual impulses, did never-ending battle. Thus one of the best of his plays, *The Moment Next to Nothing* (1958), set in Ireland at the time of Saint Patrick, is essentially a tale of a monk's discovery of the world of the flesh. The 'myth' in use here may indict the *status quo* but it lacks the power to say much about the Irish psyche or national identity. Likewise, Padraic Colum's Noh plays, written at the end of his long career, lack significant connection with Irish life in modern times. Colum successfully catches Yeats's manner, in a play such as *Moytura* (1963), in which the ghost of Oscar Wilde's father looms large, or *Cloughoughter* (1966) where Roger Casement meets the ghost of Owen Roe O'Neill. The latter play formed a triple bill, under the title *The Challengers*, at the Lantern Theatre in Dublin in February 1966, the other two plays being *Glendalough*, about Parnell, and *Monasterboice*, about Joyce. Colum also wrote a fifth play to complete the Noh cycle, entitled *Kilmore* (published in 1981) and concerned with Henry Joy McCracken. These were all, indeed, history plays, and each is firmly associated with a particular landscape resonant with associations. They remain interesting only as academic exercises. Theatrical exercises might be a better term for Ulick O'Connor's three plays in the Noh style, staged at the Dublin Theatre Festival in 1978. One of these is an interesting attempt to apply the Yeatsian format to a modern theme. *Submarine* tells the story of the attempted return of two IRA men, Frank Ryan and Sean Russell, to Ireland from Germany in August 1941. On the submarine journey Russell died and his companion returned to Germany. O'Connor has the two republicans meet the ghost of Roger Casement on board the submarine, a Chorus questions him about his motives and fate, which correspond with theirs to a large degree. As the ghost of Casement fades, the Chorus describes the coming death of Russell and the failure of Ryan to reach Ireland and organize IRA activity against British rule in Northern Ireland.

The lack of an enabling myth is acutely felt in such post-Yeatsian Noh plays, and this lack is bound up with the general fate of the hero in modern drama. Myth without irony seems no longer viable in the theatre. In Ireland drama since O'Casey has tended towards demythologising the heroic ideal. O'Casey's three Dublin plays were not, of course, history plays; yet they encapsulated history, interpreted history, and finally became history. In O'Casey, experience and history fuse, lose antiquarian bias and become armed agents of consciousness. The revolutionary achievement of O'Casey in this regard was to banish offstage the shapers and controllers, the historical leaders, and to show instead the ironic gap between their vision and the lives of the urban poor. Thus Patrick Pearse becomes a mere voice outside a public-house window in *The Plough and the Stars* (1926), while the voice to be attended to inside is that of the Covey, underlining the mistaken alliance of labour and republicansim. There is quite a complex ironic process at work in this play, however, as the Covey himself, mocking commentator though he is, is himself subject to severe criticism for his domination by political jargon. The technique is basically satiric and deflationary. Thus we hear Uncle Pether likened to Brian Boru leading the Irish forces at Clontarf; while in *The Shadow of a Gunman* (1923) we hear of Helen of Troy, Prometheus, Orpheus, Morpheus, and Cuchulain, always in a context that burlesques the mythic, and we hear of Patrick Sarsfield at the Battle of Vinegar Hill; and in *Juno and the Paycock* (1925) we hear two contradictory versions from Captain Boyle of the role played by the priests in the Great Famine, not to mention his own role in 1916. History can be nonsense, just so much fantasy as sustains a character's or a nation's self-esteem: such is O'Casey's criticism of life. When he went on to write history plays in the acceptable sense, *The Star Turns Red* (1940) and *Red Roses for Me* (1943), he wrote what might be called myths of the new Jerusalem in Ireland, as he revisited the years of the labour struggles of 1911-13 and saw therein a prophecy of glorious communist revolution. But it was the earlier Dublin plays that left their mark on the development of Irish drama, not these history plays, It was, after all, in the Dublin plays that the new Cathleen ni Houlihan is first glimpsed, 'a ragin' divil now, an' if you only looked crooked at her you're sure of a punch in th' eye'.[20]

Denis Johnston took it from there. Cathleen ni Houlihan reappeared in *The Old Lady Says 'No!'* as a Dublin harridan, a grotesque version of Emmet's beloved Sarah Curran. Using expressionist techniques, Johnston placed Robert Emmet in post-civil-war Dublin, which was thereby perceived as the nightmare of a concussed actor. *The Scythe and the Sunset* (1958), at the other

end of Johnston's career, took another look at the 1916 rebellion
and dared to revise O'Casey's verdict, as the title implies. It was
still possible at this stage for an author of powerful imagination
to seize hold of the mythic in Irish history and reinterpret it. This
capacity disappeared in the nineteen fifties. Maurice Meldon's
Aisling (1953), a vivacious dream play rather in Johnston's style, is
the last play one can point to where an author can confidently and
coherently assess the degradation of Cathleen ni Houlihan in
modern times, 'a really fine specimen of Irish woman-hood'
auctioned off to the highest bidder.[21]

One can already see the breakdown of history taking place in
the plays of Brendan Behan. Apart from *The Quare Fellow* (1954)
and in another genre *Borstal Boy* (1958), Behan's work was a dance
of death. He was a writer saturated in Irish history, but increasingly
helpless at its intuited inexorability. One of his best poems,
translated from the Irish by Donagh MacDonagh as 'The Jackeen's
Lament for the Blaskets', at once expresses Behan's elegiac sense
of a lost tradition and his uncertain or ironic warrant (as a
'Jackeen' or native Dubliner) to act as witness.[22] Such a duality
and such an uncertainty were not evident in O'Casey or
Johnston, each of whom was secure in his vision of Irish society.
Behan was torn between a commitment to republican tradition
and a perception of its hopelessness. *The Hostage* (1958), accordingly,
is a very confused play, politically. One can see this confusion
expressed in the songs to Collins, 'The Laughing Boy', the chorus
of which runs:

Ah, curse the time, and sad the loss my heart to crucify,
Than [sic] an Irish son, with a rebel gun, shot down my Laughing Boy.
Oh, had he died by Pearse's side, or in the G.P.O.,
Killed by an English bullet from the rifle of the foe,
Or forcibly fed while Ashe lay dead in the dungeons of Mountjoy,
I'd have cried with pride at the way he died, my own dear Laughing Boy.[23]

If only. If only Collins had died in the General Post Office he could
be mourned decently. But he was on the 'wrong' side in the civil
war, so in spite of his good qualities he cannot be mourned
properly by republicans. 'If only', Behan says elsewhere, 'Jim
Larkin had learnt Irish — or Collins had studied Leninism!' or if
'Collins and Griffith [had not] allowed themselves to be tricked
into Partition at the Treaty negotiations'.[24] *The Hostage* renders
the absurdity of an English hostage killed in crossfire between
legitimised ex-republicans and die-hard republicans: an image
of futility and confusion. Leslie's 'resurrection' is to declare a

plague on both their houses. Recently, in the correspondence columns of the *Irish Times* the argument was raised again whether Collins was not a terrorist in the same sense as the modern Provisionals, and whether he was murdered or killed in action. Such metaphysical questions, by no means innocent, lie at the heart of political differences today. Behan's *The Hostage*, and to an extent the unfortunate *Richard's Cork Leg* (1972), anticipate these differences.

Contemporary playwrights such as Thomas Murphy and Brian Friel do not suffer from Behan's immersion in history. Murphy sees the modern Irish consciousness as hopelessly estranged, a state from which history offers no redemption. In *The White House* (1972) a bar-room discussion on the political problems of Northern Ireland, undertaken for the benefit of a returned emigrant, reveals that some of the pub denizens 'nearly' went up to help the downtrodden Catholics; Murphy's scorn is for the mixture of sympathy and hesitancy shown by such microcosmic Irishmen. *The Blue Macushla* (1980) views the IRA ensconced in a Dublin nightclub (comparable to Behan's locating them in a whorehouse) through its possession of the soul of the ambitious but corrupt owner, Eddie O'Hara. By presenting the whole story of terrorisation, betrayal, and crookery in the style of a Hollywood gangster movie Murphy suggested the unreality of the contemporary moral consciousness when confronted by the IRA. It is simply not possible, Murphy seems to be saying, to think straight about moral questions in Ireland at present, so great is the flood of hogwash visited upon the public by public leaders, spouting history, while the newspapers are full of stories of shady business deals and doubtful alliances. History, it follows, is itself corrupt. Consequently, apart from his one history play, Murphy's plays sever the knot between history and society and suggest the preferability of the individual consciousness in honest, existential revolt. *Famine* (1968) is the great exception.

The Great Famine of 1846-8 has, of course, achieved the status of myth in the past forty years or so. In fiction Liam O'Flaherty and Walter Macken have treated it; in drama George Shiels (*Tenants at Will*, 1945) and Gerard Healy (*The Black Stranger*, 1945). As Cecil Woodham-Smith said at the end of her study, *The Great Hunger*, 'The history of what then occurred is deeply engraved on the memory of the Irish race; all hope of assimilation with England was then lost, and bitterness without parallel took possession of the Irish mind'.[25] Murphy used *The Great Hunger* as source material, but avoided polemics or the sort of conclusion Gerard

Healy had come to in his play, namely that all the suffering was
sheer waste unless a new generation was bred fired with sufficient
anger to emancipate Ireland from England. Healy, in other words,
had to see some meaning in the famine; he could accept it only as
an episode in the fight for freedom. Murphy sees no meaning in
it, beyond the study it offers of the ethical breaking point of a
peasant leader, John Connor, descended from kings of Connaught.
Famine is a condition in the play which triggers certain results,
sociologically and psychologically: it breeds dispossession,
violence, and despair. In a programme note to a revival of the play
by the Tuam Theatre Guild in 1984 Murphy drew attention to the
power of the famine as metaphor for him as a playwright of the
nineteen sixties:

I found that I was not so much interested in the crisis as a historical fact,
but that I identified with it and was peculiarly involved in that age. The
catstrophe had stopped the Irish race in its tracks (as nothing else had
done) and in the nineteen sixties I was suffering a hangover that had
lasted over a hundred years. The tangible facet of famine, physical
hunger, had been removed, but the other 'poverties' remained. Poverty
of thought; wild wisdom and native cunning stalemating a 20th century
need to open out and expand; Mother MacCree's blessings issuing from
a poor 19th century mouth; the natural extravagant vitality of youth
being frustrated and made to feel guilty by the smell of too much history.

In *Famine*, then, Murphy had found his objective correlative. In
subsequent plays, from *A Crucial Week in the Life of a Grocer's
Assistant* (1969) to *The Gigli Concert* (1983), he avoided history: his
material is an escape from history into individual experience,
clarified by the demands of form.

Friel has always been more of a nationalist writer than Murphy,
that is, his plays have been occupied more with questions of
identity and place.[26] His plays engage sooner or later with the
great Irish themes, emigration, the passion for respectability,
politics, religion, and so on, though Friel is concerned as a writer
to cast a cold eye on tradition and to fight free of conventionality
by means of irony and experiments in form. The fact that his first
noteworthy play (and the first of his early plays to be published)
was a history play is not as significant as it might appear. *The
Enemy Within* (1962) was set in the seventh century, and told a story
of Saint Columba and his struggle to find or preserve his vocation
in the face of the claims made on him as a military leader by the
clans back home. Self-realisation here connotes repudiation of
patria, a pursuit which, however sanctifying, implicates Columba

in inexorable guilt. Already we have here a concern, a scruple, which was to prove in some form or other crucial to Friel's dramaturgy. But history in itself, as a means of recording the truth is, in Friel's drama in general, suspect because its formal, objective methodology is too presumptuous to understand the experience Friel values most, namely the inner, the subjective, the lyrical. Thus the commentators in *Winners* (1967) seem crass in their attempts to describe the last hours of the teenage lovers: their history comes nowhere near the truth about the couple, any more than does the sociology of the commentator in *The Freedom of the City* (1973) reach the meaning of the lives of the three occupants of the Mayor's Parlour. The inference to be drawn is that reality, factual events, may be intuited but not known. This sceptical view is plain also from the mildly satirical portrait of the historian Hoffnung (surely an ironic name) in *Aristocrats* (1979): that play is a coming to terms with history for the O'Donnell family, but the academic historian of the family makes little headway in sorting out the various myths and fantasies which apparently sustained its members.[27] It was not until *Translations* (1980) that Friel overcame this particular bias against history, and it has to be noted that he quickly provided a counterpoint to that play with *The Communication Cord* (1982). The ground is expertly chosen in *Translations* for a siege to the famous two-culture theory: the metaphor of map-making in a Gaeltacht area in the 1833, a watershed time since it marked the transition from the old hedgeschool culture to the new, progressive, so-called National School system of education, with (once again) its presumption that it could 'interpret between privacies' like a master historian.[28] When the hedge-schoolmaster Hugh remembers 1798 it is not as an historic occasion, inspirational or meaningful in tradition, but as a Wordsworthian moment of bliss in being alive and young and strong and in good company:

We marched as far as — where was it — Glenties! All of twenty-three miles in one day. And it was there, in Phelan's pub, that we got homesick for Athens, just like Ulysses. The *desiderium nostrorum* — the need for our own. Our *pietas*, James, was for older, quieter things. And that was the longest twenty-three miles back I ever made. (*Toasts* JIMMY) My friend, confusion is not an ignoble condition.[29]

Maire and Yolland have had their brief moment too, their private history, and the confusion that follows (manifested by Maire's distracted state and Lancey's threats of retaliation) is left unresolved. Friel's tact in so ending *Translations* is beyond praise.

The rest is, one might say, our experience, our heritage. In a way what we have done with that heritage forms the subject matter of *The Communication Cord*, and the confusion it records finds its proper form in farce. Here it is as if an ersatz cottage setting for *Cathleen ni Houlihan* turned into a Hotel Paradiso; its inevitable collapse symbolises the folly of attempting to sustain a façade of culture (or communication) through mere sentiment and opportunism. In that regard, the total darkness in which the play ends is ominous.

Friel's sense of a vacuum in the contemporary historical consciousness (and in *Aristocrats* of its dangerous seductiveness) is shared by both Thomas Kilroy and Hugh Leonard. Kilroy's *The O'Neill* (1969) presented the great Earl as a man baffled and confused by the world he sees breaking up around him. He is a modern figure, like Osborne's *Luther*, unsure of his motives and of his role as saviour of his country: the very opposite of the Yeatsian hero. His virtual paralysis of will, like that of Connor in Murphy's *Famine*, serves not so much to demythologise in O'Casey's manner as to make a bridge between the historical moment and the modern temper. A bridge of a different kind is made in *Talbot's Box* (1977), where the mystic Matt Talbot, caught up in the public struggle for justice for the proletariat, goes against the tide and struggles instead to preserve his individual, eccentric vision of God as all-consuming. In covering the Dublin lockout of 1913, and the violence at the time, Kilroy's emphasis is on the isolation of Talbot who in the play as a whole is an image of the modern self under siege by mass consumerism. Modern Ireland wants to appropriate Talbot, possess him as a marketable entity, just as society wishes to possess and tame the artist and turn him into a brand name, a television personality. The history play is thus for Kilroy a means of exploring the pressures on role and identity in contemporary Ireland. This point is borne out even more clearly in Kilroy's latest play, *Double Cross* (1986), in which the inter-related studies of Brendan Bracken and William Joyce serve to interrogate the ambiguities of patriotism.

The irony which pervades Friel's *The Communication Cord*, its intellectual shudder at the vulgarisation of historical awareness, might be compared with the irony in Hugh Leonard's *The Patrick Pearse Motel* (1971). Leonard writes with a broader stroke, which is to say more obviously, than Friel, exposing the sheer hypocrisy of preserving the memory of Irish patriots only for commercial reasons. His satire goes no deeper than a laugh at ignorance and pretentiousness, for which sexual inefficiency and social *gaucherie* among the *nouveaux riches* are his favourite analogues. Leonard's use of history is, of course, indirect, both here and in a later play, *Kill* (1982), yet such plays imply a resentment of desecrated pieties, of Cathleen ni Houlihan as a harp-playing opportunist.

V

In Ireland in the early nineteen-eighties the Juggernaut of history seems strangely to have seized up. The failure of politicians to make any progress over the problem of Northern Ireland; the stagnation of the coalition government, dominated by conservatives; the obscurantism of the majority as manifested in the referenda that backfired, on the 'right to life of the unborn' and on divorce, the reluctance to liberalise laws governing homosexuality or illegitimacy, offset at the same time by a tolerance towards harsher standards of 'criminal justice'; and the general atmosphere of economic retrenchment and caution, related to high unemployment, comparatively high inflation, and a much-complained-of tax system, have all contributed to a pervasive sense of inertia in modern Ireland. In 1984 the government's three-year plan was announced under the title 'Building on Reality', but the reality envisaged is notoriously negative. In addition, the *New Ireland Forum Report* (1984), the result of all-party debates and much national soul searching, failed to get a positive British response, which means in effect that it was short-circuited. And that *Report*, it might be said, was the only bit of history with dynamic potential lying around. Not to be facetious, the *Report* is now the only history play in town.

In such an atmosphere playwrights and theatres seem unable to find coherence. Box-office considerations rule over the need to experiment and to develop new forms. Even Field Day, the company set up by Brian Friel and Stephen Rea in 1980 to tour Ireland with new and/or challenging plays, has rather run out of steam as articulator of the *contemporary* Irish consciousness — on stage, that is, for the pamphlets Field Day is issuing are another matter. With its first production, *Translations*, Field Day promised much, but the statement in that play was to some extent cancelled out by *The Communication Cord* and in 1984 the cancellation was actually within the double bill presented, a modern-dress *Antigone*, under the title *The Riot Act* by Tom Paulin, and a translation of Molière's *School for Husbands* under the title *High Time*, by Derek Mahon. The first was, necessarily, political, but surprisingly tentative in its application to Northern Ireland, if it could be said to have any real application at all; while the second, while vastly entertaining as farce, might just as well have been *The Rogueries of Scapin* with disco music added. Together, the two plays seemed to avoid rather than promote any criticism of Irish life.

Stewart Parker's *Northern Star*, staged at the Lyric Theatre, Belfast, in November 1984, serves to bear out the argument that for the contemporary Irish playwright history is a metaphor of disintegration. A play about Henry Joy McCracken, the United Irishman executed in 1798, *Northern Star* is theatrically self-conscious about its own sense of futility. In an interesting programme note Parker writes:

So how to write an Ulster history play? — since our past refuses to express itself as a linear, orderly narrative, in a convincing tone of voice? Tune into any given moment from it, and the wavelength soon grows crowded with a babble of voices from all the other moments, up to and including the present one.

He goes on to say that he has tried to 'accommodate this obstinate, crucial fact of life by eschewing any single style, and attempting instead a wide range of theatrical ventriloquism (emboldened by the knowledge that Henry Joy McCracken himself was a gifted mimic)'. Formally, this works out as a series of parodies of the styles of Synge, O'Casey, Behan and Beckett, a strategy of simultaneously employing and dismissing tradition. In content, Parker implies that 1798 could just as well be 1984, so far as the North is concerned, and that no exit is possible from what he calls (in the play) the 'dungeon' of history. Irony provides the unifying technique, for the whole play is shot through with McCracken's flippant awareness that all of his efforts are illusory: 'the cycle just goes on, playing out the same demented comedy of terrors from generation to generation, trapped in the same malignant legend' (typescript, act 2).

Parker's play was critically acclaimed in Belfast, but was a dismal failure in the Dublin Theatre Festival (1985). There is a certain irony in this, since the play itself articulates disenchantment with history. Its Dublin failure merely records Dublin's boredom with the Northern issue. The reception given Frank McGuinness's *Observe the Sons of Ulster Marching Towards the Somme* (1985), on the other hand, suggests a willingness to believe that history is, indeed, bunk, since the play illustrates the death-wish inherent in the Unionist mentality in the glorious year of 1916, and this deliberate omission suggests that the author is interested more in allegory than history.

We have reached the position, then, where the Irish playwrights of today can deal with history only in a tentative, ironic, or self-conscious way. It is largely a question of style. Novelists don't have this problem. As James M. Cahalan has shown, in *Great Hatred, Little Room: The Irish Historical Novel* (1984), historical fiction is flourishing in Ireland in modern times. But it is clear that when novelists such as William Trevor or Jennifer Johnston write for the stage their style is too literary to make their historical subject-matter convincing. An example is provided by Jennifer Johnston's play, *Indian Summer* (1984), staged by the Cork Theatre Company. Set in Cork in 1920 this was an old-fashioned three-act play which tried to capture the political atmosphere of the period by setting the action in an Ascendancy 'big house'. The effect was of artificiality, of characters over-articulate or else stagey. Yet Ms Johnston could write about this period with subtlety in her novel, *The Old Jest* (1979). Much the same point could be made about William Trevor's novel, *Fools of Fortune* (1983) when contrasted with his play staged at the Abbey, *Scenes from an Album* (1981). The novelist bears it away, perhaps because he can express or suggest breakdown more powerfully by means of narrative and description than by dialogue and action. On stage style itself must fragment under the pressure of history, a breakdown symbolised by Sarah's reversion to dumbness in *Translations*,[30] or John Connor's reduc-tion to incoherence in *Famine*,[31] for the idea of collapse must be enacted, not described.

But at the other extreme from the fiction writer turned play-wright there is the writer-collaborator, in a development which I wish now, finally, to suggest is significant for the fate of the history play in Ireland. Recently two groups have simultaneously emerged dedicated to the documentary. In each case the play-wright has but a minor role. The plays are shaped instead by the actors and grow out of improvisation, trial, error, and general collaboration. The result is in line with what O'Casey and later on Arden and D'Arcy achieved, namely, an expression of the lives of working-class people in the face of social and political changes outside their control. Dublin City Workshop, a community enterprise from the north inner city, put together with the aid of playwright Peter Sheridan the story of the notorious Monto district (closed or destroyed by the authorities in the nineteen twenties) under the title, *The Kips, The Digs, The Village* (1982), staged at the Project Arts Centre. The idea began as a youth

employment scheme, with funding from the Department of
Education, and it was therefore a cooperative enterprise involving
mainly amateurs. In working on the idea the group discovered
there was material here for a trilogy, and consequently moved on
to the nineteen forties to deal with the Dublin Docks strikes, in a
sequel entitled *Pledges and Promises* (1983), and concluded with a
piece which juxtaposed the Papal visit of 1979 and the overwhelming drugs problem of the inner city, under the title *A Hape
of Junk* (1983). The latter was very well received at the Dublin
Theatre Festival by David Nowlan, critic for the *Irish Times* (5
October), and the full trilogy played before the end of the Festival
before going on a tour extending as far as the Royal Court, London.
Episodic in form, crude in characterisation, and simple in theatrical technique though the trilogy was, it was nevertheless full of
energy, humour, and above all truth. As history it was folk drama
such as Lady Gregory never dreamed of: street-wise, demotic,
partisan but compassionate. Much the same claim could be made
for the work of Charabanc, a group which started at virtually the
same time in Belfast, exploring the working-class conditions at
the beginning of the century. Their first effort was *Lay Up Your
Ends* (1983), a study of Belfast linen workers during a strike in
1911. The cast at this time were all women, directed by Pam
Brighton, and they put the script together collectively, with the
aid of playwright Martin Lynch. Following the success of their
first effort, staged at the Belfast Civic Arts Theatre, Charabanc
scripted a play set in Belfast in the election year of 1949 under the
title, *Oul Delf and False Teeth* (1984). Pam Brighton again directed,
and she described in detail in *Theatre Ireland* the genesis and
honing of the script, which once again had the assistance of
Martin Lynch.[32] It is clear that Charabanc know very well what
they are doing, and it was with conviction one of their directors,
Ian McElhinney, claimed in a programme note to *Oul Delf and
False Teeth* that the company was 'presenting an alternative way of
looking at the history of our society'. Both of these plays toured
Ireland, playing at the Projects Arts Centre when reaching Dublin,
thus making the comparison with the Dublin City Workshop
inevitable. Charabanc is a more sophisticated, professionally
organised company, which has the capacity to grow so long as it
stays away from contemporary material (which it unfortunately
strayed into in 1985 and 1986); whereas the Dublin City Workshop
seems to be defunct, such is the state of subsidised theatre.
Charabanc was well received at the Glasgow Mayfest in May
1984, and the company undertook a tour to Russia in October.

What the company's early work conveyed was a lively set of very convincing scenes of city life, with a dialectic wittily and honestly providing a backbone, and with, of course, no heroes, no myths, and no gap between performance and audience. The fact that male roles are mostly (though not always) played by women ensures that the question of identity is kept fluid, or open. And in the end what this style of drama, the analytic form of city chronicle, supplies is the perception that past and present conditions may be equated. Perhaps in that way such new proponents of history on the stage can offer a way out of the contemporary confusion. After all, what this type of drama offers is not inspiration to revolution but education in the ways power, identity and community have been expressed in the recent past. And this is the sort of communication which theatre can do better than any other medium. Even Mr Tyrie can see that.

WOMEN'S CONSCIOUSNESS AND IDENTITY IN FOUR IRISH WOMEN NOVELISTS

TAMSIN HARGREAVES

'The self is the principle and archetype of orientation and meaning'
(C. G. Jung)

At one point in Molly Keane's novel *Good Behaviour* the huge, hopeless heroine, Aroon St. Charles remarks: 'I stood there waiting. There was nobody to tell me where to go. I was the lost girl in the fairy story. I dared myself to go forwards.'[1] Her words usefully summarise the main direction of my argument in this essay on women's consciousness in the work of four contemporary Irish women writers. The idea of the fairy story is particularly apt because the search for identity and existential meaning which informs so many of the classic fairy tales is both the dominant theme in the writing of Edna O'Brien, Julia O'Faolain, Molly Keane and Jennifer Johnston and also the subject of this essay. Despite limitations of space, it is possible to explore the 'story' about women's consciousness which informs and connects novels by these writers who, in purely literary terms, and of course in very different ways, stand as the most important contemporary Irish women novelists. They have all produced a number of very finely written novels and have firmly established themselves as writers of distinction. But, as well as this, one can trace the outline of a fictional 'argument' about a clearly discernible woman's 'problem' which might well be described as the single, most important problem for women today or indeed for women at any time of their existence.

In their different treatment of this problem, these writers offer four possible solutions: in relation to men and to sexuality in O'Brien's work; to sexuality and to religion in O'Faolain's novels; to the domestic arts in both O'Faolain and Keane; and, finally, to artistic creativity in the novels in Jennifer Johnston. For the question explored by these novels is the ancient one of 'how to be'. What is the self? How is it established? What should one do to solidify one's identity, to give it a viable and meaningful existence? These issues are implicitly raised and answered by these writers in the dramatised language of their fictions.

Because these writers, with the possible exception of Edna O'Brien, are first and foremost women writers, with the emphasis on writers, rather than women's writers with the emphasis on women (and thus on the articulation of their specific problems as women), the way they deal with their material, the way they pose questions and attempt solutions to problems, encompasses all humanity and not just women. Their fictional involvement with the nature of identity and the nature of being, relates, of course, initially to being female. But then as the matter complicates itself, the question becomes much more one about how to be a woman as well as about how to be a human being, and finally quite simply and metaphysically, about how to be. Being a woman in the world then, is for these writers and for their protagonists a specific matter within the overall question of being alive and having, or not having, a sense of identity and purpose in the world. Of course, from a woman's perspective these writers are peculiarly interesting precisely because they are important writers who are also women, whose material is infused with questions about existence which are seen primarily from the woman's point of view. Taken together, then, these novels provide, in microcosm, quite a comprehensive account of women's search for identity and meaning.

Edna O'Brien's early writing painfully articulates this funda-mental problem of loss of self. In *The Country Girls* Caithleen's potential sense of self is severely damaged when her beloved mother dies. Even before this event, however, the gradual separa-tion of the self from the mother, which has to occur in psychological and emotional maturation, has not taken place because of the mother's unwillingness to let Caithleen grow away from her emotionally. Because this psychological umbilical cord between mother and child leaves Caithleen weak and dependent, she is, upon her mother's death, stranded at an infantile emotional level and condemned to carry a painful sense of loss and need through-out her life. These emotional conditions are of primary importance in all of O'Brien's novels. Indeed, in the introduction to a collection of her novels she herself remarks on this: 'I think that loss and particularly sexual loss is my theme rather than sex itself.'[2]

O'Brien's novels may be seen as finely written psychodramas in which the protagonists desperately attempt to replace the safety and wholeness, the sense of identity and meaning found

with the mother. A sense of loss is the primary experience of the
self for Caithleen in *The Country Girls*:

> . . . I heard nothing, because you hear nothing, nor no one, when your
> whole body cries and cries for the thing it has lost. Lost. Lost. And yet I
> could not believe that my mother was gone; and still I knew it was true
> because I had a feeling of doom and every bit of me was frozen stiff. . . .
> Suddenly I knew that I had to accept the fact that my mother was dead.
> And I cried as I have never cried at any other time in my life.[3]

In this early novel we then go on to see the emergence of the
characteristic solution in O'Brien's fiction to this terrible emptiness. The self is given value, identity and meaning in being
desired and loved by another:

> He cupped my face between his cold hands and very solemnly and very
> sadly he said what I had expected him to say. And that moment was
> wholly and totally perfect for me; and every thing that I had suffered up
> to then was comforted in the softness of his soft, lisping voice . . . He
> kissed me. It was a real kiss. It affected my entire body. My toes, though
> they were numb and pinched in the new shoes, responded to that kiss,
> and for a few minutes my soul was lost.   (99)

Curiously the reverse of the painful present sense of emptiness
is not one of fulfilled presence, of self-affirmation, but one of total
absence — 'my soul was lost'. As becomes evident from several
of the novels under discussion, happiness comes in an almost
ecstatic sense of being which is also a kind of transmutation of
the self beyond the bodily self. In sexual union, in religious
ecstasy, and in artistic creativity there is a sense of almost mystical
transcendence, of individuation as well as of annihilation. But
with the difference that in artistic creation (and this is why it is
the most satisfactory human resolution presented in the work of
these four writers) the self is affirmed and made whole in a positive
and in a more lasting way than in sexual union or in religious
ecstasy where the dependence on the other, the one outside the
self, weakens the self, and creates a posture of permanent longing,
dependence and desire.

In O'Brien's novels the main theme is always concerned with
loss and with how heterosexual relations and, more specifically,
sexual relations may be used to replace the loss of the self, of the
infant's passionate sense of self in the union with the mother. At
the end of *The Country Girls* Caithleen remarks:

But all that night I slept badly. I tucked my legs up under my nightdress and I was shivering. I was waiting for someone to come and warm me. I think I was waiting for Mama.   (181)

The experience of loss so clearly articulated in *The Country Girls* is implicit in all O'Brien's subsequent novels as is the sense of self-hatred (hatred about being a woman) expressed in this novel. Significantly Caithleen describes how she is only thankful for being a woman when she partakes in the mysterious self-transformation and self-creation for the Not I, for the man in her life:

I hate being a woman. Vain and shallow and superficial. Tell a woman that you love her and she'll ask you to write it down, so that she can show it to her friends.   (171)

Girl With Green Eyes — much more appropriately first entitled *The Lonely Girl* — continues the agonising story of the quest for selfhood through another. Because Eugene Gaillard, with whom Caithleen falls in love, has all the detachment and strength she admires, she yearns for a complete identification with him. Seeing him as both a father figure and a God figure, Caithleen takes over his ways and gives her whole being into his care and direction. She longs to please him and, in return, to be protected and shielded from her fears. The psychological function he is made to perform for her is clear. In losing herself in him she will annihilate her own painful consciousness: 'I wished that somehow he would make some deep confession to me and engross me in his fears so that I could forget my own . . .'[4] Rather than self-affirmation which comes through artistic creativity, the O'Brien protagonist longs for self-annihilation. But of course the difficulty with the sexual solution to identification is that it is impermanent. The protagonist of *Girl With Green Eyes* realises this:

Up to then I thought that being one with him in bed meant being one with him in life, but I knew now that I was mistaken, and that lovers are strangers, in between times.   (314)

Consequently, the desired psychological union which would resolve Caithleen's emptiness does not occur; instead, the novel focuses, as do all O'Brien's novels, on the disappointed return to the lonely self.

The Keane, O'Faolain and Johnston novels dealt with in this essay go beyond loneliness to describe modes of coping with the basic problem of identity. In their writing, the main characters are not preoccupied with a sense of their own psychological insecurity. However, in *Girls in their Married Bliss*, Caithleen, now a married woman, whose marriage is breaking up, is acutely conscious of her psychological dilemma. She is aware that she gives herself and her things away too easily. She recognises that even psychologically in psychotherapy she cannot afford to give anything away:

Life after all was a secret with the self. The more one gave out the less there remained for the centre — that centre which she coveted for herself, and recognised instantly in others.[5]

She now sees her mother as to blame for her emotional dependence 'a blackmailer stitching the cord back on' and O'Brien shows Caithleen's husband taking their son away from her so that she doesn't turn him into 'one of those mother-smothered, emotionally sick people . . .' (156).

In *August is a Wicked Month* Caithleen is a divorced woman desperately trying to fill up her sense of emptiness with love affairs. When her son is killed his death forms yet another part of the grief-stricken scenario of the novel. It is a most depressing novel because O'Brien appears not to have a perspective beyond that of her craven heroine with which to view her desolation. Her longing for 'all the men in the world to be making love to her', her fantasies of reassurance from men or priests, her desire to vanish back to her childhood, only to remember the dark springs of her terror, leave the reader with a devastating sense of hopelessness:

She hungered for more; love, reassurance, as if what had gone in had been mysteriously drained by some sort of spiritual diabetic flow.[6]

The novel ends with Caithleen telling Baba

You know what I want . . . To cease to be me . . . I want to love someone or something, so utterly, and to ask for nothing in return and to die for loving that thing if necessary.   (166)

Self-annihilation in the identity of the loved one is the traditional posture or solution for woman in the great Romantic novels (most memorably Catherine's 'Nelly, I *am* Heathcliff' in *Wuthering Heights*) and O'Brien's heroines shares this desire. But O'Brien goes beyond this to reveal the psychological problems both at the root of the desire as well as in the postulated solution. It is ironic that her novels (which so devastatingly articulate the agony of psychic emptiness and the fallacy of the love solution but which never go beyond it) have attained a popularity and commercial success far beyond that of the other writers mentioned in this essay. The view of women offered to women readers in O'Brien's novels desperately needs to be seen within a wider perspective, a perspective which sees the consciousness embedded in her novels as part of a broader pattern and a continuing argument, an argument in which her novels are seen to articulate a problem and the fallacy of the solutions offered to it, but which go no further.

In turning to two of Julia O'Faolain's novels, *The Obedient Wife* and *The Women in the Wall*, we find that the story about how to be, about the search for identity, becomes at once both more practical, pragmatic and material than in O'Brien's novels and also at the same time more spiritual and transcendental. In *The Obedient Wife* domesticity and the domestic skills of cooking, bourgeois living and the family are seen as modes of salvation in a chaotic anarchic life. Law (rather than literature) is favoured as putting pattern into women's lives; the bonds of need and interdependence between husband and wife are seen to be the sound and sane basis for existence. Carla's love affair with a priest ends because she senses his emotional and spiritual independence, his lack of need. While she resents her husband's control over her and her dependence on him, she is unable to find her own independent emotional and psychic existence. When she makes love with her husband she tries to keep her own self separate — 'an inner image of herself tried to claw itself together'.[7] Certainly, the sense of control she gets through cooking bolsters her sense of self but she is unwilling to take on the responsibility of the man who is a priest, his church, his God and him:

I don't like that responsibility . . . It makes me feel like a seducer. Like a male . . .   (144)

When Carla's chastity in her marriage is threatened she feels her personality dissolve: 'She was dislocated, adrift.' What she hates about her husband is the way he can win her son round: 'It was as if Maurizio had no self.' (200) Cleverly, in leaving Carla alone to sort out her love affair her husband deprives her of her known function as wife and mother. In this vacuum he 'magnetised her mind', and she is insensibly pulled back to him and to her role as obedient wife. Curiously what repulses Carla in her lover, the priest, is his self-sufficiency. His own love affair

with God removes him from the secular plane of sexual and
psychological union. The egotism of the quest for religious salvation deflates the pretension or the possibility of human loving.
Whereas the temporal world of family exists in the interdependence of its members, the priest relates to an eternal impersonal
reality which undermines and is incompatible with secular life.

In these two novels O'Faolain sees only two possibilities; either
as in *The Obedient Wife* a harnessed sexuality in bourgeois domestic
life, or as in *The Women in the Wall* mystic union with the lover
Christ and total denial of the body. Hers is a peculiarly stark
vision in that she polarises the solutions to the problem of identity
so distinctly. Radegunda in *The Women in the Wall*, despite herself,
enjoyed sexuality in her marriage but longed to 'give herself
to God' which she suceeds in doing in the course of the novel,
becoming effectively both mystic and saint. Conversely, Agnes
the unwilling, or not totally committed Bride of Christ, longs
for sexuality. She finds brief ecstasy in it and then years of
agony while she watches the growth and the dying of her own
unacclaimed illegitimate daughter. In O'Faolain's fictional world,
those who can find Christ as lover and achieve mystic union are
indeed happy, if only sporadically, until the final union in death.
Those who opt for the body and sex are a prey to violence and disappointment. There seems to be a close connection in O'Faolain's
imagination between sex and violence. In *No Country for Young
Men*, of course, this connection is made explicit by the end of the
novel when it is revealed that the senile nun had murdered the
man for whom she felt both a deep sexual attraction and profound
revulsion. A distorted sexuality in O'Faolain becomes violent,
murderous or suicidal as in *The Women in the Wall*.

In this novel, then, O'Faolain's counterpart to O'Brien's solution
to the identity problem in sexual union is mystic union with
Christ. Radegunda becomes the 'passive uncritical servant of
God's will'. She waits listening with 'the more receptive part
of the mind . . . the feminine part which waited, humbly and
uncritically, to be fecundated by divine decisions, which are
unfathomable and must simply be accepted'.[8] The mystic stance
is identical to the female's posture of passive longing in O'Brien's
novels. The solutions in O'Faolain's novels are at once both more
pragmatically physical and more transcendentally spiritual.

In O'Faolain's two novels an ordered and domiciled attachment
to creatures is seen to be that which saves the secular as well as
that which damns the spiritual. The less painful way for those
who cannot manage the mundane solution of secular love is seen

to be the way of detachment: because attachments are nothing; they are frail and fleeting. But even so there is a strong sense in O'Faolain's writing that they are all the secular have, as in *The Obedient Wife*, and they should therefore be sealed and solidified as securely as possible since they are what holds the fabric of society together. But for the religious mystic happiness is not the bourgeois compromise but rather the 'shucking off of the body', the getting outside of body, the freed soul. Ingunda in *The Women in the Wall*, the illegitimate child of Agnes the nun, epitomises the split, the incompatibility between the religious solution and the temporal one. Agnes herself was unable to opt finally for the one or the other mode. She and Fortunatus sinned not for loving (Agnes comes to believe) but for not loving *enough*. She held on to the pattern and safety of administration in the convent. She could not let herself go completely in sexual human loving and as a result her daughter Ingunda immures herself, feeling the unconscious desire to punish herself for being the living proof of that unresolvable struggle. The desire to 'cease to be' takes on the most literal sense in this novel and, after her daughter's death, Agnes in turn bricks herself up to escape the split in herself between her sexuality and her spirituality. It is a conscious decision and takes place externally, as it were, outside the psychological realm of her own psyche. The painful struggle is over.

In Molly Keane's recent novels *Good Behaviour* and *Time After Time* we find the struggle is also over. But here the struggle is over before the novels even begin. The basic psychological premise of these novels is that psychological wholeness, emotional integrity, no longer exists. The self is alienated from itself; it feels itself full of self-loathing and is unable to love others or indeed the self except in a highly sublimated manner. Love and care have become sublimated into material comforts, external power over oneself, nature or other people. We see the emergence and development of this stance in *Good Behaviour* in the characterisation of Aroon St. Charles. Unloved, indeed hated, by her own mother Aroon is desperately in need of love. But since no one in this fictional world is capable of love (except the warm governess who is forced to suicide) good manners replace good feeling and good behaviour keeps life, a form of life, going. Beyond the crippled consciousness of her characters Keane offers a deeply ironic, witty and painful critique of alienated being. Aroon attempts to get a feeling of selfhood by being needed and loved by the men in her life — by her father, her brother and by Richard (her brother's homosexual lover). In being used by the latter two as a cover-up for their own

homosexual love affair Aroon gets momentary feelings of worth.
Just as she achieves moments of ecstasy from these men, she senses
her mother's draining need of her father and her determination
to have him all for herself; to prevent any living expression of the
father's love for his daughter. The novel is riddled with betrayal.
The most significant of which is Aroon's unconscious betrayal of
her own self and the transposition of emotional need into purely
physical material needs. In despair Aroon asks herself

What must I do, I thought . . . what must I do now, tomorrow and for
ever? . . . [She feels her cold hotwater-bottle] Here was something I could
change, something I must give myself . . .[9]

What we find in this novel then is the transition from identification through sex, men or through God, to identification by
means of material comforts which, to some extent, resolve the sense
of existential, psychological, purposelessness and meaningless-
ness. The climax comes when, in despair after her father's death,
Aroon hears she has been left all her father's property. Material
objects and wielding the power given her by owning them,
permanently displaces the loving, suffering, changing organism
which is a person. The self comes to operate mechanically and
automatically. Time, in which and through which we suffer, is
replaced by the time *after* that living time when people are both
psychologically and (in a symbolical representation of that)
physically maimed.

In *Time After Time* the characters, all women, except for one
homosexual man, are all maimed. April is deaf. May's hand is
deformed. June is 'a little slow', uneducated and despised, while
their brother Jasper has only one eye. Curiously here, as in Edna
O'Brien's novels, the awful mummy-love is seen to have been the
cause of these characters' inability to grow up emotionally and
psychologically. Their maiming or crippling is merely the external
aspect of a process which has been cut short in their psychological
development. Since none of the brothers and sisters in *Time After
Time* has fully experienced unconditional loving, which might
have enabled them to mature, none of them is capable of loving.
They hate one another and use their pets and their skills —
cooking, flower arranging, farming, self-adornment — as defences
behind which they may hide their inadequacies from each other
and, most of the time, from themselves. Their human needs are
almost fully sublimated into these varying activities and the
painful reasons for these sublimations have been all but lost to

their consciousness. They themselves are not conscious of pain; they are not conscious of suffering the struggle for identity and authentication any longer but they are seen to be merely shells of human beings. These characters find contentment in the perfection of their skills. Jasper's cooking is nearly an art form: '— in the most trivial cooking tasks he looked only for perfection.'[10] April's narcissism keeps her totally absorbed. Her body and her clothes are nearly perfect. May's flower arrangements represent a triumph over her deformity as well as aesthetic performances. In their heavily defended worlds 'divided from each other and following their several pursuits, each one of the family felt a different and happier person'. (61)

As well as flower arranging May is able to use her deformed hand to steal small objects she covets and Keane makes the connection between the excitement she feels and sexual excitement explicit: 'The planning and timing of the adventure meant as much to her as the first movements in a game of sex to a luckier person.' (72) In Jasper's exhilaration when gardening Keane tells us he experienced 'some of the emotion he could have known, perhaps, with an undemanding bride, had love not been so aborted in him when he was young'. (212) The implication is obvious. Potentially 'healthy' sexuality has been sublimated into ceaseless 'activity' of one kind or another. When Leda, a formerly beautiful but now blind and ugly woman out of the family's past re-enters their lives, she soon exerts her power over them all: 'Leda warmed their intimacy with her special skills to capture love in any form that she could use at her own discretion and requirement.' (129-130)

The naive hope for love and identification in the loved one which we found in O'Brien's novels has here reached its final distortion and perversion. The other is sought in order to create ammunition against others and to give a sense of power. Unconscious parasitism becomes a carefully planned and highly devious form of emotional treachery: 'all she wished for was a power over each against each, and to steal even the secrets they didn't know they kept.' (143) The orderly disciplines of the religious life in O'Faolain have been displaced here by the orderly disciplines of diets, exercises, gardening, flower arranging and so on. In this novel the criticism of the life-in-death existence of the characters is silent, or rather implicit, in Keane's skilful and subtle mode of narration. Only one character, Jasper, is made to think, 'I just wish I was more of a Human Being . . .' (214)

Johnston's dramatised meditations in fictional form, *The Old Jest*, *The Christmas Tree* and *The Railway Station Man* articulate the final and most satisfactory (both in artistic and human terms) solution to the quest for identity in the work of these four women writers. Rather than loss or transcendence of the self through men, or sexual union (as in O'Brien) or in religious ecstasy (O'Faolain) or domesticity and sublimation of the self in displacement activities (Keane), and the subsequent erosion of the self which these solutions involve, Johnston's three novels postulate the actual birth of self not at biological birth but with the birth of individual and individuating consciousness. Jung's description of his own experience of individuation seems peculiarly apposite here:

It was as if a wall of mist were at my back, and behind that wall there was not yet an 'I'. But at this moment *I came upon myself*. Previously I had existed too, but everything had merely happened to me. Now I happened to myself. Now I knew: I am myself now, now I exist.[11]

And there is a strong sense in Johnston's later novels that she is working towards a more subjective, symbolic or even expressionist mode of narration in which characters become the voices of an emerging consciousness. Almost all Johnston's novels describe the relations between a young, sensitive lost person and a much older but also 'lost' person, both of whom undergo, with the reader, some kind of revelation about the self and about the self's relation to others. In *The Old Jest* eighteen year old Nancy, on the verge of self-discovery, attempts first — in the well-worn, traditional manner — to find out who she is by finding out who her father was. But at the end of the novel, as a result of her conversations with a political fugitive on the beach and with her dear Aunt Mary, she feels that, quite irrespective of who her parents are, she will be able to find the courage to take the psychological leap into her own adult independent existence, to find herself, to find her voice in her own expression and writing.

This novel, as are the other two considered here, is as much about the making of a person as it is about the creation of a potential artist. The self is both made and found in artistic creativity. Safe, secure and well loved in her genteel home Nancy, like the fugitive on the beach, will have to leave her safety in order to find out who she is and to follow her internal vision. Like all Johnston's protagonists she fears commitment and the risk of the pain involved in commitment. But unless the self engages in the flux, the process of life, with all its risks and changes, it is in danger of petrification, of death-in-life or of eternal evasion of the self. Facing up to change means being vulnerable, losing one's certainty, one's secure knowledge as defences: 'It all drains away, leaving you alone, like standing on the top of a mountain with a cold wind blowing. No protection.'[12] Nancy, the protagonist of the novel, wonders whether other people feel this 'desolation, this isolation'. In leaving her early dependency on the house, the people who love her, she will, her middle-aged fugitive reassures her, be able to 'travel without encumbrances'. She is fearful of the exploration. But, as all Johnston's novels show, there is nothing to fear except death, and ' "Death is an old jest, but it comes to everyone" '. (85)

In this novel Nancy is lucky; she has the psychological security given her by her beloved Aunt Mary, by Bridie and her 'calm gentle way of living'. She feels she will be able to draw on the strength they have bequeathed her. What she feels most clearly is her attraction to words. She gets a thrill from them: 'Written, spoken, words just tumbling themselves round in my head . . . hardly even thought, like shadows, but making their own noise.' (58) Her desire is to know who she is and what her life and life itself are all about. The novel ends with Nancy determined to 'make sense' of it all, to find a pattern: 'If I could see the pattern, then maybe I could understand. There has to be a pattern. It can't all just be futile in the end.' (149)

The desire to find a sense of coherence in one's experience, in one's life, and the realisation that one has to take emotional risks in order to begin to 'know' anything in any real sense, combine in what is arguably Johnston's finest novel and the most achieved piece of writing among those mentioned in this essay. In *The Christmas Tree* Constance, the forty-two year old unmarried mother of an infant baby is dying of cancer and reflects on her past life. She sees her determined posture of self-isolation in order to avoid pain as deeply ironic and absurd. Not because as in Edna O'Brien's novels one can 'find counsel' or lose oneself in another person, but because only by risking relationships, by participating in life fully, can one truly be said to have lived at all. Her posture of 'eternally protecting herself' against any 'possibility of pain' meant a life of insulated reality:

I never allowed myself to know anyone very well . . . never had courage of any sort, that has been the absurdity of my life.[13]

In her comments on her parents' marriage it is made clear that the 'cushioning against loneliness that marriage is supposed to bring' (27) is not for her a viable solution to the quest for identity and meaning. It is not through relationships alone that one can cure one's own existential emptiness. She does not attempt to use her child's father in this way. She wishes, in creating a child and in creating writing, to produce a person or a piece of literature which will leave its own mark on the world; which will, through her, make connections with other people and affect their lives in some way. She remembers that the isolation she created for herself was in order to comprehend more. Now that she is dying she attempts to make her sense of it all cohere in writing, to find the pattern at the heart of it all. She realises, in retrospect, that she was wrong to put off committing herself to herself, to her confrontation with life. Her lack of involvement with relationships she sees as her lack of involvement in her own life:

All these years I have mistreated my mind, as I have mistreated my body; both are the victims of my carelessness, my sloth and my innate conviction that tomorrow would be time enough for attack, courage, commitment. (85)

Unlike the pathological dependency with which others are viewed by O'Brien's protagonists, Johnston's characters have evaded relationships in order to get through life without pain but also without living. Their moment of revelation and of freedom comes when they realise, as does Constance in *The Christmas Tree*, that the most important person to whom she has failed to commit herself is herself. At her death she realises that her failure is not her dying but her not having lived:

Here I am, eyeball to eyeball with death, and I haven't moved the world in any way. I haven't even left a footprint on its surface. (140)

The mark left by the self to which she refers is not purely an external one. It is at its source the turning of the self to pay attention to itself; to listen inwardly; to hear the voice of one's own creativity and possibly a voice beyond one's own. Constance says she's 'never heard the whisper of His voice . . . but only because I haven't known how to listen. I have never found the silence in my heart that is necessary'. (150) The truth, in Johnston's novel, is seen to lie within the self. The appropriate posture, then, is one of commitment and attention to the self. Not, as in O'Brien, escape from the self in relationships or, as in O'Faolain's portrait of religious mysticism, spiritual transcendence of the physical self but rather, as in Johnston's subsequent novel, affirmation of the creativity at the centre of being.

Johnston continues her study of self-authentication and creativity in *The Railway Station Man* where Helen, the protagonist, is aware (as was Constance at the end of *The Christmas Tree*) that isolation is an insulation from reality and prevents a painful but possibly necessary connection with reality. She also, like Constance, looks back at her mistaken posture of waiting for revelation. She didn't have 'the gumption nor the energy to realise that we have to create our own miracles'.[14] She only finds herself (quite ironically, when looked at from the perspective of the steps in the argument of this essay) when her husband dies. Unlike the desperate hope in Edna O'Brien's novels, there is no sense here of finding the self in the other. There is rather an acute awareness that relationships if wrongly used actually prevent self-discovery.

In order to be an artist, and Helen wants to be (and in the course of the novel becomes committed to being) a painter, you have to 'uproot, learn how to be alone, wrestle with the devils'. (44) Involved in the process of artistic creation, the self loses touch with the world but the result of that creativity has itself reality in the world. And the audience is an important part of the whole artistic process. So, in *The Railway Station Man* the process of de-insulation, of separation from the world, of filling the void, begins when Helen decides to paint. Having made the decision to let herself *be* born, as it were, she has a moment of ecstasy, of joy in her self-affirmation:

When she woke up the next morning and looked at the moving shadows on the ceiling, she was filled with a joy that she had never experienced before . . . Everything seemed so simple, so right. She lay and looked at the shadows and understood the meaning of ecstasy. Quite, quite abnormal for a person who had never allowed herself to be shaken radically in any way by emotion. (79)

The act of becoming fills the self. In finding one's voice one comes into being. The self is made whole by an act of affirmation and as well as this the self makes a whole — Helen's work is not just 'an illustration', it has 'an identity of its own'. (92) Rather than feeling herself, her whole being, magnetised by that of a man (as Carla does by her husband in *The Obedient Wife*) Helen feels that the canvas 'had become a magnet' (interestingly both writers use the word magnet and magnetised) 'drawing out of her head an implacable coherence that she had never felt before'. (109) The act of artistic creation, then, like Carla's marriage and Radegunda's religious ecstasy and the endless activities of Keane's characters, gives a coherence to the inner and outer chaotic and anarchic world. But the difference here is that the creating self is not evaded or sublimated or destroyed in the process. The act of artistic creativity gathers together the whole self. It both performs a healing psychological function and produces an external autonomous self in the work of art.

To be, then, in Johnston's novel, is quite clearly to be self-creative and self-created. But the doing, the creativity, if one compares it with the characters' activities in Keane's *Time After Time* which superficially might appear the same, must come out of experience, out of suffering and loving in the world, not through an evasion of it. Before the novel's ending Helen has determined not to marry Roger. She wants to own herself. She wants to love him outside what might be the prison of his 'giving himself' to her. She realises that time is made real only by recognition of one's own individual identity: 'If you're not very careful your past is empty time too and you have nothing to recognise yourself by.' (177) The kind of relationship that marriage might offer is not viewed as an antidote for loneliness. The only real cure for that, says Helen, is 'some sort of close relationship with God'. (177)

The message which emerges from an over-view of these four novelists is that the self must cure the self. Authentication and a sense of identity have to be truly self-affirming and not self-evading in order to bring contentment. For women in a Christian culture like Ireland the fictional alternatives to the problem of selfhood are obviously easily polarised into those of sex and religion and, as we have seen, these two elements play important roles in novels by contemporary Irish women writers. Indeed, if we look back to the first half of this century Kate O'Brien, (a still greatly under-rated Irish writer) in *The Land of Spices* and particularly in *That Lady*, produced two highly distinguished novels which deal most skilfully with these polarities. But in terms of the four contemporary writers considered here, only in Jennifer Johnston's novels do we find the whole question of women's search for identity and psychological independence taken beyond these polarities and seen in relation to what is arguably the most satisfactory recreation of the self — in the process of artistic creativity.

It is not, I think, surprising that Johnston's novels which radically extend the fictional treatment of women's consciousness and quest for identity are also those which are the most exploratory and, in a positive way, subjective in literary terms. O'Brien's unquestionable gift as a writer seems to have foundered on an inability to find a centre, to find a self, to find a subject. O'Faolain's writing seems to be caught hanging between violence and submission without any hope of development. Keane beautifully anatomises a lost integrity, a lost wholeness but the sheer skill and even virtuosity of her writing cannot hide the static nature of her vision. It seems to me, that among these writers, Jennifer Johnston's writing stands alone. It offers a step forward both in ways of writing this kind of fiction and in ways of seeing both the self and the world.

SHADOWS OF DESTRUCTION: THE BIG HOUSE IN CONTEMPORARY IRISH FICTION

ANDREW PARKIN

Ancestral houses have long been resonant symbols of power, class structure, and even the state itself, giving architectural expression to the rise and fall of particular families. The palace front and the fate of the families who belonged to it provided the environment and circumstances of Greek tragedy. In England, too, there has of course been a long tradition of country house literature finding expression in poetry, drama, and fiction.[1] That the houses of aristocrats should feature in so much literature is hardly surprising, since aristocracies were patrons and audiences; their fortunes and actions could deeply affect their society, and held an intrinsic fascination for those less fortunate than themselves. It is rather more intriguing that the 'Big House' theme has persisted in Irish fiction since the second world war, years after the struggle for independence had finished in the south and the political and class warfare of the troubled 1920s had destroyed many of the houses and driven a number of aristocratic families to leave Ireland. In a land of ruined hovels, the ruin of the Big House had already been chronicled before Yeats put it on stage in its briefest, perhaps most horrifying form in *Purgatory* (1938). Yet the Big House is by no means worn out as a theme in such diverse talents as those of Aidan Higgins, Molly Keane, John Banville, William Trevor, and Jennifer Johnston. Study of selected novels by several of these writers may suggest explanations.

It is worth recalling first, though, that earlier Big House novelists, beginning with Maria Edgeworth, were usually themselves Anglo-Irish in the sense that they were landowning gentry, English was their first language, and if they were formally educated it was often done in England.[2] Edgeworth's *Castle Rackrent* (1800), Somerville and Ross's *The Real Charlotte* (1894) and, after Ross's death, *The Big House at Inver* (1925) along with Elizabeth Bowen's *The Last September* (1929) are usually taken to be the landmarks in the earlier tradition. We should not, however,

306

forget Dion Boucicault's *The Colleen Bawn* (1860), although an example from drama, because it was adapted from Gerald Griffin's novel *The Collegians* (1829) and demonstrates what a powerful hold the theme had on the imagination of a non-Ascendancy, indeed decidedly flashy author. It also demonstrates the power for impressing a wide and various audience in Victorian and modern times of the theme of the declining estate and the marriage of noble with commoner.

Sinister, melodramatic elements of the theme as treated by Boucicault and Sheridan LeFanu crop up at the end of the last century in a book still very potent, but not usually seen as a Big House novel, Bram Stoker's *Dracula* (1897). It can of course readily be argued that the sanguivorous Count was Transylvanian, the action begins and ends in Transylvania, and its main setting is England. But Stoker was Irish. On the few occasions when Count Dracula speaks he is not given, like Van Helsing, a heavy foreign accent. On the contrary, he speaks of his family and tribal pride in the rhetoric of the late nineteenth century re-awakening of heroic Ireland:

When was redeemed that great shame of my nation, the shame of Cassova, when the flags of the Wallach and the Magyar went down beneath the Crescent? Who was it but one of my own race who as Voivode crossed the Danube and beat the Turk on his own ground? This was a Dracula indeed! Woe was it that his own unworthy brother, when he had fallen, sold his people to the Turk and brought the shame of slavery on them![3]

If for 'Turk' we read 'English' the Irish feeling of the passage becomes clear. But Dracula would seem also to have an aristocratic impatience with modern ideas of humanity and democracy (he is eventually defeated by their representatives, the doctor and the lawyer) which is the corollary of his fierce warrior mentality. He is eloquent in his nostalgia for the historic battles when he tells Harker:

Ah, young sir, the Szekelys — and the Dracula as their hearts' blood, their brains, and their swords — can boast a record that mushroom growths like the Hapsburgs and the Romanoffs can never reach. The warlike days are over. Blood is too precious a thing in these days of dishonourable peace; and the glories of the great races are as a tale that is told. (33)

The phrasing and the rhythms of the Count are that of an Irish speaker of English rather than a European one; they fit with the

image of Dracula as a nobleman with a 'Gothic' castle, and a
country house, as well as a London town house to which he
periodically withdraws. Peasants fear him with a superstitious
dread appropriate to such criminal aristocrats as were members
of the Hell Fire Club. The Count destroys commoners by sucking
their blood, but the vampire's kiss in Stoker's novel is clearly
meant to go beyond mere blood-letting. It is described in sexual
terms, the victims experiencing 'a langorous ecstasy' (42) before
they go wanly to their graves. The deeper foundation for this
imagery is to be found in Stoker's Irish experience. His mother's
horrific accounts of the 1832 cholera outbreak in Sligo so impressed
him that he encouraged her to write them down. Her letter
devoted to these experiences gives a sharp immediacy to the
incidents and also contains a number of images foreshadowing
the *Dracula* world. The disease itself is described in terms that
apply to Dracula himself:

It was the cholera, which for the first time appeared in Western Europe.
Its bitter strange kiss, and man's want of experience or knowledge of its
nature, or how best to resist its attacks, added, if anything could, to its
horrors.[4]

The healthy treat the disease's victims as creatures to be totally
shunned, but also as beings to be kept safely buried even while
they are still alive. She tells how a 'poor traveller' when found to
be ill was pushed with long poles into a pit and buried alive. The
poles suggest the stakes used in the novel to impale the un-dead.
And the fearsome hammer blows Van Helsing and Seward use for
these impalings are curiously anticipated by Mrs. Stoker's
account of the burial of the tall Sergeant Cullen:

The men who were putting him in, when they found he would not fit,
took a big hammer to break his legs and *make* him fit. The first blow
roused the Sergeant from his stupor, and he started up and recovered. (27)

Mrs. Stoker's abiding impression is that the town is 'a place of the
dead' (26). Her letter contains other elements of the vampire world:
sinister clouds of mist, storms, insanity, even the deaths of children,
and a pervasive aura of helplessness, suspicion, and dread. A
more obvious Irish forerunner and influence was Sheridan Le
Fanu's 1871 story of 'Carmilla' the female vampire. Although
Stoker's research into Voivode Drakula gave him major details for
the novel, its Irish origins place it well in the Gothic strain of Big
House fiction in which, as Seamus Deane recently remarked 'the

destruction or perversion of an aristocratic family or person becomes a tale of terror'.[5] A discarded early chapter of Stoker's novel described Harker straying during a snowstorm into a deserted village 'forsaken years before because of vampire trouble' (114). It is difficult to resist the conclusion that *Dracula* is a covert image of an alien aristocracy bleeding Irish peasants that it may live. That its ruthless power even preyed on children was certainly a circumstance that was not lost on the Swift of 'A Modest Proposal'. Indeed, the zoophagous Renfield is a creation worthy of Swift. In the figure of Dracula, Stoker combined the battle-thirst of the old Irish chiefs with the half-life of the Ascendancy, at once present and absent, Irish and English, and not quite either.[6] The much adapted, less often read novel, presents a striking pictorial description near its end:

The castle of Dracula now stood out against the red sky, and every stone of its broken battlements was articulated against the light of the setting sun. (416)

Only twenty-five years later, 'between 1921 and 1923, 192 Big Houses were destroyed'.

Besides the universal taste for horror, the persistence of Dracula's myth suggests the deeper connection in the popular mind between decaying aristocracy and exploitation. It is a post-revolutionary literary myth, the new world of urban professionals defeating the old rural codes and superstitions, yet it is firmly rooted in a feudal past.[8] No less than the folk material on which it draws, *Dracula* is Stoker's revenge against decadent aristocracy. It is a literary version of the traditional '*anti-seigneurial* rebellion'.[9]

More typically, the Big House novel was written from the insider viewpoint (Somerville and Ross, George Moore, Elizabeth Bowen). As Seamus Deane points out, as the Big House culture died it was resuscitated in Irish writing. Deane sees this as an 'artificial' process. It is, on the contrary, entirely natural: the corpse is exhumed by some for the purposes of revenge; by others it is resurrected in the nostalgic and ambivalent imagination, for they are its apologists and its critics. Indeed, the persistence of the genre into the post-war world does not mean that Irish fiction is now playing with old used-up themes because it is itself in decline. The literary qualities of the novels themselves refute that notion; what we are encountering is the tenacious hold of a form of rural culture over the modern imagination, however cosmopolitan. This is partly accounted for by the immense energy of pastoral — here is an Irish version of pastoral; it is also testimony to the fact that 'rural civilization has not yet lain down and died, either gracefully or ungracefully'.[10] Melusine survives in the world of post-war Irish fiction, because 'Cultures may pass, but cultural legacies remain'.[11]

The anti-seigneurial strain, stripped of Gothic trappings of course, obtains in Aidan Higgins's *Langrishe, Go Down* (1966), whose title suggests a direct command for the decline of the Langrishe family. The title also suggests Drishane, the family home of Edith Somerville, as well as echoing Lydia Languish, with her determination to match herself with 'a fellow not worth a shilling' in Sheridan's comedy, *The Rivals*. Higgins's mood, however, is not that of comedy even though he is irreverent.[12] As we might expect, his technique is modern. A first group of nine chapters is headed 1937. Third person narrative gives Helen's point of view as she rides the bus from Dublin back to the Big House, Springfield, she shares with her sisters Imogen and Lily.[13] Helen bears the news that the family fortune is now exhausted. She knows her sisters will not face reality. She is isolated from them, just as they are all isolated from the people and life beyond the demesne walls. Yet the pattern is made more unusual by the fact that these survivors of the gentry are Catholic, following their mother's conversion. Harsh and domineering, Helen is fastidious, snobbish and bitter. Her one contact with the locals is an encounter in the Catholic graveyard with an old man who celebrates the past as he remembers Springfield in its more prosperous phase. But the desolate present cannot be escaped: Helen realises her remaining family need 'to change their ways, for the old impossible life was ending'.[14] In chapter five we switch to Imogen's point of view, and then switch between Helen and Imogen until the last brief chapter of this section. Here an impersonal, choric voice, its words italicised, demonstrates time's work of decay, leaving us with a vision of the three remaining sisters, isolated victims of change:

There, each in her own room, each with her own troubles, they lie sleeping in big brass beds headed into the corners and looking as if designed for suffering — dreaming of better times, of worse times. And so all goes away. (78)

The novel is a log book of this decline. The one bright touch of life is in Imogen's affair with Otto Beck, a German student of Philology. The account of this affair at the lodge where Otto has been allowed to live rent free, occupies the second section, a flashback to 1932. A savage irony ends the section with a stillborn baby for Imogen and the demise of the affair. Death and sterility dominate section three, headed 1938. Its three brief chapters deal with the funerals of both Emily and Helen, the Anschluss, and Imogen's visit to the now decrepit lodge, perhaps inhabited by a vagrant, or even Otto. The novel ends with Imogen alone (Lily's absence is one of several loose ends in the book) facing the ruin of the estate, the ruin of Europe, about which she knows as little as she knows about Ireland, and facing ironically the beginning of Spring:

The beginning of a mild March day. On the shadowed windowsill a few dead flies remained, leftovers. Hide away here, let the days pass and hope that things will change. Clouds were slowly passing across the windows. Yes, that — or nothing at all. How the wind blows today!   (275)

Higgins's technique of framing the flashback to 1932 between the chronological periods 1937 and 1938 gives to Imogen's affair a poignancy it would not otherwise have. But it separates our slender knowledge of Helen at the beginning of the book from her funeral in chapter thirty-seven. We therefore care little about her death. Moreover, her funeral is given only a few words. It follows the much longer description of Emily's funeral in the previous chapter. The effect is an anti-climax, and two funerals back-to-back is itself a clumsy idea. Although Emily's funeral is meant as an important scene, we know even less about her than we do about Helen. We care as little about her as the inclement weather or the inept grave diggers do. It might be objected that Higgins's purpose is to make us view these aristocratic, ageing sisters as people of no consequence, feeling little for them as they go down. After all, they feel little enough for the people around them. But this is an artistic fallacy; we need to have a fuller sense of Emily as a character for her funeral to carry significance. The final section of the book fails, and its gestures towards larger significance through reference to events in Europe are not very convincing. A very much fuller novel would be needed to cut the Ascendancy down to size by contrast with the European experience of the dictatorships. The link between aristocracy and Fascist politics is a major theme needing far fuller treatment; it contains some uncomfortable ironies and exciting possibilities. Imogen's love affair, though, is strongly written: it stresses her isolation from her own class and family; it represents a longing for connection with a larger, less provincial life and mores than Ireland could provide. By contrasting her with Otto, Higgins exposes her ignorance of the Gaelic background and Catholic rural life off which she lives. Ironically, Otto, through his interest in Gaelic place names, gets closer to Irish life than she ever does. Otto's knowledge is as assured as Imogen's ignorance. She is truly parasitic, living off virtually an alien land, just as he is parasitic on Springfield's decrepit estate.

Helen's similar ignorance and isolation are still great, even though she is able to understand the plight of Springfield. In her monologue in chapter eight she muses:

. . . when we die no one will mourn for us, or afterwards remember us . . . Here I languish under blankets and eiderdown . . . I am dead with cold. (69)

The short Winter days are the last days of Helen, her family, and her class. The view from the Big House has changed:

74 acres of it mine today — a forgotten battlefield that means nothing to me. Nothing. (73)

and

History ends in me. Now. Today. (74)

Although moved by Catholicism, she perceives from the outside its rites

said in secret, [which] had held the people together, the faith of poor and oppressed Catholic Ireland in the penal times. (11)

When Helen sees a cinema poster advertising a film billed as 'Romance and pathos among four human derelicts' and another, 'Strike it Rich' (27) she, whose ancestors had struck it rich, now aligns herself and her three sisters differently:

Human derelicts, she thought grimly, it's about us. (28)

Higgins's novel is to some extent a revenge upon the class it portrays. Its technique of development through the point of view of major characters cannot compensate fully for the novel's lack of detailed portraiture of the Ascendancy class. This charge cannot be levelled at books by Elizabeth Bowen or Molly Keane. Yet Higgins's quest for a broader, historical view is responsible for at least one of the novel's strengths, the characterisation of Otto, his bohemian friends, and their graceless attitudes. Studious, cruel, predatory, parasitic Otto, regretting the loss of German whores, is a stark foil to Imogen's fastidious loneliness and ingenuousness. He is Higgins's best reminder to us that the problems of Ireland, its class war and prejudices, are just a very small part of the vast turmoil and revolution and carnage that swept Europe and the rest of the world in our century. The essentially provincial love affair suggests in this context that the descent of the Ascendancy is also essentially no more than provincial. This does not lessen the personal suffering and sense of futility of the sisters. It creates perspective, and too briefly, a context for their pain. Chekhov is, of course, the supreme master of this effect.

Working back from present to past through the points of view of main characters is also the organising principle in William Trevor's *Fools of Fortune* (1983). The major part of the book is in three sections, 'Willie', 'Marianne' and 'Imelda' in that order. The first two sections start in the present and then plunge to the crucial past through the first person narrative voice of the character whose name is the title of the section. The third section is told through a third person omniscient voice. There then follows a brief sprint to the finish: the three sections are repeated in the same order. Willie tells how he returned to his gutted house, Kilneagh. Marianne is glimpsed through a selection of diary entries, the last recording Willie's return in 1982 after a life on the run. The brief closing section, 'Imelda', again uses the authorial third person, offering a coda on Imelda as Holy Fool, juggling sanctity and madness.

Addressed to each other, the saddened voices of Willie and Marianne reveal the tragedy of Kilneagh and the Quintons who live there. The poignancy of the Irish situation is made sharper by contrast with Marianne's family home, the grander English house, Woodcombe Park.[15] The Ascendancy tradition at Kilneagh is just about dead, whereas Woodcombe Park 'bustles with life'.[16]

Fools of Fortune is, like all Big House novels, a love story as well as an anatomy of social disaster. Marianne visits Kilneagh for the funeral of Willie's father and sisters killed in the fire that gutted the house, save for one wing. Back at school in Switzerland, Marianne discovers she is pregnant by Willie, and thus becomes another of the English women from Woodcombe who over the centuries have married into the Quintons. She resolves to bear the child, goes to Ireland and lives on at Kilneagh in the hope that Willie one day must return. Willie's return is long delayed, because he left to take a bloodthirsty revenge on the Black and

Tan Sergeant Rudkin who had set fire to the house and shot two servants and the dogs. The action was itself a link in the chain of revenge: Rudkin's informer, Doyle, had been found hanged somewhere on the estate. His Irish executioners had also cut out his tongue. Doyle's motive was probably comradely feeling for the sergeant with whom he had fought his way through the Great War. Thus a network of loyalties, divisions and conflicts entraps the Quintons, killing father and daughters, making the mother a drunkard, Willie a murderer who decapitates Rudkin, and driving Imelda insane as a defence against the seemingly endless chain of suffering. As with Higgins, European events form a background to the action. Trevor also complicates the pattern by having the Protestant Quintons take in the old Catholic Father Kilgarriff, by making them Home Rulers, and showing them aiding Michael Collins. On one of Collins's clandestine visits to the house he meets Mrs Quinton, an Englishwoman from Woodcombe Park. Her 'voice conveyed no note of apology ... There was injustice in Ireland was what my mother maintained: you didn't have to be Irish to wish to expunge it' (28-29).

The implication of love with politics and so with the chain of revenge is a powerful motif. Just as Heaney puns with 'Act of Union' so Trevor makes the same point. Imelda hears her mother, Marianne, say to Mr Lanigan:

Does the map remind you curiously of an embrace? A most extraordinary embrace to throw up all this . . . Father Kilgarriff thinks so, and the others too. Yet I am a part of all this now. I cannot help my fervour.   (162)

From this embrace are spawned the 'troubles' and 'the shadows of destruction that pervade Kilneagh' (166); its children are also the Anglo-Irish and the culture of their demesnes. The furniture and setting of this culture is one concern of the Big House novel. Trevor gives us Josephine the maid's sense of the environment through Willie's memory of her when first employed at Kilneagh:

But it was my mother who made her feel at home in a world she did not know and in a house that seemed enormous to her. Its landings and half-landings, front staircase and back one, the kitchen passages, the Chinese carpet in the scarlet drawing-room, the Waterford vases in the hall, endless porcelain figures in the morning-room, the silver pheasants, the rosewood trays: all this was a strangeness that whirled about her, like colours in a kaleidoscope.   (26-27)

Thus prepared, we cannot fail to hear of the plangent past, when Marianne sees the house with 'the roof of the burnt-out gate-lodge all tumbled in' and, at the end of the unchanged avenue, 'the windowless house' which 'rose blackly from weeds and undergrowth, corrugated iron nailed over the pillared doorway'. (96) It is here that she feels a sense of belonging because of her love for Willie. This love condemns her to a long, painful wait for his return, because Willie's revenge (his mother had longed for it until her suicide) makes him a fugitive living abroad.

The lovers restored at the end of the book have survived a terrible penance. It seemed as if Imelda might have been an artist. Yeats's 'Lake Isle of Inisfree' hovers in her mind and she echoes Stephen in *A Portrait of the Artist as a Young Man*:

Imelda Quinton is my name, Ireland is my nation. A burnt house is my dwelling place, Heaven's my destination.   (p. 155)

This hints also at her other role. She possesses the power to heal; to the locals, she is a kind of saint. Imelda's condition, though a link in the chain of disaster that makes her one of the novel's 'fools of fortune', is also interestingly a symbol of the end of hatred. The conventional Ascendancy schooling her parents endured seems in no way superior to Imelda's upbringing. Her madness heals, whereas the normal world has created the shadows of destruction. Imelda's miraculous being gives the lie to the rigid teacher, Miss Halliwell, who in a letter counsels the solution that Yeats's Old Man in *Purgatory* wrongly thought could cut the chain of suffering:

If it's true, it is my duty to tell you that this child should not be given life. In such a child there is the continuation of the tragedy that made the child's father what he is. This is the most evil thing I have ever known of.   (p. 167)

Kilneagh, however, becomes a kind of shrine of Imelda to which the country people bring food. The mulberries must be picked from bushes laid out in imitation of those at Woodcombe Park.[17] The Quintons have at the last the love Josephine had advised Willie not to lose: 'It's like a gift, loving someone.' (p. 104) They also gain what Josephine's prayers had asked for: ' "Dear Mary, console them", she whispered.' (p. 182) Josephine constantly asks 'that the survivors may be comforted in their mourning. She requests God's word in Ireland'. (p. 183)

The final moving page of the novel shows the grateful lovers united at last in old age, yet seen as eternally young by their daughter, and perhaps by us, for as readers we picture them as young for the vast majority of the book. The overall effect of the novel is to celebrate love over warfare, healing over bloodshed, reconciliation over revenge. It might be thought that Trevor hopes to head off class hatred by making the Quintons Protestant supporters of Irish Nationalism, and in Willie's case capable of carrying out 'reprisals'. But this is legitimate, since historically there were Ascendancy supporters of the Irish cause. Reviewing Trevor's collections of stories, *Beyond the Pale and Other Stories* (1982) and *Scenes from an Album* (1981), a recent writer concisely stated a persistent attitude in Trevor's works that deal with Ireland:

> one must hesitate before pronouncing judgment on their collective 'meaning'; but if there is one consistent view, it seems to be that the past cannot be forgotten but that with resolution and forgiveness it need not be perpetuated.[18]

In her short, intense novels, *How Many Miles to Babylon?* (1974) and *The Old Jest* (1979), Jennifer Johnston treats the Ascendancy theme with classical restraint. *The Captains and the Kings* (1972) and *The Gates* (1973) also deal with the theme, but for reasons of space I here prefer to confine my remarks to the more recent novels. The first of these takes the form of a death cell memoir by Alexander Moore, a young officer, a gentleman, and a refugee in the trenches of the Great War from a worse fate, the icy death of the heart he sees in his mother. The ordered, leisured life he is born to on his parents' estate inculcates the familiar Anglo-Irish syndrome of raising barriers of class, education, religion, and money between the inheritors and the ordinary people whom they employ and live among. Alexander is saved from the attendant emotional attrition by his friendship with Jerry Crowe, a boy who grows up to work on the estate. This remarkable friendship outlasts Alexander's mother's warnings and even British Army war-time discipline. Boyhood games with Jerry in the leafy corners of the demesne strengthen Alexander's humanity, preserving him from the limiting prejudices of snobbery. Jerry is a good horseman. The two boys plan to be partners and breed horses when they grow up. Jerry's closeness to nature and animals, in conjunction with his friendly warmth, act therapeutically on the lonely Alexander, much as Dickon helps to transform Mary and Colin in Frances Hodgson Burnett's *The Secret Garden*.

Written in the characteristically precise and lucid style we now expect from Jennifer Johnston, the novel is full of contraries:

parent and child, gentleman and worker, officer and soldier, career officer and volunteer, soldier and writer, humane values and destruction of the culture through war, good manners and rough, instinctive behaviour, life in the Big House and life at the front. By means of such contrasts, the life on the Moores' estate gains definition. The calm self-confident power that comes with years of affluence is deftly evoked in Alicia, the mother, when she wants the dismissal of Cave, the shabby music teacher, 'ridiculously out of place'[19] in the elegant drawing room:

'Dragging his disease and poverty into my drawing room. You will write, won't you.' It was a command rather than a question. I heard a quick sigh from father. (6)

Neither parent expresses much emotion in words or tone of voice. A glacial surface must be preserved. Alexander notices though that sometimes his father can barely control his anger and frustration. Alexander escapes the rigours of English or Irish public (boarding) school life because Alicia maintains a fiction that he is delicate. This is a genteel cover for her refusal to live alone with her husband on account of some unspecified misdemeanour in his past. Our sympathy for the ineffectual father, our horror at the life-denying Alicia, and our compassion for young Alexander cannot be attributed to any note of self-pity in Alexander's memoir, or any authorial declarations to the reader. Cool, hard prose states fact, builds a context, and lets the scenes do their own work:

I had a friend. A private and secret friend. I never went to his house nor he to mine. (13)

Although she is too ignorant to realise it, Alicia's world is doomed. Even the uneducated Jerry can explain to Alexander the realities of European politics that make his father look grave:

'The Germans are going to fix all those eejits in Europe, the British are going to fix the Germans, and we . . .'
He paused for a moment and fumbled in his top pocket for a cigarette butt.
'We . . .?'
'Oh. We are going to fix the British.'
. . .
'Anyway, Mr Bingham says there will be no more wars.'
Jerry spat.
'War . . .' I said. It didn't seem possible that war could ever touch us within the magic circle of hills. (21)

Beside events in Europe, the advantages, privileges, and attendant responsibilities of his class that make Alexander's relationship with Jerry 'unsuitable' seem of no importance. His father, Frederick, knows the real importance of the landowner. He is in a marriage with the land more real than his marriage to Alicia. He is a peasant at heart. Alec's instinct is to start learning to manage the estate with his father rather than go on a European tour with Alicia or go to fight in the war. The pull of the Irish countryside and its husbandry as opposed to aristocratic manners, education and the grand tour suggest the duality of the Anglo-Irish gentry. Alec is of the Ascendancy generation that was so rapidly dispossessed. In the novel this comes not from external forces in Irish politics but from a revelation by his own mother. Alicia casually reveals that Alec is her son by another man, long dead, whom she refuses to name or remember; this suggests the English perhaps not protecting Anglo-Irish interests in Alec's generation: ' "He's dead. Like I said. Dead Alexander. N'en parlons plus." ' (47) Her frigidity, its callous terseness, the switch to French are perfect. If there is one slight false note here, it is in her use of 'Like'. An Edwardian gentlewoman would more likely have used the grammatically correct 'As' in this context.

Alec now feels like an outsider in the house. He is drawn out into the night and finds Jerry and others dancing to the music of a blind fiddler. Dressed for dinner, Alec is grotesquely an obvious outsider here too, but part of him is drawn to this older, Gaelic world, presided over by the blind prophet it seems of some ancient god. The bonds of his one friendship have been restored before he is helped back to the house, quite drunk, by Jerry. Ready to face death in the war now, Alec still retains a deep feeling for the Big House itself:

Where the path joined the avenue I stopped and looked at the house and wondered if it would ever be possible to love any person as I loved these blocks of granite, the sleeping windows, the uncompromising greyness, the stern perfection of the building in front of me.   (62)

Alec, it turns out, loves Jerry more than he loves the house, because he is willing to die on his account.

If Jerry initiated Alec's political education, the process is continued by a fellow officer, Bennett, who thinks of the people and their masters in terms of dogs and whip crackers. He foresees revolution and then its Orwellian aftermath. But Jerry knows that men will die also for men of words, like Patrick Pearse. He tells Alec:

I shit on your Home Rule. If it ever happens it will only be a sop. Keep them quiet. I believe . . . I know the only way to get them out is to shoot them out.   (102)

Jerry's loyalties are to his personal relationships and to Ireland. When he hears his father is missing elsewhere in France, he goes absent without leave to look for him. Arrested on his return, Jerry is to be shot. Alec is detailed to command the firing squad. Instead he shoots Jerry as an act of friendship. As a result, Alec at the end of the book is in a cell awaiting his own death by firing squad, as he was at the beginning. The circular structure suggests the remorseless cycle of violence and that inexorable logic of the emotions which makes Alec a traitor to his class and his regiment. His one friendship has led him to value personal loyalty above the concerns of England and Europe. He is now totally beyond the reach of his mother, and in the trenches of France Alec feels Irish. His commander, Major Glendinning, as a matter of course treats him as such. Alec has chosen sides and dies for it.

The Old Jest (1979) is set in August 1920, its events covering almost a fortnight and thus nearing the month significant in Big House fiction, September. The narrative again proceeds through the journal of a young person, this time eighteen-year-old Nancy Gulliver. Where the point of view in the previous novel was male, and its events largely those of the male world, here the point of view is female, its world female though not matriarchal. Nancy's first person journal entries are followed by sudden switches to a third person ominscient narrator. This gives the impression that the Nancy of the journals is turning her life into fiction, in accord with her ambition of becoming a writer. This device complicates and deepens the very simple plot, suggesting an ironic gap between the raw events of life (as seen in the journal's late adolescent view) and the novelist's art. The novelistic portions are fuller, more informative, and seem more real than the journal. A further irony, of course, is that both modes are equally real or unreal, being fictions of the same novelist.

Nancy is an orphan living with her grandfather and Aunt Mary. The Big House is too costly now for the family to maintain. A developer will soon acquire it and fill its park with desirable residences for professional people commuting, as it is now called, to their work in Dublin. Johnston gives a deft and convincing portrait of Nancy's erratic emotional swings; by turns she is shy and rude, vulnerable and strong-willed, sensitive and crass. When she meets a man hiding on the beach we fear violence, then her seduction, and finally suspect he may be her father. In an effective anti-climax he turns out to be a gentleman from a neighbouring Big House, but he has joined the Nationalists, using his military experience to take up arms against the British. He could be an Alec Moore come back from the Great War. Nancy does not lose her maidenhead, but she loses her political virginity. She likes the fugitive and helps him only to see him shot down on the beach after he has followed the order to drop his gun. His killing of a dozen British soldiers has been avenged. It is this political initiation rather than sexuality which brings Nancy to adulthood. The two themes of revolution and the decline of her family conjoin when Nancy feels sad at the loss of the old way of life. Her gentleman gunman tells her:

Everything has to keep changing. It's a myth that the things of value get lost with change. That's not true. Next year will always be a better year than the year before last. You have the whole bloody world waiting for you. Someone has just lifted what could only be an appalling liability from your shoulders and you want sympathy. Oh God! [20]

Nancy's Aunt Mary sees the inevitable change as a result of her own inability to face reality. Wistfully, she thinks her husband Gabriel, had he lived, might have saved the estate. Mary sees herself 'like those people pursued by wolves who throw everything out of the sledge until there's nothing left. I've kept going by selling little things'. (92) Her little acts of domestic courage demand our compassion.

Alec Moore and Nancy Gulliver are protagonists who love the Big House because it is a special kind of home with its own beauty, but they both rebel against the adult worlds that they inherit. Both are of the civil war generation, both support the Nationalist cause transcending, perhaps, rather than betraying their class, and both are horrified by what they discover in the British: determined and lethal efficiency. But where Alec, as a male, awaits a military death, Nancy is left to an uncertain future which can perhaps contain the promise and hope for the birth of a new life.

Molly Keane's remarkable comeback as a novelist in her old age has given us the most richly textured of the post-war Big House novels. In satirical bite, hawk-eyed observation, and wicked intelligence, she approaches the supreme novel of the English stem of the genre, Waugh's *Brideshead Revisited*.[21] If Molly Keane's reappearance after a gap of twenty-five years is remarkable, even more remarkable is the book that broke the silence, *Good Behaviour*

(1981), which, allusive as it is to *The Last September, Brideshead Revisited* and her own fictional world established earlier, yet creates its own detailed setting and era. The narrator, Aroon St. Charles, large, ungainly and plain is the unmarried inheritor of the Big House, Temple Alice. But the novel begins with the death of Aroon's mother in the comparatively mean dwelling, Gulls' Cry, a 'small Gothic folly of a house . . . built on the edge of a cliff'[22] and formerly inhabited only by some poor elderly cousins. The novel then flashes back to Aroon's childhood, an abiding theme of Big House fiction. Through Mrs Brock, the governess, life at Stoke Charity, a much grander English House owned by Wobbly Massingham, is splendidly evoked, along with attitudes of aristocratic patronage and disdain, and the damaging Philistinism that leads partly to Mrs Brock's disgrace and perhaps to Richard's covert homosexuality. Although Mrs Brock comes from Stoke Charity to Temple Alice, where she is dearly loved by Aroon and her older brother Hubert, when they are adults they betray her memory with Wobbly's son, Richard, as a sort of callow adult game, when the charismatic Richard spends a summer holiday at Temple Alice. The novel thus moves from the meanest house, Gulls' Cry, to the greatest, where there is, alas, not much charity, to the more modest world of good behaviour imposed by Mummie at Temple Alice. The bulk of the novel then settles down to a vividly detailed account of the rituals of life at Temple Alice until the death of Major St. Charles reveals his astonishing will leaving all to Aroon (Hubert having been killed) except for small legacies to his chilly wife and to the warmer Wild Rose, his favourite servant, willing sexual partner, and devoted nurse after his stroke.

Although Major St. Charles returns from the Great War with one leg amputated, contemporary events hardly intrude. There are no interruptions to the good-mannered routines at Temple Alice on account of the troubles. There is, however, the uncomfortable fact that as expenses mount up, the family fortunes go down, a circumstance maddeningly brought to the family's attention by their solicitor. Hubert's death is not the kind of sensational violence we might find in Elizabeth Bowen, or William Trevor, but is the result of a mere car accident. The decline of the St. Charles estate is not the result of 'Bolshie' tenant action, but of general economic forces, little unwise extravagances, a haughty disdain for facing business realities, and an absorption in the horsey pursuits of the gentry. After the Major's stroke, Mummie's response to business is to stuff all bills and official looking letters into a drawer while treating the good-tempered solicitor as at once a source of ready cash and a lower species of life. Solicitous of her husband's sexual well-being, especially with other women, indeed preferably so, she condones his flings. Her demanding code of good behaviour, though, must prevail, covering with a chill gloss of politeness all real responses to love, death, or anything else which might stimulate emotional display. Aroon remembers her mother writing daily to the Major during the Great War:

He didn't keep any of her letters, or I have never found them. I don't suppose they would tell me anything I don't know. She was so cold. (65)

The comedy of manners in the novel extends from Mummie's control of the daily rituals of meals, feeding and walking the dogs, visits to the dressmaker or to exercise the horses, to the splendour and agonies of hunt balls. There are witty accounts, rich in implication, of two visits, one with Daddy in his prime, and one with Mummy after Daddy's stroke, to the Crowhurst twins, impecunious but resourceful descendents of an ancient noble line, both of them in the Major's playful sexual thrall. Yet behind the dash and wit, the comedy of good manners, the quiet little accommodations to discreet pleasures, there are the raw and genuine feelings of Aroon as she grows lumpily and sometimes painfully towards knowledge. She clings to the fiction that Richard is her lover. There is great humour, anguish, and delicacy in the scene when Richard climbs into her bed and contemplates her enormous breasts on his last night at Temple Alice, and remains chaste. Molly Keane is a mistress of sad ironies and what might be termed 'domestic grotesque'. Aroon and later the Major take the incident as a sign of Richard's love; we suspect that it is merely another cruel game between the young men, one designed also to mask their homosexuality. Aroon is able, because of her upbringing, to rationalise the chaste occupation of her bed as an instance of good behaviour:

My anger and anxiety at the appalling noise he made going back to his room suffocated and choked down a different sense in me: one of absolute loss. But we had both known how to behave. We had behaved beautifully. No pain lasts. And another thing: I can never look on myself as a deprived, inexperienced girl. I've had a man in my bed. I suppose I could say I've had a lover. I like to call it that. I do call it that.   (108)

Beneath the self-deception there is fear of reality and the sharp emotions it provokes. This is even truer of Mummie when she first sees the Major after his stroke:

The odd thing was that she seemed to want me to go in with her. She was afraid. She wanted to pretend things were quite ordinary.   (146)

That pretence, even in the face of death, is what good behaviour is designed to preserve. This is really the domestic equivalent of the military code, necessitated by battle conditions, that one does not emote or panic but acts according to disciplined training. The irony of Temple Alice is that Daddy, a representative of a military aristocracy, is able to show warmth, relax the code, and truly love his son and daughter, whereas Mummy makes of good behaviour a steely armour to keep life away. Under cover of good behaviour Mummy can maintain a fierce rivalry with her daughter and contrive many humiliations.

Such horrors of family life are inextricably woven into the dense fabric of a largely vanished way of life meticulously observed as the background to Aroon's development. This is a major achievement. The subtle complexities of Molly Keane's art are illustrated in the painful scene when Aroon, invited to a ball given by another Big House family (much to Mummie's genuine surprise), plans to show off her dress to Daddy. When she appears in all her cosmetic glory, Mummie is sitting with him:

'Good girl,' he said. He looked over to Mummie to join him and help him elaborate his admiration. She considered me with a dull obedience.
   'Yes. Stupendous,' was what she said. I blushed as I had when Rose stopped my dancing, and this time I was choking on tears of pain and hatred. It was a shocking moment for each of us. The worst possible instance of not knowing how to behave.   (194)

The progress of the entire scene towards this climax is a demonst-ration of the immorality of Mummie's marmorean politeness. To do and say what helps people in a specific situation in such a way as to express true feeling and benevolence: this is the best behaviour.

Good Behaviour wittily recreates the past glories and present disasters of a debt-ridden Ascendancy family between the wars, ending with Aroon at her moment of triumph, the realisation that she is in charge of her mother. Her revenge is depicted in the opening scenes where the now invalid Mummie, fallen to the level of living at Gulls' Cry, gags on the rabbit she detests but

which Aroon serves with the perfect 'good behaviour' excuse
that it is good for her. Money and social caste, or the absence of
these, cannot alter the fact that we perpetuate folly and malice in
ourselves.

That families are no exception to this rule of human nature and,
indeed, may well be its happiest hunting ground, is a basic
theme in Molly Keane's work. *Time After Time* (1983) again
anatomises the family, but this time Mummie and Daddy are
already dead and we find Jasper Swift with his eternal spring of
ageing sisters, named after the months: April, May and Baby
June. The siblings keep up the Big House in the only way they are
able, by becoming its servants themselves, Jasper acting as cook,
May as housekeeper, June as farm and stable hand. Only April,
once a fashionable married woman, is exempt, shielded by
deafness, money of her own, and a strict self-imposed beauty
regimen, unbroken in her seventy-fourth year. Each is eccentric,
individualistic, and isolated despite their life together in the
decrepit house, Durraghglass. They seek safety behind closed
doors of privacy. But one can look at barriers from another
viewpoint; April's room is her refuge, but

Her key turned again in the lock, and from the wide passage-way her
door looked as obdurate as the door of any cell.[23]

The members of this family are sometimes as strangers to each
other, fellow prisoners as much as siblings. Jasper has a brief
exchange with Baby June in the kitchen, but there is no real
relationship between them:

He never suspected that her devotion to Durraghglass was not entirely
the quick and mainspring of her life. They knew almost less than
nothing about each other.   (10)

As with *Good Behaviour* the decline of the family fortunes inter-
locks with the pernicious little odious facts of human nature in
the Swift menage:

When Mummie died (too young and too cruelly) death duties depleted
the whole structure of Durraghglass, and afterwards a miasma of overdraft
and mismanagement abetted Mummie's wishes, holding brother and
sisters captive for year past forgotten year, locked in inviolable small
conflicts and old adventures.   (11)

The now elderly family, captive in a *huis clos* net of sibling rivalries,
is also captive to time, both the dusty present and the past that

lives in memories. For them, what was laid down in the past repeats itself, time and again. The interplay of time past and present can also create a timeless era with its own charm, slightly sinister: 'a now derelict clock in the archway's face had once told the time. It still looked pretty.' (18) Their lives it seems had stopped with the clock. May, born with a mutilated hand, restores broken china and demonstrates flower arrangement in the present, but behind her locked door, she enters the past through her masterpiece, a rabbit warren which in a child-adult game she peoples with 'a colony of small china rabbits'. (25) And when place is a constant, as in the Big House, times are simultaneous, a condition that has its price: 'In familiar places memories are never absolved — they contain perpetual unkindness.' (52) This proposition applies as much to a small island as it does to a demesne. It also applies to the nebulous web of class differences, and to more distant relatives as well as to the immediate family. When Leda, the Jewish foreign cousin, returns to Durraghglass, she personifies the delights of their youths when she visited them and also certain distasteful aspects of the past with uncomfortable truths: Jasper remembers she 'had cruelly disturbed his childhood and mortified his agonising boyhood' (84). Now she is blind,

an old woman only a travesty of his half-enchanted, half-forbidden memories. It was as though an interesting ghost had risen from a dead, absurd romance. (86)

She had been packed off by Mummie in disgrace for having aroused Daddy. Thinking that Leda had perished in Hitler's camps, the Swifts have made no attempts to contact her branch of the family. They have something of the shame of neutrals looking at possibly the one example of an apocalyptic struggle to defend civilised values, World War II. But Jasper's one-eyed view of the world (the result of a childhood accident) turns out to be not so bad. Leda had managed to sit out the war in relative and not very honourable comfort herself. But such historical and political tensions are in the background only.

As Leda picks up the sounds, scents, and feel of the old house, through her perceptions and memories the past recreates itself. The wonderful richness of experience this gives to the novel is expressed in simple but poignant ways, as when the brave decrepitude of old containing younger selves is rendered:

April heard a shout. 'I must tell you, Leda,' she said, 'I'm slightly deaf.' 'And I'm blind as a bat.' Some vibration from the past set them laughing together — they went on, laughing as delightedly, as irrepressibly as they had when life was all laughter, or all tears — nothing between the two to be suffered, or to outlive. (100)

The Anglo-Irish theme is constantly widened and universalised by Leda's cosmopolitan presence, but more deeply yet by the novel's roguish honesty about old age, the passage of time, the inner life of the characters which through Leda, Molly Keane has all the keys to unlock. The result is probably the finest prose we have had since the death of Waugh:

These were the submerged days that Leda's coming rescued from a deep oblivion. Since she could not see Durraghglass in its cold decay, or her cousins in their proper ages, timeless grace was given to them in her assumption that they looked as though all the years between were empty myths. Because they knew themselves so imagined, their youth was present to them, a mirage trembling in her flattery as air trembles close on the surface of summer roads. What more might she recall? What else might she show them of their lost selves? (101)

Here are the subtle cadences of true distinction. This spare but supple prose can express also the entire catalogue of the Big House, its demesne and inventory, a record of fashions, decade by decade, and the rising damp of its decline. It has the energy for satire and comedy. It renders perfectly Leda's psychological warfare, leading to her revenge on them all for her past exile at the hands of Mummie, Juno-like. Leda is also annoyed with the effeminate Jasper for his present rejection of her withered charms. Keane is also an astute recorder of humiliation. When Leda has discovered their painful secrets, she reveals all with a ruthless glee. Leda, of course, is a victim of her own malice, for the family packs her off again to her home, an institution run by nuns. Leda has demonstrated the dangers of being seduced by charm.

The Swifts at the end of the book muddle on, fitting together their lives again rather as May restores broken china, but Leda's punishment is that deaf April, insulated from hurt, joins Leda in the convent, subjecting the blind old bird to the health and beauty regime that irritates beyond endurance:

Imprisoned, Leda put her hands up to her blind eyes. There was to be no escape. (247)

Molly Keane's great achievement is that she makes the failing Ascendancy become at once a profound tragi-comic subject and a potent metaphor of all human pretensions. Old age chastens and teaches, for we become its prisoners; but to visit the cells of the past to reactivate its torments is a crime that deserves the punishment it inevitably incurs: to live blind to compassion, and deaf to agony.

Revolutions wreck and dismantle social and economic systems, making way for changed and often unforeseen conditions. But people carry the past within them, sometimes for generations, especially in rural cultures. Old patterns survive; social forms linger. The remote feudal wars of Dracula seem revived in the macabre ritual that has entered the popular imagination in our urban electronic age. How could we then suppose that the Anglo-Irish version of pastoral could disappear as suddenly as the Big Houses that were razed? Fortunately, the demise of a class that gave Ireland a number of patriotic leaders and a significant culture has furnished a powerful literary theme with rich implications; it is a vein not yet exhausted, for it reaches deeply into human nature itself, and because of the cultural hyphenation of the Anglo-Irish themselves, it reaches into the larger concerns of England and Europe. It enables Irish novelists to deal with Ireland without confining themselves to it. The Big House milieu can reach further into the past than some other modern subjects; and Ireland's past must be redeemed. Readers who are neither Anglo-Irish nor upper-class would be foolish to suppose that this recent burst of Irish fiction merely chronicles a snobbish enclave; these books and their authors, whether insiders or outsiders of the demesne, are, like the Waugh of *Brideshead Revisited*, far too interesting, far too ambivalent, and far too intelligent for that.

NOTES

ISLAND OF SAINTS AND SILICON: LITERATURE AND SOCIAL CHANGE IN
CONTEMPORARY IRELAND

Fintan O'Toole

1   *The Loves of Cass Maguire* (Dublin: Gallery Books, 1984), p. 11.
2   Flann O'Brien, *The Dalkey Archive* (London: Picador, 1976), p. 7.
3   Hugh Leonard, *Home Before Night* (Harmondsworth, Middlesex: Penguin, 1981), p. 66.
4   See Whitaker's John Snow Memorial Lecture of 1977, published in *Administration*, Vol. 26, no. 3, Dublin, Autumn, 1978, pp. 305-17.
5   (Dublin: The Dolmen Press, 1968), p. 59.
6   In *Irish Poets in English*, ed. Sean Lucy (Cork: Mercier Press, 1973), pp. 208 ff.
7   'The Irish Writer' in *Davis, Mangan, Ferguson? Tradition and the Irish Writer* (Dublin: The Dolmen Press, 1970), p. 65.
8   *The Loves of Cass Maguire*, p. 38.
9   *Ibid.*, p. 52.
10 *Ibid.*, p. 16.
11 *Downstream* (Dublin/London: The Dolmen Press/Oxford University Press, 1962), p. 48.
12 *The Selected Paul Durcan*, ed. Edna Longley (Belfast: Blackstaff Press, 1985).
13 *Dance the Dance* (London: Faber and Faber, 1969). 'An Aspect of the Rising' was reprinted in *Body and Soul*, ed. David Marcus (Dublin: Poolbeg Press, 1979), pp. 156-160.
14 *The Past* (London: Jonathan Cape, 1980), p. 217.
15 *The Selected Paul Durcan*, p. 85.
16 'Lament for Cearbhall O Dalaigh', *The Selected Paul Durcan*, p. 104.
17 'The Mystical Irish' in *The Vanishing Irish*, ed. John A. O'Brien (London: W. H. Allen, 1954), pp. 63-64.
18 *New and Selected Poems* (Dublin: Raven Arts Press, 1982), p. 80.
19 *Ibid.*, p. 85.
20 *West Strand Visions* (Belfast: The Blackstaff Press, 1974), p. 31.
21 *Poems 1963-1983* (Edinburgh/Dublin: The Salamander Press/The Dolmen Press, 1985), pp. 161-64.
22 *Sive* (Dublin: Progress House, 1959), p. 104.
23 'Getting on the High Road Again' in *The Vanishing Irish*, p. 207.
24 *A Crucial Week in the Life of a Grocer's Assistant* (Dublin: Gallery Books, 1978), p. 36.
25 *Ibid.*, p. 80.
26 *Conversations on a Homecoming* (Dublin: Gallery Books, 1986); *Bailegangaire* (Dublin: Gallery Books, 1986). Both plays were first performed by Galway's Druid Theatre Company.
27 *Three Plays: Da/A Life/Time Was* (Harmondsworth, Middlesex: Penguin, 1981), p. 83.
28 (London: Samuel French, 1971), p. 11.
29 (London: Samuel French, 1979), p. 54.

30   *Selected Poems* (Dublin: The Dolmen Press, 1982), p. 62.
31   *Collected Poems* (Dublin: The Dolmen Press, 1974), p. 173.
32   *The Pornographer* (London: Faber and Faber, 1979), p. 35.
33   'The Haulier's Wife Meets Jesus on the Road to Moone', in *The Berlin Wall Café*
     (Belfast: The Blackstaff Press, 1986), p. 4.

LITERATURE AND CULTURE IN THE NORTH OF IRELAND
Anthony Bradley

1   Nor can we equate culture with ideology, although the two do indeed overlap
     in a problematic way. Marxists might well see both cultural traditions in the
     North as deforming bourgeois ideologies, yet given such a diagnosis might
     even then concede that Ulster writing, like all literature, not only reflects but in
     some measure transcends ideologies. Althusser maintains that although art
     does not provide what Marxists can embrace as scientific knowledge, it allows
     us to penetrate an ideology in a particularly valuable way. The convoluted
     emphasis of the following passage suggests how troublesome the idea of the
     transcendence of art is for Althusser and many other Marxist thinkers:

>   What art makes us *see*, and therefore gives to us in the form of *'seeing'*,
>   *'perceiving'* and *'feeling'* (which is not the form of *knowing*), is the *ideology*
>   from which it is born, in which it bathes, from which it detaches itself as
>   art, and to which it *alludes*. Macherey has shown this very clearly in the
>   case of Tolstoy, by extending Lenin's analyses. Balzac and Solzhenitsyn
>   give us a 'view' of the ideology to which their work alludes and with
>   which it is constantly fed, a view which presupposes a *retreat*, an *internal
>   distantiation* from the very ideology from which their novels emerged.
>   They make us 'perceive' (but not know) in some sense *from the inside*, by
>   an *internal distance*, the very ideology in which they are held.

     Louis Althusser, *Lenin and Philosophy and Other Essays*, trans. Ben Brewster
     (New York and London: Monthly Review Press, 1971), pp. 222-23.
        In his *Criticism and Ideology*, Terry Eagleton points out the unsatisfactory
     nature of this passage from a Marxist point of view, yet also asserts the
     'irreducibility [of the literary work] to the historico-ideological of which it is
     the product', Terry Eagleton, *Criticism and Ideology* (London: Verso Editions,
     1978), p. 177.
2   Terence Brown's *Northern Voices: Poets from Ulster* (Totowa, New Jersey: Rowman
     and Littlefield, 1975), and John Wilson Foster's *Forces and Themes in Ulster Fiction*
     (Totowa, New Jersey: Rowman and Littlefield, 1974) are excellent and fairly
     exhaustive critical and historical accounts of, respectively, poetry and fiction
     in the North of Ireland. My approach in this essay is deliberately restricted,
     almost exclusively, to the rootedness of contemporary literature (poetry,
     prose and drama) in Ulster's two cultural traditions.
3   F. S. L. Lyons, in the chapter entitled 'Ulster: The Roots of Difference', in his
     Culture and Anarchy in Ireland 1890-1939 (Oxford: Oxford University Press,
     1979), is only one of many historians and social scientists who have described
     how the divisions of Ulster society permeate almost every aspect of life in
     that part of the world.
4   Michael Longley, 'The Neolithic Night: A Note on the Irishness of Louis
     MacNeice', in *Two Decades of Irish Writing: A Critical Survey*, ed. Douglas Dunn
     (Chester Springs, PA: Dufour, 1975), p. 104.
5   Seamus Heaney, 'The Fire I' the Flint', in *Preoccupations: Selected Prose 1968-
     1978* (New York: Farrar, Straus, Giroux, 1980), p. 84.

6   The following are very helpful, in different ways, in shedding light on the
     Ulster Protestant mentality: F. S. L. Lyons in the chapter of *Culture and Anarchy*
     previously cited, Desmond Bowen in two lectures on the history of Ulster
     Protestantism given at Queen's University, Belfast, in 1983, and Geoffrey Bell,
     The Protestants of Ulster (London: Pluto, 1976).

7   Terence Brown, 'W. R. Rodgers and John Hewitt', in *Two Decades of Irish Writing:*
     A Critical Survey, ed. Douglas Dunn (Chester Springs, PA: Dufour, 1975),
     p. 86.

8   Terence Brown, 'An Ulster Renaissance?' in *Concerning Poetry*, 14, No. 2 (1981),
     p. 16.

9   John Cronin, 'Prose', in *Causeway: the Arts in Ulster* (Belfast and Dublin: the
     Arts Council of Northern Ireland and Gill and Macmillan, 1971), p. 71.

10   John Hewitt, *The Rhyming Weavers, and other country poets of Antrim and Down*
     (Belfast: Blackstaff, 1974).

11   Cited in Introduction, *The Selected John Hewitt*, ed. Alan Warner (Belfast:
     Blackstaff, 1981), p. 6.

12   Leslie A. Fiedler, *Love and Death in the American Novel* (New York: Criterion,
     1960), p. 120. There is, indeed, a residual and crude form of Gothic fiction
     published in contemporary Ulster in Reverend Ian Paisley's *Protestant*
     Telegraph, with its lurid and titillating tales of the sexual intrigues of priests
     and nuns, and its paranoid accounts of the Catholic Church's political
     machinations and lust for power.

13   The influence of the bible as literary source is evident in the titles and
     tendency toward parable and allegory of, for example, the poems of W. R.
     Rodgers and the short stories of Anthony C. West.

14   Steiner's comments are suggestive not only of the cultural situation of the
     Ulster Catholic but of the whole process of the making of modern Ireland: 'A
     society requires antecedents. Where these are not naturally at hand, where
     a community is new or reassembled after a long interval of dispersal or
     subjection, a necessary past tense to the grammar of being is created by
     intellectual and emotional fiat.'
         George Steiner, *In Bluebeard's Castle: Some Notes towards the Redefinition of*
     Culture (New Haven: Yale University Press, 1971), p. 3.

15   W. B. Yeats and Thomas Kinsella, *Davis, Mangan, Ferguson? Tradition and the*
     Irish Writer (Dublin: The Dolmen Press, 1970), p. 59.

16   The other archaeological impulse behind Heaney's *North* (1975), which
     connected Ireland's present with its Viking antecedents, is also at work in
     Brian Friel's play *Volunteers*, first performed in 1975, in which the excavation
     of a Viking archaeological site (presumably in Dublin) brings modern
     Irishmen face to face with urgent social and political issues of the present.

17   Cited in Timothy Kearney, 'Beyond the Planter and the Gael: Interview with
     John Hewitt and John Montague on Northern Poetry and the Troubles', in *The*
     Crane Bag Book of Irish Studies 1977-1981, eds. M. P. Hederman and R. Kearney
     (Dublin: Blackwater Press, 1982), p. 726.

18   The epigraph to Heaney's good-natured but firm assertion of his Irishness in
     the Field Day pamphlet *An Open Letter* (1983) is taken from Gaston Bachelard;
     it is significant in the context of my remarks about the difficulty of articulation
     for Ulster Catholics: 'What is the source of our first suffering? It lies in the
     fact that we hesitated to speak . . . It was born in the moment when we
     accumulated silent things within us.'

19   Robert Fisk, *In Time of War: Ireland, Ulster and the Price of Neutrality 1939-45*
     (London: André Deutsch, 1983), p. 248.

20   Heaney refers to Louis MacNeice, W. R. Rodgers and John Hewitt as representa-
     tive of Northern Protestants in being 'born to a sense of two nations', in
     'Belfast', *Preoccupations*, p. 32.
21   Raymond Williams, *The Country and the City* (New York: Oxford University
     Press, 1973), p. 248.
22   The hedge-schools, Engels wrote in a letter to Jenny Longuet (Feb. 24, 1881)
     were the 'truly national schools [which] did not suit English purposes. To
     suppress them, the *sham* national schools were established'. *Ireland and the
     Irish Question: A Collection of Writings by Karl Marx and Frederick Engels* (New
     York: International Publishers, 1972), p. 329.
23   Seamus Heaney, Introd., *Collected Short Stories*, by Michael MacLaverty (Dub-
     lin: Poolbeg, 1978), p. 9.
24   Frank Ormsby, ed., *Poets from the North of Ireland* (Belfast: Blackstaff, 1979), p. 12.
25   Tom Paulin, *A New Look at the Language Question* (Derry: Field Day Theatre
     Company Limited; Field Day Pamphlet Number 1, 1983).
26   Mary Eagleton and David Pierce, *Attitudes to Class in the English Novel* (London:
     Thames and Hudson, 1979), p. 114.
27   See, for example, Henry Patterson, *Class Conflict and Sectarianism: The Protestant
     Working Class and the Belfast Labour Movement 1868-1920* (Belfast: Blackstaff,
     1980).
28   'The Unpartitioned Intellect' is the title of a lecture given by John Montague
     as part of the national conference of the American Committee for Irish
     Studies at the University of Vermont in April, 1982.
29   Johnston Kirkpatrick, 'Another Country' in *Trio Poetry 3* (Belfast: Blackstaff,
     1982).
30   Michael Longley, cited in Brown, *Northern Voices*, p. 213.
31   John Montague, *The Book of Irish Verse: An Anthology of Irish Poetry from the Sixth
     Century to the Present* (New York: Macmillan, 1974), p. 37.

IRISH CULTURE: THE DESIRE FOR TRANSCENDENCE
Walentina Witoszek and Patrick F. Sheeran

 1   *A Guide for the Perplexed* (London: Sphere, 1977), p. 9. The visit took place in
     August 1968 during the Soviet invasion of Czechoslovakia.
 2   Vivian Mercier, *The Irish Comic Tradition* (London: Oxford University Press,
     1962).
     Seamus Deane, 'The Literary Myths of the Revival: A Case for their Abandon-
     ment', in *Myth and Reality in Irish Literature*, ed. Joseph Ronsley (Waterloo,
     Ontario: Wilfrid Laurier University Press, 1977), pp. 317-329.
     F. S. L. Lyons, *Culture and Anarchy in Ireland 1890-1939* (London: Oxford
     University Press, 1979).
     David Krause, *The Profane Book of Irish Comedy* (Ithaca and London: Cornell
     University Press, 1982).
 3   M. P. Hederman and R. Kearney, eds. *The Crane Bag Book of Irish Studies 1977-
     1981* (Dublin: Blackwater Press, 1982), pp. 10-11.
 4   p. 173.
 5   René Guénon's most concise treatment of the subject is to be found in 'L'idée
     du Centre dans les Traditions Antiques', first published in *Regnabit*, Mai 1926
     and collected in René Guénon, *Symbol Fondamentaux de la Science Sacrée* (Paris:
     Gallimard, 1962), pp. 83-93. The relevant passage goes:

         Le Centre est, avant tout, l'origine, le point de départ de toutes choses;
         c'est le point principiel, sans forme et sans dimensions, donc indivisible,

et, par suite, la seule image qui puisse être donnée de l'Unité primordiale. De lui, par son irradiation, toutes choses sont produites, de même que l'Unité produit tous les nombres, sans que son essence en soit d'ailleurs modifiée ou affectée en aucune façon . . . le point central, c'est le Principe, c'est l'Être pur; et l'espace qu'il emplit de son rayonnement, et qui n'est que par ce rayonnement même (le *Fiat Lux* de la *Genèse*), sans lequel cet espace ne serait que 'privation' et neant, c'est le Monde au sens le plus étendu de ce mot, l'ensemble de tous les êtres et de tous les états d'existence qui constituent la manifestation universelle.

6 *Crane Bag Book of Irish Studies*, p. 8.
7 Nina Witoszek and Pat Sheeran, 'From explanation to intervention', *The Crane Bag*, IX, No. 2 (Summer, 1985), pp. 83-86.
8 Tom Paulin, *Ireland and the English Crisis* (London: Bloodaxe Books, 1984), p. 17.
9 See, for example, the review of Paulin's book by Frank Callanan, 'The idiom of Irishry', *New Hibernia*, April 1985, p. 28.
10 Franklin Merrell-Wolff, *Pathways Through to Space*, 2nd ed. (New York: Julian Press, 1983), p. 282.
11 *The Unconscious God: Psychotherapy and Theology*, (London: Hodder, 1977), pp. 24-31, 51-75.
12 *States of Mind: A Study of Anglo-Irish Conflict 1780-1980* (London: Allen and Unwin, 1983), pp. 6-7. The relevant passage goes:
    Such a view appears to me to approximate to the concept of the past which infused Irish historiography at the modern commencement and which still infuses the historical assumptions of most ordinary Irish people. Of course, this rendered and renders the past an arsenal of weapons with which to defend both inveterate prejudice and that ignorance which wishes only to remain invincible. But it also implies historical interpretation in terms of law and morals. In such a view, no statute of limitations softens the judgement to be made upon past events, however distant. In such a view, no prescriptive rights can be established by the passage of time, however lengthy.
13 In Projective Geometry three-dimensional space is formed from the plane inward rather than the point outward. Happily for our metaphor the point is the quintessence of contraction, the plane of expansion. And Projective Geometry includes the infinitely distant, 'the ideal elements' of space as well as finite distances. It focuses too on mobile types of form which undergo transformations rather than fixed entities such as the square or circle.
14 Sean Ó Tuama and Thomas Kinsella, *An Duanaire 1600-1900: Poems of the Dispossessed* (Dublin: The Dolmen Press, 1981), pp. 308-309.
15 *Collected Poems* (London: Macmillan, 1963), pp. 213-214.
16 *Selected Writings of Ralph Waldo Emerson*, ed. William H. Gilman (New York: Signet, 1965), p. 265.
17 'Amor Fati Contemptus Mundi' in *The Crane Bag Book of Irish Studies*, p. 188. See also Walentina Witoszek's 'Cutluromachia in Modern Irish and Polish Drama' in volume two of *Literary Interrelations: Ireland, England and the World*, 3 Vols. ed. with introd. by Wolfgang Zach and Heinz Kosok (Tubingen, West Germany: G. Narr Publ., 1987).
18 Kolakowski, Leszek, *Marxism and Beyond: On Historical Understanding and Individual Responsibility* (London: Oxford University Press, 1971), p. 55.
19 *Station Island* (London: Faber and Faber, 1984), p. 107.
20 ' "Far-off, most secret, and inviolate Rose" ' in *The Crane Bag Book of Irish Studies*, p. 115.

21 *Ibid.*, p. 118.
22 *Door into the Dark* (London: Faber and Faber, 1969), pp. 55-56.
23 *The Sanctuary Lamp,* revised edition (Dublin: Gallery Press, 1984), p. 53.
24 *Talbot's Box* (Dublin: Gallery Press, 1979), p. 17.
25 *Ibid.*, author's stage direction, p. 11.
26 'The Source' in *The Rough Field* (Dublin: The Dolmen Press, 1972), p. 49.
27 Part XI of 'Station Island' (London: Faber and Faber, 1984), pp. 89-91.
28 *Selected Poems 1956-1968* (Dublin: The Dolmen Press, 1973), pp. 58-9.
29 *New Poems 1973* (Dublin: The Dolmen Press, 1973), p. 32.
30 Patrick F. Sheeran, 'The Identity of Anglo-Irish Fiction in the Nineteenth
    Century', *Cahiers du Centre d'Etudes Irlandaises de l'Université de Paris III,* II
    (Autumn 1982), pp. 22-50.
31 Richard Chase, *The American Novel and its Tradition* (New York: Doubleday,
    1957), p. 13.
32 *Cold Heaven* (London: Triad/Panther Books, 1985), p. 284.
33 *Literature and Revolution* (New York: University of Michigan Press, 1960), p. 183.

'WHEN DID YOU LAST SEE YOUR FATHER?': PERCEPTIONS OF THE PAST IN
NORTHERN IRISH WRITING 1965-1985
Edna Longley

 1 *The South Country* (London: J. M. Dent, 1909), p. 109.
 2 'The Sense of the Past', *Ulster Local Studies,* 9, No. 20 (Summer, 1985), p. 109.
 3 Samuel Hynes, *The Pattern of Hardy's Poetry* (Chapel Hill, N.C.: University of
    North Carolina Press, 1961), p. 4.
 4 David Martin, *The Ceremony of Innocence* (London: Martin Secker and Warburg,
    1977), p. 32.
 5 For example, autobiographies, books about historical Belfast or rural com-
    munities, more specialised social and economic histories. The Blackstaff
    Press's list includes, for instance: *Out of My Class,* the autobiography of John
    Boyd (socialist, playwright, BBC producer), and *Voices and the Sound of Drums,*
    autobiography of Paddy Shea (a Catholic civil-servant at Stormont); John
    Hewitt's autobiographical sonnet sequence *Kites in Spring;* Sam McAughtry's
    family memoir of the thirties and Second World War, *The Sinking of the Kenbane
    Head;* Jonathan Bardon's *Belfast;* Michael J. Murphy's *Tyrone Folk Quest;* Brian
    M. Walker's *Sentry Hill;* Alan McCutcheon's *Wheel and Spindle;* Paddy Devlin's
    Yes, We Have No Bananas: Outdoor Relief in Belfast, 1920-39; and R. M. Arnold's
    seductively titled *The Golden Years of the Great Northern Railway* — in two vol-
    umes.
 6 Sam Keery, *The Last Romantic Out of Belfast* (Belfast: Blackstaff, 1984), p. 174.
 7 David Marcus, ed. *Irish Poets, 1924-1974* (London: Pan Books Ltd., 1984), p. 16.
 8 Printed in *Theatre Ireland,* 6 (April/June 1984), pp. 119-142.
 9 In *A Time to Dance* (Belfast: Blackstaff Press, 1982).
10 Brian Moore, *The Emperor of Ice-Cream* (Toronto, Ontario: McClelland and
    Stewart, 1965), p. 33.
11 *Ibid.*, p. 250.
12 Maurice Leitch, *The Liberty Lad* (Belfast: Blackstaff Press, 1985), p. 208.
13 Maurice Leitch, *Stamping Ground* (London: Sphere Books Ltd., Abacus edition,
    1984), p. 30.
14 *Ibid.*, pp. 41-42.
15 Seamus Heaney, *Preoccupations* (London: Faber and Faber, 1980), p. 57.
16 See the section 'The authoritarian strain in Irish culture' in Chapter 1 ('Some
    Traditions of Irish Catholicism') of J. H. Whyte, *Church and State in Modern*

Ireland, 1923-1979 (Dublin: Gill and Macmillan, 1980), pp. 21-23. This section includes a reference to rural father-son relations, and ends: 'deference to authority has been a feature not just of Irish ecclesiastical life, but of Irish life in general'.

17   *Why Brownlee Left* (London: Faber and Faber, 1980), p. 13.
18   *Ibid.*, p. 20.
19   Interview with John Haffenden, *Viewpoints: Poets in Conversation with John Haffenden* (London: Faber and Faber, 1981), p. 130.
20   *Selected Plays of Brian Friel* (London: Faber and Faber, 1984), p. 294.
21   *Ibid.*, p. 418. Hugh's description of the Irish language evidently applies to his own speech.
22   *Ibid.*, p. 446.
23   Derek Mahon, *Poems 1962-1978* (London: Oxford University Press, 1979), p. 31.
24   'Once Alien Here', *The Selected John Hewitt* (Belfast: Blackstaff Press, 1981), p. 20.
25   *Poems 1963-1983* (Edinburgh/Dublin: Salamander/Gallery, 1985), p. 151.
26   *Ibid.*, p. 48.
27   *Ibid.*, p. 86.
28   Paul Fussell, *The Great War and Modern Memory* (London: Oxford University Press, 1975), p. 325.
29   *Stamping Ground*, p. 101.
30   *Field Work* (London: Faber and Faber, 1979), p. 59.
31   John Montague, *The Rough Field* (Dublin: The Dolmen Press, 1972), p. 41.
32   *Stamping Ground*, pp. 31-32.
33   *Mules* (London: Faber and Faber, 1977), pp. 53-59.
34   James Randall, 'An Interview with Seamus Heaney', *Ploughshares*, 5, No. 3 (1979), p. 18.
35   Friel, *Selected Plays*, p. 11.
36   *Ibid.*, p. 17.
37   Oliver MacDonagh, *States of Mind* (London: Allen & Unwin, 1983), p. 119.
38   Tom Paulin, *Ireland and the English Crisis* (London: Bloodaxe Books, 1984), p. 17.
39   *A New Look at the Language Question* (Derry: Field Day Theatre Company Limited; Field Day Pamphlet Number 1, 1983), p. 13.
40   ' "The Dissidence of Dissent": John Hewitt and W. R. Rodgers', in *Across a Roaring Hill: The Protestant Imagination in Modern Ireland*, Gerald Dawe and Edna Longley, eds. (Belfast: Blackstaff Press, 1985), p. 151.
41   *Poems 1962-1978*, p. 67.
42   *Ibid.*, p. 69.
43   *Ibid.*, p. 79.
44   *Ibid.*, p. 48.
45   *Poems 1963-1983*, p. 84.
46   *Ibid.*, p. 198.
47   *Field Work*, p. 15.
48   'Red Branch (A Blessing)', *The Dead Kingdom* (Belfast/Dublin: Blackstaff Press/ The Dolmen Press), p. 51.
49   *The Rough Field*, p. 60, p. 67; *The Dead Kingdom*, p. 25.
50   *The Dead Kingdom*, p. 18.
51   *Stamping Ground*, p. 202.
52   *Ibid.*, p. 47.
53   David Martin, *The Road to Ballyshannon* (London: Sphere Books Ltd., Abacus edition, 1983), p. 155.
54   *The Ceremony of Innocence*, p. 280.
55   *The Road to Ballyshannon*, p. 156.

56 Bernard MacLaverty, *Lamb* (Harmondsworth, Middlesex: Penguin Books Ltd.), p. 152.
57 Bernard MacLaverty, *Cal* (Belfast/London: Blackstaff Press/Jonathan Cape, 1983), p. 170.
58 *Door into the Dark* (London: Faber and Faber, 1972), p. 27.
59 'Mossbawn', *Preoccupations*, p. 20.
60 'Broagh', *Wintering Out* (London: Faber and Faber, 1972), p. 27.
61 *Preoccupations*, p. 57.
62 '*North*: "Inner Emigré" or "Artful Voyeur"?' in *The Art of Seamus Heaney*, Tony Curtis, ed. (Brigend: Poetry Wales Press, 1982).
63 'Mossbawn', *Preoccupations*, p. 20.
64 *Ulster Local Studies*, 9, No. 20 (Summer, 1985), p. 114.
65 *Ibid.*, p. 112.
66 *Ibid.*, p. 113.
67 Louis MacNeice, *Collected Poems* (London: Faber and Faber, 1966), p. 450.
68 *Poems 1962-1978*, p. 35.
69 *Ibid.*, p. 78.
70 *Poems 1963-1983*, p. 156.
71 *The Selected Paul Durcan* (Belfast: Blackstaff Press, 1985), p. 55.
72 *Station Island* (London: Faber and Faber, 1984), p. 93.
73 Seamus Deane, *Celtic Revivals* (London: Faber and Faber, 1985), p. 186.
74 Brian Moore, *Fergus* (London: Jonathan Cape, 1971), p. 31.
75 *Forces and Themes in Ulster Fiction* (Dublin: Gill and Macmillan, 1974), p. 174.
76 *Fergus*, p. 37.
77 *Ibid.*, p. 227.
78 Brian Moore, *The Mangan Inheritance* (London: Jonathan Cape, 1979), p. 308.
79 *Forces and Themes in Ulster Fiction*, p. 179.
80 *Ibid.*, p. 184.
81 *Quoof*, p. 29.
82 *Why Brownlee Left*, p. 27.
83 *Mules*, p. 11.
84 In 'The More a Man Has', *Quoof*, p. 63.
85 *Mules*, p. 38.
86 *Why Brownlee Left*, p. 38.
87 *Quoof*, p. 7.
88 *States of Mind*, p. 6.
89 *Why Brownlee Left*, p. 22.
90 *Quoof*, p. 25.

YEATS, JOYCE AND THE CURRENT IRISH CRITICAL DEBATE
Terence Brown

1 For studies of Irish Ireland see F. S. L. Lyons, *Ireland Since the Famine* (Glasgow: Fontana, 1973), pp. 224-46 and *Culture and Anarchy in Ireland, 1890-1939* (Oxford: Clarendon Press, 1979), pp. 57-83. See also my *Ireland: A Social and Cultural History, 1922-79* (Glasgow: Fontana, 1981), pp. 45-78.
2 Daniel Corkery, *The Hidden Ireland* (Dublin: Gill and Macmillan, 1967), p. 62.
3 *Ibid.*, p. 64.
4 C. P. Curran, 'On the North Side', *The Irish Statesman*, July 10, 1926, p. 484.
5 Thomas McGreevy, 'Anna Livia Plurabelle', *The Irish Statesman*, February 16, 1929, pp. 475-76.
6 *Ibid.*, p. 476.
7 *Ibid.*

8   James Devane, 'Is an Irish Culture Possible?' *Ireland To-day*, Vol. 1, No. 5, October 1936, p. 29.

9   *Ibid.*, pp. 30-31.

10 Robert Lynd, 'Anglo-Irish Literature', *Saorstat Eireann Official Handbook* (Dublin: The Talbot Press, 1932), p. 280.

11 L. A. G. Strong, *The Sacred River: An Approach to James Joyce* (London: Methuen and Co. Ltd.), p. 13.

12 Frank O'Connor, 'The Future of Irish Literature', *Horizon*, Vol. V, No. 25, January, 1942, p. 58.

13 *Ibid.*, p. 59.

14 Sean O'Faolain, 'Fifty Years of Irish Writing', *Studies*, Spring, 1962, pp. 100-101.

15 Sean O'Faolain, 'Yeats and the Younger Generation', *Horizon*, Vol. 5, No. 25, January, 1942, p. 50. For a fuller treatment of O'Faolain's critique of Yeats and the Revival see my 'After the Revival: The Problem of Adequacy and Genre', in *The Genres of the Irish Literary Revival*, ed. Ronald Schlieffer (Norman, Oklahoma: Pilgrim Books, 1980), pp. 153-77.

16 The argument was present, however, in an inchoate form in Kavanagh's critical comments on Yeats and on Joyce, whose *Ulysses* was one of his sacred books. See Alan Warner, *Clay is the Word: Patrick Kavanagh, 1904-1967* (Dublin: The Dolmen Press, 1973), pp. 82-85.

17 Thomas Kinsella, 'The Irish Writer', in *Davis, Mangan, Ferguson? Tradition and the Irish Writer*, writings by W. B. Yeats and Thomas Kinsella (Dublin: The Dolmen Press, 1970), p. 62.

18 *Ibid.*

19 *Ibid.*, p. 64.

20 *Ibid.*, pp. 64-65.

21 *Ibid.*, p. 65.

22 *Ibid.*

23 Declan Kiberd, 'Inventing Irelands', *The Crane Bag*, Vol. 8, No. 1, 1984, pp. 11-12.

24 *Ibid.*, p. 13.

25 Richard Kearney, *Myth and Motherland* (Derry: Field Day Theatre Company Limited; Field Day Pamphlet Number 5, 1984), p. 18.

26 *Ibid.*

27 Seamus Deane, *Celtic Revivals: Essays in Modern Irish Literature* (London and Boston: Faber and Faber, 1985), p. 36. This volume usefully collects some of Deane's scattered essays (with some alterations) on Irish writing which he has published since 1975.

28 *Ibid.*, p. 112.

29 *Ibid.*

30 *Ibid.*, p. 49.

31 Seamus Deane, *Heroic Styles: the Tradition of an Idea*, (Derry: Field Day Theatre Company Limited; Field Day Pamphlet Number 4, 1984), pp. 7-8.

32 *Ibid.*, p. 10.

33 Deane, *Celtic Revivals*, p. 97.

34 *Ibid.*, p. 107.

35 Deane, *Heroic Styles*, pp. 16-17.

THE TREASURE OF HUNGRY HILL: THE IRISH WRITER AND THE IRISH LANGUAGE
Colbert Kearney

1   See Anne Clissman, *Flann O'Brien: A Critical Introduction to his Writings* (Dublin: Gill and Macmillan, Dublin, 1975), p. 77.

2 Seán Ó Tuama, *Nuabhéarsaíocht* (Dublin: Sáirséal agus Dill, 1950), p. 9f. My translation.
3 (Dublin: An Press Náisiúnta, 1941), p. 41. My translation.
4 *Ibid.*, p. 89f. My translation.
5 In gaol he meets his father for the first time; his father has just completed a similar sentence.
6 Clissman, p. 238.
7 See Colbert Kearney, *The Writings of Brendan Behan* (Dublin: Gill and Macmillan, Dublin, 1977), p. 26 and *passim*.
8 Máirtín Ó Cadhain, *The Road to Brightcity and Other Stories*, trans. Eoghan Ó Tuairisc (Dublin: Poolbeg Press, 1981), p. 9f.
9 'Brendan Behan and the Gaelic Tradition', *Journal of the American Irish Historical Society*, New York, 1982, Vol. 43, pp. 84-97.
10 Ó Cadhain, p. 10.
11 *Borstal Boy* (London: Hutchinson, 1958), p. 81.
12 Rutherford [*sic* for Eugene R.] Watters, *Murder in Three Moves* (Dublin: Allen Figgis, 1960).
13 *Ibid.*, p. 269.
14 A special Eugene Watters issue of *Poetry Ireland Review*, 13, Dublin, Spring 1985, contains the text of *The Week-End*, as well as 'Comes the Experiment: Notes Towards a Reading of *The Week-End of Dermot and Grace*' by Sean Lucy, and an essay on Watters' Irish poetry, especially *Aifreann na Marbh*, by Colbert Kearney. See also Alan Titley, 'Contemporary Irish Literature', in *The Crane Bag Book of Irish Studies* (Dublin: Blackwater Press, 1982), pp. 890-896. The October 1985 issue of *Comhar* was dedicated to his work. Martin Nugent's *Drámaí Eoghain Uí Thuairisc* (Maynooth: An Sagart, 1984) is not a very exciting study of his plays in Irish but may indicate a growing interest.
15 *The Week-End of Dermot and Grace* (Dublin: Allen Figgis, 1964).
16 *Dialann sa Diseart* (Dublin: Coiscéim, 1981), preface.
17 Anonymous (Ó Riada himself?) sleevenote on Gael-Linn record of music for film of *The Playboy of the Western World*, CEF 012.
18 W. B. Yeats and Thomas Kinsella, *Davis, Mangan, Ferguson? Tradition and the Irish Writer* (Dublin: The Dolmen Press, 1970), p. 59.
19 Seamus Heaney, *Preoccupations: Selected Prose 1968-1978* (London: Faber and Faber, 1980), p. 20.
20 See *ibid.*, p. 17.
21 *Sweeney Astray* (Derry, Field Day, 1983), p. ix.

LANGUAGE AND AFFECTIVE COMMUNICATION IN SOME
CONTEMPORARY IRISH WRITERS
Michael Toolan

1 James Joyce, *Portrait of the Artist as a Young Man* (Harmondsworth, Middlesex: Penguin Books Ltd., 1960), p. 189. All further references to this work appear in the text.
2 Edward Said, *The World, the Text and the Critic* (London: Faber and Faber, 1984), p. 48.
3 Thus Declan Kiberd charts some major literary debunkings of time-honoured Irish/English antithesis in his Field Day pamphlet no. 6, *Anglo-Irish Attitudes* (Derry: Field Day Theatre Company Limited, 1984), and Richard Kearney probes the mythic/anti-mythic opposition in pamphlet no. 5, *Myth and Motherland* (Derry: Field Day Theatre Company Limited, 1984).

But the allegedly quaint Irishism, *tundish*, merits re-examining. Just whose property it is remains unclear: it turns up frequently in Lawrence, occurs in *Measure for Measure* (III, ii, 162), and its first element is traced by the Oxford Dictionary to Old English *tunne*. It is, as Stephen later discovers, 'good old blunt English'. (p. 251). *Funnel*, however, seems to have entered Middle English from Old French: *funnel*, in these terms is more foreign than *tundish*. It may be that *tundish* is a shaming reminder of provincial archaism of Irish English, and more particularly of the colonial violation that planted such words in Ireland in the Elizabethan period, but I have my doubts: by those lights, shouldn't the sensitive Englishman smart at the reminder of the Norman conquest every time he uses the word *funnel*? And if *tundish* is an Elizabethan fossil in Irish English, how can Stephen consistently think of the dean (who rejects the word), rather than himself (who does not), as a country-man of Ben Jonson?

4   Montague, *The Rough Field* (Dublin: The Dolmen Press, 1972), p. 7.
5   Heaney, *Preoccupations* (London: Faber and Faber, 1980), p. 132.
6   George Watson, *Irish Identity and the Literary Revival* (London: Croom Helm, 1979), p. 33.
7   'The Irish Writer', in *Davis, Mangan, Ferguson? Tradition and the Irish Writer*, writings by W. B. Yeats and Thomas Kinsella (Dublin: The Dolmen Press, 1970), p. 65.
8   Kinsella, 'The Divided Mind', in *Irish Poets in English*, ed. Sean Lucy (Cork: Mercier Press, 1973), p. 217.
9   *Selected Poems* (London: Oxford University Press, 1982), p. 108.
10   *Ibid.*, pp. 110-111.
11   'A Severed Head', *The Rough Field*, 3rd ed. (Dublin: The Dolmen Press, 1979), p. 40.
12   London: Faber and Faber, 1983.
13   *Translations* (London: Faber and Faber, 198), p. 40. All further references to this work will appear in the text.
14   A major dilemma, raised by the Tobair Vree example, concerns the degree to which personal memory is in fact a shared memory. This is an abiding theme in Friel, whose *Translations* contains a mocking corrective to bogus Dublin bourgeois assertions of an ancestral share in the peasant cottage, as 'our first cathedral, [which] shaped all our souls.' And *Philadelphia, Here I Come* (London: Faber and Faber, 1965) is partly structured around Gar's efforts to have affirmed (beyond the habitual mould of everyday interaction) a deeper bond between himself and his father. His major effort in that direction fails poignantly, when he finds that a particular cherished memory he has, of a day out fishing with his father, is one which the latter cannot recall (pp. 104-105).
15   *Field Work* (London: Faber and Faber, 1979), p. 34.
16   On Heaney's reaction to the violent enforcement of tribal loyalty, see his poem 'Punishment', *North*, and the later 'Casualty' in *Field Work*, interestingly discussed by Blake Morrison, in *Seamus Heaney* (London: Methuen, 1982), pp. 78-80.
17   M. Bakhtin, *Problems of Dostoyevsky's Poetics*, trans. R. W. Rotsel (Ann Arbor: Ardis, 1973).
18   B. L. Whorf, *Language, Thought and Reality*, ed. J. B. Carroll (New York: 1956).
19   Not all see the word *bog* so positively however: P. F. Sheeran finds it used by English outsiders, a reflex of their lack of inward understanding of the native culture. See his 'Colonists and Colonized; Some Aspects of Anglo-Irish Literature from Swift to Joyce', in *The Yearbook of English Studies*, vol. 13 (1983), ed.

G. K. Hunter and C. J. Rawson (London: MHRA), pp. 97-115.

20 Hederman, 'Seamus Heaney, the Reluctant Poet', *The Crane Bag Book of Irish Studies*, eds. M. P. Hederman and R. Kearney (Dublin: Blackwater Press, 1981), p. 486. The Heaney quotation is from an interview with Seamus Deane in the same text, p. 70.

21 *Preoccupations: Selected Prose, 1968-1978* (London: Faber and Faber, 1980), p. 35.

22 R. Harris, *The Times Literary Supplement*, 20 May 1983, p. 524.

23 Tom Paulin, *A New Look at the Language Question* (Derry: Field Day Theatre Company Limited; Field Day Pamphlet Number 1, 1983), p. 13. All further references to this work will appear in the text.

24 *Preoccupations*, p. 197.

25 R. Quirk, 'Language and Nationhood', in *Style and Communication in the English Language* (London: Ed. Arnold, 1982), p. 65.

26 Sheeran, *op. cit.*

27 Noted in Declan Kiberd, 'Writers in Quarantine', *The Crane Bag Book of Irish Studies*, p. 348.

28 A phrase here is taken from, in my view, one of Heaney's finest, most technically assured reflections on his own position, the opening Glanmore sonnet in *Field Work*, p. 33. 'Now the good life could be to cross a field / And art a paradigm of earth new from the lathe / Of ploughs'.

29 F. S. L. Lyons, *Ireland Since the Famine* (London: Fontana, 1973), p. 244.

30 Kiberd, 'Writers in Quarantine', p. 350.

31 Heaney's notes to 'Station Island', *Station Island* (London: Faber and Faber, 1984), p. 122.

POST-WAR ULSTER POETRY: A CHAPTER IN ANGLO-IRISH LITERARY RELATIONS
John Wilson Foster

1 A. Alvarez, 'A Fine Way with the Language', *The New York Review of Books* (March 8, 1980).

2 As reported by Graham Martin in *The Review*, I, No. 8 (August 1963), p. 18.

3 By Terence Brown, for instance, in his *Northern Voices: Poets from Ulster* (Dublin: Gill and Macmillan, 1975).

4 Robert Herring, 'Reflections on Poetry prompted by the Poets of 1939-1944', *Transformation Three*, eds. Stefan Schimanski and Henry Treece (London: Lindsay Drummond Ltd., 1945), p. 183.

5 Herring, p. 183.

6 *Lyra: An Anthology of New Lyric* (Billericay, Essex: Grey Walls Press, 1942), p. 13.

7 Robert Greacen, 'The Belfast Poetry Scene 1939-1945', *The Honest Ulsterman* (Winter 1984), p. 19.

8 Brown, pp. 128, 132. At the same time, Greacen wanted Ulster poetry to 'act as the bridgehead between Ireland and Great Britain, and to suck the best out of the English, the Gaelic and the Anglo-Irish culture', quoted by Brown, p. 129.

9 Greacen, p. 21.

10 *Irish Literary Portraits* (London: BBC, 1972), pp. 132, 176.

11 Quoted to this effect in *The Poet Speaks: Interviews with Contemporary Poets*, ed. Peter Orr (London: Routledge & Kegan Paul, 1966), p. 207.

12 There are two valuable memoirs of the Forties poetry scene in London: Wrey Gardiner's *The Dark Thorn* (1946) and Derek Stanford's *Inside the Forties* (1977).

13 'Ulster Bull: The Case of W. R. Rodgers', *Essays in Criticism*, III, No. 4 (October 1953), pp. 470-475.

14 I discuss Rodgers's world-view in more detail in 'The Dissidence of Dissent: John Hewitt and W. R. Rodgers' in *Across a Roaring Hill: The Protestant Imagination in Modern Ireland*, eds. Edna Longley and Gerald Dawe (Belfast: Blackstaff Press, 1985), pp. 139-160.

15 However, 'I've always been right-wing', Larkin told an *Observer* interviewer; the interview is reprinted in Philip Larkin, *Required Writing: Miscellaneous Pieces 1955-1982* (London: Faber and Faber, 1983), p. 52.

16 *Poets of the 1950s: An Anthology of New English Verse*, ed. D. J. Enright (Tokyo: Kenkyusha Ltd.), pp. 8-9.

17 Blake Morrison has already made this very point, in *The Movement: English Poetry and Fiction of the 1950s* (Oxford: Oxford University Press, 1980), p. 93.

18 See Herring's article in *Transformation Three*; the quotation, however, is from Denys Val Baker's article, 'A Review of War-Time Reviews', also in *Transformation Three*, p. 199.

19 Morrison, pp. 60-62.

20 Larkin's 'Homage to a Government' accrues a deeper post-imperial sadness when we set it beside 'Going, Going' (both from *High Windows*, 1974). Larkin alludes to the first poem in his *Observer* interview just before proclaiming the right-wing nature of his politics, *Required Writing*, p. 52.

21 *Required Writing*, p. 55.

22 This is from Kavanagh's poem 'To Hell with Commonsense', reprinted in his *Collected Poems* (New York: Norton, 1973), p. 155. Kavanagh includes an unflattering reference to Enright in his poem 'Sensational Disclosures'.

23 When reviewing *The Oxford Book of Contemporary Verse*, edited by Enright, in *The Irish Times*, Montague took the opportunity to denounce the provincialism of the Movement and of recent English poets generally. Montague, born in the USA, grew up in Ulster, but he is not a Northern Irish writer in the way Heaney, Muldoon or Longley are Northern Irish. This is partly to do with the fact that he is closer generationally to pre-partition Ireland, that his politics are (or seem) more republican than theirs, and that his education pre-dates the Butler Education Act from which Heaney, Muldoon and Longley, as British subjects, benefitted.

24 *Springtime: An Anthology of Young Poets*, eds. G. S. Fraser and Iain Fletcher (London: Peter Owen, 1953), p. 12. In the 'Editors' Introduction', Larkin is grouped with the 'Regionalists'!

25 'Tell me a bit about your childhood', the *Observer* interviewer asked Larkin. 'Oh, I've completely forgotten it', he replied: *Required Writing*, p. 47.

26 From an interview with *Paris Review*, reprinted in *Required Writing*, p. 68.

27 See Derek Mahon, 'Poetry in Northern Ireland', *20th Century Studies* (November 1970), pp. 90-91; also my article on Heaney, 'The Poetry of Seamus Heaney', *Critical Quarterly*, XVI, No. 1 (1974), pp. 35-48.

28 The Ulster neo-romantics of the 1940s fell silent around 1947 or 1949 and kept their heads down for a quarter of a century until the Movement was no longer recognisable as such. After *The Undying Day* (1948), Greacen did not publish a full-length volume of poetry until *A Garland for Captain Fox* (1975); after *The Heart's Townland* (1947), McFadden did not publish a full-length volume until *The Garryowen* (1971); John Gallen was killed in a climbing accident in 1947. Barring John Hewitt, little happened in Ulster poetry after 1948 until the appearance of John Montague, who was in no simple sense an Ulster poet. It was really with Hobsbaum's Belfast Group that Ulster poetry reawakened.

29   See Hobsbaum's articles, 'The Present State of British Poetry', *Lines Review*, No. 45 (June 1973) and 'The Growth of English Modernism', *Wisconsin Studies in Contemporary Literature*, VI (1965).

30   From 'The Sea in Winter' in *Poems, 1962-1978* (Oxford: OUP, 1979). Like Larkin, Mahon peppers his verse with vulgarisms: in both cases they are there less to shock than to re-establish a lost connection with readers.

31   'I Am Raftery', of course, is an updating of a Gaelic original.

32   'The Attic' in *Poems*, p. 102.

33   *The Ironic Harvest: English Poetry in the Twentieth Century* (London: Edward Arnold, 1974), pp. 142-43.

34   The class dimensions of the Movement are too complicated to be gone into here; suffice it to say that I think the lower middle-class nature of the Movement has been somewhat exaggerated and that I would describe Larkin's background as thoroughly middle class.

35   Morrison, p. 93.

36   Where Heaney is concerned, the angular approach may derive as much from the example of Patrick Kavanagh: see my article, 'The Poetry of Patrick Kavanagh: A Reappraisal', *Mosaic*, XIII, No. 3 (1979), which discusses Kavanagh's influence on Heaney.

37   'New Lines in English Poetry', *Hudson Review*, IX, No. 4 (Winter 1956-57), p. 593.

38   I have discussed the connection between Calvinist and Movement aesthetics in the article mentioned in footnote 14. In that article I suggest Donald Davie (Movement poet, ex-Baptist) as the mediating figure between Nonconformism and the Movement. Hewitt, the ex-Methodist Ulster poet, shows in his verse some Movement characteristics, but would have been too regionalist for Movement poets and critics.

39   And it *is* just a literary posture. The no-nonsense approach is not serviceable in the most serious arena of Ulster life — the struggle over the national identity of the province — for the writers are not extremists or even highly committed politically, and it is hard to maintain a tough pose in the cause of moderation.

40   James Fenton has recently satirised Alvarez's critical posture in 'Letter to John Fuller', a poem in *Children in Exile: Poems 1968-1984* (New York: Vintage, 1984).

41   See Hughes's *Poetry in the Making* (London: Faber and Faber, 1967), pp. 55-58.

42   See my *Critical Quarterly* article cited above in footnote 27. Indeed, the American critic, Calvin Bedient, in a deflationary assessment of Heaney in the course of a review of *Field Work* (*Parnassus*, Fall/Winter 1979, pp. 108-22), brackets me with Alvarez as the only two critics who up until then had expressed reservations about Heaney's poetry.

43   To be fair to Heaney, stanza nine of *An Open Letter* suggests that it is simply the offending word *British* in the Penguin title that has caused his dismay (possibly even his sense of betrayal, if Heaney granted permission under the impression that the anthology was to be called *Opened Ground*, a phrase that is Heaney's own). Would Heaney's pamphlet not have appeared then if Motion and Morrison had taken Michael Schmidt's precaution of calling his alternative anthology *Some Contemporary Poets of Britain and Ireland* (1983)? Possibly, though the word *British* is sometimes a hard one to replace (as in *the British Isles*) and often means less than it implies. In any event, its use by Motion and Morrison is as debatable as the national identity of Northern Ireland; Longley would probably not baulk at its use in the title of the anthology, but Muldoon or even Mahon might (but then again they might not). And how many of the Ulster poets contemplated reversing their decision to appear in the anthology, before or after Heaney's verse epistle?

In the light of the problematic involved, the word *British* seems less a text than a pretext for Heaney's *Open Letter*. This pamphlet, after all, fits the pattern established by the first six Field Day pamphlets, which all contain an apparently pre-requisite anti-colonialist attack on Britain.

THE GO-BETWEEN OF RECENT IRISH POETRY
Dillon Johnston

1 William Butler Yeats, *The Poems*, a new edition, ed. Richard J. Finneran (New York: Macmillan, 1983), p. 182.
2 James Joyce, *Ulysses* (New York: Modern Library, 1961), p. 309.
3 Seamus Deane, *Heroic Styles: The Tradition of an Idea* (Derry: Field Day Theatre Company Limited; Field Day Pamphlet Number 4, 1984), p. 5.
4 Deane, p. 18.
5 Carl Jung, *Alchemical Studies*, vol. 13 of *Collected Works* (Princeton: Princeton University Press, 1967), p. 233; also see Michael Grant and John Hazel, *Gods and Mortals in Classical Mythology* (Springfield, Mass: G. & C. Merriam Co., 1973); H. T. Peck, ed., *Harper's Dictionary of Classical Literature and Antiquities* (New York: Cooper Square, 1963).
6 At the conclusion of this paper, I suggest other earlier Irish 'Hermetic' poets. Actually, in some of her functions, Crazy Jane could be seen as an hermetic narrator. To the extent that Yeats distances himself from her, however, to that extent she does not affront the reader as do the mysterious narrators we are considering here.
7 Thomas Kinsella, *A Technical Supplement* (1976), in *Peppercanister Poems 1972-1978* (Winston-Salem: Wake Forest University Press, 1979), p. 77. Hereafter, references to this volume and to *The Messenger* (1978) in *Peppercanister Poems* will be given, within parentheses in my text, as KPP with page number.
8 Hugh Kenner, *Joyce's Voices* (London: Faber and Faber, 1978), p. 49.
9 Seamus Heaney, *Station Island* (London: Faber and Faber; New York: Farrar, Straus, Giroux, 1984), p. 83. Hereafter, cited parenthetically in my text as HSI with page number.
10 Geoffrey Stokes, 'Bloody Beautiful', *Voice Literary Supplement*, March, 1984, p. 15.
11 Paul Muldoon, *Quoof* (Winston-Salem: Wake Forest University Press; London: Faber and Faber, 1983), p. 32; hereafter, cited parenthetically within my text as Q with page number.
12 Paul Muldoon, *Why Brownlee Left* (Winston-Salem: Wake Forest University Press; London: Faber and Faber, 1980), p. 22; hereafter, cited parenthetically in my text as WBL with page number.
13 John Montague, *The Great Cloak* (Winston-Salem: Wake Forest University Press; Dublin: The Dolmen Press, 1978), p. 29; hereafter, cited parenthetically within my text as MGC with page number.
14 John Montague, 'American Pegasus', *Studies* 48 (Summer 1959), pp. 183-91.
15 Thomas Dillon Redshaw, 'John Montague: Appreciation', *Eire-Ireland*, XI, 4 (Winter, 1976), pp. 122-33, 124.
16 Daniel O'Hara, 'An Interview with Thomas Kinsella', *Contemporary Poetry*, IV, 1 (1981), pp. 1-18, 6.
17 William Carlos Williams, *Selected Essays* (New York: New Directions, 1969), p. 288.
18 James Joyce, *A Portrait of the Artist as a Young Man* (New York: Viking Press, 1968), p. 189.
19 Robert Duncan, 'Introduction', *Bending the Bow* (New York: New Directions, 1968), pp. ix-x.

20 Seamus Heaney, *Field Work* (London: Faber and Faber; New York: Farrar, Straus, Giroux, 1979), p. 31.
21 Karl Kerenyi, 'The Trickster in Relation to Greek Mythology', trans. R. F. C. Hull in Paul Radin's *The Trickster: A Study in American Indian Mythology* (London: Routledge and Kegan Paul, 1956), pp. 171-192, 189.
22 'Paul Muldoon writes . . .', *The Poetry Book Society Bulletin*, #118 (Autumn 1983), p. 1.
23 Adrian Frazier, 'Juniper, Otherwise Known: Poems by Paulin and Muldoon', *Eire-Ireland* XIX, #1 (Spring, 1984), pp. 123-133, 133.
24 Paul Radin, *The Trickster*, p. 18.
25 *Ibid.*, p. 164.
26 *Ibid.*, p. 19.
27 Kerenyi, p. 181.
28 John Kerrigan, 'The New Narrative', *London Review of Books*, 16-29 February 1984, pp. 22-23.
29 Kerenyi, p. 185.
30 James Randall, 'An Interview with Seamus Heaney', *Ploughshares*, 5, #3 (1979), p. 17.
31 Kerenyi, p. 190.
32 James Joyce, *Ulysses*, p. 191; *Finnegans Wake* (New York: Viking Press, 1959), p. 489.

A QUESTION OF IMAGINATION — POETRY IN IRELAND TODAY
Gerald Dawe

 1 Osip Mandelstam, *The Complete Critical Prose and Letters*, ed. J. G. Harris (Ann Arbour, Michigan: Ardis, 1979), p. 119.
 2 Flannery O'Connor, 'Writing Short Stories', in *Mystery and Manners: Occasional Prose* (London: Faber and Faber, 1972), p. 104.
 3 Seamus Heaney, 'Gifts of Rain: IV', *Wintering Out* (London: Faber and Faber, 1972), p. 25.
 4 Daniel Hoffman, *Barbarous Knowledge: Myth in the Poetry of Yeats, Graves and Muir* (London: Oxford University Press, 1970), p. 21.
 5 Cf. Raymond Williams's remark, 'Nostalgia, it can be said, is universal and persistent: only other men's nostalgias offend,' in *The Country and the City* (London: Paladin, 1975), p. 21.
 6 See Brian Torode's 'Ireland the Terrible' in *Culture and Ideology in Ireland*, eds. Curtin, Kelly and O'Dowd (Galway: Galway University Press, 1984), pp. 20-29.
 7 Heine, *Die Bader von Lucca*, in H. H. Samtliche Werke, ed. Hans Kaufman (Kindler Verlag: Munich 1964), Vol. V, pp. 234-44. I am indebted to Dr Eoin Bourke of the German Department, University College Galway for this reference.
 8 Terry Eagleton, 'New Poetry', in *Stand Magazine*, 25, No. 3 (Summer, 1984), pp. 76-80.
 9 Terry Eagleton, *Literary Theory: An Introduction* (Oxford: Basil Blackwell, 1983), p. 114.
10 Tom Paulin, 'A Nation, Yet Again', *Liberty Tree* (London: Faber and Faber, 1983), p. 45.
11 John Montague, 'Last Journey', *The Dead Kingdom* (Belfast: Blackstaff Press; Dublin: The Dolmen Press, 1984), pp. 74-75.
12 Seamus Heaney, 'Anahorish', *Wintering Out*, p. 16.
13 A useful comparison can be made with Derek Walcott's *Midsummer* (London: Faber and Faber, 1984).

14 Seamus Heaney, *Station Island* (London: Faber and Faber, 1984).
15 *Ibid.*, pp. 32-33 (my italics).
16 *Ibid.*, p. 24.
17 I have looked at this viewpoint elsewhere: 'A Question of Convenants: Modern Irish Poetry', *The Crane Bag*, 3, No. 2 (1979); 'Checkpoints: The Younger Irish Poets', *The Crane Bag*, 6, No. 1 (1982); 'Convention as Conservatism', *The Crane Bag*, 7, No. 2, (1984); 'Poetry and the Public: Solitude and Participation', *The Crane Bag*, 8, No. 2 (1984); and 'The Permanent City: The Younger Irish Poets' in *The Irish Writer and the City*, ed. Maurice Harmon (Gerrards Cross: Colin Smythe; Totowa, New Jersey: Barnes & Noble, 1984), pp. 180-190.
18 Sean O'Faolain, *The Irish*, (Harmondsworth, Middlesex: Penguin Books, 1969), p. 143.
19 Thomas Kinsella, 'Nightwalker', *Poems 1956-1973* (Dublin: The Dolmen Press, 1980), p. 105.
20 Thomas Kinsella, 'The Irish Writer' in *Davis, Mangan, Ferguson? Tradition and the Irish Writer* (Dublin: The Dolmen Press, 1970), p. 66.
21 Derek Mahon, 'The Sea in Winter', *Poems 1968-1978* (London: Oxford University Press, 1979), p. 111.
22 Padraic Fiacc's books include: *By the Black Stream: Selected Poems 1947-1967* (Dublin: The Dolmen Press, 1969); *Odour of Blood* (Newbridge, Co. Kildare: The Goldsmith Press, 1973, reprinted 1984); *Nights in the Bad Place* (Belfast: Blackstaff Press, 1977); *The Selected Padraic Fiacc* (Belfast: Blackstaff Press, 1979).
23 Blake Morrison and Andrew Motion, *The Penguin Book of Contemporary British Poetry* (Harmondsworth, Middlesex: Penguin Books, 1982), p. 16.
24 Raymond Williams, *Politics and Letters: Interviews with New Left Review* (London: N.L.B. Verso ed. 1981), p. 246.
25 The young Belfast poet and editor, Damian Gorman, pertinently remarks on this matter: '. . . part of the reason why so many of our local poets are so wellknown across the water is that this is a troubled region, deserving media attention. Thus poets are to some degree indebted to the situation. Our most urgent trouble at present is a complete lack of political imagination . . . It seems to me that men and women of poetic imagination might make a greater contribution to those reserves of conjury which will be needed to spirit us out of a state of attrition.' 'Does Poetry Matter in Northern Ireland?', *Fortnight: An Independent Review for Northern Ireland*, No. 217 (April, 1985), p. 19.
26 Padraic Fiacc, *Nights in the Bad Place*, p. 37.
27 Milan Kundera, 'Afterword: A Talk with the Author by Phillip Roth', in *The Book of Laughter and Forgetting* (Harmondsworth, Middlesex: Penguin Books, 1983), p. 235.
28 'Missa Terribilis: A Sequence', *Paris/Atlantic; An Irish Issue*, (American College in Paris, Paris, Summer 1985).

HEARTH AND HISTORY: POETRY BY CONTEMPORARY IRISH WOMEN
Arthur E. McGuinness

1 Roger McHugh and Maurice Harmon, *Short History of Anglo-Irish Literature*, (Dublin: Wolfhound Press, 1982), p. 321.
2 Eithne Strong, *Songs of Living*, (Dublin: Runa Press, 1961), pp. 7-8.
3 *Sarah, In Passing*, (Dublin: The Dolmen Press, 1974), pp. 60-1.
4 *Night Feed*, (Dublin: Arlen House, 1982), p. 44.
5 *In Her Own Image*, (Dublin: Arlen House, 1980), p. 9.
6 *Venus and the Rain*, (Oxford: Oxford University Press, 1984), p. 41.

7   *Jan Toorop: Impressioniste, Symboliste, Pointilliste,* (Paris: Institut Neerlandais, 1977).

8   *The Flower Master,* (Oxford: Oxford University Press, 1982), p. 32; *Venus and the Rain,* p. 31.

9   *Trio Poetry 2* (Belfast: Blackstaff Press, 1981).

IRELAND'S *ANTIGONES*: TRAGEDY NORTH AND SOUTH

Anthony Roche

My thanks to Tom Paulin, Aidan Carl Mathews and Brendan Kennelly for providing me with encouragement and copies of their scripts. I would also like to thank Stephanie McBride of the Irish Film Institute for arranging a screening of *Anne Devlin*.

1   Brian Friel, *Translations* (London and Boston: Faber and Faber, 1981). The play's direct quotations from George Steiner, *After Babel: Aspects of Language and Translations* (London and New York: Oxford University Press, 1975) are recorded by Christopher Murray in his review, *Irish University Review,* 11, 2 (Autumn 1981), p. 239. See also Richard Kearney, 'Language Play: Brian Friel and Ireland's Verbal Theatre', *Studies,* 72, 285 (Spring 1983), pp. 20-56, especially the Appendix, pp. 54-55.

2   George Steiner, *Antigones* (Oxford: Clarendon Press, 1984).

3   Oliver Taplin, 'Difficult Daughter', review of George Steiner's *Antigones, The New York Review of Books,* December 6, 1984, p. 16.

4   Tom Paulin, *The Riot Act: A Version of Sophocles' 'Antigone'* (London and Boston: Faber and Faber, 1985). All future page references are to this edition and will be incorporated in the text.

5   Steiner, *Antigones,* p. 138.

6   Conor Cruise O'Brien, 'Views', *The Listener,* 24 October 1968, p. 526.

7   In *States of Ireland* (London: Hutchinson and Co., 1972; rev. ed. 1974), p. 158.

8   Review of Conor Cruise O'Brien, *Neighbours: The Ewart Biggs Memorial Lectures, 1978-1979;* reprinted as 'The Making of a Loyalist' in Tom Paulin, *Ireland and the English Crisis* (Newcastle-upon-Tyne: Bloodaxe Books, 1984), pp. 23-38.

9   *Ibid.,* p. 29.

10   O'Brien, *States of Ireland,* p. 159.

11   Paulin, 'Introduction', *Ireland and the English Crisis,* p. 16.

12   Fintan O'Toole, 'Field Day: On The Double', *The Sunday Tribune,* Dublin, 23 September 1984.

13   Mitchell Harris, 'Friel and Heaney: Field Day and the Voice of the Fifth Province', MLA paper, Washington D.C., December 1984, p. 10.

14   Interview with Tom Paulin, Belfast, July 1985.

15   Paulin, *Ireland and the English Crisis,* p. 33.

16   Richard Kearney, *Myth and Motherland,* Field Day Pamphlet 5 (Derry: Field Day, 1984); reprinted in *Ireland's Field Day,* introd. Denis Donoghue (London: Hutchinson and Co., 1985), p. 67.

17   Sophocles, *The Three Theban Plays: Antigone, Oedipus the King, Oedipus at Colonnus,* translated by Robert Fagles, introd. and notes by Bernard Knox (London: Allen Lane, 1982; Middlesex: Penguin Classics, 1984), p. 106.

18   W. B. Yeats, *The Poems: A New Edition,* ed. by Richard J. Finneran (London: Macmillan, 1983), p. 182.

19   Tom Paulin, 'Under Creon', *Liberty Tree* (London and Boston: Faber and Faber, 1983), p. 13.

20   Paulin, *Ireland and the English Crisis,* p. 17.

21   *Ibid.,* p. 17.

22 Paulin, 'Under Creon', *Liberty Tree*, p. 13. Henry Joy McCracken, James Hope and Joseph Biggar were all Belfast presbyterians involved in the republican struggle for Irish independence. Paulin identifies the first of the three in the 'Brief Lives' at the close of *Ireland and the English Crisis:* 'Henry Joy McCracken (1767-1798). Northern Irish republican leader executed after the failure of the 1798 rebellion', p. 217. In the Antrim insurrection led by McCracken, 'a party of the insurgents, "the Spartan band", led by James Hope, a weaver, displayed[ed] outstanding determination'. (R. B. McDowell, *Ireland in the Age of Imperialism and Revolution* [Oxford: Clarendon Press, 1979], p. 637). *The Northern Star* was their newspaper. Joseph Biggar became M.P. for Cavan in 1874; on p. 145 of *Ireland and the English Crisis*, Paulin cites James Joyce's description of Biggar as 'the inventor of parliamentary obstructionism'.
23 Interview with Aidan Carl Mathews, Dublin, August 1985.
24 Aidan Carl Mathews, *Antigone*, unpublished script, Dublin, July 1984. Page references will be incorporated in the text.
25 Aidan Carl Mathews, 'The Antigone', *Theatre Ireland*, 7 (Autumn 1984), p. 18.
26 Aidan Carl Mathews, 'Annotations on *Antigone*', unpublished typescript, 1984, p. 3.
27 See Steiner, *Antigones*, pp. 141-143.
28 See René Girard, *Violence and the Sacred*, translated by Patrick Gregory (Baltimore and London: The Johns Hopkins University Press, 1977): 'In Greek tragedy violence invariably effaces the differences between antagonists . . . the resemblance between the combatants grows ever stronger until each presents a mirror image of the other' (p. 47).
29 Mathews, 'Annotations on *Antigone*', p. 1.
30 Steiner, *Antigones*, p. 121.
31 Cf. the ending of Jean Genet, *The Balcony* (London and Boston: Faber and Faber, 1958; rev. ed. 1966): 'Irma: In a little while, I'll have to start all over again . . . put the lights on again . . . dress up . . . ah, the disguise! Distribute roles again . . . assume my own . . . *(She stops in the middle of the stage, facing the audience.)* . . . Prepare yours . . . judges, generals, bishops, chamberlains, rebels who allow the revolt to congeal. I'm going to prepare my costumes and studios for tomorrow . . . You must now go home, where everything — you can be quite sure — will be falser than here . . . You must go now. You'll leave by the right, through the alley . . . *(She extinguishes the last light.)* It's morning already. *(A burst of machine-gun fire).*'
32 Interview with Brendan Kennelly, Dublin, June 1985.
33 Brendan Kennelly, *Antigone: A Version*, unpublished script, Dublin, 1984, p. 2. All future references are to this script and will be incorporated in the text. Kennelly's version, the last of the three to be staged, was produced at the Peacock Theatre in Dublin, May 1986.
34 Brendan Kennelly, *Cromwell: A Poem* (Dublin: Beaver Row Press, 1983). Page references will be incorporated in the text. It will be clear from the context in each case whether the page reference is to *Antigone* or *Cromwell*.
35 Brendan Kennelly, 'Louis MacNeice: an Irish outsider', *Irish Writers and Society at Large*, ed. Masaru Sekine (Gerrards Cross: Colin Smythe, 1985), p. 100.
36 Steiner, *Antigones*, p. 95.
37 *Ibid.*, p. 235.
38 *Ibid.*, p. 241.
39 *Ibid.*, p. 238.
40 *Ibid.*, p. 134.

41 On the film, see Kevin Barry, 'Cinema and Feminism: The case of *Anne Devlin', The Furrow*, 36, 4 (1985), pp. 244-249; review by Verina Glaessner and Julian Petley's interview with Pat Murphy, *Monthly Film Bulletin*, 53, 624 (January 1986); and Luke Gibbons, 'The Politics of Silence: *Anne Devlin, Women and Irish Cinema'*, *Framework* 30/31, pp. 2-15. I am indebted to my reading of these, and to the unpublished MA thesis of Stephanie McBride.

42 Pat Murphy's term for the last section of the film. See interview, *Monthly Film Bulletin*.

43 See Luke Gibbons, 'The Politics of Silence': 'the view from the wings . . . exposes the artifice of spectacle, the contrived nature of dramatic action' (p. 7). Murphy's film thus builds on Mathews's critique of conventional dramatic forms.

44 Interview with Julian Petley, *Monthly Film Bulletin*.

45 Steiner, *Antigones*, p. 304.

THE MARTYR-WISH IN CONTEMPORARY IRISH DRAMATIC LITERATURE
Claudia W. Harris

1 Daniel Magee, *Horseman Pass By* (Playscript, 1983), p. 70. Further page numbers noted in text. This paper retains Magee's unique spelling. The play was published in *Theatre Ireland*, 6 (April/June, 1984), pp. 119-142.

2 Hugh Dalziel Duncan, *Symbols in Society* (New York: Oxford University Press, 1968), p. 144.

3 Henri Hubert and Marcel Mauss, *Sacrifice: Its Nature and Function* (Chicago: Univ. of Chicago, 1964), p. 97.

4 René Girard, *Violence and the Sacred* (Baltimore: Johns Hopkins Univ., 1972), pp. 1, 19, 17, 8.

5 Hubert and Mauss, p. 97.

6 Tomas MacAnna, Interview, 12 October 1983, Dublin.

7 Girard, p. 7.

8 During a conversation — and, I believe, misunderstanding my approach — Seamus Heaney objected strongly to the idea that the Irish practise a death cult. Apparently during the hunger strike period in 1981 this was an accusation frequently levelled by the English. Heaney pointed out that one need only visit Westminster Abbey to see a demonstration of a death cult.

9 'A paradigm of this sort goes beyond the cognitive and even the moral to the existential domain; and in so doing becomes clothed with allusiveness, implications, and metaphor — for in the stress of action, firm definitional outlines become blurred by the encounter of emotionally charged wills. Paradigms of this type, cultural root paradigms, so to speak, reach down to irreducible life stances of individuals, passing beneath conscious prehension to a fiduciary hold on what they sense to be axiomatic values, matters literally of life and death.' Victor Turner, *From Ritual to Theatre: The Human Seriousness of Play* (New York: Performing Arts Journal Pub., 1982), p. 73.

10 In Belfast, if I ever deplored the killing, those knowing I came from Atlanta would laugh. How could *I* talk about murder and mayhem! When I tried to explain that what went on in Atlanta was either crimes for gain or crimes of passion, they would deplore our situation: 'But that's awful, people dying for no purpose!'

11 Girard, pp. 47, 49.

12 Frank Wright, Interview, 7 November 1983, Belfast. Further references are to this interview.

13 Desmond Fennell, Interview, 13 November 1983, Dublin.

14 Richard Schechner, *Essays on Performance Theory, 1970-1976* (New York: Drama Books, 1977), p. 164.
15 Tom Paulin, *The Riot Act* (Unpublished playscript, 1984), p. 19. Further page numbers noted in text.
16 Fintan O'Toole, 'Field Day: On the Double', *The Sunday Tribune* (Dublin, 23 September 1984). Further references are to this review.
17 Keith Jeffery, 'In Defence of Decency', *Times Literary Supplement* (London, 19 October, 1984).
18 John Keegan, Interview, 8 November 1983, Belfast.
19 Frances Quinn, Interview, 20 October 1983, Belfast.
20 Peter Sheridan, *Diary of A Hunger Strike* (Unpublished playscript, 1982), p. 45. References are to either the original script or the production script with page numbers noted in text.
21 Conor Farrington, *Aaron Thy Brother* (Newark, Delaware: Proscenium Press, 1975), p. 82. First performed at the Peacock, 6 August 1969. Further page numbers noted in text.
22 Jennifer Johnston, *Indian Summer* (Unpublished playscript, 1983).
23 Graham Reid, 'The Hidden Curriculum' in *The Plays of Graham Reid* (Dublin: Co-op Books, 1982).
24 Lynda Henderson, Interview, 25 October 1983, Belfast.
25 Brian Friel, *Translations* (London: Faber and Faber, 1981).
26 John Boyd, *Collected Plays 1: The Flats, The Farm, Guests* (Dundonald, N.I.: Blackstaff, 1981), p. 2.
27 Martin Lynch, *The Interrogation of Ambrose Fogarty* (Dundonald, N.I.: Blackstaff, 1982).
28 Patrick Galvin, *Three Plays by Patrick Galvin: The Last Burning, Nightfall to Belfast, We Do It For Love* (Belfast: Threshold, 1976), pp. 165-166.
29 Conor Farrington, *Grey Eye: A Play for Radio* (Unpublished playscript, 1984), pp. 25, 28. Further page numbers noted in text.
30 Frank McGuinness, *Observe the Sons of Ulster Marching Towards the Somme* (London: Faber and Faber, 1986), p. 74. First performed February 1985.
31 Christina Reid, *Tea in a China Cup* (Unpublished playscript, 1983).
32 Galvin, pp. 95-96.
33 Victor Power, *Who Needs Enemies?* (Unpublished playscript, 1971), p. 91. First performed by University of Iowa, 1971.
34 Martin Lynch, *Castles in the Air* (Unpublished playscript, 1983).
35 Thomas Murphy, *Famine* (Dublin: Gallery Press, 1977). p. 85.
36 Sam Thompson, *Over the Bridge* (Dublin: Gill and MacMillan, 1970), pp. 42, 44. First performed in 1960 in Belfast.
37 Martin Lynch, *Dockers* (Belfast: Farset, 1982), p. 90.
38 Brian Friel, *The Communication Cord*(London: Faber and Faber, 1983).
39 Seamus Deane, 'In Search of a Story', in *The Communication Cord* Field Day Theatre Company program (1982), [no page numbers].

THE HISTORY PLAY TODAY
Christopher Murray

1 *This is It!* by Andy Tyrie, Sam Duddy, Michael Hall, in *Theatre Ireland*, 7 (Autumn 1984), p. 31.
2 David H. Greene and Edward M. Stephens, *J. M. Synge 1871-1904* (New York: Macmillan, 1959), p. 248. Yeats's reminder came during the debate on the *Playboy* on Monday night, 3 February 1907.

3   Conor Cruise O'Brien, 'An Unhealthy Intersection', *The New Review*, 2, No. 16 (July 1975), pp. 3-8.
4   Denis Johnston, *The Moon in the Yellow River*, in *The Dramatic Works of Denis Johnston*, Volume 2 (Gerrards Cross: Colin Smythe, 1979), p. 152.
5   W. B. Yeats, *Uncollected Prose*, eds. John P. Frayne and Colton Johnson, Volume 2 (London: Macmillan, 1975), p. 298.
6   Lady Gregory, *Our Irish Theatre* (Gerrards Cross: Colin Smythe, 1972), p. 20. Subsequent quotations are from this edition.
7   Daniel Corkery, *Synge and Anglo-Irish Literature* (Cork: University Press, 1931), pp. 19-21.
8   Lady Gregory, *Our Irish Theatre*, p. 62.
9   Benilde Montgomery, 'The Presence of Parnell in Three Plays by Lady Gregory', in *Irish Renaissance Annual III*, ed. Dennis Jackson (Newark: University of Delaware Press, 1982), pp. 106-23.
10 Lennox Robinson, *The Dreamers: A Play in Three Acts* (London and Dublin: Maunsel, 1915), no pagination.
11 *The Collected Plays of W. B. Yeats* (London: Macmillan, 1952), p. 705.
12 M. J. Molloy, 'The Making of Folk-Plays', in *Literature and Folk Culture: Ireland and Newfoundland*, eds. Alison Feder and Bernice Schrank (St. John's: Memorial University of Newfoundland, 1977), p. 66.
13 *The Wood of the Whispering* (Dublin: Progress House, 1961), no pagination.
14 Eugene McCabe, *Pull Down a Horseman/Gale Day* (Dublin: Gallery Press, 1979), p. 17.
15 *Ibid.*, p. 35. The following quotations from *Gale Day* are also from this edition.
16 John Arden, *To Present the Pretence* (London: Eyre Methuen, 1977), pp. 103-4. 'A Socialist Hero on the Stage' was written in collaboration with Margaretta D'Arcy. Subsequent citations from this source will be indicated parenthetically in the text.
17 Margaretta D'Arcy and John Arden, *The Non-Stop Connolly Show, Parts One and Two* (London: Pluto Press, 1977), p. v.
18 *Ibid.*, p. 58. For a contrary view of the cycle to the one I take, see Elmar Lehmann, 'England's Ireland: An Analysis of Some Contemporary Plays', in *Studies in Anglo-Irish Literature*, ed. Heinz Kosok (Bonn: Bouvier Verlag Herbert Grundmann, 1982), pp. 437-8.
19 *The Non-Stop Connolly Show, Part Six: World War and the Rising: 1914-1916* (London: Pluto Press, 1978), p. 106.
20 Sean O'Casey, *The Shadow of a Gunman*, in *Collected Plays*, Volume One (London: Macmillan, 1949), p. 132.
21 Maurice Meldon, *Aisling: A Dream Analysis* (Dublin: Progress House, 1959), p. 78.
22 In *Modern Irish Poetry*, ed. Derek Mahon (London: Sphere Books, 1972), p. 150.
23 Brendan Behan, *The Hostage* (London: Methuen, 1962), p. 17.
24 *Brendan Behan's Island* (London: Hutchinson, 1962), pp. 87, 88.
25 Cecil Woodham-Smith, *The Great Hunger* (New York: New American Library, 1964), p. 405.
26 See the recent doctoral dissertation by Ulf Dantanus, 'Brian Friel: The Growth of an Irish Dramatist', Göteborg University, 1984.
27 One of the characters, the embittered Eamon, says to Hoffnung that his history will have to be a romantic fiction about a family 'brushing against reality occasionally by its cultivation of artists', but in the main living 'in total isolation . . . without passion, without loyalty, without commitments'. Brian Friel, *Aristocrats* (Dublin: Gallery Press, 1980), p. 53.
28 Brian Friel, *Translations* (London: Faber and Faber, 1981), p. 67.

29 *Ibid.* See also Eitel F. Timm, 'Modern Mind, Myth, and History: Brian Friel's *Translations*', in *Studies in Anglo-Irish Literature*, ed. Heinz Kosok, pp. 450-3.

30 Referring to Sarah's regression to dumbness in act 3 Seamus Heaney said: 'It is as if some symbolic figure of Ireland from an eighteenth-century vision poem, the one who once confidently called herself Cathleen Ni Houlihan, has been struck dumb by the shock of modernity'. Review of *Translations* at the Dublin Theatre Festival, *Times Literary Supplement*, 24 October 1980, p. 1199.

31 (Dublin: Gallery Press, 1977), p. 81: 'And I'll not go. Not for landlord, devil, or the Almighty himself! I was born here, and I'll die here, and I'll rot here! . . . Cause there's food to be . . . The roadmaking is to . . Cause there's . . . Cause I'm right.'

32 Pam Brighton, 'Six Characters in Search of a Story', *Theatre Ireland*, 6 (April/ June 1984), pp. 144-7. See also Lynda Henderson, 'Charabanc Theatre Company', *Theatre Ireland*, 3 (June/September 1983), p. 132.

WOMEN'S CONSCIOUSNESS AND IDENTITY IN FOUR IRISH WOMEN NOVELISTS

Tamsin Hargreaves

1 Molly Keane, *Good Behaviour* (London: Sphere Books Ltd., Abacus edition, 1984), pp. 196-97.

2 Edna O'Brien, *Seven Novels and Other Short Stories* (London: Collins, 1978), p. 8.

3 Edna O'Brien, *The Country Girls* (Harmondsworth, Middlesex: Penguin Books Ltd., 1960), pp. 49-51. Further page references to this text will be cited parenthetically.

4 Edna O'Brien, *The Girl With Green Eyes* in *Seven Novels and Other Short Stories* (London: Collins, 1978), p. 260. Further page references to this text will be cited parenthetically.

5 Edna O'Brien, *Girls in Their Married Bliss* (Harmondsworth, Middlesex: Penguin Books Ltd., 1967), p. 122. Further page references to this text will be cited parenthetically.

6 Edna O'Brien, *August Is a Wicked Month* (Harmondsworth, Middlesex: Penguin Books Ltd., 1967), p. 93. Further page references to this text will be cited parenthetically.

7 Julia O'Faolain, *The Obedient Wife* (Harmondsworth, Middlesex: Penguin Books Ltd., 1983), p. 193. Further references to this text will be cited parenthetically.

8 Julia O'Faolain, *The Women in the Wall* (Harmondsworth, Middlesex: Penguin Books Ltd., 1978), p. 197.

9 Molly Keane, *Good Behaviour*, p. 212.

10 Molly Keane, *Time After Time* (London: Sphere Books Ltd., Abacus Edition, 1984), p. 46. Further references to this text will be cited parenthetically.

11 C. G. Jung, *Memories, Dreams and Reflections* (London: Fontana Flamingo, 1983), p. 49.

12 Jennifer Johnston, *The Old Jest* (London: Fontana/Collins, 1979), p. 78. Further references to this text will be cited parenthetically.

13 Jennifer Johnston, *The Christmas Tree* (London: Fontana/Collins, 1982), pp. 2 and 3. Further references to this text will be cited parenthetically.

14 Jennifer Johnston, *The Railway Station Man* (London: Hamish Hamilton, 1984), p. 5. Further references to this text will be cited parenthetically.

SHADOWS OF DESTRUCTION: THE BIG HOUSE IN CONTEMPORARY IRISH
FICTION
Andrew Parkin

1   Estates and gardens as well as houses themselves have inspired writers. I am
    personally indebted to the late Edward Malins who, in conversation, first
    aroused my interest in the topic. See Edward Malins, *English Landscaping and
    Literature* (London: O.U.P., 1966) and for an elegant, authoritative treatment of
    Irish gardens, see the same author with the Knight of Glin, *Lost Demesnes, Irish
    Landscape Gardening, 1660-1845* (London: Barrie & Jenkins, 1976). Of consider-
    able interest too are Maurice Craig, *Classic Irish Houses of the Middle Size* (London:
    The Architectural Press, 1976), Caroline Walsh, *The Houses of Irish Writers*
    (Dublin: Anvil Books, 1982) useful for its photographs, and William Trevor's
    A Writer's Ireland (London: Thames & Hudson, 1984). The key survey of litera-
    ture centring on the country house is Richard Gill, *Happy Rural Seat, The
    English Country House and the Literary Imagination* (New Haven and London: Yale
    University Press, 1972). This includes useful discussion of works by Anglo-
    Irish writers, and nobody interested in the genre should ignore Gill's book.

2   A major distinguishing factor in defining the Anglo-Irish was that they were
    a discrete class. They were not all Protestants, nor were they all Loyalists.
    Brendan Behan's pungent definition of an Anglo-Irishman as a 'Protestant
    with a horse' is quoted in Terence de Vere White's *The Anglo-Irish* (London:
    Gollancz, 1972). See also J. C. Beckett, *The Anglo-Irish Tradition* (Ithaca, N.Y.:
    Cornell University Press, 1976). Terence Brown puts the Anglo-Irish into the
    context of modern Irish history and society in his concise and useful *Ireland:
    A Social and Cultural History 1922-1979* (London: Fontana, 1981). See especially
    pages 110-121. Anglo-Irish literature, however, is not only work written by
    members of a class known as the Anglo-Irish or Ascendancy. Definitions of
    Anglo-Irish literature range from the notion that it expresses in English the
    Irish experience or spirit, to the simpler idea that it is work in English written
    by Irishmen. See Alan Warner's *A Guide to Anglo-Irish Literature* (Dublin: Gill
    and Macmillan, 1981) for a brisk discussion of definitions in the opening
    chapter. Anthony Cronin's sprightly and readable essays get rid of many of
    the cobwebs clinging to this topic; see his *Heritage Now* (Dingle, Co. Kerry:
    Brandon, 1982). Two seminal and moving essays are Elizabeth Bowen's 'The
    Big House' in *Collected Impressions* (London: Longmans Green & Co., 1950)
    and T. R. Henn's 'The Big House' in *Last Essays* (Gerrards Cross: Colin
    Smythe, 1976). See also Sean O'Faolain *The Irish* (Harmondsworth: Penguin,
    1981; 1st pub. 1947) for a concise, eloquent discussion. The best scholarly
    account of the ambivalent position of Anglo-Irish writers is Henn's essay
    'The Weasel's Tooth' in his *Last Essays*.

3   Bram Stoker, *Dracula* (New York: Modern Library, n.d. 1932?), p. 32. Further
    references to this text will cite page number only.

4   Quoted in Harry Ludlum, *A Biography of Dracula: The Life Story of Bram Stoker*
    (London: W. Foulsham & Co., 1962), p. 25. Further references to this text will
    cite page numbers only.

5   See Seamus Deane, 'Jennifer Johnston' in *Bulletin of the Department of Foreign
    Affairs*, Government of the Irish Republic, number 1015, February, 1985.
    Readers should note, however, that it was Somerville, not Ross who survived
    to write *The Big House of Inver* (1925). See also Deane's perceptive but not
    totally convincing attack on the Ascendancy myth in 'The Literary Myths of
    the Revival' in J. Ronsley (ed.) *Myth and Reality in Irish Literature* (Waterloo,
    Ontario: Wilfred Laurier University Press, 1977), pp. 317-329.

6 See Ann Power's definition of the Anglo-Irish in her 'The Big House of Somerville and Ross' in *Dubliner*, Spring 1964, pp. 43-44. The Anglo-Irish, however, were not a *race*. The contradictions in the Anglo-Irish are also discussed by J. White, *Minority Report: the Protestant Community in the Irish Republic* (Dublin: Gill and Macmillan, 1975), pp. 53-69.

7 Seamus Deane, *op. cit.*

8 Emmanuel leRoy Ladurie observes in *The Territory of the Historian* (Hassocks, Sussex: The Harvester Press, 1979; 1st. pub. Gallimard, 1973), pp. 101-102: '. . . peasant legends are full of stories about the wicked landlord who exploits or deceives his tenants and underlings. If he should perjure himself, swearing he has always dealt honestly with his people, he is immediately struck by a thunder-bolt and transformed into a black dog or a wolf — doomed for ever to be an ancestor-totem for his descendants. On stormy nights, he will return in his beastly form to haunt the family hearth.'

9 Ladurie's phrase. See his stimulating discussion of 'Rural Civilization' in chapter six of *The Territory of History*, pp. 79-110.

10 *Op. cit.*, p. 109.

11 *Op. cit.*, p. 80.

12 The most irreverent and hideously comic treatment of the Big House is that meted out by Brendan Behan in his radio play, *The Big House*, in which a Dubliner and a cockney conspire and cheat the owners of the house by stripping it of all valuables, especially the lead roof. The owners are swindling upstarts rather than true gentry. See *Evergreen Review* (1957), pp. 40-63 for this text. More general discussion of the house as symbol in modern Irish drama occurs in the present writer's 'Imagination's Abode' in J. Ronsley (ed.) *Myth and Reality in Irish Literature* (Waterloo: Wilfred Laurier University Press, 1977), pp. 255-263.

13 Another sister, Emily, is apparently dead already in the 1937 chapters, yet her funeral scene is described in the 1938 section.

14 Aidan Higgins, *Langrishe, Go Down* (New York: Grove Press, 1966), p. 12. Subsequent references to this text will cite page numbers only.

15 This accords with the norm for Irish country houses. See E. Bowen's essay 'The Big House' already cited in note 2. For a concise and masterly analysis of Bowen's 'natural artistic power' see Angus Wilson's Introduction to *The Collected Stories of Elizabeth Bowen* (London: Jonathan Cape, 1980). For an intelligent reassessment of Bowen see Hermione Lee, *Elizabeth Bowen: an Estimation* (London: Vision Press, Barnes and Noble, 1981).

16 William Trevor, *Fools of Fortune* (Harmondsworth: Penguin, 1984; 1st. pub. Bodley Head, 1983), p. 9. All further references to this novel will be to the Penguin text, citing page number only. For a good discussion of Trevor's fiction in general see Robert E. Rhodes, 'William Trevor's Stories of the Troubles' in James D. Brophy and Raymond I. Porter, *Contemporary Irish Writing* (Boston: Twayne and Iona College Press, 1983), pp. 95-114.

17 The detail of the mulberry bushes recalls Elizabeth Bowen's essay 'The Mulberry Tree' in *Collected Impressions*. See note 2.

18 Robert E. Rhodes, 'Two of William Trevor's Latest' in *Irish Literary Supplement* (Vol. 2, No. 2), p. 28.

19 Jennifer Johnston, *How Many Miles to Babylon?* (London: Fontana, 1984; 1st pub. Hamish Hamilton, 1974), p. 3. Further references will be to this Fontana text, citing page numbers only.

20 Jennifer Johnston, *The Old Jest* (London: Fontana, 1984; 1st pub. Hamish Hamilton, 1979), p. 102. Further references will be to the Fontana text, citing

Notes to pages 320-324

page numbers only.
21   Waugh's novel, of course, does not concern the fate of the Anglo-Irish; but the
     decline of aristocracy set against the turmoil of modern history is a large,
     international theme, whether anchored in Britain, Ireland, or Russia.
     Brideshead is in my view its best modern fictional expression; Chekhov's *Three
     Sisters* and *The Cherry Orchard* are its masterpieces in the modern drama.
22   Molly Keane, *Good Behaviour* (London: Sphere Books, 1982; 1st pub. André
     Deutsch, 1981), p. 4. Further references will be to the Sphere text, citing page
     numbers only.
23   Molly Keane, *Time After Time* (London: Sphere Books, 1984; 1st pub. André
     Deutsch, 1983), p. 8. Further references will be to the Sphere text, citing page
     numbers only.

NOTES ON CONTRIBUTORS

ANTHONY BRADLEY was born in Ireland. He holds degrees from Queen's University, Belfast, and the State University of New York at Buffalo. He is Professor of English at the University of Vermont, where he teaches Modern Irish Literature; in 1982-83, he was a Fellow at the Institute for Irish Studies at Queen's University, Belfast. He is author of a critical introduction to Yeats's plays, *William Butler Yeats*, has edited *Contemporary Irish Poetry: An Anthology*, and has written numerous articles and reviews on Irish literature.

TERENCE BROWN is Director of Modern English and a Fellow of Trinity College, Dublin. He is the author of *Louis MacNeice: Sceptical Vision; Northern Voices: Poets from Ulster; Ireland: A Social and Cultural History, 1922-79* and co-editor of *The Irish Short Story*.

GERALD DAWE was born in Belfast in 1952. Educated at Orange-field Boys' School, the New University of Ulster and University College Galway, he has received a Major State Award for research (1974-77), an Arts Council Bursary for poetry (1980) and in 1984 he was awarded the Macaulay Fellowship in Literature. He has published two collections of poetry: *Sheltering Places* (1978) and *The Lundys Letter* (1985) as well as editing an anthology *The Younger Irish Poets* (1982) and, with Edna Longley, *Across a Roaring Hill* (1985), a collection of essays on the Protestant imagination in Modern Ireland. He is currently completing *Servitudes of Time*, a chronicle of poetry in Ireland (1975-1985).

JOHN WILSON FOSTER teaches in the Department of English at the University of British Columbia, Vancouver. A native of Belfast, he has lectured and written on many aspects of modern Irish literature and culture. He is the author of *Forces and Themes in Ulster Fiction* (1974) and *Fictions of the Irish Literary Revival* (1987).

TAMSIN HARGREAVES: Lecturer in English at Trinity College, Dublin University. B.A. Hons. Trinity College, Dublin. M. Litt. Cambridge. Has published articles on Kate O'Brien and is at present completing a book on the imagination of Kate O'Brien.

CLAUDIA HARRIS of Emory University is currently at work on a full-length study of contemporary Irish drama.

DILLON JOHNSTON teaches English at Wake Forest University in North Carolina. Through his involvement with the Wake Forest University Press, he has been instrumental in making the work of several contemporary Irish poets available to North American readers. His book, *Irish Poetry After Joyce*, was published by Notre Dame Press in 1985.

COLBERT KEARNEY teaches English at University College, Cork, and has written and lectured widely on various topics in Anglo-Irish literature. He is particularly interested in the cultural confusion in which the Irish writer begins.

EDNA LONGLEY is a senior lecturer in English at Queen's University, Belfast. Her annotated edition of Edward Thomas's *Poems and Last Poems* appeared in 1981 and she has also edited his critical prose in *A Language Not to be Betrayed: Selected Prose of Edward Thomas* (1981). She has written extensively on contemporary Irish and English poetry and edited the works of James Simmons and Paul Durcan. With Gerald Dawe, she has co-edited a collection of critical essays, *Across a Roaring Hill: The Protestant Imagination in Modern Ireland* (1985). In 1986, her collection of interconnected essays, *Poetry in the Wars*, was published by Bloodaxe Books.

ARTHUR E. McGUINNESS, Professor of English at the University of California, Davis, is the author of *George Fitzmaurice* (1975) and of other essays on Irish and other contemporary writers which have appeared in *Irish University Review, Eire-Ireland, Yearbook of English Studies*, and *Themes in Drama*. He has just completed work on a book titled *Indomitable Irishry: Yeats, Clarke, Kinsella, Heaney*.

CHRISTOPHER MURRAY teaches English at University College, Dublin. He has written extensively on Irish drama and has collected materials for an Irish Theatre Archive. He is editor of the *Irish University Review*.

FINTAN O'TOOLE is theatre critic of *The Sunday Tribune*. From 1981 to 1983 he was theatre critic of *In Dublin* magazine. He was Arts Editor of *The Sunday Tribune* from 1983 to 1985, and editor of *Magill* magazine from 1985 to 1986. His study of the theatre of Tom Murphy was published by Raven Arts Press in 1987 and his other publications include *A Fair Day* with photographer Martin Parr.

ANDREW PARKIN was educated at Pembroke College, Cambridge, where he won an Open Exhibition in English, and at the Drama Department of Bristol University. He has taught in England, Hong Kong and Canada. A specialist in modern drama and Anglo-Irish literature, he has edited *The Canadian Journal of Irish Studies* since 1975, has published books and numerous articles and reviews, and has held a Humanities Research Centre Fellowship in Canberra at the Australian National University. He currently teaches English at the University of British Columbia. His first volume of poems appeared in 1987.

ANTHONY ROCHE divides his time between Ireland, where he was born, and the U.S., where he teaches. He holds a First Class Honours B.A. for Trinity College, Dublin, and a Ph.D. from the University of California at Santa Barbara. He is a co-editor of the *Irish Literary Supplement* and has published articles on Synge, Joyce, Beckett, Friel, Kilroy and Murphy.

PATRICK F. SHEERAN is a Statutory Lecturer in the Modern English Department at University College, Galway. He is the author of *The Novels of Liam O'Flaherty* and a forthcoming study of the sense of place in Ireland.

MICHAEL J. TOOLAN lectures at the University of Washington, Seattle. His work, on such Irish writers as Thomas Kinsella, Brian Moore and John McGahern, has appeared in *Eire-Ireland, Journal of Literary Semantics, Poetics Today* and *The Canadian Journal of Irish Studies*.

NINA WITOSZEK is a Research Assistant at Stockholm University. She is completing a book on contemporary Polish and Irish culture and drama entitled, *The Theatre of Recollection*.

INDEX